Aleutian Is.
(U.S.)

Midway Is.
(U.S.)

Wake Is.
(U.S.)

CYPRUS

PAKISTAN

INDIA

HONG KONG

NORTHERN
MARIANAS

MARSHALL
ISLANDS

BANGLADESH

PHILIPPINES

SUDAN

Andaman Is.
(Ind.)

Guam (U.S.)

SOUTH
SUDAN

SRI LANKA

BRUNEI

PALAU

MICRONESIA

KIRIBATI

UGANDA

KENYA

MALDIVES

MALAYSIA

NAURU

WANDA

SINGAPORE

SOLOMON
ISLANDS

RUNDI

SEYCHELLES

Chagos Is. (U.K.)

PAPUA
NEW GUINEA

TANZANIA

Diego Garcia (U.K.)

TUVALU

AMBIA

Cocos Is.
(Austl.)

Christmas Is.
(Austl.)

MALAWI

MAURITIUS

ZIMBABWE

VANUATU

FIJI

MOZAM-
BIQUE

SWANA

ESWATINI

LESOTHO

AUSTRALIA

Norfolk Is.
(Austl.)

ITH
RICA

Kermadec Is.
(N.Z.)

Lord Howe Is.
(Austl.)

Prince Edward Is.
(S. Afr.)

NEW
ZEALAND

McDonald Is.
(Austl.)

Chatham Is. (N.Z.)

Auckland Is.
(N.Z.)

Bounty Is. (N.Z.)

Macquarie Is.
(Austl.)

Antipodes Is. (N.Z.)

0   1000   2000   3000 km

Name Dependent territories of Commonwealth states (in brackets)   **(as of 01/2021)**

Blue Line 5

Ausgabe für Bayern (Mittelschulen) Klasse 9 R-Zug

Die Mediencodes (Beispiel: ⊕ Find more online: nd4r3a) enthalten zusätzliche Unterrichtsmaterialien, die der Verlag in eigener Verantwortung zur Verfügung stellt.

Im Lernmittel wird in Form von Symbolen (⊙/▱) auf Medien verwiesen. Diese umfassen – bis auf die Hörverstehens-übungen – ausschließlich optionale Unterrichtsmaterialien und unterliegen nicht dem staatlichen Zulassungsverfahren.

Zusatzmaterial für Schülerinnen und Schüler u.a.:
Blue Line 5 Bayern R-Zug Workbook mit Audio-CD (ISBN 978-3-12-548355-2)

1. Auflage   1 ⁵ ⁴ ³ ² ¹ | 25 24 23 22 21

Herausgeber: Wolfgang Hamm, Marktredwitz
Autorinnen und Autoren: Daniel Shatwell, Hanau; Wolfgang Hamm, Marktredwitz sowie
Sheila McBride, Leinfelden-Echterdingen; Chris Caridia, Frankfurt; Monika Münzenloher, Dorfen; Joanne Popp, editing etc., Korntal-Münchingen
Beratung: Michaela Cavallucci, München; Gaby Fruhmann, Parsberg; Michael Meisenzahl, Karlstadt;
Lisa Schubert, Altdorf; Anna Weber, Taufkirchen
Externe Redaktion: Birgit Piefke-Wagner, Korntal-Münchingen; Anette Dralle, Stuttgart

Entstanden in Zusammenarbeit mit dem Projektteam des Verlages.

Umschlaggestaltung und Gestaltungskonzept: know idea, Freiburg; Koma Amok, Stuttgart
Umschlagfotos: Avenue Images GmbH (Dave and Les Jacobs), Hamburg; plainpicture GmbH & Co. KG
(Angela Elbing), Hamburg
Satz: graphitecture book & edition; Fotosatz Kaufmann, Stuttgart
Reproduktion: Schwabenrepro GmbH, Stuttgart
Druck: Firmengruppe APPL, aprinta druck, Wemding

Printed in Germany
ISBN 978-3-12-548265-4

9 783125 482654

Inhalt

L = Listening   M = Mediation   R = Reading   S = Speaking   V = Viewing   W = Writing

L = Listening   M = Mediation   R = Reading   S = Speaking   V = Viewing   W = Writing

So lernst du mit Blue Line

So lernst du mit deinem Buch.
Das Buch hat vier *Units* (Kapitel).
Jede *Unit* ist gleich aufgebaut.

Intro

Hier steigst du in das neue Thema ein.
Dazu gibt es auch einen kurzen Film.

Im gelben Kasten siehst du, was du in
der *Unit* lernen wirst.

Topics

In jeder *Unit* gibt es zwei *Topics*.
Hier kannst du erkennen, wie schwer
eine Übung ist:

● schwer ◑ mittel ○ leicht

In der *Task* kannst du zeigen, dass du alles
verstanden hast, und deine eigenen Ideen
einbringen.

Text

Auf den *Text*-Seiten findest du spannende
Geschichten, Sachtexte und Artikel.

Mediation/Film

Auf der linken Seite geht es darum,
englische Informationen auf Deutsch
wiederzugeben und zwischen englisch- und
deutschsprechenden Personen zu vermitteln.
Das nennt man *Mediation*.

Auf der *Film*-Seite geht es um einen
Film in englischer Sprache.

Checkout

Auf dieser Seite findest du eine Übersicht über die
Kompetenzziele der *Unit*.

Die Abschlussaufgabe (*Unit task*) könnt ihr meist
zu zweit oder in der Gruppe lösen.

Look at …

Hier kannst du Australien, Indien, Südafrika und Neuseeland weiter entdecken.
Schau genau hin. Vieles kannst du verstehen oder erraten.

Skills

Auf jede *Unit* folgt eine Doppelseite, auf der du eine bestimmte Fertigkeit (*Skill*) oder Lernstrategie besonders trainieren kannst.

Test practice

Hier kannst du für eine schriftliche Abschlussprüfung trainieren.

Symbol	Erklärung
○ ◑ ●	leicht/mittel/schwer (Niveaudifferenzierung)
✿	individualisierende Aufgabe (natürliche Differenzierung)
→ ○ p.120	Verweis auf leichtere Parallelübung auf der *Diff corner*-Seite
OR	Aufgabe zur Auswahl (Wahldifferenzierung)
⌐○	Entwicklung von Schlüsselkompetenzen für Ausbildung und Beruf
P	Hier entsteht ein Produkt für das Portfolio.
4/3 ↗	Verweis auf eine Übung im *Workbook*
→ G1, p.127	Verweis auf den Grammatikanhang (*Grammar*)
→ M	Verweis auf die Methodenseiten (*Methods*)
→ V	Verweis auf eine *Word bank* im Vokabular (*Vocabulary*)
☺☺	Partnerarbeit
☺☺☺	Gruppenarbeit
📀	Verweis auf die Lehrer-CD (Audio)
🎞	Verweis auf die Lehrer-DVD (Film)
⊕ Find more online: 3h58uu	Code auf www.klett.de eingeben und Zusatzinformationen erhalten

Grammar   Methods   Vocabulary

Im Anschluss an die vier *Units* gibt es noch weitere nutzliche Seiten:

Grammar: Hier findest du alle Regeln und Erklärungen zur Grammatik, Übungen und eine Liste der unregelmäßigen Verben.

Methods: Manche Übungen könnt ihr auf eine bestimmte Art und Weise bearbeiten.
Das erkennst du an diesem Symbol: → M.
Wie es genau funktioniert, kannst du hier nachlesen.

Vocabulary: Im *Vocabulary* findest du alle neuen Wörter in der Reihenfolge, in der sie in der *Unit* auftauchen, sowie *Word banks*, die dir bei der Bearbeitung der *Task* helfen.
Im *Dictionary* sind die Wörter noch einmal alphabetisch aufgelistet: zuerst Englisch–Deutsch und dann Deutsch–Englisch.

1,1 ☞ Zoom in – A world language

1 Over a billion people all around the world speak English, and it is an official language in 67 countries. The majority of these speakers have learned English as a second language. So you can often talk to people in English when you don't know their language.

Top 5 languages by number of speakers (native and non-native)

Language	Number of speakers in millions
English	1,121
Chinese	1,107
Hindi	537
Spanish	513
French	285

Number of speakers in millions

Source: SIL International, Dallas

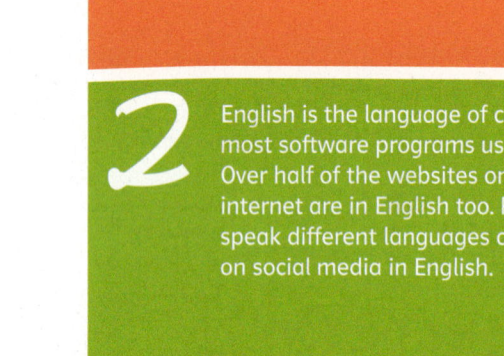

2 English is the language of computers – most software programs use English. Over half of the websites on the internet are in English too. People who speak different languages can also chat on social media in English.

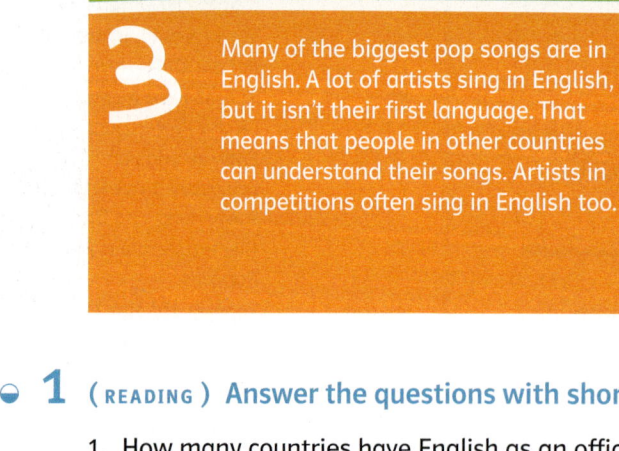

3 Many of the biggest pop songs are in English. A lot of artists sing in English, but it isn't their first language. That means that people in other countries can understand their songs. Artists in competitions often sing in English too.

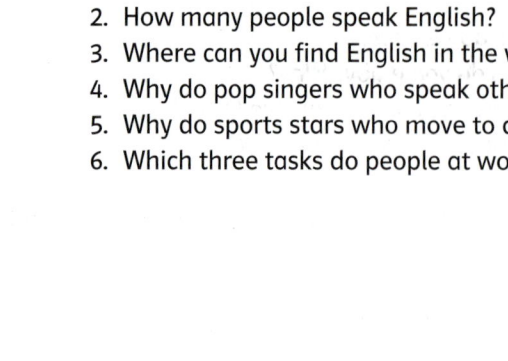

● 1 (READING) **Answer the questions with short answers.**

1. How many countries have English as an official language?
2. How many people speak English?
3. Where can you find English in the world of computers?
4. Why do pop singers who speak other languages often sing in English?
5. Why do sports stars who move to different countries use English?
6. Which three tasks do people at work sometimes have to do in English?

4 Sports stars often move to play in other countries. When they need to communicate with fans or the people in their new team, it's easier for them to use English. Sports stars often use English like this when they aren't in an English-speaking country.

5 English is the language of international business. Many people write e-mails, give presentations and meet other employees in their job. If they work with companies and customers from other countries, they often have to do these tasks in English.

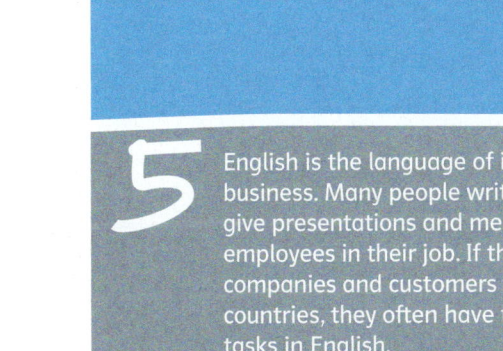

2 (SPEAKING) Find examples.

a) Talk in a group. Think about these questions.

1. Which programs, websites and social media sites do you use?
2. Which songs and artists do you like? Which series do you enjoy? Why?
3. Which international sports stars do you know and like? Why do you like them?
4. Which international companies do you know? What do they make or sell?

b) Collect new English words for each of these topics. Add to the lists during the year. (You can make lists for other topics too!)

computers   music   sport   work and business

Unit 1 Intro

Around Australia

G'day! My name is Penny and I live near Canberra. That's the capital of Australia. Spring begins in September in Australia and Christmas is in the summer. So people often celebrate Christmas on the beach!

1

2

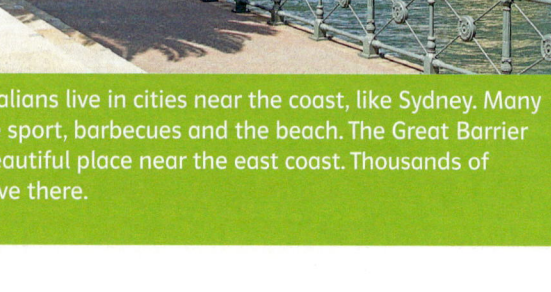

Most Australians live in cities near the coast, like Sydney. Many people love sport, barbecues and the beach. The Great Barrier Reef is a beautiful place near the east coast. Thousands of creatures live there.

1 (SPEAKING) **Choose a photo and tell your partner about it.**

a) Describe the photo.

There is / There are ….
A person is …ing …. / Some people are …ing.

b) Would you like to travel to Australia? Why or why not?

> cool beaches   beautiful animals
> very hot   expensive   . . .

2 (READING) **Which three sentences are right?**

2/1

1. The capital of Australia is Sydney.
2. In Australia spring starts in September.
3. Many animals live in the Great Barrier Reef near the east coast.
4. Fifty thousand years ago Australia was a part of Antarctica.
5. Many Aboriginal people were killed after the British settlers came.
6. There are a lot of schools in the centre of the country.

Am Ende dieser Unit kann ich ...
- Informationen über Australien verstehen.
- einen Blogeintrag über eine Reise schreiben.
- darüber sprechen, wenn ich krank bin.
- Texte über Umweltprobleme verstehen.
- Informationen in einer Apotheke weitergeben.
- einen Film über Tiere in Australien verstehen.

3

Australia is one of the largest countries in the world. It broke away from Antarctica millions of years ago. There are many animals that only live in Australia, like the koala and the kangaroo.

4

Aboriginal people have lived in Australia for over 50,000 years. In the 18th century the first British settlers arrived. Thousands of Aboriginal people were killed after that. They have struggled for their rights since then.

5

The flat, hot centre of Australia is called the 'outback'. Not many people live there, and they live a long way away from each other. That's why children have their school lessons online at the School of the Air.

3 (LISTENING) Listen to Peter's talk about the School of the Air.

1,3
2/2

a) There is one mistake in each sentence. Listen and find the word which is wrong.

1. I'm a Year 10 student at the School of the Air.
2. I sit in front of the TV when the lesson begins.
3. There isn't any time for online shopping, computer games or videos.
4. I have the same homework as other students in Australia.
5. Three times a year the students spend a month together in town.
6. The music day is the best part of the school year.

b) Write the correct sentences in your exercise book.

Ich kann Informationen über Australien verstehen. ✔

A trip to Uluru

1 Find Uluru on the map of Australia at the back of the book.

What is the nearest large town?

2 (READING) Read Koa's blog post about his visit to Uluru.

1,4
3/1

INTERNET

1 **25th September 2021**
Hi everyone!
I really enjoyed my visit to Uluru, the big, beautiful rock in the Australian outback. I come
5 from Perth on the west coast of Australia. My father is from an Aboriginal tribe near there, but we have a modern lifestyle. So I didn't know much about Uluru before the trip. I was very excited on the journey.
10 Uluru is a famous sight for tourists. But did you know that they aren't allowed to climb the rock any more? That's because Uluru is an important place for Aboriginal people. Some tourists are disappointed when they find out. But they can
15 do other things. The guides can show them how to look for water or make a fire. There are walks around Uluru and helicopter flights too. The tribes have a lot of traditions. I saw some Aboriginal dances and they played the
20 didgeridoo last night. It sounds cool!

I also saw some very colourful Aboriginal dot paintings of birds and other animals.
After the music we sat around the fire and
25 listened to some Aboriginal stories. (It was a dark night, but I wasn't afraid!) The Aboriginal people believe that giant creatures came here a long time ago. They made the mountains, rocks and rivers. That's why the Aboriginal people
30 want to protect Uluru and other places in the outback.
Before I left, I tried kangaroo meat. My father asked me, "What did you think of it?" It was delicious. I was surprised!
35 So did I enjoy my time at Uluru? Yes, I did! And I won't forget what I learned about the Aboriginal people. Will I cook kangaroo meat at home in Perth? Well, maybe. ☺
I'll write more tomorrow.
40 Bye!

CULTURE

Der Uluru ist für die Aborigines ein heiliger Ort. Nach ihrem Glauben ruhen dort die Geister ihrer Vorfahren. Der Berg wurde den Aborigines im Jahr 1985 zurückgegeben. Der Berg ist 863 Meter hoch. Die Aborigines haben sich dafür eingesetzt, dass Menschen den Uluru nicht mehr besteigen dürfen. 2019 wurde der Aufstieg geschlossen. Kennst du andere Orte, an denen Besucher nicht zugelassen sind oder bestimmte Regeln beachten müssen?

3 Work with the text.

a) Copy and complete the notes about Koa and his trip.

Comes from: …   Listened to: …
Father is from: …   Tried: …
Saw (two things): …   Won't forget: …
Aboriginal people played: …

b) Which of the things in the text would you do at Uluru? Which wouldn't you do? Say why.

3/2 **4 Work with adjectives from the text.** → **M** Bus stop, p.140

a) Read what people at Uluru said. Put in the words. You don't need all of them. → ○ p.114

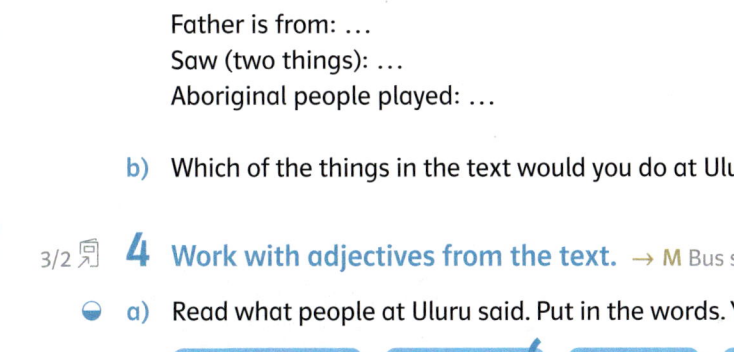

1. "Look at the evening sun on Uluru! It's <u>beautiful</u>!"
2. "Later we can eat some kangaroo meat. It's —— !"
3. "Tourists aren't allowed to climb Uluru. I was —— when I found out. ☹"
4. "It was my friend's birthday yesterday. She was —— when the guide gave her a small present!"
5. "Aboriginal people have a lot of traditions. But many have a —— lifestyle."
6. "Uluru is a safe place. You needn't be —— !"

b) Write a sentence with each of the adjectives that you didn't use in a).

5 (SOUNDS) **Read, say and listen.**

a) Say the words. Where does the stress go? Copy the table and put them in the right group.

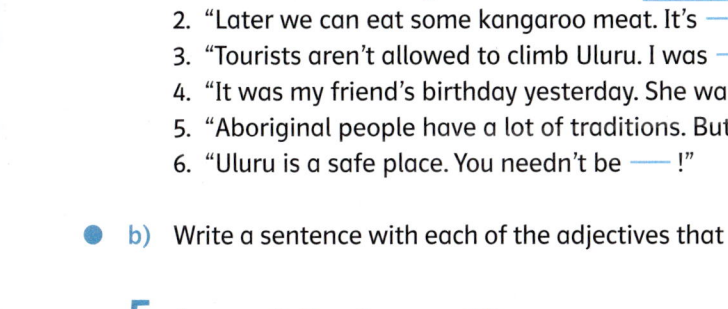

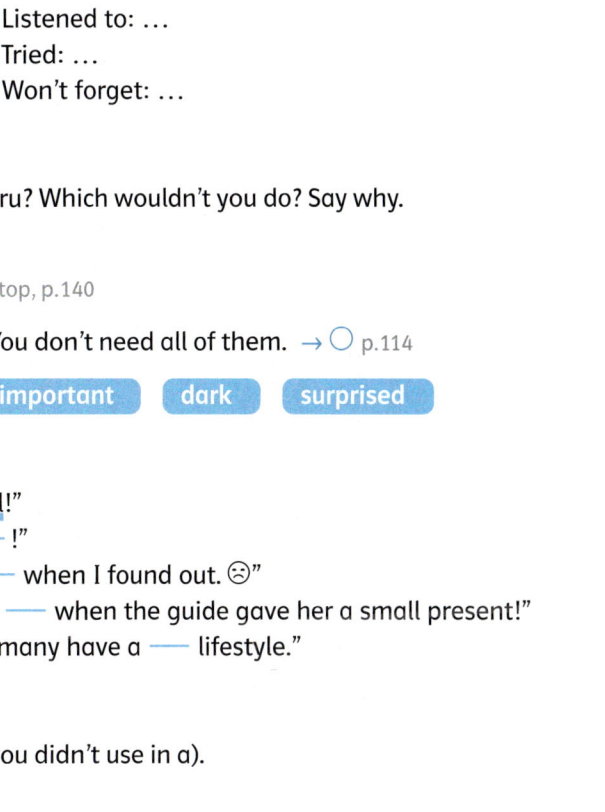

STUDY SKILLS

Du kannst die Betonung der Wörter (Englisch: „stress") in den Wortlisten ab S.154 oder in einem Wörterbuch nachschlagen. Ein senkrechter Strich vor einer Silbe zeigt an, dass dieser Teil des Wortes betont wird (z. B. colourful [ˈkʌləfl]) oder amazing [əˈmeɪzɪŋ]).

1st part of word	2nd part of word	3rd part of word
colourful	amazing	Aboriginal

1,5 b) Now listen to the words and check your answers.

Language detectives → **G1, p.127**

They <u>played</u> the didgeridoo <u>last night</u>.
Giant creatures <u>came</u> here <u>a long time ago</u>.
I <u>didn't know</u> much about Uluru.
"What <u>did</u> you <u>think</u> of it?"

In welcher Zeitform sind diese Sätze? Achte auf die <u>Signalwörter</u>!

4/3 **6 Complete the story about Omeo, a tour guide at Uluru.** → M Peer correction, p.141

a) Put in the right form of the words in brackets. → ◯ p.114

Last week a group of tourists from Germany (1) <u>visited</u> (visit) Uluru. They (2) —— (arrive) at three o'clock on Monday afternoon and they (3) —— (go) on a helicopter flight around the rock. It (4) —— (be) very exciting! After that they (5) —— (ask) Omeo a lot of questions. They (6) —— (sing) songs with Omeo in the evening, but he (7) —— (not play) the didgeridoo for them. Later the tourists (8) —— (try) some delicious Aboriginal food.

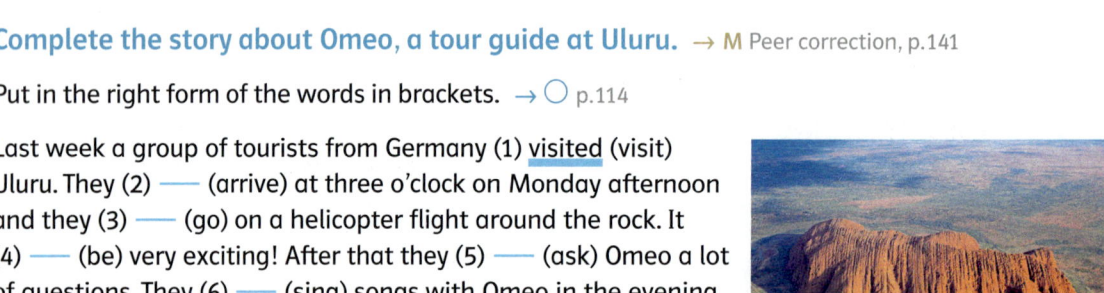

b) Make more sentences about the tourists' visit to Uluru.

1. climb the rock (✗) They <u>didn't climb</u> ....
2. enjoy the helcopter flight (✔) They ....
3. listen to stories (✔) They ....
4. leave rubbish there (✗)
5. take photos of Uluru (✔)
6. see any koalas (✗)

4/4 **7 Make the questions and find the right answers.** → M Bus stop, p. 140

a) Make the questions that Koa's friend asked. Then find the right answers. → ◯ p.114

Friend:
1. Uluru? · visit · did · when · you
    <u>When did you visit Uluru?</u>
2. did · there? · how long · stay · you
3. around Uluru? · go · you · on a walk · did
4. like · did · best? · you · what
5. you · to Uluru? · travel · did · how
6. go · did · on a helicopter tour? · you

Koa:
a. We went by plane.
b. Yes, we did. We walked for three hours!
c. No, we didn't. The flights are expensive.
d. We stayed for five days.
e. <u>We went to the rock in September.</u>
f. I liked the didgeridoo music best!

b) Write the questions for these answers.   visit Uluru?   play the didgeridoo?   take photos?

1. No, we didn't. But we listened to an Aboriginal man who played it!
2. Because I wanted to know more about Aboriginal culture and traditions.
3. Yes, I did. I took more than a hundred. I can show them to you now.

Language → G 2, p.128

I'll write more tomorrow.
I won't forget what I learned.
Will I cook kangaroo meat at home in Perth?

8 (SPEAKING) Talk about the future.

a) Think about these questions. Make notes.
You can use a dictionary for help.

> What kind of job will you have in ten years?
> Where will you live?
> What will you do in your free time?

b) Ask your classmates the questions from a) and answer them. → M Milling around, p.141

I think I'll …   Maybe I'll …   work as a ….   live in ….
I won't …   play … / watch … / make ….

9 Choose the right words for Koa's blog post.

Yesterday I **talk** · **talked** (1) to my friend Daku about the future. Daku **wants** · **want** (2) to be a
guide at Uluru. Then he **take** · **will take** (3) tourists on tours. He thinks that the job is interesting
before · **because** (4) you work with people. **Next year** · **Last year** (5) I want to look for a job at a
supermarket in Perth **so that** · **but** (6) I can travel to the USA. Maybe I **will** · **doesn't** (7) spend a
year there and see **many** · **much** (8) great places!

✿ 10 (TASK) A blog post → V Talking about experiences, p.146

a) Think of a class trip or another interesting journey. Make notes in your exercise book for a blog post.

Trip to: …			
How did you travel?	Who went with you?	How long?	What did you see?
– …	– …	– …	– …

b) Add to your notes. How did you feel when you
were there?

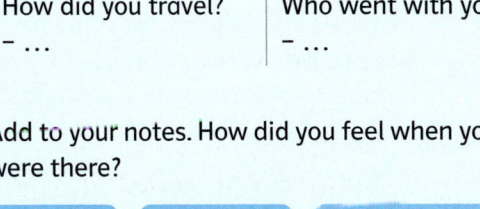

excited   surprised   disappointed

afraid   …

When did you arrive and leave?

c) Use your notes to write a blog post about the
trip. Look at the checklist on page 145 to check
your draft.

d) Share your blog post with a partner. Give feedback. → M Tip top, p.143

BLOG

Hi everyone!
This was my first trip to …. We stayed there for
… days. I went with my class and our teachers,
Mr … and Mrs …. We went by ….
I was very … when I saw ….
I won't forget …. It was great!
Maybe I'll go again one day.
Bye,
…

> **Ich kann einen Blogeintrag über eine
> Reise schreiben.** ✔

A few days in bed

1 Talk about the photo.

What do you think the woman's job is?

2 (READING) Read the dialogues.

1,6

1 Penny doesn't feel very well and is at the doctor's.

1.
Receptionist: Hello, how can I help you?
5 Penny: Hello. My name is Penny Watkins. I have an appointment at 11 o'clock to see Doctor Robson.
Receptionist: I can't find you in our list of patients. Are you new in Canberra?
10 Penny: Yes, my family moved here from Sydney two months ago.
Receptionist: If you're new, you have to register with us as a patient. If you register, we can get your medical records from your last
15 doctor.
Penny: OK.

2.
Doctor: Hello Penny, take a seat. How are you today?
20 Penny: Hello Doctor Robson. I feel really ill.
Doctor: Oh dear. What's the matter?
Penny: I have a bad headache and a cold.
Doctor: Do you have a high temperature?
Penny: I don't know. I feel quite hot.
25 Doctor: Well, let's look at you. ... OK, Penny, I think you've caught the flu.

Penny: Oh no. I want to go surfing tomorrow. If I miss the trip, my friends will be sad.
Doctor: If you go surfing, the flu will get much
30 worse.
Penny: What? You mean I can't go surfing?
Doctor: I'm afraid not. You'll have to stay in bed for a few days if you want to get better. You'll have to drink lots of water too.
35 Penny: Well, OK. Do I have to make another appointment?
Doctor: Call us if you're not better on Monday. Here's a prescription for some medicine. Take one tablet every morning before breakfast.
40 There's a pharmacy on Darwin Road.
Penny: Thank you.
Doctor: You're welcome. Goodbye Penny, and get well soon.

3 Choose the right answers.

1. There is a problem because Penny **forgot her last appointment** • **is a new patient**.
2. She has a headache and a cold. She also feels **hot** • **tired**.
3. The doctor thinks that Penny has **the flu** • **a bad cold**.
4. Penny wants to go **rafting** • **surfing**.
5. The doctor gives Penny **some medicine** • **a prescription**.
6. She should take a tablet every **morning** • **evening**.

5/1 **4 Work with the words.** → M Think – pair – share, p.143

a) Make a mind map with the words and phrases.
→ ○ p.115

> a headache · take tablets · being ill ✓
>
> a high temperature · drink tea · tired
>
> stay in bed · the flu · a cold

STUDY SKILLS

Du kannst neue Wörter besser behalten, wenn du sie mit Wörtern verbindest, die du schon kennst. Sammle sie in Wörternetzen und ergänze neue Wörter.

ill
I feel ....   being ill   I can ....
                          I have ....

b) Add more words and phrases to the mind map.

5 (SPEAKING) Sort out the mixed-up dialogue.

a) Put the phrases in the right order. Act the dialogue. → ○ p.115 → M Read and look up, p.142
5/2

Receptionist:

1 Can you come today at 2:30 p.m.?

2 No problem. Goodbye.

3 Hello. How can I help you?

4 Good. What was the name again?

5 OK, Mr Hogan. See you at 2:30 p.m.

Patient:

6 Thank you. Goodbye.

7 Yes, I can.

8 Hogan. That's H-O-G-A-N.

9 Hello. My name is Mr Hogan. I would like to make an appointment. I have a high temperature.

b) Change the name, the time and the problem. Act the new dialogue.

6 (LISTENING) Listen to the dialogue between Penny and her father.

1,7
6/3–4

Complete the sentences. You don't need all the words.

> a breakfast · swimming · last · sad · surfing · happy · first · a barbecue

1. Penny feels … about the trip to the beach.
2. It's the … time. All her friends are going.
3. She will miss … with her friends too.
4. Her father will go … with her one day.

LISTENING SKILLS

Achte beim Hören darauf, wie die Sprecherinnen und Sprecher klingen. Wann geht die Stimme nach oben oder nach unten? So kannst du erschließen, wie sich die Personen fühlen.

Language detectives → G 3, p.129

If I <u>miss</u> the trip, my friends <u>will be</u> sad.
If you <u>go</u> surfing, the flu <u>will get</u> much worse.
You'll <u>have</u> to stay in bed for a few days if you <u>want</u> to get better.

In diesen Sätzen findest du eine Bedingung und die Folge davon. In welchem Teil des Satzes steht die Bedingung, in welchem Teil die Folge? Wo findest du immer das will-future?

7 Choose the right answers.

6/5

1. If Penny goes to the pharmacy, they **give** · **will give** her the tablets.
2. If she takes the tablets and stays in bed, she **will get** · **gets** better soon.
3. If she **stays** · **will stay** at home tomorrow, she will sleep a lot.
4. Dad: If you go surfing tomorrow, you **will be** · **are** very ill!
5. But if you **will call** · **call** Lara, she will tell you the news.
6. Penny: If I **don't feel** · **won't feel** better on Monday, I will go to the doctor's again.

6/6 ## 8 Write sentences about Penny. → M Bus stop, p.140

a) Complete the sentences. → ○ p.115

1. If Penny goes to school on Monday, she —— cricket (play)
   If Penny goes to school on Monday, she <u>will play</u> cricket.
2. If she wants to talk, she —— her friends. (call)
3. They will have a barbecue too if they —— longer. (stay)
4. Penny will work with her best friend if she —— a project at school. (do)
5. If her dad isn't too busy, they —— surfing in a few weeks. (go)
6. She will take photos if she —— her cousin in Sydney next month. (visit)
7. Her cousin will come to Canberra in December if she —— time. (have)

b) Write four sentences about yourself. Use these ideas.

... if my grades are good next week ...
... if there is enough time on Saturday ...

... will watch a film tomorrow if ...
... will help my ... at the weekend if ...

Wie bildet man solche Sätze aus Bedingung und Folge im Deutschen? Wie bildet man sie in anderen Sprachen, die es in eurer Klasse gibt?

9 Put in the right words to complete the message. You don't need all of them.

come   hours   visited   if   was   where   you ✔   barbecue

were   because

E-MAIL

Hi Penny,

Are you (1) feeling better now? I hope so!

The surfing trip —— (2) fun yesterday. But we missed you! ☹ The waves —— (3) very big and we spent two —— (4) at the beach. I wore a hat —— (5) the sun was very hot. If you —— (6) next time, I'll show you the café —— (7) we had a burger. I'll visit you —— (8) you're better tomorrow.

See you,

Lara

10 Match the sentence halves.

7/7–8

1. If my leg doesn't hurt any more,
2. If I don't sleep much,
3. If you need some medicine,
4. If you work hard at school,
5. If the doctor doesn't speak so fast,
6. If we are late,

a. I get tired.
b. wait for us.
c. you can get a good grade.
d. Penny can understand her.
e. go to the pharmacy.
f. I can play basketball at the weekend.

Language → G 3, p.129

If you're new, you have to register with us.

If you register, we can get your medical records.

Call us if you're not better on Monday.

❋ 11 (TASK) A dialogue → V Talking about being ill, p.147

a) Use the phrases to make a dialogue. Partner B doesn't feel well. Partner A gives advice.

7/9

A: Hi, …

B: Hi. …

A: Oh dear. …

B: I … . And my … . …

A: Maybe you should … .

B: OK, I'll do that.

A: … ((Give more advice.))

B: Thanks. That's good advice!

A: … ((Look at page 16 to see how you can finish the dialogue.))

How are you today?

I feel really ill.   I don't feel very well.

What's the matter?   What's the problem?

I have a bad … .   My … hurts.   …

… go to the doctor's   … take medicine

… go to the pharmacy   …

If you drink …, you'll … .   …

b) Change roles.

Ich kann darüber sprechen, wenn ich krank bin. ✔

Great Barrier Reef in danger

 1 What do you already know about the Great Barrier Reef? → **M** Think – pair – share, p.143

 2 (READING) Read the online article and the letter.

1,8–9

A INTERNET

9 June 2019

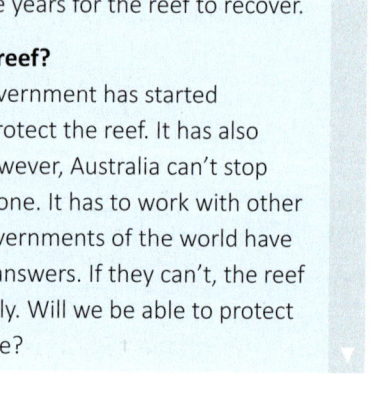

1 **A beautiful place**
The Great Barrier Reef is one of the most beautiful places on earth. It has thousands of reefs and hundreds of islands. The Great
5 Barrier Reef is 2,300 kilometres long. More than 400 kinds of coral and hundreds of kinds of fish and birds live here. But the Great Barrier Reef is in danger.

Climate change and coral bleaching
10 Climate change causes warmer water temperatures and 'coral bleaching'. When the water gets warmer, it destroys the algae on the coral. The coral loses its beautiful colours and there is coral bleaching. Large areas of the reef
15 have already died.

Ships and oil spills
A lot of ships go past the Great Barrier Reef. The worst accident happened in 2010, when a Chinese ship hit the reef. This caused damage
20 to three kilometres of coral and there was a big oil spill. It will take years for the reef to recover.

Can we save the reef?
The Australian government has started programmes to protect the reef. It has also
25 changed laws. However, Australia can't stop climate change alone. It has to work with other countries. The governments of the world have struggled to find answers. If they can't, the reef may die completely. Will we be able to protect
30 this beautiful place?

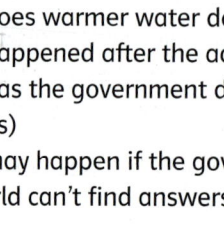

3 Write short answers. Use information from the texts.

a) Use information from the article.

1. How many kinds of coral live on the reef?
2. What does warmer water do to the algae?
3. What happened after the accident in 2010?
4. What has the government done? (Two answers)
5. What may happen if the governments of the world can't find answers?

b) Use information from the letter.

1. Who sent the letter?
2. In which city does he or she live?
3. When did he or she write the letter?
4. When did the person visit the reef?
5. How does the person feel about the future of the reef?

READING SKILLS

Du kannst neue Wörter auch ohne Wörterbuch verstehen, wenn du dir den Inhalt anschaust. Vielleicht kennst du das Wort „bleaching" (Zeile 11) nicht. Im Text steht aber „the coral loses its beautiful colours". Daraus kannst du erschließen, dass es „die Farbe verlieren" bedeutet.

B

1

Robert Phillips
XX Martens Place
Brisbane
QLD X000

Australian Government
5 Department of the Environment and Energy
Barbara Thompson
GPO Box XXX
Canberra ACT XXXX   10th October 2019

Dear Mrs Thompson,

10 I am writing to protest about the destruction of the Great Barrier Reef. Last month I visited the reef. In the past there were beautiful colours. But some parts of the reef look awful now!

Coral bleaching is a very big problem. The coral and the animals that live on the reef are dying because the water is getting warmer. The government has changed some laws but it 15 can do much more.

Oil spills from ships are a problem too. It takes years for the reef to recover from a bad oil spill. Why can't ships avoid the reef completely?

I am very worried about the future of the Great Barrier Reef. We must try to save the reef before it is too late. If we don't do anything now, we will lose this amazing place forever.

20 Yours sincerely,

Robert Phillips
Robert Phillips

4 Choose one of these tasks.

9/1–2 a) Give a short presentation about the Great Barrier Reef and its problems.
→ M 1-minute-presentation, p.140

Use information from the texts and find more photos. Say how you feel about the problems and where the photos are from.

OR

b) Write a short letter about the reef to Mrs Thompson. Say:

– why you are writing and how you feel
– how you heard about the problem
– what the government should do

There is more about letters on pages 106 and 107.

Ich kann Texte über Umweltprobleme verstehen. ✔

At the pharmacy

Du bist in einer Apotheke in Bayern. Du triffst eine englischsprachige Touristin, die nicht so gut Deutsch spricht. Hilf ihr dabei, Medikamente zu kaufen.

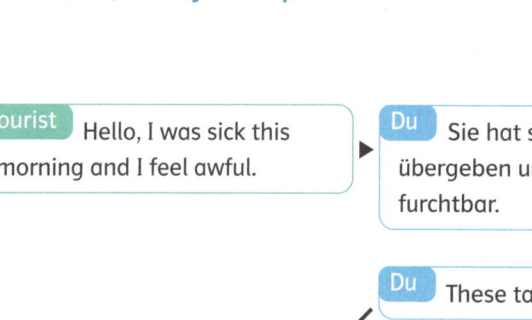

⌐ 1 (MEDIATION) Can you help?

Tourist	Du	Apotheker/in
Tourist Hello, I was sick this morning and I feel awful.	**Du** Sie hat sich heute Morgen übergeben und fühlt sich furchtbar.	**Apotheker/in** Diese Tabletten sind gut, wenn man sich übergeben hat. Sie sollte morgens und abends eine nehmen.
	Du These tablets ….	
Tourist How much are they?	**Du** Wie viel …?	**Apotheker/in** Sie kosten 15 € für eine 10er Packung.
	Du They cost ….	
Tourist OK. Here you are.	**Du** ….	**Apotheker/in** Vielen Dank. Wenn es in zwei Tagen nicht besser ist, soll sie zum Arzt gehen.
	Du You should ….	
Tourist Thank you very much.	**Du** ….	**Apotheker/in** Dann wünsche ich gute Besserung.
	Du Get ….	
Tourist Thank you. Goodbye.	**Du** ….	

⌐ 2 (SPEAKING) Spielt weitere Dialoge.

8/1

Nutzt die Informationen in der Tabelle und spielt zu dritt weitere Dialoge.

have a headache	take tablets / medicine
have a high temperature	drink water
have a cold	stay in bed

Ich kann Informationen in einer Apotheke weitergeben. ✔

Amazing creatures

1 **What Australian animals do you know?**

→ **M** Think – pair – share, p.143

How many Australian animals do you and your class know?
Make a list.

2 **(VIEWING)** **Watch the film.**

a) Match the fact cards (1–4) with the photos (A–D) from the film.

1
– Kakadu National Park
– very dangerous

2
– live in families
– love to swim and play with tourists

3
– 7 metres wide
– from May to November

4
– Ningaloo Reef
– the world's largest fish

whale shark saltwater crocodile dolphin manta ray

b) Watch the film again. Take notes to complete the sentences.

1. Saltwater crocodiles are one of the most … in the world.
2. The dolphins are full of … .
3. Manta rays look like they're … when they're eating.
4. Whale sharks can be as much as … metres long.

VIEWING SKILLS

Dieser Film ist ein Dokumentarfilm. Auf Englisch nennt man diese Art von Film „documentary". In einem Dokumentarfilm werden interessante Fakten zu einem bestimmten Thema präsentiert. Welche Dokumentarfilme kennst du noch?

3 **(SPEAKING)** **Talk about the animals in the film.**

Have you seen animals like these in real life? Where?
Which of the animals would or wouldn't you like to see? Say why.

I have/haven't seen … .
I saw it/them … (at the zoo in …/in …)
I'd like to see … … (interesting/beautiful/…)
I wouldn't like to see … … (dangerous/scary/…)

Ich kann einen Film über Tiere in Australien verstehen.

Checklist 🌐 Find more online: nd4r3a

✔ **Ich kann Informationen über Australien verstehen.**

Canberra is the capital of Australia. •
The Great Barrier Reef is a beautiful
place near the east coast. •
Aboriginal people have lived in
Australia for over 50,000 years. 10 ↗

✔ **Ich kann einen Blogeintrag über eine Reise schreiben.**

Hi everyone! • I really enjoyed my
visit to Uluru. • I didn't know much
about Uluru before the trip. • I'll
write more tomorrow. • Bye! 10 ↗

✔ **Ich kann darüber sprechen, wenn ich krank bin.**

I have a bad headache and a cold. •
If I miss the trip, my friends will be
sad. • Call us if you're not better on
Monday. • Get well soon. 10 ↗

✔ **Ich kann Texte über Umwelt-probleme verstehen.** 11 ↗

✔ **Ich kann Informationen in einer Apotheke weitergeben.** 11 ↗

✔ **Ich kann einen Film über Tiere in Australien verstehen.**

👥 ❋ (UNIT TASK) # A class event

Organisiert einen australischen Nachmittag oder
Abend mit der Klasse. Ihr könnt eure Familie,
Freunde und andere Leute aus der Schule
einladen. Ihr könnt euch auch eine Idee aussuchen
und sie innerhalb des Unterrichts umsetzen.

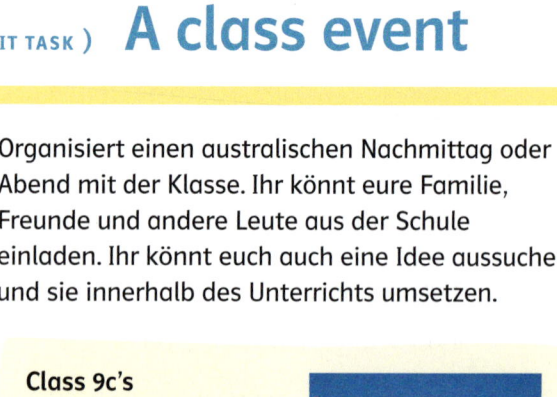

Class 9c's
AUSTRALIAN EVENING
When? Tuesday 18th
October at 5:00 p.m.
Where? Room 14
See you there!

Step 1

Make a plan for the event.

a) Collect ideas for the programme.
→ M Placemat, p.142

music/dance?   a video?   a quiz?

a short talk / a reading?   …

Denkt daran, das Thema der Veranstaltung ist Australien!

b) Find a location and a date.

c) Copy the table and make a plan like this:

What?	Time needed?	Who can do it?
Introduction	5 minutes	Tim and Julia
1. …		
2. …		
Break (with food and drink?)		
…		

Step 2

Plan your event in more detail.

a) What will you have to do? Make a list of jobs. Here are some ideas.

- Who can be the presenter?

- Who can design the poster and share it?

- Who can organize the break (if you have one)?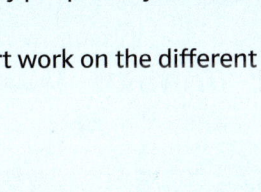

- Are there any special guests? Who can send the invitations?

- Who can tidy the room after the event?

- Who can organize decorations?

- Who can take photos and write a report?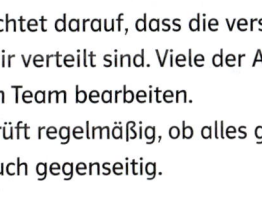

- Who should get a present or a 'thank you' at the end? Who can organize this?

b) Decide in class who can do which job. How many people do you need for each job?

c) Start work on the different jobs.

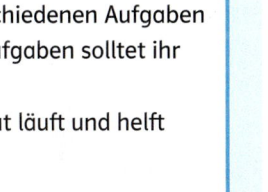

Thanks!

STUDY SKILLS

Achtet darauf, dass die verschiedenen Aufgaben fair verteilt sind. Viele der Aufgaben solltet ihr im Team bearbeiten.
Prüft regelmäßig, ob alles gut läuft und helft euch gegenseitig.

Step 3

Hold your event. Good luck!

Step 4

Talk about the event.

a) Say what you think in one sentence. The groups can take turns to talk about it.
   → **M** Round robin, p.142

b) Talk about these questions together.

- Which parts of the project went well?
- What could you do better?
- What did you learn?

Life in Australia

1 Match each heading with a photo.

A A road train
B Be careful! There could be a fire!
C When you're ill in the outback
D Drive carefully! There may be kangaroos!
E An Aboriginal dot painting
F Sydney Harbour Bridge
G The music of the Aboriginal people
H Scary creatures?

INFO

Australien ist ein sehr großes Land. Von Perth an der Westküste bis Brisbane an der Ostküste sind es mehr als 4.300 Kilometer auf der Straße. Im Vergleich dazu beträgt die Entfernung auf der Straße von München nach Hamburg rund 800 Kilometer.

2 (SPEAKING) Talk about the photos.

Which of the things in Australia would or wouldn't you like to see or do? Say why.

I'd like to

I wouldn't like to

see ....   look at ....   go to ....
ride on ....   listen to ....

I like ....
I'm interested in ....

I don't like ....
I'm not interested in ....

A picture-based interview

A

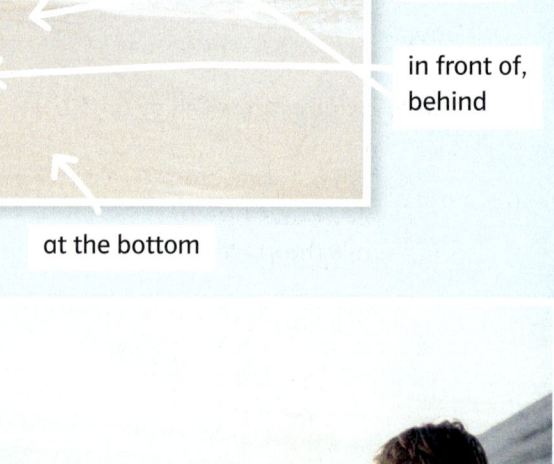

in the right/left corner

on the right, at the top

in the background

on the left

next to

in front of, behind

in the middle

in the foreground

at the bottom

B

1 **Look at photo A and talk about it.**

Describe the people in the picture.

Sprich über das Bild. Wähle eine sinnvolle Reihenfolge im Bild, um Einzelheiten zu beschreiben:
This photo/picture shows ....
There is ... / There are ....
He/She is about ... years old.

2 **Now talk about the photo in detail.**

a) Where are the people? Describe the place. What's in the background?

b) Describe what the people are doing and what they are wearing.

c) How do you think the people feel? Explain.

d) Describe other things in the photo. Example:
   – Talk about the different colours in the photo.
   – What's the weather like?

So kannst du dein Interview beginnen:
He/She is in the middle / at the bottom / on the right / ....
It's next to / between / behind / ....
In the background you can see ....

Benutze das present progressive und sprich in ganzen Sätzen:
He/She is standing/talking ....
He/She is wearing ....

I think he/she is happy/sad/ ....
Maybe he/she is thinking about ....

There is a blue/green/ ....
It's sunny/cold/rainy/ ....
Maybe it's summer.

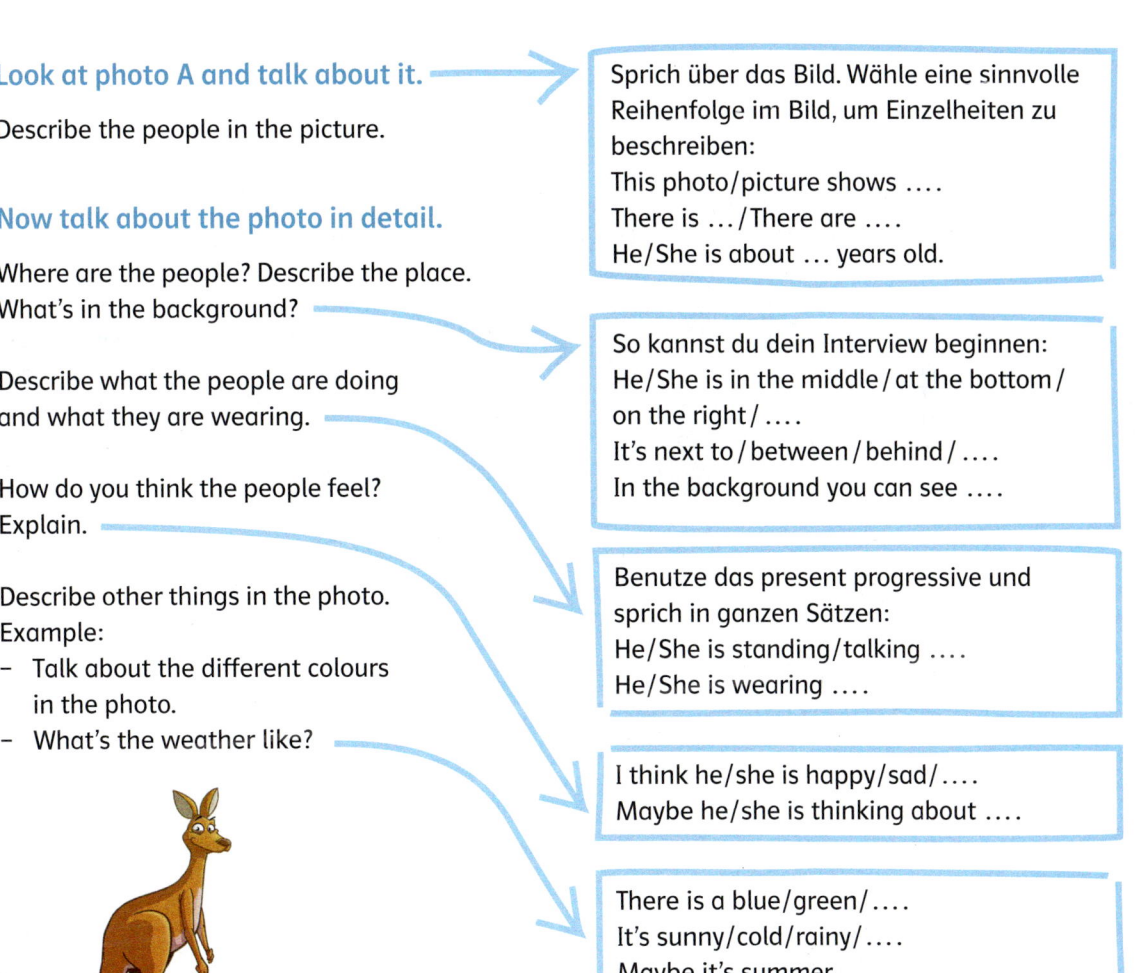

Stoppe die Zeit! Du solltest mindestens 1 Minute reden!

3 **What about you?**

   – Would you like to go surfing or camping? Why? Why not?
   – What kind of activities would you like to do with your friends?

I would/wouldn't like to ... because ....
I would like to play ... / visit ... / ....
I usually wear ... in summer.

4 **Now talk about photo B in the same way.**

Language → G 4, p.130
He <u>is wearing</u> a T-shirt.
They <u>are sitting</u> around the fire.

Ein zweisprachiges Wörterbuch in Printform ist für die gesamte schriftliche Prüfung erlaubt.

A Listening Comprehension (Hörverstehen)

You will hear the recordings twice.

1,10  **1** **Read the sentences. Then listen to the teenagers. Are the sentences true (T) or false (F)? There is an example (0.) at the beginning.**

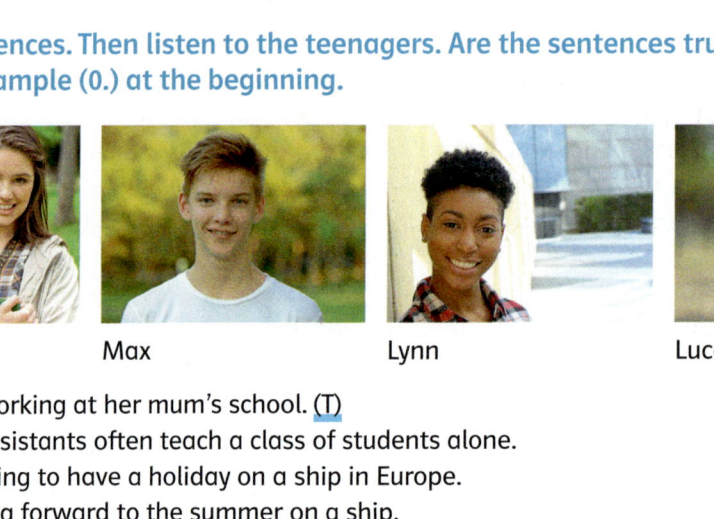

Katie   Max   Lynn   Lucas

0. Katie liked working at her mum's school. (T)
1. Classroom assistants often teach a class of students alone.
2. Max is planning to have a holiday on a ship in Europe.
3. Max is looking forward to the summer on a ship.
4. Lynn wants to work as an assistant in a sports shop.
5. Shop assistants only have to work during the day.
6. Lucas is going to leave for Brisbane next year.
7. The most important thing for Lucas is that he can go surfing in Brisbane.

1,11  **2** **Read the sentences. Listen to the four Australian teenagers again and fill in the information. There is an example (0.) at the beginning.**

0. Last year Katie did work experience at a school. Many of the children aren't good at reading or writing.
1. Katie will probably not work at a school ——.
2. Before Max starts his training, he wants to travel around —— ——.
3. Life on a ship is hard. Maybe Max will be ——.
4. Lynn says that shop assistants have to listen carefully to the ——.
5. Yesterday Lynn —— for the job online.
6. During his work placement Lucas will change departments every —— ——.
7. Lucas will have a room in the hotel so he will —— some money.

B Use of English (Sprachgebrauch)

1 Read the text about food in Australia. Find <u>nine</u> mistakes and write the correct word. There is an example (0.) at the beginning.

Eating in Australia

1 People who are on holiday in other countries think <u>different</u> about food	0 <u>differently</u>
and eating. Some are interested in trying new food. Others likes going	1
to the fast food restaurants they know from there home country.	2
If you travelled to Australia, you will not be disappointed. Australian	3
5 food is not at all boring. There are much immigrants in Australia and	4
they brought their multicultural influences to the country. So you will	
find Chinese and Bavarian restaurant, for example. But of course, there	5
are a lot of British traditions in Australia food too!	6
Australians are famously for their barbecues, and there are many free	7
10 barbecue grills. If you eat a meal like this at Sydney or another city, you	8
will understanding why barbecues are popular with Australians.	9

2 Read the text about Australia's capital and complete it with words from the box. Use one word for each gap. There is an example (0.) at the beginning.

> about · again · because · do · did · for · however · isn't · means · more · most ✔ ·
> new · quiet · quite · since · too · when

Australia's capital

Which city is Australia's capital? Sydney or Melbourne is what (0) <u>most</u> people would probably say. But Canberra is the capital of Australia. How (1) —— that happen?
In 1908 the Australian people decided to have one capital for all the Australian states. At first they talked (2) —— Sydney and Melbourne, but finally they decided on a (3) —— capital, Canberra. The name (4) —— 'meeting point'. That's (5) —— a good name because they planned and built the city as the business and cultural centre of Australia. Canberra has been the official capital (6) —— 1927. (7) ——, Canberra (8) —— a spectacular city. People say that it hasn't got enough character and that it is (9) —— small with its population of only 322,000 people.

C Reading Comprehension (Leseverstehen)

Work and travel in Australia

1 **An online guide**

Would you like to visit Australia? Would you like to see the outback and visit the Great Barrier Reef? Worried that it could be too

5 expensive?
The Australian Working Holiday visa can help you. It gives young people between 18 and 30 the chance to have an adventure for up to 24 months. More than 200,000 young people get

10 one every year.
This is what you need: a Working Holiday visa and enough money to live until you find a job. The visa allows you to work in Australia, but you're only allowed to work at each job for six

15 months.
What type of work can you do? A lot of jobs are on farms. Many farms in the outback are 100 kilometres away from the nearest neighbour or supermarket, so finding workers

20 is a problem.
Also, a lot of the work, like fruit picking, is seasonal. Farm work can be fun, and you don't need to have experience. But don't forget, it's hard work and you will get dirty.

25 They also need teachers in the outback who live with families on large farms and teach small groups of children. You should like kids and be flexible. Children often help on the farm during busy times, so they have lessons

30 in the evenings.

If you're not very interested in the outback, you can find factory jobs, office jobs or jobs in restaurants (like waiters, etc.) in towns. There are many organizations in Australia

35 which help people when they first arrive. They welcome you at the airport and find you a place to stay for the first few nights. They also give you information about the job market, places to stay, travel and safety.

40 But you won't just come to Australia to work. You'll do some exploring between your jobs, so it's often best to plan what you want to see. This will help you to find job locations that are best for your travel plans.

45 Linda (18): I took a job on a sheep farm with 6,000 sheep. I worked with an Italian girl and an English girl. I've never worked so hard in my life, and it really brought us together. I'm so thankful for those three months in the

50 outback.

1 Answer the questions. Short answers are possible.

1. How many people get a holiday visa each year? more than 200,000
2. Why is it difficult for many farms in the outback to find workers?
3. What is working on a farm like? (3 aspects)
4. What can a child's day in the outback look like at busy times?
5. How can the organizations help people when they arrive?

2 In which line or lines of the text do you find the following information?

1. The Australian Working Holiday visa gives young people the chance to stay in Australia for up to two years. → lines 7–9
2. It's difficult to find workers for farms in the outback.
3. The children sometimes have to help on farms, so people who give lessons in the evenings are needed.
4. You can find jobs in towns as well as in the outback.
5. There are organizations which can help you from the beginning of your visit.
6. If you want to explore and work in Australia, you should plan it well.

D Text Production (Schreiben)

1 Du bewirbst dich auf einen Ferienjob in Australien.

Du hast vor, nach Australien zu reisen, aber du weißt noch nicht, wie du die Reise bezahlen sollst.
In einer Zeitung hast du folgende Anzeige gelesen und du willst diese Gelegenheit nutzen.
Schreibe einen Brief, in dem du
– eine passende Einleitung schreibst und dich vorstellst (Name, Alter, Hobbys)
– über deine Vorkenntnisse berichtest: Arbeit mit Kindern/Tieren, Aushilfsjobs, usw.
– über deine Erwartungen sprichst: dein Englisch verbessern, neue Leute treffen, usw.
– nach den Arbeitszeiten und deiner freien Zeit fragst
– weitere Fragen stellst: Dauer deines Aufenthalts, Entfernung vom Flughafen, usw.
– einen geeigneten Schlusssatz findest.

Sheep farming family is looking for help

Are you flexible and interested in helping on a farm and earning some money
for free-time activities? If so, then we'd like to hear from you!

Who?   We are a nice sheep farming family and we are looking for someone to help us
on the farm.

Where?   About 100 km west of Brisbane

What?   – We need help with the sheep: counting, feeding, shearing[1],
– helping in the fruit and vegetable garden and at the market,
– babysitting and helping the children with their homework,
– cooking and helping in the house. You can live and eat with us for free.

When?   – We need help during the summer.

Send your application to Tim Baker at …

1 to shear – *scheren*

Schreibe einen Brief von ungefähr 100 Wörtern auf ein gesondertes Blatt. Achte auf eine ansprechende äußere Form und eine gut lesbare Handschrift.

E Mediation (Sprachmittlung)

1 Situierung und Text

Deine Schule veranstaltet eine Projektwoche zum Thema Umwelt. Deine Klasse hat sich für das Land Australien entschieden. Du findest Informationen dazu im Internet. Lies die Website aufmerksam durch.

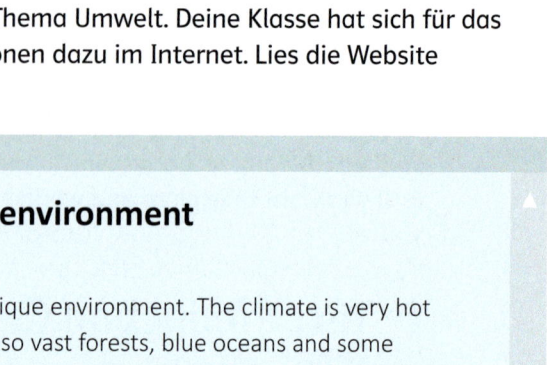

INTERNET

Australia and the environment

1 **Beautiful Australia**

Australia is a huge country (and continent) with a unique environment. The climate is very hot and dry – especially in the outback – but there are also vast forests, blue oceans and some amazing food. It attracts a lot of tourists who like eating fish and go diving to see the coral. This
5 experience should still be available to our children and grandchildren as well, so we need to take action now to save it for the future.

Climate change

Everyone is talking about climate change. One major cause concerns the fuel we burn. Using coal, for example, means that our atmosphere is being polluted by CO_2. This leads to rising
10 temperatures. It also makes people ill and kills the beautiful coral on the Great Barrier Reef. We should act now and find new energy sources so that we can close coal mines around the world.

Deforestation

Many of the world's forests have been destroyed and we should protect those which are left. Thousands of trees are cut down every year to make space for new houses as well as factories.
15 But trees are important for producing fresh air. They are also home to many species of animals. For every tree that is cut down, new ones should be planted.

Blue oceans

There are a lot of blue oceans around Australia. Oceans are important for our health – they give us food and a space for free-time activities. A lot of people have jobs connected with the ocean.
20 Governments set limits about how many fish can be taken from our oceans, both by individual fishermen and by industries. These limits need to be kept to and checked so that our oceans stay alive.

2 Aufgabe

Verwende die Informationen von der Website, um deine Klasse über die Situation in Australien zu informieren. Lies dafür die folgende Zusammenfassung auf Deutsch. Suche dann die fehlenden Informationen im englischen Text und ergänze die Lücken 1–10 mit Angaben in deutscher Sprache. Schreibe die Angaben in dein Heft.

Australien und seine Umweltprobleme

Wunderschönes Australien
Australien hat ein heißes, trockenes Klima, es gibt dort aber auch riesige Wälder, blaue Ozeane und unglaublich tolles Essen. Viele Touristen wollen ihren Urlaub in Australien verbringen. Diese (1) —— sollte auch für unsere Kinder und Enkelkinder noch (2) ——. Deshalb müssen wir jetzt beginnen, sie für die Zukunft zu bewahren.

Klimawandel
Leider wird häufig (3) —— als Brennstoff benutzt. Das macht Menschen krank und tötet die (4) —— am Great Barrier Reef. Es wird nach anderen Energiequellen gesucht, die die Umwelt nicht schädigen. Wenn das gelingt, können die Kohlebergwerke (5) —— werden.

Abholzung der Wälder
Viele Wälder (6) ——, um Platz zu machen für den Bau neuer Häuser und Industrieanlagen. Wir sollten also die verbleibenden (7) ——, da sie wichtig sind für unsere frische Luft. Auch geben sie vielen (8) —— ein zu Hause.

Blaue Ozeane
Es gibt viele schöne blaue Ozeane rund um Australien. (9) —— setzen Grenzen, wie viele Fische aus dem Meer gefischt werden dürfen. Diese Grenzen sollten (10) —— und kontrolliert werden, damit unsere Meere am Leben bleiben.

That's the end of Test practice 1!

Exploring India

1

India is more than nine times the size of Germany. It has a population of more than a billion people. New Delhi and Mumbai are the biggest cities. Tourists can see beautiful buildings like the Taj Mahal. But millions of poor people live in slums in big cities.

2

Most people in India work on farms, but jobs with computers are important too. India is less expensive than Europe. English is one of India's 22 official languages, and most Indians speak it. So India is an interesting place for international companies.

1 (SPEAKING) **Talk about the photos.**

Choose a photo and describe it to your partner.

There is a ....
He is .... She is .... It is ....
There are ....
They are ....
The photo shows a/some ....

2 (READING) **Read and take notes.**

22/1 ↗

What do you find out about these things?

1. India's population
2. the Taj Mahal
3. languages in India
4. India's independence
5. water in India
6. Holi
7. weddings in India

Am Ende dieser Unit kann ich ...
- Informationen über Indien verstehen.
- eine Firma vorstellen.
- ein Poster über Nachhaltigkeit gestalten.
- einen Text über eine berühmte Person verstehen.
- Informationen über verschiedene Jobs weitergeben.
- einen Film über einen Lieferservice verstehen.

3

India was a British colony for many years. But an Indian man, Mahatma Gandhi, led protests against the British. He helped India become an independent country in 1947. Gandhi died a few months after independence.

4

India has a lot of environmental problems. Many parts of the country are very dry, and sometimes people don't have enough water. There are also problems with pollution and waste in India. This is because so many people live together.

5

Family is very important in India, and young and old people often live together. There are many Indian traditions. One of them is Holi, the festival of colours. There are a lot of arranged marriages, and Indian weddings can last for several days.

3 (LISTENING) **Listen to an Indian girl and her grandmother.**

1,13

a) Find the missing information.

1. There will be a —— next week.
2. Grandma thinks there will be —— guests.
3. Amita and Krish first met at ——.
4. Young people in India are —— now.
5. When she was younger, Grandma didn't meet people from ——.

b) How does the girl feel about the event?

Ich kann Informationen über Indien verstehen. ✔

Working in India

1 (SPEAKING) **Look at the photos. What are they doing?**

I think he is working in a ....
Maybe she is working with ....

factory   computers   tourists   ...

2 (READING) **Read the internet page about different jobs in India.**

1,14
23/1

INTERNET

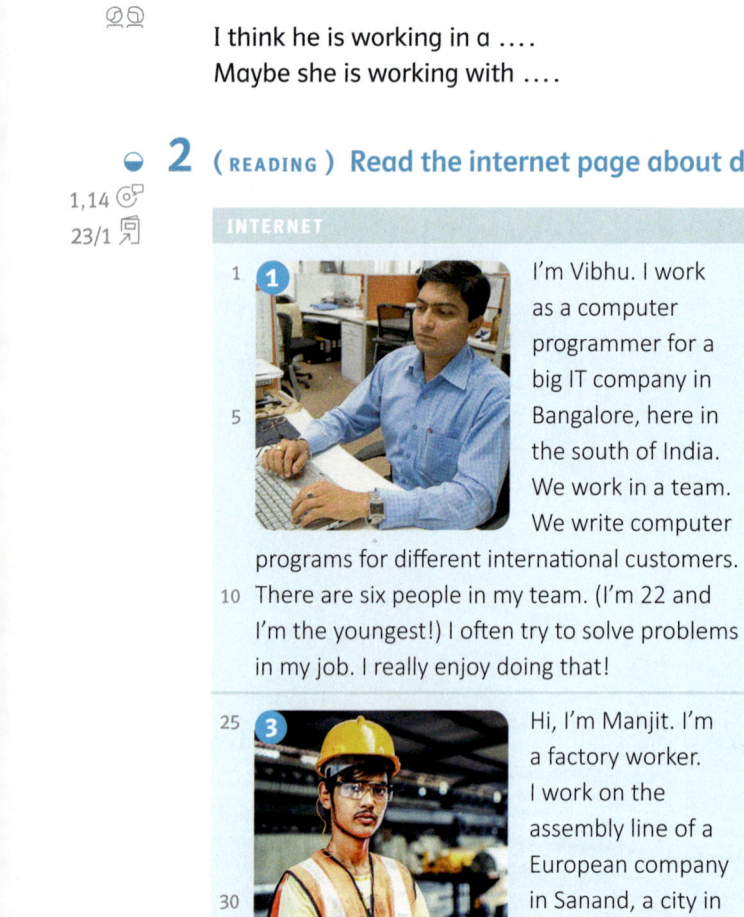

1 **1** I'm Vibhu. I work as a computer programmer for a
15 big IT company in Bangalore, here in the south of India.
   We work in a team. We write computer
20 programs for different international customers.
10 There are six people in my team. (I'm 22 and
   I'm the youngest!) I often try to solve problems
   in my job. I really enjoy doing that!

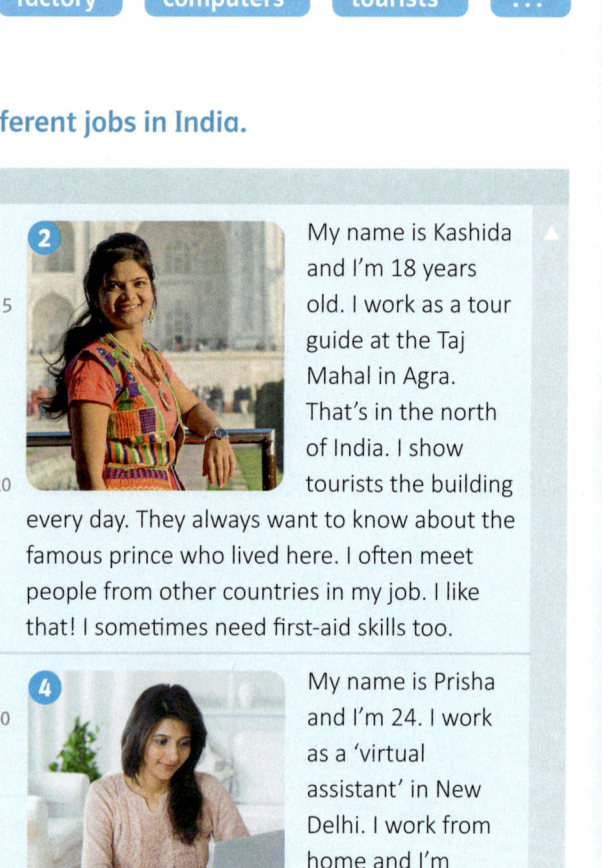

2 My name is Kashida and I'm 18 years
15 old. I work as a tour guide at the Taj
   Mahal in Agra. That's in the north
   of India. I show
20 tourists the building every day. They always want to know about the
   famous prince who lived here. I often meet
   people from other countries in my job. I like
   that! I sometimes need first-aid skills too.

25 **3** Hi, I'm Manjit. I'm
40 a factory worker. I work on the assembly line of a European company
30 in Sanand, a city in the north of India.
45 We make car parts.
   The company produces its goods in India and
   sells them all over the world. Sometimes
35 people are late for work. My boss doesn't like
   that! He sometimes gets very angry. Today
   machines do a lot of things. I'm 24, so I'm fit.
   But it's true that the work is very hard.

4 My name is Prisha
40 and I'm 24. I work as a 'virtual
   assistant' in New Delhi. I work from
   home and I'm
45 always online. I help different companies
   with their office jobs. For example I write
   e-mails and organize trips for my customers.
   I like working from home, but I don't usually
50 meet my customers. I never travel to work.
   That saves me a lot of time.

CULTURE

Arbeitsbedingungen in Indien unterscheiden sich sehr von denen in Europa. Rangordnungen sind sehr wichtig in der indischen Kultur und das zeigt sich in den Firmen. Für Europäer erscheinen indische Chefs manchmal sehr unhöflich und unfreundlich gegenüber ihren Angestellten. Was könnt ihr über Arbeitsbedingungen wie z. B. Arbeits- und Urlaubszeit in Firmen in eurer Nähe herausfinden?

3 Collect information about the people.

Copy the table and put in the information.

Name	How old	Job	One fact about job
Vibhu			
Kashida			
…			

4 (SPEAKING) Talk about the jobs with a partner.

Which of the jobs would or wouldn't you like to do? Say why. Use the information from Ex. 3.

I'd like to work as a … because … .
I wouldn't like to work as a … because … .

23/2 ⚐ ### 5 Work with words for jobs. → M Peer correction, p.141

a) Match the sentence parts to say what the people do. → ◯ p.116

1. A computer programmer
2. A farmer
3. A tour guide
4. A virtual assistant
5. A chef
6. A factory worker
7. A nurse

a. makes meals in a restaurant.
b. makes car parts, for example.
c. produces food and keeps animals.
d. shows interesting sights to tourists.
e. does office work for different people.
f. looks after people who are ill.
g. writes computer programs.

b) Find the words in the text.

1. A group of people who work or play together
2. A visitor from another country, for example
3. The things that a company makes and sells
4. Another word for a journey

6 (LISTENING) Listen to Kashida at the Taj Mahal. Choose the right answers.

1,15 ☉
23/3 ⚐

1. The prince met the girl at a **market** · **school**.
2. The wedding was five **months** · **years** later.
3. They **were happy** · **often had arguments**.
4. They designed **cities** · **buildings** together.
5. They had **four** · **fourteen** children.
6. The prince died in **1666** · **1696**.

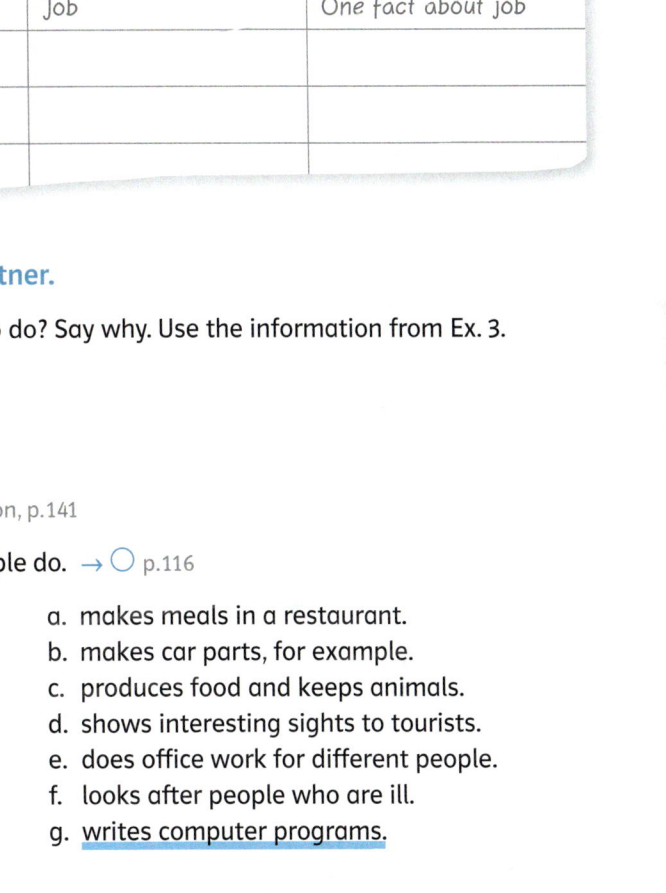

Language detectives → G 5, p. 131

I <u>show</u> tourists this in the building <u>every day</u>.
He <u>gets</u> very angry.
I <u>often</u> <u>solve</u> problems in my job.
I <u>don't</u> <u>usually</u> <u>meet</u> my customers.
My boss <u>doesn't like</u> that!

Schau dir die Sätze und die Signalwörter an.
Was drückst du mit dieser Zeitform aus?
Was musst du bei *he*, *she* und *it* beachten?
Wie bildest du die Verneinung?

7 Complete what Manjit says about his work.

a) Complete the sentences. Where do you need the -s? → ◯ p.116

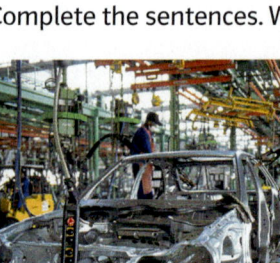

Manjit: I (1) <u>work</u> (work) between 40 and 65 hours every week. But I (2) —— (like) my job. I often (3) —— (listen) to music on the assembly line. Our boss (4) —— (visit) us most days. He (5) —— (work) in an office near the assembly line. He sometimes (6) —— (shout) at people when they (7) —— (arrive) late. Every Friday I (8) —— (finish) work at six o'clock. I (9) —— (go) home and the weekend (10) —— (start). No more work until Monday!

b) Use the notes to give more information.

1. more than 500 people – work – factory
2. boss – often – show – visitors – factory
3. we – not talk – to visitors (loud machines!)
4. best friend – work – another factory

8 Complete the sentences about the others.

a) Complete the sentences. → ◯ p.116

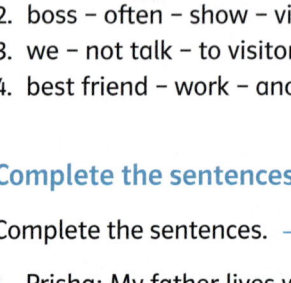

24/4–5
25/6

1. Prisha: My father <u>lives</u> with me. (live)
2. My father —— any more. (not work)
3. Vibhu —— for an IT company. (work)
4. He —— programs with other workers. (write)
5. They —— computers. (not repair)
6. Kashida —— tourists the Taj Mahal. (show)
7. She —— souvenirs. (not sell)

Language → G 5, p. 131
She likes ... ☺
She <u>doesn't like</u> ... ☹

b) Tell your partner three things about your daily routine. Two are true, one isn't true. Can your partner guess which thing isn't true? You can use these ideas:

A: I sometimes .... I don't .... I often ....
   (I never .... My brother .... My sister ....)
B: I think that's true! / I don't think that's true!
A: You're right!

9 Match the questions and the answers.

1. <u>What's your job?</u>
2. How do you travel to work?
3. How many hours do you work every week?
4. What does your company make?
5. Where are your customers?
6. Do you work from home?
7. What time do you usually start work?
8. Do you work in a team?

a. We have customers all around the world.
b. Yes, I do. There are six people in my team.
c. No, I don't. I work in an office.
d. <u>I work as a receptionist.</u>
e. I travel by bus.
f. I usually start work at 9 a.m.
g. I work 40 hours every week.
h. My company makes computer parts.

10 (SPEAKING) Act an interview about work.

25/7

Your partner asks you five questions from Ex. 9. You can use the answers from the exercise or make up your own answers. Start and finish like this:

A: Excuse me, can I ask you about your job, please?
B: Yes, of course. What would you like to know?
…
A: Thank you for the interview!
B: You're welcome!

Language → G 5, p.131
How <u>do</u> you <u>travel</u> to work?
<u>Do</u> you <u>work</u> from home?

SPEAKING SKILLS

Falls du deine Partnerin oder deinen Partner nicht sofort verstehst, helfen dir Fragen wie „What do you mean?" oder „Sorry, can you say that again?"

11 (TASK) A presentation about a company → V Presenting a company, p.148

a) Choose a company. It can be a local, national or international company.

b) Find information about the company. Search online. Take notes about the company.

What does the company make or do?
Where does the company produce its goods?
Where does it sell its goods?
How many people work there?

STUDY SKILLS

Überlege dir zunächst, welche Quellen du verwenden kannst. Du solltest nicht nur auf der Website der Firma nachschauen, sondern z. B. auch Zeitungsartikel und Berichte lesen.

c) Organize your information and make a plan. Find pictures of the things that the company makes.

1. Say what my presentation is about
2. Give information about the company
3. Answer questions about my presentation

d) Present the company. → M 1-minute-presentation, p.140

Today I'd like to tell you about ....
It's a company in .... It ....

Ich kann eine Firma vorstellen. ✔

In the country

● **1** (READING) **Read this article from a British youth magazine.**

1,16 ☞
26/1

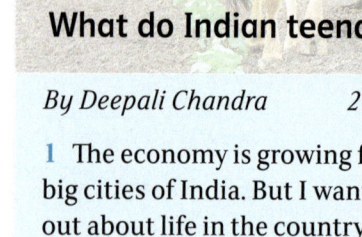

Deepali Chandra

What do Indian teenagers think?

By Deepali Chandra   *20th August 2021*

1   The economy is growing fast in the big cities of India. But I wanted to find out about life in the country and on farms, where most people still live. What environmental problems do teenagers in Indian villages worry about? I spoke to Kyra, Tanvi and Moti, three teenagers from villages in different parts of India.

2   Kyra is a 16-year-old girl from a village in the north of India. She told me, "We need to make farming more sustainable so that we can grow food in the future too. There is a lot of pollution. We use fertilisers that help the crops to grow. But they are slowly damaging the soil. Another problem is that there are more people, so we need more food for them. We grow two or three different crops in the same field every year. This is not good for the soil. The crops don't grow well here."

3   I also spoke to Tanvi (15), from the east of the country. She said, "Villages in India don't have good sanitation. Many houses don't have bathrooms or toilets. People wash themselves and their clothes in rivers every day. Waste pollutes the soil and water."

4   Sixteen-year-old Moti is a boy from a village in Gujarat, in the west of India. "Our village doesn't have good drinking water," Moti said. "We have to walk to another village every day, so we use the water very carefully."

5   Indian villages have many problems. However, the situation is changing. Sustainable living is important for the young people there. Some villages have changed their crops, and this has helped the soil. Others have raised money for better sanitation and drinking water. What about where you live? What can you do to help the environment?

READING SKILLS 👁

Wenn du dir die Struktur eines längeren Textes anschaust, kann sie dir helfen den Text leichter zu verstehen. Versuche als erstes zu erkennen, welche Aufgabe jeder Abschnitt hat. (Dieser Text hat fünf Abschnitte: eine Einleitung, drei Abschnitte, die zeigen, was die Teenager der Reporterin gesagt haben, und am Schluss eine Zusammenfassung.)

2 Match the headings with the parts 1–5 of the text. You don't need all of the headings.

A A walk to get water
B Things are getting better!
C Problems with farming

D Can machines help?
E Pollution in rivers
F What do they worry about?

3 Work with the text.

a) Answer the questions. You can use short answers. → p.117

1. What kind of problems did Deepali ask about?
2. What is the problem with fertilisers?
3. What can happen when there are two or three crops in the same year?
4. Why is bad sanitation a problem?
5. Why do they use water carefully in Moti's village?
6. What have some villages done to get better sanitation and drinking water?

b) Use information from the text to complete these sentences.

1. Most Indian people still ….
2. Crops grow better when ….

3. People wash themselves in rivers because ….
4. Young Indian people think ….

4 Work with words from the text.

a) What is it? Put in the right words. You don't need all of them. → p.118

drinking   teenagers   sustainable   field   fertilisers   environment   village

1. People who are between 13 and 19 are —— .
2. A —— is a group of houses and other buildings in the country.
3. Farmers use —— to help plants to grow.
4. Water that is safe to drink is called —— water.
5. If farming is —— , we will have food in the future too.
6. The —— is another word for the world around us.

b) Find the words in the text for these definitions.

1. plants which a farmer grows (Part 2)
2. where plants grow (Part 2)

3. the smallest room in the house (Part 3)
4. make something dirty (Part 3)

5 (SOUNDS) Listen, read and say.

1,17
26/2

1. There is a lot of pollution.
2. Many houses don't have bathrooms.
3. We have to walk to another village every day, so we use the water very carefully.
4. Some villages have changed their crops, and this has helped the soil.

SPEAKING SKILLS

Höre dir die Sätze genau an und versuche, sie nachzusprechen. Lange Sätze bestehen aus mehreren Abschnitten, die sinnvoll zusammenhängen (z. B. Verb und Objekt). Beim Zuhören kannst du diese Abschnitte erkennen.

The economy is growing <u>fast</u> <u>in the big cities</u>.
The crops don't grow <u>well</u> <u>here</u>.
We walk <u>to another village</u> <u>every day</u>.

Schau dir die Sätze an. Wo im Satz stehen die Adverbien <u>der Art und Weise</u> und wo stehen die Angaben <u>des Ortes</u> und <u>der Zeit</u>?

6 **Copy the table. Put the words and phrases in the right groups.** → M Peer correction, p.141

27/3

every day · fast · in the evening · at home ✓ · yesterday · well · here

every morning · carefully · in other countries · slowly · in India

Where?	When?	How?
at home	…	…
…		

27/4 **7** **Write sentences about village life in India.**

a) Use the words to write a sentence for each photo. Put the parts of the sentences in the right order.
→ ○ p.118

1. The people have breakfast at home every day.

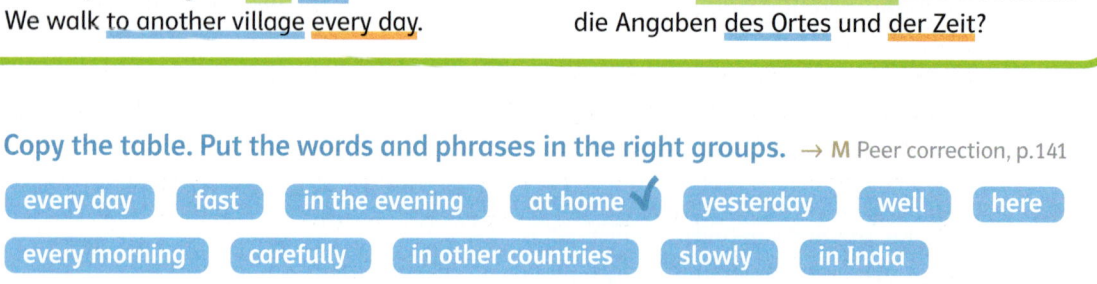

The people **every day** · **at home** · **have breakfast**

They **in the river** · **wash clothes** · **in the morning**

People **very hard** · **every day** · **work**

They **to get drinking water** · **a long way** · **walk**

Moti **on the farm** · **feeds the goats** · **every evening**

Crops **don't grow** · **in the soil** · **very well**

b) Write five sentences about your daily routine. Use two words or phrases from Exercise 6 in each sentence.

28/5 **8 Deepali's blog** → M Bus stop, p.140

a) Choose the right answers. → ◯ p.119

> **BLOG**
>
> Hi everyone!
> Village life in India **am** • **is** • **are** (1) very different from in Europe. Most houses have chickens, so the people can get eggs **easiest** • **easy** • **easily** (2). They know each other **good** • **well** • **best** (3) and chat with **their** • **them** • **they** (4) neighbours.
> Most people in villages **work** • **works** • **working** (5) on farms. Many **don't have** • **doesn't have** • **didn't have** (6) drinking water so they have to **getting** • **get** • **gets** (7) it from another village. Tomorrow **I talked** • **I talk** • **I'll talk** (8) to two other teenagers in Gujarat.
> What do you like about where you live?
> Bye,
> Deepali

b) Write a short comment about Deepali's blog and answer her question.

9 Find the right words for the gaps. You don't need all the words.

28/6

> are · is · lot ✔ · make · many · money · most · much · next

Kyra: Many farmers grow crops which need a <u>lot</u> (1) of water. Then the villages don't have enough water. That's why some farmers —— (2) now growing more crops which don't need so —— (3) water. Also, —— (4) villages don't have good sanitation. This causes water pollution, which can —— (5) people very ill. But things are changing. They have raised —— (6) to build new houses with bathrooms and toilets.

✳ 10 (TASK) A poster about sustainable living → V Sustainable living, p.149

a) Work in groups of four. What can you and your family do to help the environment? Collect topics and ideas. → M Placemat, p.142

28/7

Topics: Ideas:
pollution   waste   farming   use ...   buy more/less ...   travel by ...
    holidays   traffic   shopping   ...   save ...   ...

b) Find pictures for your ideas. Organize your information and make a poster about sustainable living.

c) Look at the other posters. Which posters have the best ideas? → M Gallery walk, p.141

d) Talk in the group about how you worked together. What would you do again, and what would you do differently another time?

> **Ich kann ein Poster über Nachhaltigkeit gestalten.**   ✔

Mahatma Gandhi and the Salt March

● **1** (SPEAKING) **Talk about the photo of Gandhi.**

What kind of person do you think he was? `strong?` `friendly?` `...?`

● **2** (READING) **Read the article about Gandhi and the Salt March.**

1, 18

2nd October 1869	1	Mohandas Gandhi was born in Porbandar, a city in the west of India, in 1869.
1870s–1914		Gandhi was the youngest of four children. He wasn't always good at school and he didn't 5 like sport. He was very small and didn't look strong. But when Gandhi wanted something, he certainly fought hard to get it. When he left school, he trained as a lawyer. India was a British colony at this time. Many 10 Indians were very poor and had to work very hard. Gandhi saw this and wanted to change the lives of the poorest people in India.
1914–1929		Gandhi decided to help India become an independent country. He believed in non-violent protest. He wasn't afraid to break the law and he was sent 15 to prison several times. Gandhi was a vegetarian. He never wore expensive clothes and he wasn't interested in money. Indians started to call Gandhi 'Mahatma'. This means 'great soul'.

● **3** **Work with the text.**

30/1–2 **a)** Check your answers to Ex. 1. Were you right?

b) Complete the sentences about Gandhi and India.

1. Gandhi's parents had ... children.
2. Gandhi trained as ... after he left school.
3. Gandhi didn't eat ....
4. The first Salt March started because there was ....
5. Indians had to ... from British shops.
6. Thousands of Indians ... the march.
7. More than 60,000 were ... after the march.
8. India got its ... in August 1947.
9. Gandhi ... a Hindu extremist in 1948.

c) Find the parts of the text which show that Gandhi was popular with most people in India.

Indien war eine der wichtigsten Kolonien Großbritanniens. Von 1858–1947 gehörte es zum britischen Weltreich („British Empire"). Als Indien 1947 unabhängig wurde, forderten auch andere Kolonien ihre Unabhängigkeit. Es war der Anfang vom Ende des British Empire.

March 1930

In 1930 Gandhi started the first 'Salt March', a protest against the British. After a new law Indians weren't allowed to make their own salt. They had to
20 buy expensive salt from British shops. So Gandhi and 78 followers decided to send a peaceful message to the British. They walked 400 kilometres together. More and more Indians joined the march.

When they arrived at the coast, thousands of people were with Gandhi. He showed them how to make salt. When he did this, he broke the law. The
25 British put Gandhi and more than 60,000 other Indians in prison after the march. The British used violence at another march, but the Indians did not use violence.

August 1947

India became an independent country in 1947. Unfortunately there was violence between Hindus and Muslims in India when independence came.

30th January 1948

30 Gandhi was a Hindu, and he respected other religions and cultures. Some Hindus were angry when he was friendly to the Muslims in India. A few months after independence Gandhi was shot and killed by a Hindu extremist.

4 Choose one of these tasks.

31/3–5

a) Take notes from the text and write your own timeline about Gandhi.
Use the internet to find this information: Which other countries did Gandhi live in, and when? → M Writers' conference, p.143

OR

b) Think about what you have learned in this unit. Collect information about one of these aspects of India.

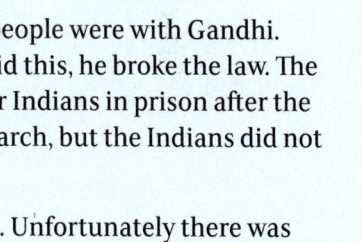

Use the information to give a topic-based talk. → M 1-minute-presentation, p.140

Ich kann einen Text über eine berühmte Person verstehen. ✔

Jobs around the world

Sanjay is a shop assistant in Mumbai in India. He works in a large supermarket. He often has to help customers. Sanjay works in the evening and at weekends. He works with many different products. He has to know all their prices, be quick and be good with numbers.

Sanjay

Hannah is a cook. She works in a restaurant in Toronto in Canada. She helps to plan menus and she cooks meals. Her food always has to taste and look good. She works every evening from 5:00 p.m. until 11:00 p.m. and she often has to work at weekends. She has to stand for long hours in her job.

Hannah

Jasmine is an assistant gardener who lives near Cambridge in England. She usually works outdoors in gardens and parks. But she often works in greenhouses in the winter. Jasmine helps to take care of plants. Jasmine has to be fit and she often uses machines in her job.

Jasmine

1 (MEDIATION) Du informierst dich über verschiedene Berufsbilder.

29/1

Auf einer Website für Jugendliche aus der ganzen Welt hast du diese drei Profile von jungen Menschen und ihren Berufen gefunden. Übertrage die Tabelle in dein Heft und ergänze die Informationen auf Deutsch.

	Beruf	Tätigkeiten	Besondere Anforderungen
Sanjay	Verkäufer		
Hannah			
Jasmine			

Ich kann Informationen über verschiedene Jobs weitergeben. ✔

Feeding Mumbai

1 (SPEAKING) **Talk about delivery services for food.** → M Think – pair – share, p.143

What delivery services for food do you know? Think about these questions.

What kind of food?
Who delivers it?
How do the people deliver the food?
Where and when do the people work?

2 (VIEWING) **Watch the film about a delivery service in Mumbai.**

a) Put the photos from the film in the right order.

b) Watch again. Take notes to answer these questions.

1. Who makes the meal?
2. Where does he or she make it?
3. How do the people who deliver the food travel? (three ways)
4. How do they know who gets which meal?
5. How does the man feel when he gets his meal?

VIEWING SKILLS

In Dokumentarfilmen werden verschiedene Szenen häufig aneinandergereiht. Damit kann man längere Zeitabschnitte zusammenfassen. Am Anfang einer Szene wird oft im Untertitel angezeigt, wo und wann die Szene spielt.

CULTURE

In Indien sitzt man beim Essen oft auf dem Fußboden. Vieles wird ohne Besteck gegessen. Es wird aber nur die rechte Hand benutzt, die linke gilt als unrein. Welche Nahrungsmittel isst du mit der Hand?

3 (SPEAKING) **Talk about the delivery service in the film.**

How is the delivery service different from what you talked about in Ex. 1? What things are the same? Use your notes from Ex. 2b).

don't travel by ...   travel by ...   don't make ...   don't use ...   ...

Ich kann einen Film über einen Lieferservice verstehen. ✔

Checklist  Find more online: nd4r3a

✔ **Ich kann Informationen über Indien verstehen.**

India has a population of more than a billion people. • English is one of India's 22 official languages.
32 ⇗

✔ **Ich kann eine Firma vorstellen.**

We work in a team and we write computer programs. • The company produces its goods in India. • I don't usually meet my customers.
32 ⇗

✔ **Ich kann ein Poster über Nachhaltigkeit gestalten.**

We need to make farming more sustainable. • The crops don't grow well here. • People wash themselves in rivers every day.
33 ⇗

✔ **Ich kann einen Text über eine berühmte Person verstehen.** 33 ⇗

✔ **Ich kann Informationen über verschiedene Jobs weitergeben.**
33 ⇗

✔ **Ich kann einen Film über einen Lieferservice verstehen.**

✱ (UNIT TASK) # An e-mail project

In diesem Projekt könnt ihr eine Partnerschule in Indien finden, der ihr E-Mails und Videos schicken könnt.

Step 1

Find out about schools in India.

Search online and find schools in India. Look for a school in India that matches your school or class.

STUDY SKILLS

Schaut euch die Websites der Schulen an, die ihr im Internet findet. Wählt diejenigen aus, die euch ansprechen. Speichert die Seiten als Favoriten, damit ihr sie jederzeit wieder finden könnt.

Step 2

Make a list of schools that you could write to.

Look at the school websites again and take notes about how to contact them.

Step 3

Plan your e-mail. Make a mind map.

Work in groups of three or four.
What can you say about your school?
What would you like to ask the school in India?

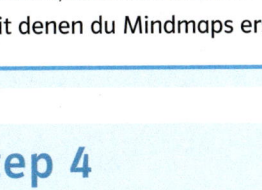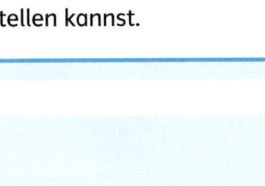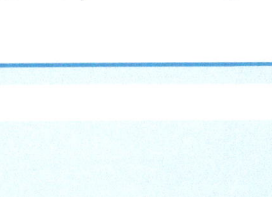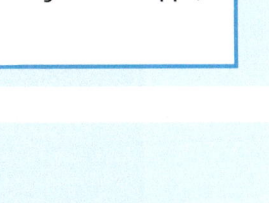

school life
clubs
weather
topics
subjects
holidays
food
nearest town/city

STUDY SKILLS

Eine Mindmap oder ein Wörternetz kann dir helfen, deine Ideen zu ordnen. Verwende zunächst einen Bleistift, damit du leichter etwas ändern kannst. Schreibe Stichpunkte auf Englisch. Es gibt auch Apps, mit denen du Mindmaps erstellen kannst.

Step 4

Write a draft.

Check your spelling, your grammar and the content.

WRITING SKILLS

Nutzt die Checkliste auf S.145, um euren Entwurf zu überprüfen. Schaut dann in einem Wörterbuch nach, wie man die Wörter richtig schreibt.

Dear friends, / Hi everyone,
We are ....
Our school is .... There are ... students.
Could you tell us something about ...?
Could you send us ...? / What about ...?
What is ... like?
Bye,
Your friends at ... School

Step 5

Read the e-mails from two other groups. → M Tip top, p.143

Give feedback. What is good about the e-mails? What could be better?

Step 6

Send your e-mails to the school or schools that you found in Step 1.

Be patient if you don't get an answer right away. There are also websites that help you find penfriends all over the world.

Out and about in India

👥 **1** (SPEAKING) **Talk about the photos with a partner.**

Think about these questions.

What is happening?
What people can you see?
Where are they?
What are they doing?
What can you see in the background?
Could you see things like this in Germany?

| train, station | cricket, slum | cow |
| Holi | tea | wedding | dance |

 2 (SPEAKING) **Talk about India.**

What do or don't you like about India? Explain why you like or don't like it.

I like … because ….
I don't like … because ….

| loud | pollution | exciting | food | clothes |
| colours | many people | … |

INFO

Der Großteil der Menschen in Indien sind Hindus und alle Hindus sind Vegetarier, sie essen also auch kein Rindfleisch. Die Kuh hat allerdings auch eine besondere Bedeutung im Hinduismus – sie ist ein Symbol des Lebens und Kühe werden wertgeschätzt. Der Verkehr steht also still, wenn eine Kuh auf der Straße ist.

A picture-based story

Sieh dir die Bilder an und schreibe eine Geschichte auf Englisch. Beginne wie folgt:

Just in time
Mr and Mrs Singh and their daughter Layla live in England. They flew to India last month for the
wedding of Layla's cousin Chandran. When the Singh family arrived at the airport in London …

Schreibe eine Geschichte von ungefähr 12 Sätzen bzw. etwa 100 Wörtern auf ein gesondertes Blatt.

1.

2. 10 hours later

3. 2 hours later

4. The next day

36/1 🗇 **1 Look, think and take notes.**

First look at the pictures and read the signs.
Take notes.

> People: Layla Singh, …
> Places: London, airport, …
> What happens: fly to India, plane is late, …

Überlege dir zuerst, um was es in der Geschichte geht. Wer sind die Personen und an welchen Orten spielt die Geschichte? Die **Überschrift**, hier: Just in time („Gerade noch rechtzeitig") gibt einen guten Hinweis auf die Handlung.

36/2 🗇
37/3 🗇 **2 Start writing.**

Write a first draft. Do not worry if the story is not perfect. You can add details later.

Use the speech bubbles.

Schreibe die Geschichte im **simple past** (saw, were, waited, landed, felt, phoned). Verwende auch die **Zeitangaben** in den Kästchen.

Verwende auch die **Sprechblasen**. Oft ist es einfacher, die Personen in einer Geschichte miteinander sprechen zu lassen. (He/She said, "….")

37/4–5 🗇 **3 Read your text again and check it.**

– Did you use the simple past?

– Is your text interesting to read?

– Did you use the English word order?

– Is your text easy to read?

– Correct your text.

So machst du deine Geschichte spannend:
1. Benutze **Adjektive** um die Personen und die Sachen zu beschreiben: Layla was annoyed. The people were all happy.
2. Verwende auch **Adverbien** um zu beschreiben, wie jemand etwas tut: They ran quickly. He shouted loudly.

Denke an die **Satzstellungsregel**: Ort vor Zeit: They arrived in New Delhi ten hours later.

Verbinde die Sätze mit **Bindewörtern**. Sie machen den Text verständlicher und leichter lesbar: and/or/but/because/however/so/then …

4 Ask for feedback.

Show your text to your partner.
What tips can he or she give you?

Überprüfe die richtige **Schreibweise** mit Hilfe eines Wörterbuchs.

Ein zweisprachiges Wörterbuch in Printform ist für die gesamte schriftliche Prüfung erlaubt.

A Listening Comprehension (Hörverstehen)

You will hear the recordings twice.

1,19 **1 Listen to text 1. Choose the right answer. There is an example (0.) at the beginning.**

You will hear five short announcements from India.

0. At the pool this afternoon at 3:30 there will be —— .
   a) cakes and cookies
   b) activities only for children
   c) boring games
   d) drinks

1. You have to call Doctor Harris on —— .
   a) 504-374-23
   b) 54-274-23
   c) 94-374-33
   d) 54-274-83

2. Mumbai zoo will be closing in —— .
   a) 45 minutes
   b) 30 seconds
   c) half an hour
   d) one hour

3. You can save money on —— at the Kumar Shopping Mall.
   a) clothes
   b) vegetables
   c) fruit
   d) drinks

4. Trains from platforms 5–7 to Delhi will be leaving —— .
   a) earlier
   b) an hour later
   c) from different platforms
   d) tomorrow

1,20 **2 Listen to text 2 and write the missing information. There is an example (0.) at the beginning.**

Maya is a girl from India who talks about her life in a radio interview.

0. Maya works at a clothes factory in Bangalore.
1. Most girls in her village marry when they are ….
2. Maya's dad said that he wanted her to see ….
3. The journey to Bangalore by train was exciting but ….
4. Now she lives with a lot of ….
5. Maya didn't like the factory because it was ….
6. Her boss spoke a different ….
7. She has to work for ….
8. In the evenings she is always ….

B Use of English (Sprachgebrauch)

1 Write the right form of the verb. There is an example (0.) at the beginning.

Trains in India

India (0 have) <u>has</u> an amazing railway system. We (1 visit) —— India last summer and (2 see) —— its busy railway stations but we still (3 think) —— that travelling by train would be a great experience. (4 see) —— you ever —— a photo of a crowded train like this one? Sometimes people (5 sit) —— on top. A year ago, we (6 choose) —— the fastest of the many types of trains. Our journey (7 take) —— four hours and cost as much as €10, but the same journey could take nine hours and be a lot cheaper. Don't forget that there (8 be) —— a special reservation for seats on certain trains. If you (9 not have to) —— travel quickly, it's best to (10 take) —— the night train from city centre to city centre. We (11 go) —— from New Delhi to Mumbai last year. That (12 not be) —— expensive, but we (13 not sleep) —— a lot. Next year we (14 do) —— it again.

2 Write the word that matches the definition. There is an example (0.) at the beginning.

0. Something that you think is really special is <u>amazing</u>.

1. When a lot of people and cars in the streets of a city are moving around, it is ——.

2. To remember their holidays, many people use their camera to take a lot of ——.

3. When there are no more seats and people have to stand the train is ——.

4. When you travel from A to B, you go on a ——.

5. You should make a —— if you want a seat on a train.

6. When you go from one place to another, for example by train, you ——.

7. The building where a train arrives and leaves is a railway ——.

8. This train doesn't go very fast. It is ——.

9. Many train journeys in India don't cost much. They are very ——.

C Reading Comprehension (Leseverstehen)

Tigers in trouble

1 India is home to most of the world's wild tigers today, but their numbers have gone down a lot. At the time of independence from Britain, in 1947, there were about 40,000
5 tigers in India. Today, there may be less than 2,000. Some people believe that in the future the only tigers left will be the tigers living in zoos.

India's economy is growing fast, which means
10 that more space is needed for cities, factories, roads and railway systems. Unfortunately, the areas where tigers can live and move about are getting smaller every year. The growing economy is not only a big threat to
15 tiger reserves, but also to the areas of woods between them. These areas are extremely important because they mean tigers can move to new areas and find different partners. This is important to keep the tiger population
20 healthy.

As the areas where tigers can live are getting smaller, they are moving closer to people and towns and cities. They sometimes hunt farm animals or even kill people living in
25 villages. Farmers often kill tigers to protect themselves, their animals and their family. Tigers are also hunted and killed so that people can earn money. The black market for tiger body parts is growing all over Asia. Some
30 tiger body parts are sold as medicine.

There have been surveys recently with good news. Between 2011 and 2014 the population of tigers increased to about 2,220. It is too early to celebrate as there was a similar
35 increase in the past but it unfortunately stopped.

India has tried very hard in the past to increase the tiger population by improving how and where tigers live. For a time this was
40 very successful.

In the 1970s the number of tigers was not high. But between then and 1984 there was a huge increase in the population (to about 4,000). This was after important conservation
45 work, which cost millions of dollars. However, between 1984 and 2008 cities grew and people hunted tigers. The number of tigers dropped again, this time to about 1,400.

It seems that the growing economy is good
50 for companies but not for the environment. Governments must do something soon to protect these amazing animals. If they don't, it will be too late. There will be no tigers left in the wild.

55 **Could zoos be the answer?**
Wildlife groups and tiger experts are working hard to protect tigers, but it is very expensive. Some people believe that zoos are the answer:
– new generations can grow up safely,
60 – scientists can find out about animal food and health,
– animals which are born in zoos can be let into the wild.

But there are also people who see the
65 problems of keeping animals in zoos:
– the cages and areas they live in are often too small for the animals,
– the animals are often bored or under a lot of stress.

70 *Jeff Sparks (2016) in 'The Conservationist'*

1 Read the text about tigers in India and decide if the following statements are true, false or not in the text. There is an example (0.) at the beginning.

0. There are <u>more</u> tigers today than in 1947. → <u>fewer</u>
1. People think that in the future you will only be able to see tigers in zoos.
2. More space is needed for parks and farms.
3. Tigers have less space to live than in the past.
4. Tigers sometimes kill cows, pigs, sheep and people.
5. Between 2011 and 2016 there was the first increase in the tiger population in India.
6. It is easy to protect tigers.
7. Everyone agrees about zoos.

2 Copy the table into your exercise book. Use the information from the text to complete the table with the right number of tigers.

Year	1947	1984	2008	2011–2014
Number of tigers (about …)				

D Text Production (Schreiben)

1 Du hast eine E-Mail von Tariq aus Indien erhalten. Schreibe ihm eine Antwort.

Du hast dich auf einer Plattform angemeldet, die Kontakte zu Jugendlichen aus anderen Ländern vermittelt, und hast eine E-Mail von Tariq aus Indien erhalten.
Antworte ihm auf Englisch und gehe dabei auf seine E-Mail ein. Stelle ihm auch Fragen, z. B. zum Schulalltag und zum Essen in Indien. Schreibe eine E-Mail von ungefähr 100 Wörtern auf ein gesondertes Blatt. Achte auf eine ansprechende äußere Form und eine gut lesbare Handschrift.

E-MAIL

Hi there,
I'm Tariq. I'm 16 and I'm from Surat in the state of Gujarat in India. Surat is one of the largest cities in India and it is 289 miles north of Mumbai. Over 4.4 million people live in Surat. I play cricket and love watching the boats on the river in the city centre. I want to work on a boat when I leave school.
I'd like to hear more about you. Please tell me about where you live and go to school in Bavaria. What are your interests and your plans for the future? And why do you want a penfriend from India?
Hope to hear from you soon.
Bye for now,
Tariq

E Mediation (Sprachmittlung)

1 Situierung und Text

Deine Klasse vergleicht die beiden Länder Indien und Deutschland. Du interessierst dich für das Thema Umwelt und hast diesen Zeitungsartikel über Neu-Delhi gefunden. Lies ihn aufmerksam durch.

Zeitungsartikel

Air pollution in Delhi

1 Air pollution in the north of India reached new heights last month. The levels in many areas were so dangerous that they
5 were causing people in the country's capital extreme breathing problems. Measurements of the air quality showed that the number of toxic particles in the air was nine times above the limit.
10 The government have said that the air is so bad that there is a serious health emergency in the city at the moment.

Short-term action

Schools were closed for two days and
15 people were advised not to go outside. Building sites were closed as they were too dangerous – the workers couldn't breathe, and they couldn't see what they were doing.
20 Rules were introduced to reduce the number of cars on the road. People nowadays do anything to make money and in 2019 a bar

in Delhi started to sell fresh air to its
25 customers – at a very high price, obviously. The government has been handing out millions of masks. They filter the air that people breathe.

Long-term action

30 There are plans to replace the polluting diesel buses with 500 electric buses. But this is only a start. Delhi's taxis are often toxic auto rickshaws. The government wants to replace them with 1.5 million
35 electric rickshaws.
There are already solar-powered underground stations. These are the world's first stations that work with new energy sources only.
40 In a statement the Indian government say that by 2030 CO_2 emissions will be reduced by 30 %, although more energy will be needed.
They argue that their pollution affects the
45 whole world so everyone should help.

2 Aufgabe

Lies den Zeitungsartikel. Schreibe anschließend auf Deutsch in dein Heft, mit welchem Problem Delhi im Moment konfrontiert ist und was unternommen wird, um die Bewohner davor zu schützen. Nenne kurz- und langfristige Hilfen.

a) Problem:

b) Kurzfristige Hilfen (5)

(1) Kneipen verkaufen frische Luft.
(2) …

c) Langfristige Hilfen (4)

(1) …

That's the end of Test practice 2!

Discover South Africa ——————————

1

South Africa has three capitals: Pretoria, Cape Town and Bloemfontein. The parliament is in Cape Town. The city is also famous for Table Mountain, one of South Africa's most beautiful sights. The population of the country is 80% African and 20% European and others.

2

After independence from Britain in 1934, apartheid started in South Africa in the 1940s. This separated black and white people. Black people had to live in 'townships'. Apartheid ended in 1994, and a black man, Nelson Mandela, became president.

1 (SPEAKING) **Talk about the photos.**

a) Describe one of the photos to a partner.

There is …. There are ….
Photo … shows ….

b) Talk about the photo. Would you like to spend a holiday in South Africa? Why? Why not?

You can use these words:

beautiful   hot   modern

poor

2 (READING) **Correct the sentences.**

38/1 ↗

1. Table Mountain is in Bloemfontein. That's wrong. Table Mountain is in ….
2. In 1934 Nelson Mandela became president of South Africa.
3. South Africa is often called the rainbow nation because it has interesting weather.
4. Many rich people still live in townships.
5. Tourists can see farm animals in South Africa's national parks.

Am Ende dieser Unit kann ich …
- **Informationen über Südafrika verstehen.**
- **über einen Unfall sprechen.**
- **einen Text über mein Vorbild schreiben.**
- **Texte über das Leben junger Menschen verstehen.**
- **Informationen in einem Krankenhaus weitergeben.**
- **einen Film über das Leben in Kapstadt verstehen.**

3

3
There are eleven official languages and many traditions in South Africa. That's why it is often called the 'rainbow nation'. Many young people have moved to the cities to find work. However, many black South Africans don't finish high school.

4
Some people in South Africa are very rich. But many parts of the country are still poor, and many black people still live in townships in or near the cities. A lot of the houses there don't have sanitation or electricity.

5
Many tourists visit South Africa. They go on safari in the national parks and see wild animals like lions, elephants and buffaloes. Kruger National Park is the largest park. It has an area of 19,485 square kilometres.

3 (LISTENING) **Listen to a South African radio news programme.**

2,2

Choose the right answers.

1. There was a large **concert** • **protest** in Cape Town yesterday.
2. The woman is **worried** • **happy**.
3. Rangers in Kruger National Park found five dead **elephants** • **buffaloes** yesterday.
4. A new programme will help young people for **a year** • **six months**.
5. The man **is looking forward to** • **isn't sure about** the programme.
6. The weather in Cape Town will be **cold and wet** • **hot and sunny** today.
7. Steve has the news about **traffic** • **sport**.

Ich kann Informationen über Südafrika verstehen. ✔

After the accident

1 (SPEAKING) **Why do road accidents often happen?**

People drive too …   They look at …   There is too much …   …

2 (READING) **Read the report and the text message.**

2,3

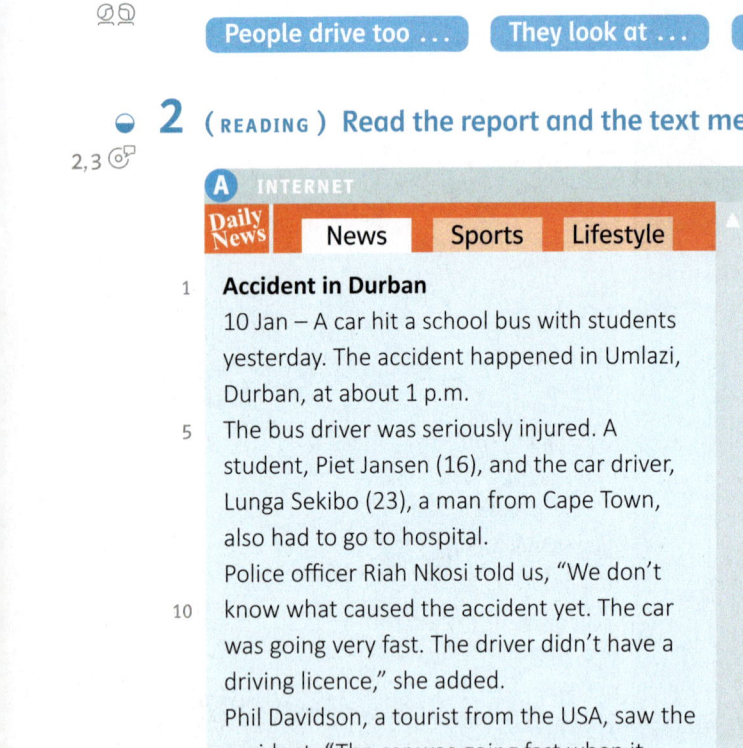

A INTERNET

Daily News   **News**   Sports   Lifestyle

1 **Accident in Durban**

10 Jan – A car hit a school bus with students yesterday. The accident happened in Umlazi, Durban, at about 1 p.m.

5 The bus driver was seriously injured. A student, Piet Jansen (16), and the car driver, Lunga Sekibo (23), a man from Cape Town, also had to go to hospital.

Police officer Riah Nkosi told us, "We don't

10 know what caused the accident yet. The car was going very fast. The driver didn't have a driving licence," she added.

Phil Davidson, a tourist from the USA, saw the accident. "The car was going fast when it

15 happened," Phil said. "The driver braked and the car skidded. It crashed into the bus."

The police are looking for more information about the accident.

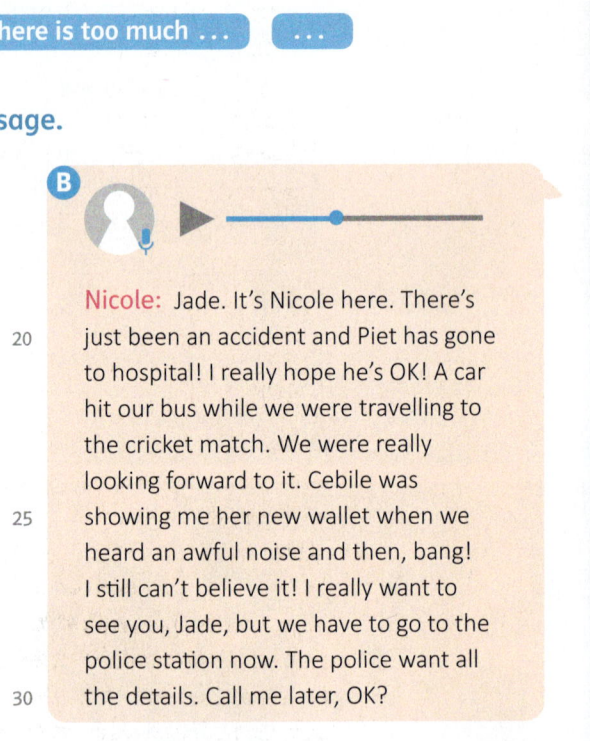

B

Nicole: Jade. It's Nicole here. There's
20 just been an accident and Piet has gone to hospital! I really hope he's OK! A car hit our bus while we were travelling to the cricket match. We were really looking forward to it. Cebile was
25 showing me her new wallet when we heard an awful noise and then, bang! I still can't believe it! I really want to see you, Jade, but we have to go to the police station now. The police want all
30 the details. Call me later, OK?

INFO

In Südafrika herrscht Linksverkehr, wie in Großbritannien und Australien. Das stammt noch aus der Zeit Südafrikas als britische Kolonie und zeigt, wie die Kolonialzeit das Leben dort bis heute beeinflusst.

3 **Work with the texts.**

a) Match the parts of the sentences. → ◯ p.119

1. **Text A:** Piet and the two drivers
2. Phil Davidson
3. Riah Nkosi
4. **Text B:** Nicole
5. Nicole and Cebile
6. Jade

a. is looking for more information.
b. tells Jade about the accident.
c. saw the car hit the bus.
d. should phone Nicole later.
e. were injured in the accident.
f. were on the bus when it happened.

b) Find the parts of the text that give you the information. Write the lines.

1. Nicole is worried about Piet.
2. The students are interested in sport.
3. Nicole is surprised about what happened.
4. Jade is one of Nicole's best friends.

4 **Work with words from the text.** → **M** Bus stop, p.140

39/1

a) Complete the online comment about the report. → ○ p.120

Why are there so many car (1) <u>accidents</u> 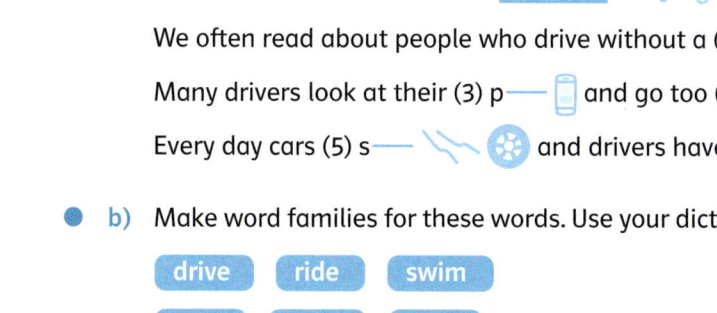 on South Africa's roads?

We often read about people who drive without a (2) d— l— 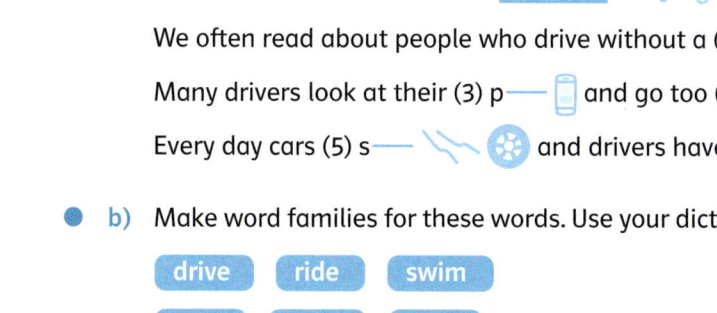.

Many drivers look at their (3) p— and go too (4) f—.

Every day cars (5) s— ✳ and drivers have to (6) b— hard.

b) Make word families for these words. Use your dictionary to find suitable words.

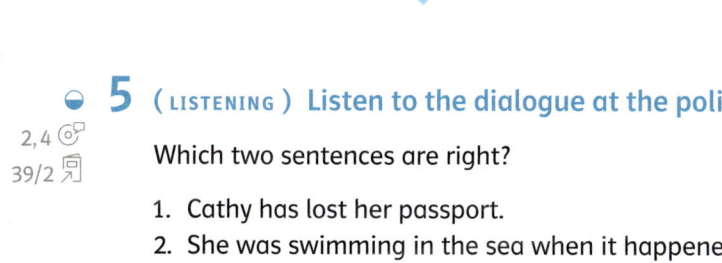

drive   ride   swim   visit   read   play

1. drive

driver — **drive** — driving licence

STUDY SKILLS

Wörternetze können dir helfen, deinen Wortschatz zu erweitern. Du kannst auch später immer wieder Wörter aus der gleichen Wortfamilie ergänzen.

5 (LISTENING) **Listen to the dialogue at the police station.**

2,4
39/2

Which two sentences are right?

1. Cathy has lost her passport.
2. She was swimming in the sea when it happened.
3. Cathy is staying at a hotel in Durban.
4. She will be there for one more week.
5. She should come back to the police station before she leaves.

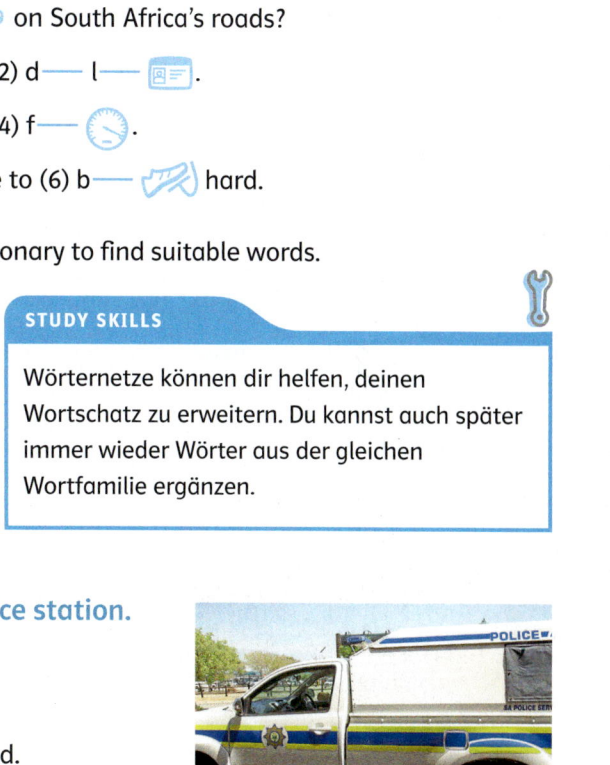

LISTENING SKILLS

Manchmal sind Namen oder Adressen schwer zu verstehen. Wenn man nicht nachfragen kann, schreibt man sie am besten so auf, wie man sie hört. Das ist besser, als gar keinen Anhaltspunkt zu haben.

6 (SOUNDS) **Read, say and listen.** → **M** Peer correction, p.141

39/3

a) The words below are spelled with the letter 'o' but sound different. Make a chart. Say the words to a partner and put them in the right group.

/ɒ/	/əʊ/
on	know

told   gone   know ✓   so   Nicole   won't
hospital   not   on ✓   going   from

2,5   b) Listen to the words and check the chart.

40/4 **7** **What did they do?**

a) What did they do on the morning of the accident? → ◯ p.120

1. Piet <u>walked</u> to school after breakfast. (walk)
2. Cebile and Nicole —— at break. (talk)
3. They —— Piet in the cafeteria at lunchtime. (meet)
4. Nicole's phone —— at 12:22 p.m. (ring)
5. She —— it. (not hear)
6. Phil —— his hotel at about 11:30 a.m. (leave)
7. He —— to his friend in the USA. (not talk)

Language → **G1**, p.127

The accident happen<u>ed</u> yesterday.
Phil <u>saw</u> the accident.
The driver <u>didn't have</u> a driving licence.

b) What did or didn't you do last weekend? Use the pairs to write five or more sentences.

play / not play …   go to / not go to …   eat / not eat …   meet / not meet …

Language detectives → **G7, p.133**

The car <u>was going</u> fast when the accident <u>happened</u>.
Cebile <u>was showing</u> me her new wallet when we <u>heard</u> an awful noise.
A car <u>hit</u> our bus while we <u>were travelling</u> to the cricket match.

Schau dir die Sätze an. Welche Handlung war noch nicht zu Ende und dauerte noch an, als etwas Neues passierte? Wie wird <u>die Zeitform</u> gebildet? Achte auf Einzahl (<u>was</u>) und Mehrzahl (<u>were</u>).

40/5 **8** **Use the words and the pictures below to write what they were doing at 2 p.m. on Saturday.**

was   were   looking for   playing   talking to   swimming   working   visiting

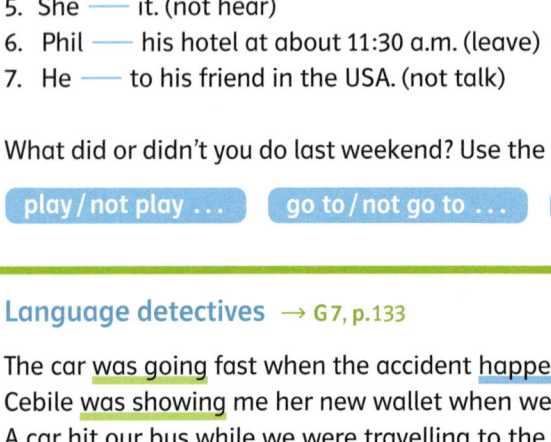

1 Nicole … her friend

2 Phil Davidson … a museum

3 Cebile … a new wallet

4 Riah Nkosi … at the police station

5 Jade and her mum … in the sea

6 Piet and his friends … on the beach

1. At 2 p.m. on Saturday Nicole <u>was talking to</u> her friend.

9 (SPEAKING) What were you doing?

41/6

a) Think about what you were doing at 8 p.m. yesterday. Make notes. Use these ideas:

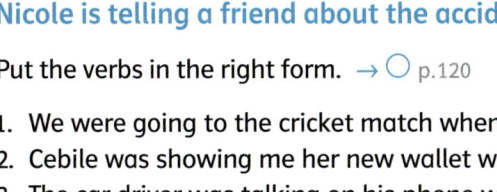

I was + listening to …   watching …   playing …   + with my brother/sister.
       making …   talking to …   …   with my friend. ….

b) Ask other students what they were doing. → M Milling around, p.141

A: What were you doing at 8 p.m. yesterday?
B: I was listening to music with my brother. We were listening to ….

41/7–8 ## 10 Nicole is telling a friend about the accident. Complete her sentences.

a) Put the verbs in the right form. → ◯ p.120

1. We were going to the cricket match when a car crashed into the bus. (crash)
2. Cebile was showing me her new wallet when we —— a loud bang. (hear)
3. The car driver was talking on his phone when the police ——. (arrive)
4. While the police officer —— to the car driver, the witness came to help. (talk)
5. While I —— in the police car, I sent a message to Jade. (sit)
6. While I —— at the police station, my parents arrived. (wait)

b) Complete the sentences.

1. Piet —— (listen) to music when the car —— (hit) us.
2. Jade —— (get) the message while she —— (talk to) her mum in the kitchen.
3. I —— (go) home with my parents when I —— (get) a message from Cebile.

11 (TASK) A role play at the police station → V Talking about an accident, p.150

a) Look at the texts about the accident on page 64. What happened? What did the different people see? What does the police officer want to know? Take notes.

b) Decide who is the police officer and who is the witness. Use your notes to make a dialogue. The phrases will help.

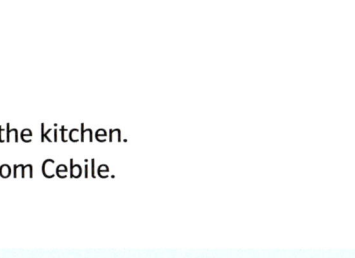

Police officer Riah Nkosi

Phil Davidson   Nicole   Piet Jansen

Police officer:
What is your name?
Please tell me what you saw.
Was the … travelling fast? …
What other information can you give us?
Thank you. You may leave now.

Witness:
My name is ….
I saw a ….
Yes, it was.
I think …. There was ….
You're welcome!

c) Present your dialogue to the class. → M Tip top, p.143

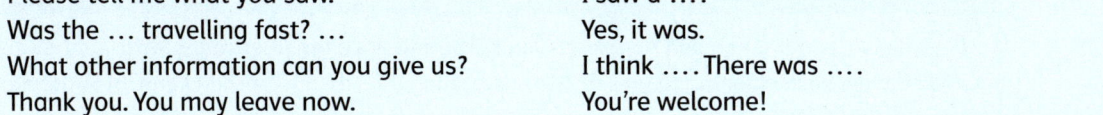

Ich kann über einen Unfall sprechen. ✔

South African role models

1 (READING) **Read the dialogue.**

2,6

Miriam Makeba

Zackie Achmat

1 **Kungawo:** Hi everyone and welcome to our podcast about inspiring South Africans. With me now is Mia, who is going to tell us about her very special South African role model.

5 **Mia:** Yes, Kungawo. We've already talked about music on the show. My role model is the South African singer and songwriter Miriam Makeba.

Kungawo: Miriam Makeba? OK, tell us more.

10 **Mia:** Well, she became famous all around the world during apartheid. Life was hard for black people in South Africa at that time. They had to live in townships and many other places were for white people only. I admire

15 Miriam Makeba because she fought against apartheid. The government took away her passport when she left South Africa. She couldn't go home.

Kungawo: That sounds awful!

20 **Mia:** Yes, it was. Her life has been an inspiration for a long time. She achieved a lot. What about you? Who do you admire?

Kungawo: My role model is Zackie Achmat.
Mia: Who's he?

25 **Kungawo:** Zackie Achmat is a South African film director. He fought against apartheid and has fought for gay and lesbian rights too. He has helped many South Africans with HIV and AIDS. He has made films about people

30 who have the diseases.

Mia: HIV and AIDS have been serious problems in South Africa for many years.

Kungawo: That's right. There is medication for HIV, but at first it was very expensive.

35 Zackie Achmat has been HIV-positive since 1990 but he didn't take medication right away. He fought for cheaper drugs. He only took medication in August 2003, when it was cheaper, and poorer people could pay for it

40 too.

Mia: He was really brave. South Africans have achieved a lot since 1994 and before that.

Kungawo: Yes, there's a lot that this country can be proud of.

INFO

HIV ist ein Virus, der durch den Austausch von Körperflüssigkeiten übertragen wird. Aids ist die Krankheit, die nach einer längeren Zeit der Ansteckung mit HIV ausbrechen kann. In Südafrika waren 2018 mehr als 7 Millionen Menschen entweder HIV-positiv oder aidskrank. Heutzutage kann man mit HIV und Aids ein weitgehend normales Leben führen. Seit Längerem gibt es wirkungsvolle Medikamente, aber erst seit 2003 sind günstige Medikamente in Südafrika für alle zugänglich.

2 Complete the sentences. → ○ p.121

42/1

1. Mia's role model is a <u>South African singer and songwriter</u>.
2. During apartheid Miriam Makeba became famous —— .
3. Miriam Makeba couldn't go back to her country when the government —— .
4. Zackie Achmat's films are about —— .
5. At first medication for HIV —— .
6. Zackie Achmat was brave because he only took medication when —— .

3 Work with words from the text. → M Bus stop, p.140

a) Put the words into the right groups (nouns, verbs or adjectives). → ○ p.122

`brave` `achieve` `inspiration` `sing` `admire` `proud` `role model`
`singer` `inspiring`

Du kannst manchmal eine Silbe an den Anfang oder an das Ende eines Wortes stellen, um neue Wörter zu bilden.

b) Use the endings to make new words. Use your dictionary if you are not sure.

`admir(e)` `pay` `music` `achieve` `help` `-ment` `-ful` `-ian` `-ation`

4 Choose the right answers to complete Mia's blog.

INTERNET

Today we talked about Miriam Makeba, the (1) **sing** · **singer** and songwriter. I really (2) **admire** · **achieve** her. She has been an (3) **inspiration** · **inspiring** to many South (4) **Africa** · **African** people. Miriam Makeba fought (5) **again** · **against** apartheid. She couldn't go home when the government took (6) **away** · **out** her passport. That was (7) **awesome** · **awful**!

5 (LISTENING) Listen to another podcast. Which three sentences are right?

2,7
42/2

1. Nelson Mandela trained as a doctor when he was young.
2. He was sent to prison near Cape Town.
3. He worked with the government to end apartheid.
4. He was president until 2002.
5. He helped to fight against AIDS and HIV.
6. He was 90 when he died. That was in 2013.

6 **What has Zackie Achmat done in his life? Complete the sentences.**

43/3

1. Zackie Achmat has worked with poor people in South Africa. (work)
2. He —— to many people with AIDS and HIV. (talk)
3. He —— for gay and lesbian rights. (fight)
4. He —— several prizes for his work. (win)
5. He —— concerts for people with AIDS and HIV. (not organize)
6. He —— many young South Africans. (help)
7. He —— a film about music. (not make)

Language → G 8, p.134

We've already talked about music on the show.
He has helped South Africans with HIV.
They haven't made a podcast about animals yet.

Language detectives → G 8, p.134

Miriam Makeba's life has been an inspiration for a long time.
HIV and AIDS have been serious problems in South Africa for many years.
South Africans have achieved a lot since 1994.

Schau dir die Sätze an. Wie würdest du die Sätze auf Deutsch sagen?
For und since sind wichtige Signalwörter für das present perfect. Welches Wort verwendest du für eine Zeitspanne, welches für einen Zeitpunkt?

43/4 **7** **How long have they done it?** → **M** Peer correction, p.141

a) Make sentences with for or since. Put in the right form of the verb. → ○ p.122

1. Mia – (be) in Cape Town – two days
   Mia has been in Cape Town for two days.
2. She – (live) in her flat – January
3. She – (work) at a hairdressing salon – two years
4. Her parents – (be) on holiday in Durban – last Friday
5. Kungawo – (share) a flat with his friend – six months
6. He – (work) at a large supermarket – November last year
7. Kungawo and Mia – (make) podcasts together – they met
8. Mia – (be) interested in music – a long time

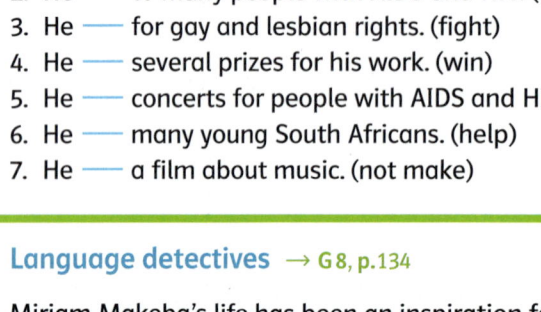

Mia, 18

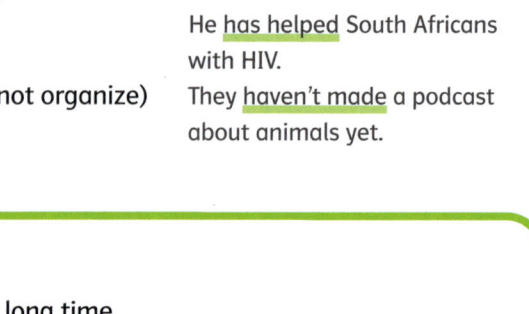

Kungawo, 19

b) How long? Make a sentence with each verb.

| live in ... | be interested in ... | know ... | have ... | enjoy ... |

I've lived in ... for ..../ since ....
I've ....

8 (SPEAKING) Ask a partner. → M Milling around, p.141

a) Ask your partner questions. → ○ p.122

43/4

| listen to South African music | meet a famous person |

| see a lion | organize a flea market | work with … | … |

Language → G 8, p.134

<u>Have</u> you ever <u>seen</u> this film?
<u>Yes, I have.</u> / <u>No, I haven't.</u>

A: Have you ever listened to …?   B: Yes, I have. / No, I haven't. Have you …?

b) Ask another partner about his or her interview.

A: Has Sophia ever listened to …?   B: Yes, she has. No, she hasn't.

9 Find the right words for the gaps. You don't need all the words.

| for | from | has | have | hears | her | his | listens ✓ | many |

| much | of | since |

Mia often <u>listens</u> (1) to different kinds of South African music. She's a big fan —— (2) the singer Karen Zoid, for example. Mia —— (3) heard all Karen Zoid's songs and has been to —— (4) of her concerts. Karen Zoid has been a big star —— (5) many years. She played with —— (6) band at the Nelson Mandela HIV / AIDS charity concert in 2005.

10 (TASK) An e-mail to a magazine → V Describing a role model, p.151

You have seen a competition in a magazine to win a 'meet and greet' with your favourite star.

a) Which star would you like to meet? Think of someone from music, film and TV or sport.

b) Think about why you are a fan. Make notes. Use these ideas:

| have watched his/her films | read his/her updates on … |

| want to go to his/her concerts |

| have liked him/her since/for … | … |

Karen Zoid

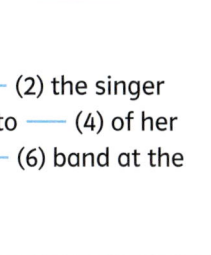

Meet & Greet

Send us an e-mail.
Say why you think
Karen Zoid is great!

c) Find out about other reasons why your star is great.

| has helped with … | has done a lot for … |

| has worked with … | … |

d) Use your notes and the phrases on the right to write an e-mail to the magazine. Explain why you should win the 'meet and greet'. Use the checklist on page 145. → M Peer correction, p.141

Dear …,
I want to meet and greet … because … . … …
I look forward to hearing from you.
Yours sincerely,

Ich kann einen Text über mein Vorbild ✔ schreiben.

Young people in South Africa

1 (READING) **Read the texts from a magazine article about young South Africans.**

2, 8–11

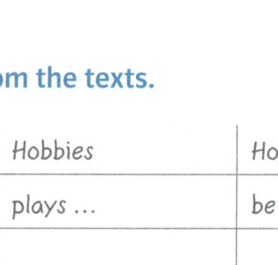

1 Hi, I'm Shaka and I live in Durban. Many young black South Africans are poor and unemployed. It's also not easy for me because I am in a wheelchair. But I was lucky because I got a job as an office worker with the organization *Working For Water*. Our workers cut down trees and control the plants in the area. We have a problem with plants and trees that aren't from here. These need much more water than local ones, so we cut some of the trees down. One day I'd like to be in charge of the office. In my free time I play the guitar a bit.

Shaka, 19

2 My name is Keeya and I work as a nurse at Tshepong Hospital in Klerksdorp. That's a town in the north of South Africa. My partner Bertha and I would like to share a flat together next year when we have saved some money. Fortunately my parents will help me with that. I speak English and Afrikaans. I enjoy working as a nurse – I like working with other people and it's great to help them. I don't think I could work at a desk all the time. I play hockey with the hospital team every week. We always have a lot of fun.

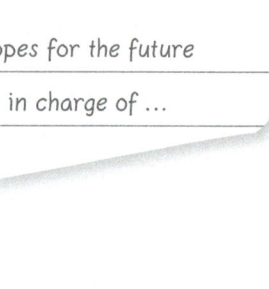

Keeya, 21

2 **Copy the table and put in the information from the texts.**

Name	Where they live	Job	Hobbies	Hopes for the future
Shaka	Durban	office ...	plays ...	be in charge of ...
Keeya				
Uuka				
Amahle				

3 **Choose the right meaning in German for these words from the texts.**

1. plant (... control the **plants** in our area)
2. save (... when we have **saved** some money)
3. programme (a new preschool **programme**)
4. use (... things that people don't **use** ...)
5. train (... to **train** as an engineer ...)

a. Pflanze
a. retten
a. Programm
a. verwenden
a. (Sport) trainieren

b. pflanzen
b. sparen
b. Sendung
b. Gebrauch
b. eine Ausbildung machen

20 3 I'm Uuka and I live in Soweto, a township in Johannesburg. I was born in Soweto too. I speak the Sesotho language at home but English at work. I work as a kindergarten teacher in a new preschool programme here in Soweto. A good preschool education is very important for poor children. Then they are **25** ready for primary school and life outside the home. At the kindergarten I often do handicrafts with things that people don't use any more, like cans or boxes. I also enjoy painting pictures after work. One day I hope to sell my pictures at markets.

Uuka, 19

30 4 My name is Amahle and I live with my family in Makhanda, a town in the Eastern Cape. I'm still at school. I have two younger sisters and a younger brother. My father left us eight years ago, so I have to help my mother at home. I have school five days a week and lots of homework too, so **35** it's quite hard. I often worry about my family because we don't have medical insurance. It's too expensive. My big hope for the future is this: I'd like to train as an engineer one day and build bridges. I like playing football too.

Amahle, 16

4 Choose one of the tasks.

45/1–2

a) Write a short text like the ones in the article **OR** about your own life. Write 10–12 sentences. You can use these ideas:

→ M Writers' conference, p.143

I live in ....   I was born in ....

That's ....   I live with ....

I speak ....   I ... in my free time.

I also like ....   I worry about ....

My hope for the future is this: ....

... is great.   ...

b) Work in groups of three. Copy the table in Ex. 2 and do a survey with students in your class.

Ask them questions in English and make a chart with the most popular answers.

Where do you live?

What job do you want ...?

What are your ...?   What ...?

...

Ich kann Texte über das Leben junger Menschen verstehen. ✔

At the hospital

Du bist mit deiner Familie im Urlaub in Südafrika. Deine Mutter hat sich am Arm verletzt. Leider kann sie nicht so gut Englisch sprechen. Hilf ihr dabei, sich in der Notaufnahme im Krankenhaus zu verständigen.

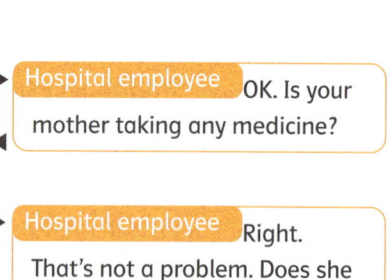

◗ 1 (MEDIATION) Can you help?

Mutter Kannst du ihnen bitte sagen, was passiert ist?

Du Hello. My mother has hurt her arm.

Hospital employee Oh dear! OK. I need to know if you have medical insurance if you're not from South Africa.

Du Sie wollen wissen, ob ....

Mutter Ja, sag Ihnen, dass wir eine weltweite Reiseversicherung haben. Hier sind die Papiere.

Du Yes, we have ... for .... Here ....

Hospital employee OK. Is your mother taking any medicine?

Du ....

Mutter Eigentlich nicht. Aber ich habe heute Morgen Kopfschmerztabletten genommen.

Du No, ... But she ....

Hospital employee Right. That's not a problem. Does she have any allergies?

Du ....

Mutter Ja, ich habe eine Katzenhaarallergie.

Du ....

Hospital employee OK. She should sign this form here. If you just wait over there, the doctor will come and see you. It may take twenty minutes.

Du ....

Mutter Haben Sie vielen herzlichen Dank!

Du ....

Du Sie sagt: ....

Hospital employee You're welcome.

◗ 2 (MEDIATION) Erkläre auf Deutsch, welche Vorschriften es im Krankenhaus gibt.

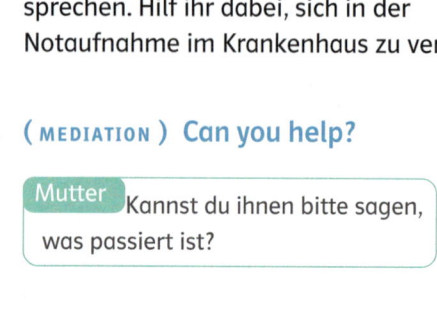

44/1–2

Die Krankenhausangestellte erklärt dir, was im Krankenhaus erlaubt ist und was nicht. Gib die Informationen für deine Familie auf Deutsch wieder.

Hospital employee: There is no food and drink allowed in the hospital. Visitors can come and visit between 2–4 p.m. and 7–8 p.m.

Ich kann Informationen in einem Krankenhaus weitergeben. ✔

Different faces of Cape Town

1 (SPEAKING) **Talk about where you live.**

a) What do you think about the city, town or village where you live?

I like …. I don't like ….
The … is cool/OK. …

b) What would you show a visitor? Why?

I would show a visitor … because ….

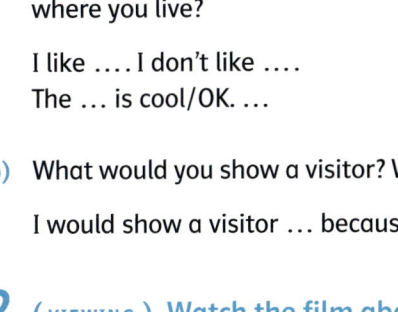

2 (VIEWING) **Watch the film about Cape Town.**

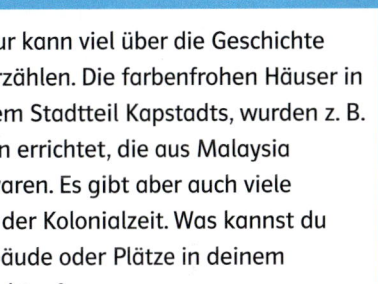

6  a) Which of these things is **not** in the film?

animals   a hospital   a mountain

people in a factory   colourful buildings

a football game on a beach

> **CULTURE**
>
> Die Architektur kann viel über die Geschichte einer Stadt erzählen. Die farbenfrohen Häuser in Bo-Kaap, einem Stadtteil Kapstadts, wurden z. B. von Menschen errichtet, die aus Malaysia gekommen waren. Es gibt aber auch viele Gebäude aus der Kolonialzeit. Was kannst du über alte Gebäude oder Plätze in deinem Wohnort berichten?

b) Watch the film from 01:25 to 02:10. Answer the questions (short answers).

1. What do the baboons in the film do?
2. Who can help with the problem?

> **VIEWING SKILLS**
>
> Am Anfang des Dokumentarfilms werden die Gesichter verschiedener Menschen gezeigt, die direkt in die Kamera sehen. Mehr erfährt man über sie jedoch nicht. Dennoch erhalten die Zuschauer einen ersten Eindruck von der Stadt und ihren Menschen. Achte darauf, welchen Eindruck die Bilder bei dir als Zuschauer oder Zuschauerin erwecken.

3 (SPEAKING) **Talk about the film.**

a) What do you think life in Cape Town is like? How do the people there feel?

b) Compare Cape Town to your city, town or village.

people   flowers and mountains   colourful buildings   animals in the roads

different kinds of people   …

In Cape Town there is/are …. We have … / We don't have … where I live.

> Ich kann einen Film über das Leben in Kapstadt verstehen. ✔

Checklist ⊕ Find more online: nd4r3a

✔ **Ich kann Informationen über Südafrika verstehen.**

South Africa has three capitals. • Apartheid separated black and white people. • South Africa is often called the 'rainbow nation'.

46 ↗

✔ **Ich kann über einen Unfall sprechen.**

The accident happened in Umlazi, Durban, at about 1 p.m. • The driver braked and the car skidded. • A car hit our bus while we were travelling to the cricket match.

46 ↗

✔ **Ich kann einen Text über mein Vorbild schreiben.**

My role model is Miriam Makeba. • Her life has been an inspiration for a long time. • Zackie Achmat has helped many South Africans with HIV and AIDS.

47 ↗

✔ **Ich kann Texte über das Leben junger Menschen verstehen.**

47 ↗

✔ **Ich kann Informationen in einem Krankenhaus weitergeben.**

47 ↗

✔ **Ich kann einen Film über das Leben in Kapstadt verstehen.**

❀ (UNIT TASK) A feature story

Du bist Reporterin oder Reporter für deine englische Partnerschule. Du sollst einen Artikel über deine Stadt schreiben und Fotos machen. Stellt anschließend alle Artikel zu einer Wandzeitung zusammen und hängt sie in der Klasse auf.

Das ist eine „feature story". Das Thema ist „early birds" (Frühaufsteher). Die Autorin beschreibt darin eine Situation, die zum Thema passt: Leute warten vor einer Imbissbude auf ihr Frühstück. Mit einer feature story kannst du deine Leserinnen und Leser auf ein Thema aufmerksam machen, über das sie vorher noch nicht nachgedacht haben.

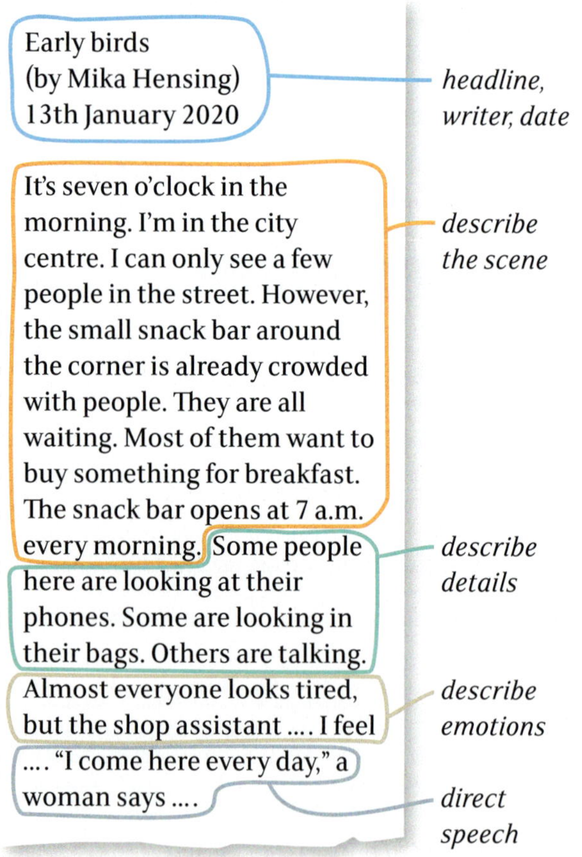

Early birds
(by Mika Hensing)
13th January 2020 — *headline, writer, date*

It's seven o'clock in the morning. I'm in the city centre. I can only see a few people in the street. However, the small snack bar around the corner is already crowded with people. They are all waiting. Most of them want to buy something for breakfast. The snack bar opens at 7 a.m. every morning. — *describe the scene*

Some people here are looking at their phones. Some are looking in their bags. Others are talking. — *describe details*

Almost everyone looks tired, but the shop assistant …. I feel …. — *describe emotions*

"I come here every day," a woman says …. — *direct speech*

Step 1

Choose a topic.

students on their journey to school   alone in the city

an afternoon in the park   ...

Step 2

Choose a place and a time.

Choose a place in your town or village and a time.
Go there, watch the people and take notes.
What can you see, hear, smell, feel?
How do you think the people feel? Why?
What do people there say?
Take photos.

STUDY SKILLS

Du kannst z. B. tagsüber die Leute an einer Bushaltestelle, auf dem Schulhof oder im Park beobachten. Finde andere Schülerinnen und Schüler, die den gleichen Ort ausgewählt haben. Geht gemeinsam dorthin. Wenn du Fotos von einer einzelnen Person oder einer kleinen Gruppe machst, musst du sie vorher um Erlaubnis fragen.

Step 3

Use your notes to write a draft. You can use these phrases:

It's ... in the morning/afternoon/evening.
I'm in ....
There is ..../There are .... I can also see ....
Some people are ....

One person is .... He/She looks/feels ....
Maybe he/she wants to ....
"...," says one ....

Step 4

Write your feature story.

Check your draft and write the feature story. Ask the other people in your group for help.

→ M Writers' conference, p.143

STUDY SKILLS

Nutze diese Liste, um deinen Entwurf zu prüfen:
– Hast du eine Überschrift, einen Einleitungssatz und ein Foto? ✔
– Hast du deinen Namen und das Datum angegeben? ✔
– Hast du alle Wörter richtig geschrieben? ✔
– Hast du die richtige Grammatik verwendet? ✔

Step 5

Make a wall newspaper in class. → M Gallery walk, p.141

South Africa – People and places

1 Work with photos 1–6.

a) Look at the photos. Match each photo with a caption on the right.

b) Describe one of the photos to a partner.

This is a photo of …. It's ….
There is / There are….
The people are …
In the foreground / In the background …

The Cape Town Cycle Tour

The Cape of Good Hope – where two oceans meet

Rock art in a cave near Cape Town

South Africa's rugby team after the 2019 World Cup

A safari in Kruger National Park

A football stadium in Durban

South Africa: Home languages

7.50 %

4.20 %

8 %

8.30 %

8.80 %

9.50 %

12.10 %

24.60 %

17 %

- isiZulu
- isiXhosa
- Afrikaans
- Sepedi
- Setswana
- English
- Sesotho
- Xitsonga
- Other languages

Source: Stats SA's Community Survey, 2016

2 Look at the chart.

a) Which language is used at home by the largest group of South Africans?

b) What do you find most interesting about the chart? Why?

c) What languages are spoken at home by the students in your class? Use a dictionary if you need to.

INFO

Englisch ist die meist gesprochene Sprache im öffentlichen Leben (Wirtschaft, Politik und Medien) in Südafrika. Aber es ist nicht die meist gesprochene Sprache zu Hause. Die meisten Südafrikaner sind mehrsprachig und sprechen zwei oder mehr Sprachen.

Visiting a national park

Du machst gerade Urlaub in Südafrika mit deinem Onkel. Heute wollt ihr den „Kruger National Park" besuchen. Am Eingang gibt euch ein Park Ranger Auskunft. Dein Onkel, der nicht so gut Englisch spricht, hat ein paar Fragen. Er bittet dich, diese dem Ranger auf Englisch zu stellen und seine Antworten dann auf Deutsch wiederzugeben.

KRUGER GATE

Onkel Hallo. Ich habe eine Frage. Wir wollen jetzt in den Park fahren. Kann man aus dem Auto aussteigen, wenn man Fotos von den Tieren machen will?

▶ **Du** My uncle asks if we can ....

▶ **Park ranger** No, sorry. You have to stay in your car all the time with the doors closed. But you'll find signs which show the distance to the nearest camp.

Du Der Ranger sagt, dass wir ....

Onkel OK. Können wir im Park mit dem Handy telefonieren?

▶ **Du** He asks: "Can we ...?" / He wants to know if we ....

Park ranger No, you can only use your phones in camps, at gates or in emergencies.

Du Er betont, dass wir ....

Onkel Frage ihn doch mal, ob man die Tiere im Park füttern darf.

▶ **Du** He asks: "...?" / He also wants to know if we ....

▶ **Park ranger** Of course not. Never feed or disturb the animals.

Du Er weist darauf hin, dass wir ....

Onkel Das verstehe ich. Mir liegt die Natur ja sehr am Herzen. Frage ihn doch noch, ob es im Park gefährlich werden kann.

▶ **Du** He says: "..." / He says that he ....

▶ **Park ranger** You'll be safe as long as you follow all the rules. You must be at your camp before the gates close. They are closed to protect visitors against wild animals. But I've worked in the park for five years. There has never been a dangerous situation.

Onkel Vielen Dank für die Informationen! Thank you.

◀ **Du** Er sagt, dass wir ....

50/1 **1** **Read the dialogue on the left and the tips about how to pass on information.**

My uncle asks: "…" / My … wants to know if/when/what ….
He says: "…"

Der Ranger sagt/erklärt/betont, dass ….

> Bei „Mediation" vermittelst du zwischen zwei Gesprächspartnern. Dabei kannst du – wie im Beispiel – die Fragen und Sätze mit verschiedenen Ausdrücken einleiten.

50/2 **2** **Tips and tricks**

a) „Mir liegt die Natur ja sehr am Herzen."
(He says) he likes nature very much.

> Versuche niemals, alles wortwörtlich zu „übersetzen". Vereinfache die Aussagen, ohne wichtige Infos auszulassen.

b) … as long as you follow the rules.
… man muss die Regeln befolgen./
Man darf nur tun, was erlaubt ist.

> Wenn dir einmal ein Wort (z. B. follow) unbekannt ist, solltest du versuchen, es im Zusammenhang mit bekannten Wörtern zu erraten oder ein Ähnliches im Deutschen denken: z. B. distance – Distanz, Entfernung

3 **Be careful with verb forms.**

a) My uncle ask**s** ….
He want**s** to know if ….

b) I've worked … <u>for</u> five years.
Er sagt, er arbeitet schon <u>seit</u> fünf Jahren.

> Denke auch daran, die richtige Form des Verbs zu verwenden, besonders nach he/she/it.
> **Beachte:** Verben im present perfect mit for/since werden auf Deutsch mit der Gegenwartsform wiedergegeben.

50/3 **4** **Ask for help.**

Could you repeat that, please?
Could you speak more slowly, please?
I'm sorry, but could you explain that again, please?

> Bitte deinen Gesprächspartner darum, langsam zu sprechen oder etwas zu wiederholen, wenn du etwas nicht verstanden hast.
> Du kannst auch bitten, das Gesagte anders auszudrücken oder zu umschreiben.

5 **Your turn**

Gestaltet nun das Gespräch mit drei Personen.
→ **M** Peer correction, p.141

Ein zweisprachiges Wörterbuch in Printform ist für die gesamte schriftliche Prüfung erlaubt.

A Listening Comprehension (Hörverstehen)

You will hear the recordings twice.

2,12 **1** **Listen to text 1. There is one mistake in every sentence. Write the wrong words in your exercise book and then write the correct ones. There is an example (0.) at the beginning.**

0. It's quite difficult to get around in South Africa if you travel on your own.
    difficult → easy

1. There are almost 19 smaller airports.

2. Travel by train or taxi if you want to meet South Africans.

3. You need an international driving licence to buy a car in South Africa.

4. Watch your things, especially when you are alone.

5. It's very important to start learning English before you leave your country.

2,13 **2** **Listen to text 2 and complete the sentences with the information you hear. You don't need all the sentence parts on the right. There is an example (0.) at the beginning.**

0. The name of the airline is … → c   a) Pretoria.

1. You need gate 41 for the flight to …   b) hat.

2. The L&G train is travelling to …   c) SunAirlines.

3. There has been an accident on the …   d) train.

4. Don't forget to watch your bag at the …   e) Johannesburg.

5. Don't forget to wear a …   f) N12.

                                               g) football stadium.

                                               h) coat.

B Use of English (Sprachgebrauch)

1 Read the interview. Write the correct questions to complete the interview. There is an example (0.) at the beginning.

	Charlie:	With me in the studio today is Tony, a ranger at Kruger National Park.
0.	Charlie:	<u>Why do you work as a ranger?</u>
	Tony:	I work as a ranger because I love wild animals and being outdoors.
1.	Charlie:	—— ?
	Tony:	It was in 1898 that President Paul Kruger started a nature reserve which later became Kruger National Park.
2.	Charlie:	—— ?
	Tony:	Kruger National Park is in the northeast of South Africa, near the border with Zimbabwe.
3.	Charlie:	—— ?
	Tony:	Today Kruger National Park is almost 20,000 square kilometres in size.
4.	Charlie:	—— ?
	Tony:	For many years most tourists have wanted to see the 'Big Five' on their safaris.
5.	Charlie:	—— ?
	Tony:	There are more than eleven thousand elephants at the moment in Kruger National Park.
6.	Charlie:	Thank you for answering my questions. I have just one more. —— ?
	Tony:	That's difficult – I like all the animals, but I think my favourite is the lion.
	Charlie:	Thanks Tony.

2 Find a synonym (=) or an opposite (↔) for the underlined words. There is an example (0.) at the beginning.

0. From Table Mountain you get a <u>bad</u> view of the city. (↔) good
1. Tourists from all over the world <u>hate</u> the beaches. (↔)
2. Last year many people <u>started</u> their tour of South Africa at Robben Island. (=)
3. It is <u>wrong</u> that Cape Town is a beautiful city. (↔)
4. My <u>mum and dad</u> visited the Two Oceans Aquarium. (=)
5. We arrived <u>a day ago</u>. (=)
6. We think that South Africans drive really <u>fast</u>. (↔)
7. Our holiday in South Africa was <u>worse</u> than last year's at home. (↔)

C Reading Comprehension (Leseverstehen)

A surprise at the beach – a story

1 **A** It had been a hard time at school in Munich for Daniel, and he was glad that he had finished. Now he could start planning his future. **(x)** But first he needed a break.

5 **B** Then Daniel got a text message from his cousin Leo in Cape Town: *Just off to the beach. Great surf. A bit boring. Friends all away. Come visit!*
This was an exciting idea.
10 Cape Town. Some time in a foreign country would be the best medicine. And he could practise his English too.

C Daniel's parents protested at first. "South Africa is too expensive. And I don't think you
15 really want to practise your English!" said his dad. "You only liked the word 'beach' in Leo's message."
"And it could be quite dangerous," his mum said. But Daniel told her, "Don't worry, Mum.
20 I'm going to stay with Leo and his parents."

D He found a good price for a flight to Cape Town and a few days later he was on his way to South Africa. **(x)**
Finally he was there in Hout Bay and his
25 holiday started. Daniel felt at home right away. He loved the climate, and he had all the same interests as his cousin Leo. Leo lived with his parents in a small house about ten minutes from the beach by car. 'The perfect
30 place to be,' thought Daniel.
He sent his parents text messages every day and told them they needn't worry. **(x)**
One morning Leo borrowed his dad's car and they went surfing.

35 **E** After surfing for an hour, the boys were sitting on the sand. Over to his right, Daniel saw some strange clouds. As he watched, the sky went darker and darker over the sea. "I'm so hungry!" Leo said. **(x)**
40 "Wait!" said Daniel as he took Leo's arm. Daniel saw that the waves were bigger now. Leo looked at the waves too.
Leo saw the clouds and suddenly knew what was going to happen. He took a deep breath
45 and tried to think quickly. 'What happens if this storm hits the beach? Will we be OK?' **(x)** He saw that Daniel was scared. "Stay cool, Daniel," he said. "Leave everything where it is and run for the car … as fast as you can."
50 Thankfully Daniel was better at running than he was at surfing, and he didn't need Leo to tell him again. The boys got to the car as the rain started. **(x)**

F As soon as the rain stopped, the sun came
55 out again. Daniel couldn't believe what had happened. "The sky is blue now and the sea is flat and perfect," shouted Daniel happily. "Even our things are still on the beach – all wet." **(x)**

1 Match the headings to the right parts of the text (A–F). You don't need all the headings. There is an example (0.) at the beginning.

0. School is over → A
1. The storm is over
2. Peaceful days in South Africa
3. What next?
4. What the parents said
5. Going on holiday with Leo
6. The weather changes

2 Find the right places (x) in the text for the missing sentences. There is an example (0.) at the beginning.

0. But first he needed a break. → line 4
1. He looked back at Daniel.
2. So much rain in five minutes – that was new for Daniel.
3. *Hout Bay is a peaceful place. No problems!* he wrote.
4. Then they had lunch on the beach.
5. The flight was great and his aunt met him at the airport.
6. "Let's get something to eat," Leo said, and started to get up.

D Text Production (Schreiben)

1 Robin und seine Familie machen eine Safari im „Kruger National Park". Schreibe eine Geschichte auf Englisch, in der du alle Bilder berücksichtigst. Beginne wie folgt:

The family was excited when their car arrived for the safari on the first day of their holiday in Kruger National Park. They …

Schreibe eine Geschichte von ungefähr 100 Wörtern auf ein gesondertes Blatt. Achte auf eine ansprechende äußere Form und eine gut lesbare Handschrift.

E Mediation (Sprachmittlung)

1 Situierung und Texte

Du träumst von einer Reise nach Südafrika mit deiner Familie. Du surfst im Internet und schaust nach Übernachtungsmöglichkeiten in Kapstadt. Lies die Beschreibungen aufmerksam.

Beschreibung der Unterkünfte

The Beach Hotel ★★★★	Happy Rhino Manor B&B	Lakeside View Hostel
Our hotel is directly on the Waterfront and it has a view of the harbour, Table Mountain and the Atlantic Ocean. Our pool and wellness area are open to all our guests. All rooms have free Wi-Fi, air conditioning, flat screen TV, tea and coffee making facilities and an en-suite bathroom. Breakfast is included and you can also have lunch, afternoon tea and evening meals in our restaurant or grill, which both serve regional dishes.	All the rooms at our B&B have a balcony or terrace. Our pool and children's playground can be used by all our guests. We also organize cycling and hiking tours in the surrounding area. All rooms have free Wi-Fi, air conditioning, flat screen TV and an en-suite bathroom with a hairdryer. You can enjoy an exceptional breakfast in our breakfast room with a view of the surrounding mountains.	Our hostel offers perfect family rooms with wooden floors. All our rooms are non-smoking rooms. Pets are allowed. From here you can explore Cape Town and the surrounding area, which is great for cycling and fishing. Our outside pool can be used by all our guests. We have free Wi-Fi in the communal lounge and kitchen. Shared bathroom with bath and shower. There is a grill in the garden where the guests love to get together in the evenings.
30 km to Cape Town airport €1435: four nights, 2 adults + 2 children: 2 twin/double rooms	12 km from Waterfront and Robben Island ferry 13 km to Cape Town airport, free transfer available €684: four nights, 2 adults + 2 children: 1 family room	24 km from Waterfront and Robben Island ferry 20 km to Cape Town airport, free transfer available €375: four nights, 2 adults + 2 children: 1 family room

2 Aufgabe

Lies die Beschreibungen der drei Unterkünfte. In deiner Familie überlegt ihr, wo ihr am liebsten übernachten möchtet. Schreibe anschließend die Angaben (1-7), die in dem Dialog ergänzt werden sollen, in dein Heft.

	Lage
Mutter	Mein Favorit ist das Beach Hotel, weil es so zentral an der Waterfront liegt.
Vater	Ja, das stimmt. Außerdem hat man von dort einen guten Blick auf den Tafelberg, (1) ….
	Aktivitäten in und außerhalb des Hotels
Du	Hm, genau. Das Beach Hotel ist aber bestimmt nicht so passend für Kinder. Ich finde das Happy Rhino Manor B&B am besten, weil man dort viel machen kann. Alle Gäste dürfen (2) …, und es gibt sogar ….
Deine Schwester	Wir sollten auf jeden Fall unsere Badesachen mitnehmen. Schließlich ist das Wetter ja in Südafrika viel sonniger und wärmer als bei uns. Mir gefällt das Lakeside View Hostel am besten. Vielleicht gibt es dort ja Hunde oder Katzen, weil (3) ….
	Flughafen/Transfer
Mutter	Wir werden doch unterwegs auch viele Tiere sehen. Aber immerhin ist das Hostel näher am Flughafen als das Beach Hotel.
Du	Ja, aber guck mal: Das Happy Rhino (4) ….
	Zimmerausstattung
Mutter	Ich glaube nicht, dass die paar Kilometer Unterschied ein Problem sind. Wir buchen ja ohnehin einen Mietwagen. Die Zimmer im Beach Hotel bieten gute Extras, wie kostenloses WLAN und Klimaanlage, und man kann sich auf dem Zimmer zum Trinken (5) ….
Deine Schwester	Schon, aber wir wollen ja nicht die ganze Zeit im Hotel sein. Wenn wir den ganzen Tag unterwegs sind, wäre doch ein einfacheres Zimmer auch in Ordnung.
	Preis
Vater	Also, das Beach Hotel ist mit Abstand (6) …. Und wir müssen noch die Kosten für die Flüge und den Mietwagen mit einkalkulieren!
Du	Warum einigen wir uns dann nicht auf einen Kompromiss und schicken eine Anfrage an das Happy Rhino Manor B&B? Das kostet für uns alle zusammen für vier Nächte (7) ….
Alle	Gute Idee, das machen wir!

That's the end of Test practice 3!

News from New Zealand

1

Hi! My name is Liam and I live in Wellington. That's in New Zealand. I'm still at school but I'm thinking about what career I can have. I'm going to talk to the careers advisor at our school next week.

2

New Zealand is about 1,000 miles (1,600 km) from Australia, its nearest neighbour. There are two large islands. About 4.7 million people live in New Zealand. A third of them live in Auckland, the biggest city. The capital of New Zealand is Wellington. Farming and tourism are important industries in New Zealand.

1 (SPEAKING) Talk about the photos.

Would New Zealand be an interesting place to visit? Say why or why not.

I think … because there is/are … in photo … .
Photo … shows that … .
Maybe … .
I would/wouldn't like (to) …

2 (READING) Read and take notes.

58/1–2

a) Write the information as notes:

- the capital
- industries
- the population and groups of people
- clubs and sport
- languages
- the 'Ring of Fire'

b) Check with a partner. Do you have the same information?

Am Ende dieser Unit kann ich ...
- Informationen über Neuseeland verstehen.
- über Jobmöglichkeiten und Fähigkeiten sprechen.
- einen Bericht über ein Praktikum schreiben.
- eine Geschichte über verschiedene Generationen verstehen.
- Informationen über einen Verein weitergeben.
- einen Film über Vulkane und Erdbeben verstehen.

3

New Zealand has many organizations with volunteers, and many young people are members of clubs. Rugby is a popular free-time activity and the national sport. The New Zealand rugby team is one of the best in the world.

4

The Maori people came to New Zealand from islands in the Pacific Ocean more than 700 years ago. Today about 15 % of the population say they are Maori. English and Maori are official languages in New Zealand.

5

New Zealand has amazing landscapes. It is part of the 'Ring of Fire'. This is an area around the Pacific Ocean where there are many volcanoes. Earthquakes often happen there too.

3 (LISTENING) Listen to the radio interviews with young people.

2,15

a) Copy the table in your exercise book. Listen and fill in the information.

Name:	Mason	Hazel
How old:		
Free-time activity:		
Why they like it:		

b) Talk about the free-time activities. Which would you like to do? Why or why not?

Ich kann Informationen über Neuseeland verstehen.

Thinking about a career

1 (SPEAKING) **Collect words about jobs and careers with a partner.**

Think about:

| where you can work | names of jobs | what you need when you apply | people at work |

2 (READING) **Read the dialogue and the form.**

2,16

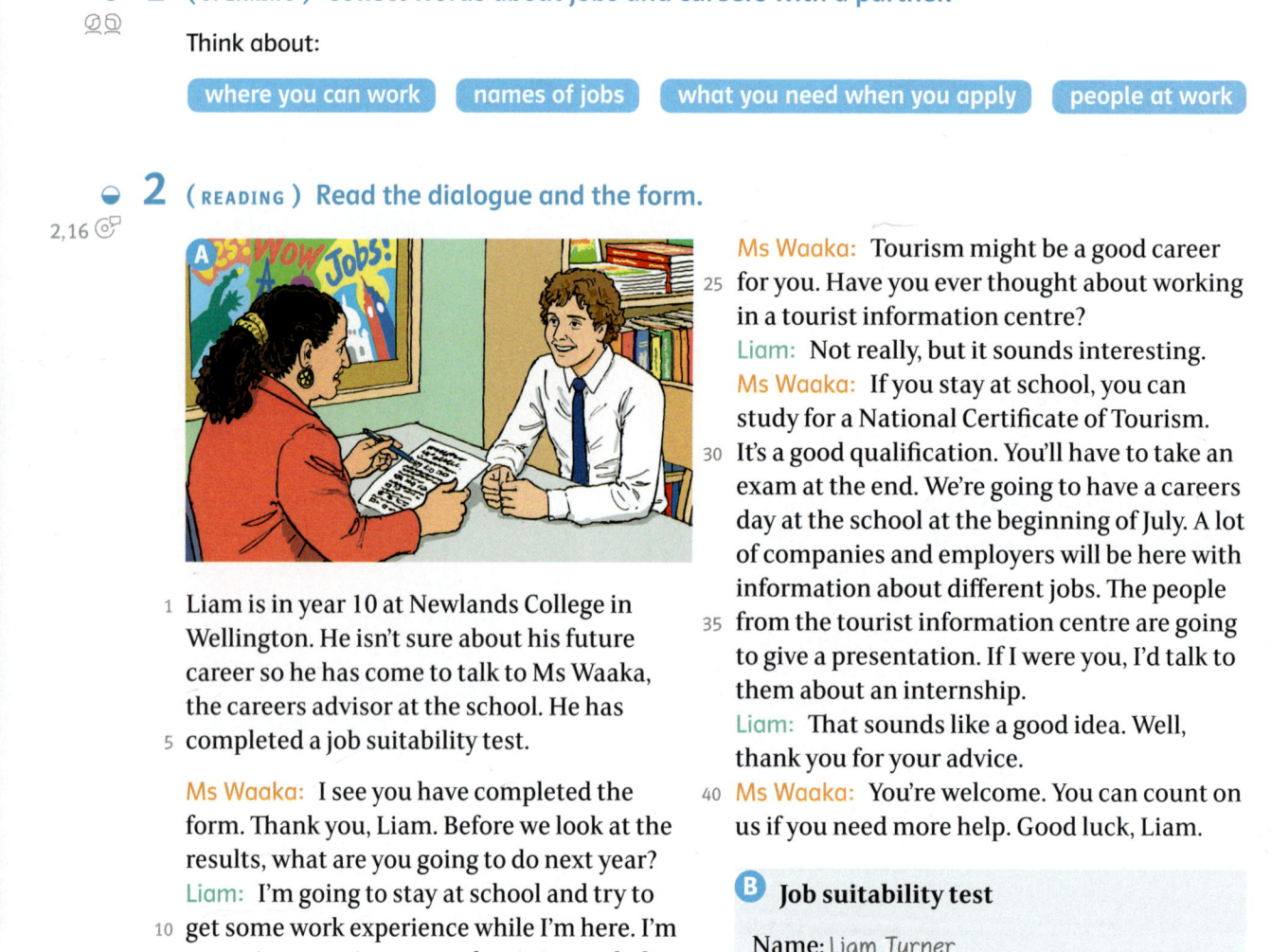

1 Liam is in year 10 at Newlands College in Wellington. He isn't sure about his future career so he has come to talk to Ms Waaka, the careers advisor at the school. He has
5 completed a job suitability test.

Ms Waaka: I see you have completed the form. Thank you, Liam. Before we look at the results, what are you going to do next year?
Liam: I'm going to stay at school and try to
10 get some work experience while I'm here. I'm not going to train as a mechanic in my dad's garage.
Ms Waaka: Well, it's a good plan to try different internships. I'm going to look at
15 your test now. I see you find it easy to talk to people that you don't know. And when things go wrong, you usually stay calm. If someone is feeling sad, you can give them support. So you have good customer service
20 and communication skills. But you don't like working with machines. Hm. Are you interested in sights and events in your town?
Liam: Yes, I am.

Ms Waaka: Tourism might be a good career
25 for you. Have you ever thought about working in a tourist information centre?
Liam: Not really, but it sounds interesting.
Ms Waaka: If you stay at school, you can study for a National Certificate of Tourism.
30 It's a good qualification. You'll have to take an exam at the end. We're going to have a careers day at the school at the beginning of July. A lot of companies and employers will be here with information about different jobs. The people
35 from the tourist information centre are going to give a presentation. If I were you, I'd talk to them about an internship.
Liam: That sounds like a good idea. Well, thank you for your advice.
40 **Ms Waaka:** You're welcome. You can count on us if you need more help. Good luck, Liam.

B **Job suitability test**

Name: Liam Turner

1. I don't mind talking to people that I don't know.
45 ☑ ☺ ☐ ☺ ☐ ☹

2. I am usually calm when things go wrong.
☑ ☺ ☐ ☺ ☐ ☹

3. If someone is feeling sad, I give them
50 support.
☐ ☺ ☑ ☺ ☐ ☹

4. I like working with machines and tools.
☐ ☺ ☐ ☺ ☑ ☹

3 Right, wrong or not in the text? → M Peer correction, p.141

1. Liam wants to leave school in the summer.
2. He finds it easy to meet new people.
3. He also has good computer skills.
4. He has always wanted a job in tourism.
5. Ms Waaka will be at the careers day.
6. Liam can find out about internships there.

59/1 **4 Work with words from the text.**

a) Choose the right words to complete Liam's e-mail about his interview. → ◯ p.123

> **E-MAIL**
>
> Hi Ella,
> I wanted to get some **information** • **advice** • **news** (1) about my career so I talked to Ms Waaka, the careers advisor. First I **completed** • **looked at** • **designed** (2) a job suitability test. Ms Waaka thinks I should study for a **question** • **qualification** • **quiz** (3) in tourism. Then I could work as an **interviewer** • **assistant** • **artist** (4) in a tourist information **building** • **centre** • **company** (5). They're going to have a **jobs** • **sports** • **careers** (6) day at the school in July. There will be a lot of **teams** • **companies** • **schools** (7) with information about jobs.
> What about you? How did your interview go?
> Bye,
> Liam

b) Find the words in the text. Look at the lines.

1. How you feel when you are quiet or not excited (16–17)
2. What you give when you try to help somebody (17–19)
3. Another word for a test (30–31)
4. A person or company that gives you work and pays you for it (32–34)

5 Work with job words.

a) Match the jobs with what the people say. You don't need all the words.

chef • vet's assistant • hotel manager • hairdresser • check-in agent
mechanic • farmer • nurse

1. "It's great when I find out what's wrong with the car!"
2. "I sometimes have to tell people that their flight is late."
3. "I have to stay calm and help the doctor."
4. "I help people with their pets every day."
5. "I sometimes don't leave the restaurant before 1 a.m."
6. "We have guests from all around the world."

b) Write a sentence like the ones in a) for each of the jobs that you didn't need.

SPEAKING SKILLS

Wenn du das Wort für eine bestimmte Berufsbezeichnung oder Ausbildung auf Englisch nicht kennst, kannst du sie auch umschreiben. Sage: „It's a job where you …" oder „It's a kind of training that …"

6 (LISTENING) **Listen to the dialogue between Liam and Ella.**

2,17
59/2–3

Which three sentences are right?

1. Ella finds out about a job at the tourist information centre in Auckland.
2. The tourist information centre in Christchurch has a lot of international visitors.
3. Ms Waaka thinks Ella should work in tourism too.
4. Ella wants to work in her aunt's hairdressing salon.
5. Liam isn't sure about his career yet.

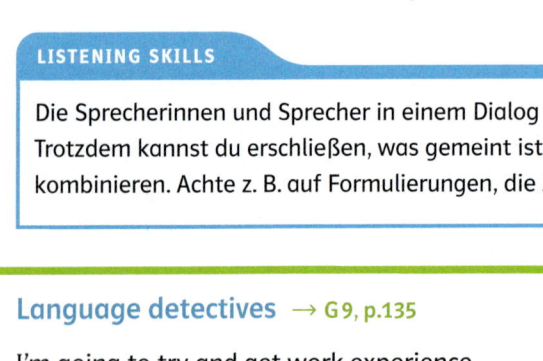

LISTENING SKILLS

Die Sprecherinnen und Sprecher in einem Dialog sagen oft nicht direkt, was sie denken und fühlen. Trotzdem kannst du erschließen, was gemeint ist. Oft musst du dafür mehrere Aussagen im Dialog kombinieren. Achte z. B. auf Formulierungen, die Zustimmung oder Ablehnung ausdrücken.

Language detectives → G 9, p.135

I'm going to try and get work experience next year.
I'm not going to train as a mechanic in my dad's garage.
We're going to have a careers day at the beginning of July.

Wenn du über Pläne für die Zukunft sprechen willst, verwendest du going to. Achte auf die Signalwörter!
Wie drückst du es im Deutschen oder in deiner Muttersprache aus, wenn du über Pläne sprichst?

7 **Talk about plans.** → M Bus stop, p.140

a) Make sentences about Ella and Liam's job plans. → ○ p.123

60/4

1. Ella (find out) about jobs as a hairdresser.
   Ella is going to find out about jobs as a hairdresser.
2. Liam (talk) to different employers next week.
3. Liam: I (apply) for jobs in tourism.
4. Liam (not work) with his dad.
5. Ella: I (train) in a hairdressing salon.
6. Ella and Liam (look) for jobs on the internet.
7. Ella and Liam (not leave) school next year.
8. Ella and Liam: We (visit) a careers day soon.

Remember the forms of 'to be'?
I am ....
He/She is ....
We are ....
They are ....

b) Write about your plans for these times. Write about two things that you are going to do and two things that you aren't going to do.

this afternoon   this evening   tomorrow   on Saturday   next week

8 (SPEAKING) **Talk about plans with a partner.**

What are your job plans? Look at the ideas.

A: I'm going to complete a job suitability test.
And you?
B: Good idea. I'm going to do that too. / I'm not
going to do that (I've already done that.)
I'm (also) going to ....

complete a job suitability test
write my CV
speak to a careers advisor
find out about internships at …
go to a careers day
apply for a job at …

60/5 **9** **Write questions and find the answers.**

a) Write questions about job plans. → ○ p.123

1. Where / you / find out about jobs?
   Where are you going to find out about jobs?
2. What / Liam / do next year?
3. When / you / leave school?
4. Who / Liam / meet at the careers day?
5. When / you / write your CV?
6. Who / you / ask about your career?

Language → G 9, p.135
What are you going to do next year?

b) Match the answers to the questions in a). Which answer don't you need?

a. The careers advisor.
b. He wants to learn new things.
c. This afternoon.
d. At the careers day.

e. He's going to study for a National Certificate in Tourism.
f. Different companies.
g. Next year.

10 (TASK) **A dialogue about jobs and qualities** → V Jobs and qualities, p.152

61/6-7

a) Work with a partner. Copy the job suitability test into your exercise book and complete it for yourself.

b) Talk to your partner about the results. What kind of job do you think is best for you? What is best for your partner?

A: I like working with animals. I'm going to train as a vet's assistant.
B: But you like working outside …

1. I like working with people.
   ☺ ☺ ☹
2. I like working outside.
   ☺ ☺ ☹
3. I can listen to people and give them support.
   ☺ ☺ ☹
4. I like working with animals.
   ☺ ☺ ☹

Maybe you could … | … might be a good career. | Why don't you …? | …

Ich kann über Jobmöglichkeiten und Fähigkeiten sprechen. ✔

A job in retail?

1 (READING) **Read the dialogue.**

2,18

1 Some students from Newlands College are talking to the store manager of a supermarket in Wellington. They want to find out what it's like to work there. Later they are going to
5 write a report.

Mr Roberts: Welcome everyone. My name is John Roberts. I'm going to talk to you about the exciting jobs in retail today. We offer jobs and apprenticeships in customer service,
10 communication and IT. But before we start our tour, are there any questions?
Rose: Yes, I have a question. What do shop assistants do in their job?
Mr Roberts: Shop assistants do many
15 different things. They help customers find the right products in the store and they work at the checkouts. Shop assistants also fill the shelves and help present the products.
Nikau: Can you tell us how a supermarket
20 works?
Mr Roberts: Well, supermarkets buy their products from other local companies. These companies are called suppliers. Stores order large numbers of products from suppliers so
25 that the prices are cheaper. Then the products are sold to customers.
Nikau: When did this store open?
Mr Roberts: It opened in 2008. It's one of the largest stores in Wellington. We have over
30 60,000 products – not only food, but also clothes and many other goods. But we work in the community too. We donate food to local charities to reduce food waste, for example.

Oliver: That's cool! How much food did you
35 donate last year?
Mr Roberts: Well, last year we donated over NZ$3 million's worth of food.
Rose: Do you sell bread here?
Mr Roberts: Yes, we do. All our bread is made
40 in the store.
Grace: Do you offer internships?
Mr Roberts: Yes, internships are offered here. You can apply for one in our office or you can visit us at the job fair next month.
45 We're always looking for interns to help our fantastic team. We also offer summer jobs for students. You get a good salary and training is included.
Grace: Did you start your career here as a
50 shop assistant?
Mr Roberts: Yes, I did. Although I've been at this company for ten years, I'll never forget what I learned in my first six months. Let's start our tour now.

2 **Find the information in the text. Take notes under these headings.** → **M** Peer correction, p.141

1. Different jobs at the company
2. When this store opened
3. The number of products

4. How the shop helps the community
5. Internships and summer jobs

2/1–2 **3 What do they do?**

a) Match the parts of the sentences. → ◯ p.124

1. The store manager is talking to
2. Stores order
3. The suppliers deliver
4. Shop assistants fill
5. Customers pay
6. The company donates

a. for products at the checkouts.
b. food to local charities.
c. products from suppliers.
d. products to the store.
e. students about jobs in retail.
f. the shelves every day.

b) Complete these sentences using the verbs and information in the text.

1. Companies which sell products to supermarkets .... (call)
2. Food, clothes and many other things .... (sell)
3. The supermarket's bread .... (make)
4. Apprenticeships, internships and summer jobs .... (offer)

Language → **G 10, p.136**
The products are sold to customers.

62/3  **4 Choose the right meaning in German.** → M Bus stop, p.140

1. Mr Roberts knows how supermarkets **work**.
2. He started his **career** ten years ago.
3. **Training** is included.
4. There's a job **fair** next month.
5. Stores **order** large numbers of products.
6. Let's start our **tour**.

a. (*v.*) arbeiten
a. (*n.*) Karriere
a. (*n.*, Sport) Training
a. (*adj.*) fair, gerecht
a. (*n.*) Reihenfolge
a. (*n.*) Führung

b. (*v.*) funktionieren
b. (*n.*) Beruf
b. (*n.*) Ausbildung
b. (*n.*, Handel) Messe
b. (*v.*) bestellen
b. (*n.*) Reise

STUDY SKILLS

Viele englische Wörter haben mehr als eine Bedeutung. Dein Wörterbuch gibt an, in welchem Zusammenhang (z. B. Schule, Sport) das Wort verwendet wird, und ob es sich um ein Nomen (n.), ein Verb (v.) oder ein Adjektiv (adj.) handelt. So kannst du das richtige Wort für das finden, über das du sprechen willst. Nimm nicht immer die erste Bedeutung, die dir das Wörterbuch anbietet!

5 (SOUNDS) Read, say and listen.

62/4

a) Make a chart in your exercise book and put the words into the right groups.

work | find | exciting | customer service | retail | price
waste | apply | internship | training | worth | donate

/ɜː/ learn	/eɪ/ day	/aɪ/ mine

2,19 b) Listen and check your answers.

Language detectives → G 1, p.127

This store <u>opened</u> in <u>2008</u>.
<u>Did</u> you <u>start</u> your career as a shop assistant?
– Yes, I <u>did</u>.

Welche Zeitform ist das? Wann benutzt du sie?
Welches Wort verwendest du, um Fragen
und Kurzantworten zu bilden?

6 **Talk about the first day of Grace's internship.**

In the morning

learn about the company

After that

do office work for Mr Roberts

Then

help with different jobs

In the afternoon

phone three different people

Then

write four e-mails

After that

make two appointments

1. In the morning Grace <u>learned</u> about the company.
2. After that she ....

63/5 **7** **Complete the questions about Grace's internship.** → M Peer correction, p.141

a) Ask the questions with the right form. → ○ p.125

1. What —— you —— first? (do)
   What <u>did</u> you <u>do</u> first?
2. When —— you ——? (start)
3. How —— you —— to work? (travel)
4. —— you —— with a computer? (work)
5. What —— you —— at lunchtime? (do)
6. When —— you —— the internship? (apply for)
7. —— you —— your internship? (enjoy)

b) Write Grace's answers to the questions. Use the pictures in Ex. 6 and the words below.

by bus • yes ... • go to café with other interns • six weeks ago • 9 a.m.

8 (SPEAKING) **Ask your partner about last weekend.**

63/6

A: <u>Did you have a nice weekend?</u>
B: Yes, thanks. / Yes, it was OK, thank you.
A: <u>What did you do?</u>
B: Well, I …. Then I …. I …. And you?

| Where did you go? | Who did you visit? |

| Did you stay long? | … |

| watched | stayed | went to | … |

64/7 **9** **A report about a job fair**

a) Read Oliver's report. Put in a suitable form of the word in brackets. → ○ p.125

Last week I (1) <u>visited</u> (visit) a job fair at the Adelphi Hotel in
Auckland. There (2) —— (be) many companies at the fair. There
were also a lot of young people who were (3) —— (interest) in
the companies. I wrote a list of questions before I (4) —— (go) to
the fair. I also (5) —— (take) my CV with me. I talked to three
employers and I want to apply for an (6) —— (intern) with one of
them. I stayed at the fair for about two (7) —— (hour). It's the
(8) —— (good) way to find out about jobs.

b) Write the questions that Oliver's friend asked him after the job fair.

1. when – the job fair – start?
2. meet – other students from our school?
3. talk to – employers – from Wellington?
4. what – wear – to the fair?

---

10 (TASK) **A report about an internship** → V Talking about an internship, p.153

64/8

a) Think about your internship. Make notes:

Where did you do the internship?
When did you do it?
What did you do?
What did you learn?
What did you like most?

> **WRITING SKILLS**
>
> Es gibt verschiedene Möglichkeiten, deine
> Notizen zu ordnen. Du kannst dafür eine
> Mindmap oder eine Tabelle erstellen. Schreibe
> Stichwörter auf.

b) Use your notes from a) to write a draft of a
report. Write about 80 words.

These phrases can help:
I worked with …. I helped …. I also ….
I learned about ….

c) Check your draft. Use the checklist on page 145
and a dictionary. Then write your report on
another page.

… was great / interesting / ….
On the first day / At the end I felt ….

d) Read your reports in a group. Choose the best report. → M Writers' conference, p.143

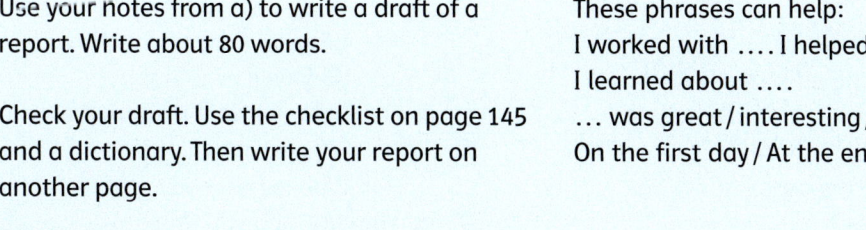

Ich kann einen Bericht über ein
Praktikum schreiben.   ✔

The Whale Rider

1 **Work with the photos.** → M Think – pair – share, p.143

Look at the photos of the people in the story. Who is who? What do you think will happen?

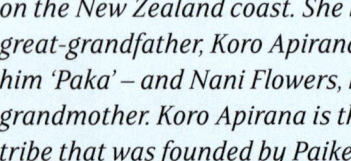 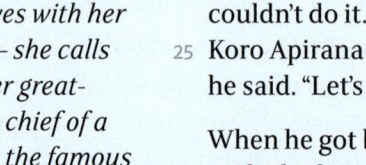 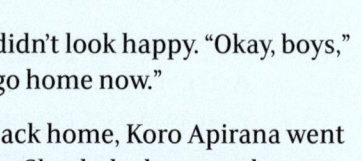

2 (READING) **Read the story.**

2,20

1 *Kahu lives in Whangara, a Maori community on the New Zealand coast. She lives with her great-grandfather, Koro Apirana – she calls him 'Paka' – and Nani Flowers, her great-*
5 *grandmother. Koro Apirana is the chief of a tribe that was founded by Paikea, the famous 'whale rider'. In the past the chief was always a man. But Kahu will be the next chief, and Koro Apirana doesn't think that a girl can do the job.*
10 *Kahu's uncle, Rawiri, tells the story.*

Two weeks after the beginning of the school holidays, Koro Apirana took the young boys from the school to the sea. It was early morning. He put them in his boat and went
15 past the bay.
Koro Apirana began a prayer. He had a flat stone in his hand. Suddenly he threw it into the water.
"One of you must bring that stone back to
20 me," Koro Apirana said. "Go now."
But the stone was too deep. Some of the boys were afraid. Others weren't able to swim so far down. Although they tried very hard, they couldn't do it.
25 Koro Apirana didn't look happy. "Okay, boys," he said. "Let's go home now."

When he got back home, Koro Apirana went to the bedroom. Slowly, he began to lament. "Is something wrong with Koro?" Kahu asked.
30 We were sitting outside. "Is it because of the stone?"
"How did you know about that?" I asked.
"One of the boys told me," Kahu said. "I wish I could make Paka happy again." Her eyes
35 looked sad.

The next morning Rawiri goes for a ride in his boat. Kahu and Nani Flowers come too.

We went past the bay and Kahu asked again about the stone.
40 "What stone?" Nani Flowers said.
So I told her. Nani wanted to see the place. We went out into the sea.

3 **Work with the text.**

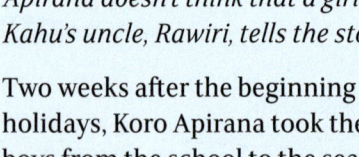 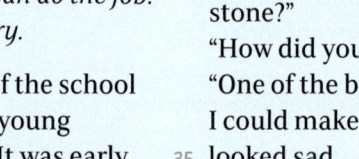 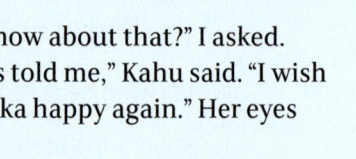

a) Put the headings in the right order.

   A A ride with Rawiri
   B A stone and a fish for Paka
   C Unhappy
   D Some help for Kahu
   E A test for the boys
   F Is she okay?

b) Answer the questions with short answers.

   1. Why did Koro test the boys?
   2. Why was he unhappy?
   3. How did Nani Flowers feel when Kahu jumped in?
   4. Who is not ready at the end?
   5. What do you think: Will Kahu become the chief of the tribe?

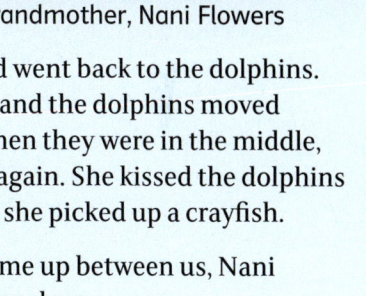

Kahu and her great-grandfather, Koro Apirana

Kahu's great-grandmother, Nani Flowers

"Well," Nani said. "No wonder those boys couldn't get it. This is deep."
45 Kahu said, "I'll get it."
She stood up and jumped.
Nani's mouth made a big 'O'. Then she shouted, "Oh, no! Go after her, Rawiri. Go."

Rawiri puts on a mask and jumps in. He sees
50 *Kahu swimming. Then Nani Flowers jumps in too.*

"Where is she?" Nani Flowers shouted. "Oh, my Kahu!"
She took the mask and put it on. I pointed.
55 Kahu was swimming slowly around the coral. She was looking for the stone, but she couldn't find it. Then a group of dolphins came towards her. They swam around Kahu and seemed to talk to her. The dolphins took her to another
60 area of the reef. Kahu seemed to say, "Here?" and the dolphins seemed to nod. Suddenly Kahu moved. She picked something up,

looked at it and went back to the dolphins. Slowly the girl and the dolphins moved
65 towards us. When they were in the middle, Kahu stopped again. She kissed the dolphins goodbye. Then she picked up a crayfish.

When Kahu came up between us, Nani Flowers held her close.
70 "I'm okay, Nani," Kahu laughed. She showed the crayfish to us. "This is for Paka's tea, and you can give him back his stone." She put the stone in Nani Flowers' hands.
Nani Flowers looked at me quickly.
75 We got back into the small boat and she said, "Not a word about this to Koro Apirana."
I nodded. I looked back to the island and saw the carving of Paikea on his whale.

When we got to the beach, Nani Flowers said
80 again, "Not a word, Rawiri. Not a word about the stone or our Kahu." She looked up at Paikea. "He's not ready yet," she said …

Adapted from: The Whale Rider by Witi Ihimaera, 2008.

4 Choose one of the tasks.

a) How did Kahu tell a friend about what happened? Write her story.
Start like this:

Paka was unhappy because …. So the next morning I …. When we got to the place I jumped … and …. I saw … and …. They helped …. I picked up … and …….

 OR

b) What other stories or films do you know where someone gets help from an animal? Research and give a short presentation.
Start like this: → M 1-minute-presentation, p.140

My story/film is ….
The animal is a …. It ….
It's exciting/interesting because …….

66/1–2
67/3–4

Ich kann eine Geschichte über verschiedene Generationen verstehen. ✔

Joining a club

| Home | What's new? | Gallery | Club history | Links |

1 **Auckland Hockey Club**

We are a large sports club on Auckland's North Shore. We have more than 450 members.

Looking to play hockey next year? Register now!

Open training for girls and boys:
5 Tuesday, 12 March 5:30 – 6:45 p.m.
Girls' trials:
Sunday, 17 March 9:00 – 10:15 a.m.
Boys' trials:
Sunday, 17 March 10:30 a.m. – 12:00 p.m.

10 We provide hockey sticks if you don't have one, but please bring your own shoes and mouthguard.
New players are welcome!
Fees: Youth players: NZ$ 250 per year; junior players: NZ$ 100 per year, due by 10 April

> I started playing hockey here two years ago.
> Since then, I have made a lot of new friends.
> 15 It wasn't always easy. I had to train hard to
> become a good player. Members have to help
> at events every month. It feels great to be part
> of a team and we have lots of fun together!

At last year's summer fete we raised NZ$ 3,000 for our trip!

20 Leo, 14, member

1 (MEDIATION) Du möchtest wissen, was Jugendliche in Neuseeland in ihrer Freizeit gerne machen.

65/1

Auf der Website eines Hockey-Clubs in Auckland findest du diese Informationen über das Vereinsleben. Ergänze die Lücken 1–7 mit Angaben auf Deutsch.

Der Auckland Hockey-Club ist —— (1) am North Shore von Auckland. Wenn man —— (2), muss man sich registrieren. Einen Hockeyschläger kann —— (3). Schuhe und Mundschutz muss jeder —— (4). Der —— (5) beträgt NZ$ 100 oder NZ$ 250 und muss bis —— (6). Mitglieder müssen einmal im Monat —— (7).

CULTURE

Das Vereinsleben spielt in Neuseeland eine wichtige Rolle. Die ehrenamtlichen Mitarbeiter engagieren sich im Verein, da sie dort Freunde gewinnen und wertvolle Arbeitserfahrungen sammeln. Welche Vereine gibt es in deiner Umgebung?

Ich kann Informationen über einen Verein weitergeben. ✓

The natural violence of New Zealand

1 (SPEAKING) Describe the photo of New Zealand with a partner.

How is this part of New Zealand different from where you live?

This photo shows . . . .   mountains   the sea   beach   lake   . . .

VIEWING SKILLS

In Dokumentarfilmen werden oft Grafiken und Computeranimationen verwendet. Diese können dir helfen, zu verstehen, worum es geht, auch wenn du nicht alle Wörter verstehst.

2 (VIEWING) Watch the film.

a) Choose the right answer.

1. New Zealand has mountains because there are **two** · **three** plates in the earth's crust under the country.
2. Mount Tongariro is a volcano on the **North Island** · **South Island**.
3. The North Island is famous for its **cold** · **hot** pools.
4. The film shows houses and roads after an earthquake in **Christchurch** · **Wellington**.
5. The earthquake happened in **2011** · **2016**.

A map of the plates in the earth's crust

b) Watch the film again from 3:45. How do people In New Zealand help each other after an earthquake? Name three things from the film.

3 (SPEAKING) Talk about natural disasters.

Imagine you have to live without electricity for a few days. What problems will there be?
→ **M** Think – pair – share, p.143

I'll miss …
I won't have ….
I won't be able to ….
… will be awful./ … won't be so bad.

CULTURE

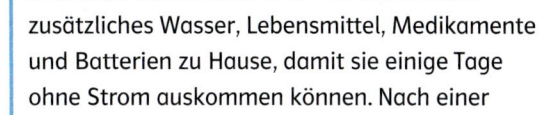

Die Menschen in Neuseeland sind gut auf Erdbeben vorbereitet. Viele von ihnen haben zusätzliches Wasser, Lebensmittel, Medikamente und Batterien zu Hause, damit sie einige Tage ohne Strom auskommen können. Nach einer Naturkatastrophe helfen ihnen diese Dinge wieder in ihren Alltag zurückzukehren.

Ich kann einen Film über Vulkane und Erdbeben verstehen. ✔

Checklist 🌐 Find more online: nd4r3a

✔ **Ich kann Informationen über Neuseeland verstehen.**

New Zealand is about 1,000 miles (1,600 km) from Australia, its nearest neighbour. • Today about 15% of the population say they are Maori.

68 ↗

✔ **Ich kann über Jobmöglichkeiten und Fähigkeiten sprechen.**

I'm going to try to get some work experience. • When things go wrong, you usually stay calm

68 ↗

✔ **Ich kann einen Bericht über ein Praktikum schreiben.**

Supermarkets buy their products from other local companies. • This store opened in 2008.

69 ↗

✔ **Ich kann eine Geschichte über verschiedene Generationen verstehen.**

69 ↗

✔ **Ich kann Informationen über einen Verein weitergeben.**

69 ↗

✔ **Ich kann einen Film über Vulkane und Erdbeben verstehen.**

✳ (UNIT TASK) # A job interview

Stell dir vor, du hast dich im Auckland Zoo auf eine Stelle als Aushilfe beworben. Nun wurdest du zu einem Vorstellungsgespräch eingeladen. Bereite das Gespräch vor und führe es zusammen mit einer Partnerin oder einem Partner durch.

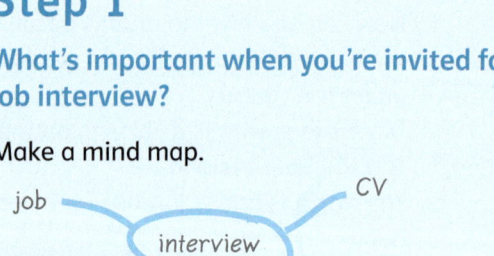

Zoo helper wanted!
Contact Matt Campbell at info@xyz.nz

Step 1

What's important when you're invited for a job interview?

 Make a mind map.

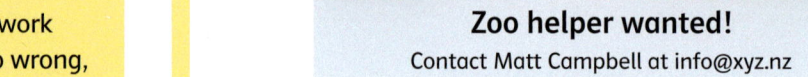

job   CV
interview
questions   clothes

Step 2

Prepare for the role of the interviewer.

→ **M** Think – pair – share, p.143

Work in groups of four. Think of questions that the interviewer can ask.

- Have you ever worked with animals before?
- Why are you interested in this job?
- Can you tell us about your work experience/internship?
- Where did you hear about …?
- …

Step 3

 Work with a partner. Agree on the five most important questions.

Choose five questions from Step 2 that are most important to you. Write them on cards.

Step 4

Prepare for the role of the applicant.

Think of your answers to the questions.
Make notes.

> 1. worked with animals? – No, but …
> 2.

SPEAKING SKILLS

Es ist wichtig, sich bewusst zu machen, mit wem man spricht. Sei immer höflich und lächle. Rede deine Gesprächspartner mit „Mr …", „Ms …" oder „Mrs …" an. Sage nicht einfach nur „Hello". Vergiss nicht, dich am Ende des Gesprächs zu bedanken.

Step 5

Practise the interview with your partner.

Act the dialogue. Then change roles and act the dialogue again.

SPEAKING SKILLS

Wenn du eine Frage nicht verstehst, sei ehrlich. Sage, dass du die Frage nicht verstanden hast („I'm sorry, I didn't understand that.") oder bitte die Person darum, die Frage zu wiederholen („Could you say that again, please?").

Step 6

Act the interview in front of the class.

Step 7

Give feedback.

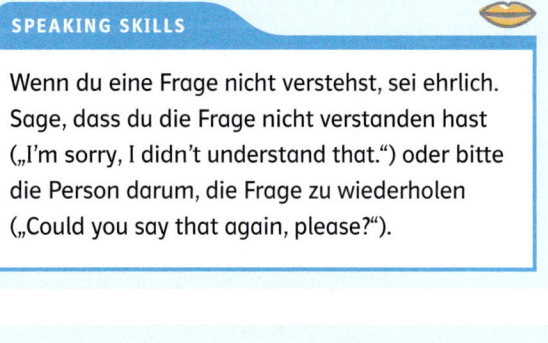

What was good about the interview? What could be better next time? Do you think that the applicant will get the job? → **M** Tip top, p.143

SPEAKING SKILLS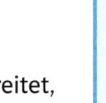

Wenn du zu einem Bewerbungsgespräch eingeladen wirst, sei pünktlich und trage angemessene Kleidung. Sei darauf vorbereitet, Fragen zum Job und zur Firma zu beantworten. Vergiss vor allem nicht, dein Handy auszuschalten.

More about New Zealand

1

1 (SPEAKING) Talk about photo 1 with a partner.

Look at the photo from New Zealand.
Think about these questions.

Where is the person? (Describe the place.)
What is the person doing?
What is he or she wearing?
What is the weather like?
How do you think the person feels?
Do you like to spend time in the mountains?
(Say why or why not.)

INFO

Die Neuseeländer werden auch als „Kiwis"
bezeichnet. Der Kiwi ist eine in Neuseeland
heimische Vogelart. Wie der australische Emu,
kann der Kiwi nicht fliegen. Kiwis sind normalerweise nachtaktiv, deshalb ist es nicht einfach sie
in freier Natur zu sehen. Die Vögel können 20 bis
30 Jahre alt werden.

2 Work with photos 2–5.

a) Match photos 2–5 with the headings A–F. There are more headings than you need.

A A young Maori at a festival
B Life in the city
C The 'All Blacks'

D On the road
E Farming in New Zealand
F Earthquake!

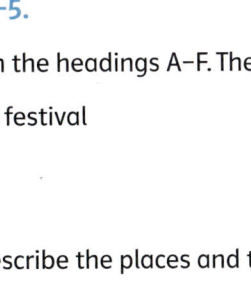 b) Talk with a partner. Describe the places and the people in the photos.

There's a … and a ….
He/She is …. They are ….

Applying for a job

Text 1: An ad

We make Kiwis' lives better every day.
Our supermarkets in Christchurch, Wellington and Auckland are looking for:

Young shop assistants
Apply to Joan Miller for jobs and internships with our company.

Text 2: An enquiry[1]

Dear Ms Miller,

I read your ad for young shop assistants on your website and I am very interested in an internship with your company. I live in Bavaria, Germany and will finish school this summer.
Could you please tell me more about this internship?
I look forward to hearing from you.

Yours sincerely,
Hannah Fischer

1 enquiry – *Anfrage*

Text 3: A form

Name: Hannah Fischer	**Qualifications:** Secondary leaving certificate
Address: xxxxx	
xxxxx	**Skills:** Good computer and communication skills;
Germany	languages: German, English
Phone: +49 987654321	**Experience:** Internship at a travel agent's
E-Mail: xyz@xyz.de	

Text 4: A letter of application

1 (Your address)

(Date)

2 (The person and address that you are writing to)
c/o Mr/Ms …

3 RE: Your ad for young shop assistants

4 Dear xxx,
I would like to apply for the job as a young shop assistant.
My first internship was at a travel agent's. During the internship I worked with customers and helped in the office. I liked the job very much.
I think I am qualified for this job because I have good communication skills and I enjoy working in a team. I am also flexible and I stay calm when things go wrong.
5 You will find more information in my CV. I look forward to hearing from you.
6 Yours sincerely,
(Your name)

Enclosed: CV

1 Work with the texts.

a) Take notes from the ad and the enquiry.

1. Where and what is/are the job(s)?
2. Who is interested and applies?
3. Who will get the enquiry?

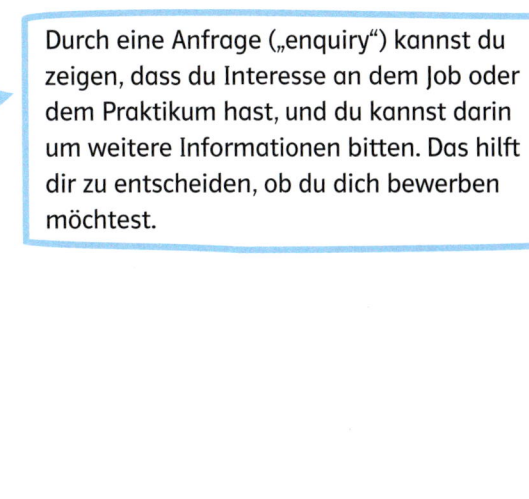

Durch eine Anfrage („enquiry") kannst du zeigen, dass du Interesse an dem Job oder dem Praktikum hast, und du kannst darin um weitere Informationen bitten. Das hilft dir zu entscheiden, ob du dich bewerben möchtest.

b) Look at the form and the letter. Complete the sentences.

1. The person has done an internship ….
2. The person is qualified because ….
3. The person sends … with the letter.

2 Copy and complete the form.

Copy and complete the form with your information. You can use the form on page 106 as a model.

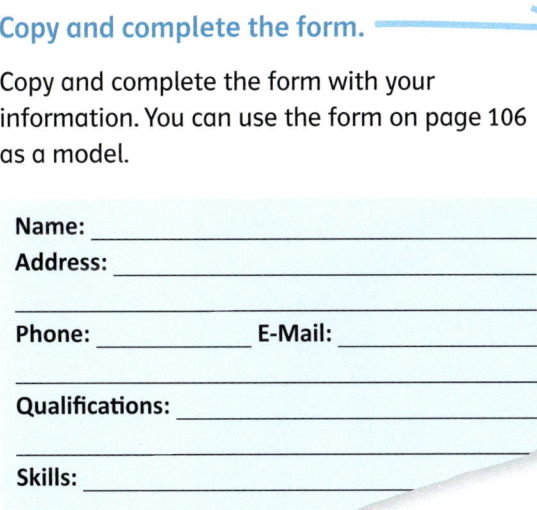

Name: _____

Address: _____

_____

Phone: _____ E-Mail: _____

_____

Qualifications: _____

_____

Skills: _____

_____

Experience: _____

_____

Bevor du ein Formular ausfüllst, überlege dir, was du schreiben möchtest. Du musst keine vollständigen Sätze schreiben. Formuliere deine persönlichen Angaben so kurz wie möglich. Schaue dir das Geschriebene am Ende noch einmal genau an und überprüfe es auf Fehler.

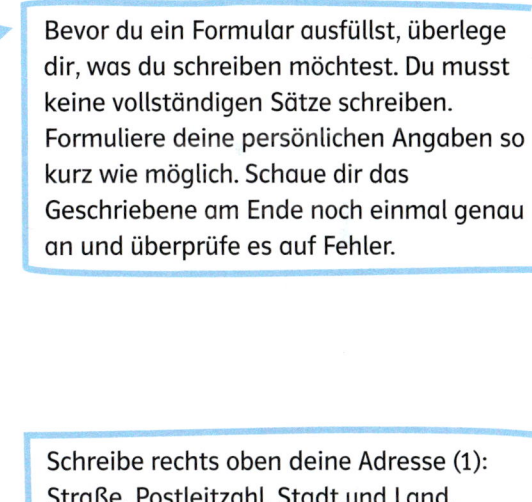

Schreibe rechts oben deine Adresse (1): Straße, Postleitzahl, Stadt und Land. Schreibe links die Anschrift der Firma (2). c/o bedeutet „care of", d.h. diese Person erhält deine Bewerbung. Vergiss nicht, rechts das Datum zu schreiben. RE (3) bedeutet: „Reference" (Betreff). Verwende die Anrede (4) mit Mr oder Ms + Name.

72/1 ## 3 Write a letter of application.

a) Write a letter of application in English for a job or internship you are interested in. Use the letter on page 106 as a model.

b) Show your letter to a partner. What tips can he or she give you?

→ M Tip top, p.143

Schreibe am Schluss, dass du dich auf eine Antwort freust (5). Schließe deine Bewerbung (6) mit „Yours sincerely", deiner Unterschrift und deinem Namen ab. Erwähne, wenn du z.B. deinen Lebenslauf hinzufügst.

Ein zweisprachiges Wörterbuch in Printform ist für die gesamte schriftliche Prüfung erlaubt.

A Listening Comprehension (Hörverstehen)

You will hear the recordings twice.

2,21 **1** Listen to Justine talking at a school in New Zealand. Write short answers. There is an example (0.) at the beginning.

0. What is Justine going to talk about?
   – Project Jonah, a project that saves whales.
1. Where in Auckland does Justine work?
2. What does Justine do in her free time?
3. What did Justine do the first time she helped?
4. How long has Justine been a volunteer?
5. Give two examples that show how whales are intelligent animals.
6. What is the goal of Project Jonah?

2,22 **2** Listen to Justine. There is one mistake in each sentence. Write down the wrong word and the correct information. There is an example (0.) at the beginning.

0. The first person with a question is a girl.
   girl → boy
1. They need more doctors to tell them about stranded whales.
2. You can visit an event at your school to raise money.
3. The girl with a question is wearing a blue skirt.
4. Justine says that some volunteers have been hurt.
5. Don't go near a whale's mouth.
6. Justine has got a podcast with more information.

B Use of English (Sprachgebrauch)

1 Read the text about the Maori. Choose the right word that fits in the sentence. There is an example (0.) at the beginning.

What do you know about the Maori?

Maori is the name of the (0) **person** · **people** who have lived in New Zealand the longest. They (1) **arrived** · **arrive** by canoe from islands in the Pacific Ocean. About 15% of (2) **New Zealands'** · **New Zealand's** population say they are Maori.

Maori is one of the official languages in New Zealand. The Maori speak this special language and it is also (3) **taught** · **thought** in many schools. (4) **English** · **England** is also an official language in New Zealand.

Also (5) **famous** · **most famous** in New Zealand is the 'haka' dance. It is danced before the national team's rugby games and the players learn it (6) **easy** · **easily**. The players, who are really (7) **big** · **bigger**, are very serious when they do this dance.

Maori also love (8) **there** · **their** body art. You see it all around the world. People who (9) **have** · **had** this body art on their faces or arms look (10) **strong** · **strongly** but also scary.

2 Put the words in the right order to make sentences about the Sky Tower. There is an example (0.) at the beginning.

0. <u>You can see the Sky Tower in Auckland</u>
1. Because the floor is made of glass,
2. If the weather is good,
3. Many people came
4. We know the Sky Tower is very popular
5. The Sky Tower is 328 m high,
6. If you ever go to Auckland on 31st December,
7. The best attraction is the SkyJump,
8. If people do the SkyJump,

a) they can go up to 85 km/h.
b) when the Sky Tower opened on 3rd August 1997.
c) which you can do from the highest viewing platform.
d) which makes it the tallest building in New Zealand.
e) <u>if there aren't any clouds.</u>
f) visitors can look through it.
g) because it had more than 415,000 visitors last year.
h) you can see up to 82 kilometres into the distance.
i) don't miss the party at the top of the tower.

C Reading Comprehension (Leseverstehen)

Is there life after rugby?

1 As Jacob was lying in hospital, he kept thinking about last Saturday's rugby game. His team was winning and Jacob was brilliant. No wonder he was captain! Jacob heard

5 everyone shout and cheer as he scored again and again. Then it happened. He couldn't remember what, but when he woke up, he hurt: hurt like he'd never hurt before. The doctor told him that he had injured his leg

10 seriously.

Everyone visited him: his parents, his little brother, his friends and the whole rugby team. They all told Jacob what a fantastic player he was. He loved what they told him. But what

15 he wanted to know was when he could start training again. Rugby was Jacob's life. And he was really good at it. Even the famous All Blacks were interested in him.

Then, on Tuesday, his dad came to visit him

20 earlier than expected. The doctor was with him. They couldn't look Jacob in the eye. "I'm afraid I have some bad news," the doctor began. "We've done a lot of tests. You will get better, and in a few months walking and even

25 running won't be a problem. But you can't play rugby ever again. If you have another accident like that, you will probably never walk again." After the doctor left, Jacob's dad spoke to him. "Your mum and I talked lots before your

30 accident. You play too much rugby and your school marks are getting worse. We want you to stop playing rugby too. You need to think about your future."

Jacob didn't understand. Never play rugby

35 again? That couldn't be true!

"I know this is bad news for you, Jacob," his dad added. "But we will all help you." Sometimes Jacob was angry, sometimes he was very sad. And it only got worse.

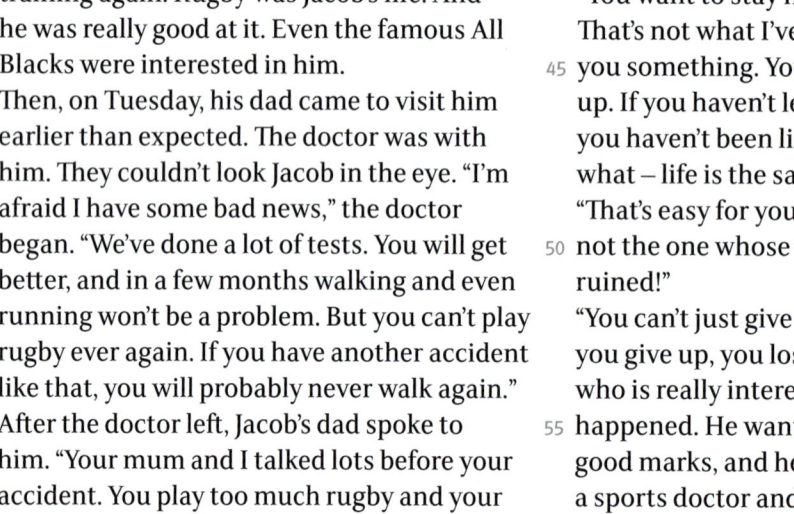

40 After a while he stopped talking to his visitors and he was happy when they left.

Then, one afternoon, his coach walked in. "You want to stay here not talking to anyone? That's not what I've taught you. Let me tell

45 you something. You fall down, you get back up. If you haven't learned that from the game, you haven't been listening. And you know what – life is the same."

"That's easy for you to say," Jacob said. "You're

50 not the one whose whole future has been ruined!"

"You can't just give up," the coach said. "When you give up, you lose. I was talking to a friend who is really interested in you and what has

55 happened. He wants you to finish school, with good marks, and he will give you a job. He is a sports doctor and he needs someone who knows rugby as well as you do to help him motivate injured players. You'll get special

60 training, don't worry."

"Really? Someone wants to offer me a job?" "Your situation has changed. Find out what's important to you in life and find a different way for yourself. Think about it, kid." And then

65 the coach walked out of the door. Jacob began to think ….

1 Answer the questions using information from the text. Write short answers. There is an example (0.) at the beginning.

    0. When was Jacob hurt? <u>last Saturday</u>

    1. Why were the All Blacks interested in Jacob?

    2. What did the doctor and Jacob's dad tell him about playing rugby again?

    3. How did Jacob feel after he heard the news?

    4. What did the coach say about life?

    5. What did the coach have for Jacob?

2 Which line(s) in the text tell you these things? There is an example (0.) at the beginning. Which sentence tells you …

    0. Jacob has had an accident. → <u>lines 6–10</u>

    1. Jacob is a good rugby player.

    2. Jacob loves playing rugby.

    3. he is not doing as well at school as he used to.

    4. Jacob's dad knew how he felt.

    5. that Jacob was surprised he had a future.

D Text Production (Schreiben)

1 Schreibe eine Geschichte auf Englisch, in der du das Bild und alle Angaben berücksichtigst. Beginne wie folgt:

Not enough money!

Last Saturday I was at the supermarket and saw a group of students. They …

supermarket   to empty their pockets   think about   party   decide   pay

Schreibe eine Geschichte von ungefähr 100 Wörtern auf ein gesondertes Blatt. Achte auf eine ansprechende äußere Form und eine gut lesbare Handschrift.

E Mediation (Sprachmittlung)

1 Situierung und Text

Du bist im Internet auf Sarahs Blog gestoßen. Sie ist gerade auf einer dreiwöchigen Sprachreise in Neuseeland. Lies den Text aufmerksam durch. Als Übung für eine englische Klassenarbeit hat dein Freund Tim das Wichtigste aus dem Text auf Deutsch zusammengefasst und bittet dich, es nochmals durchzulesen.

> **INTERNET**
>
> 1 **My adventure has begun …**
>
> This was my timetable when I left Germany:
> 11:30 (Saturday): left home town near Oberstdorf
> 13:45 (Saturday): arrived at Munich Airport
> 5 16:45 (Saturday): flight left Munich
> 23:00 (Saturday): arrived in Doha, Qatar (four-hour stopover)
> 4:45 (Monday): arrived in Auckland (17:45 (Sunday) German time)
>
> Now that I am in New Zealand my everyday life will be in English – including this blog.
>
> We flew over the sea, which was a beautiful colour as we came in to land. My guest family met me at
> 10 the airport. They don't live far from the language school. I knew Auckland was bigger than where
> I live in Bavaria, but it made me speechless.
>
> Today is Wednesday, and I woke up early, ready for my first day at the language school. The first
> three days will be great because we'll do a lot of excursions and the lessons only start next Monday.
> We had to be there at 9 and we met everyone in our class for the first time – there are only 15 of us!
> 15 After that, we went to Viaduct Harbour to see the sights. I talked to Nicole from France and we have
> the same hobbies. Tomorrow we are going to the Auckland Museum to find out about the history of
> New Zealand and the Maori. On Friday we are going to climb on the Rangitoto volcano, and on
> Saturday there is a barbecue with the rest of the school at the beach. On Sunday I'm going to visit
> Hobbiton, where *The Lord of the Rings* (my favourite film) was filmed, with my guest family.
>
> 20 And next Monday the first real English language lessons are going to start. I think they will be fun as I
> have started talking to everyone in English already. It feels good.
>
> I'll write more next week.
> Sarah

2 Aufgabe

Lies den englischen Text sowie die Zusammenfassung auf Deutsch durch. Notiere die falschen Informationen in Tims deutscher Zusammenfassung in dein Heft. Schreibe anschließend stichpunktartig auf Deutsch die richtigen Informationen. Eine berichtigte Information (0.) ist bereits vorhanden.

Tims Zusammenfassung auf Deutsch:

<blockquote>

1　Sarah hat ihre Heimatstadt am Samstag verlassen, um zum Münchner Flughafen zu fahren. Es dauerte über <u>vier</u> Stunden und ihr Flug ging um 16:45. Sie ist in Auckland um 4:45 deutscher Zeit gelandet.

Da sie nun in Neuseeland ist, wird sie nur ihren Blog auf Englisch schreiben.

5　Sie ist über das Meer geflogen und ihre Gastfamilie hat sie am Busbahnhof abgeholt. Obwohl Sarah wusste, dass Auckland richtig schön ist, war sie dann doch ganz sprachlos.

Am Donnerstag hatte sie ihren ersten Tag an der Sprachschule. In den ersten drei Tagen machen sie viele Ausflüge. Es sind nur 15 Studenten in Sarahs Klasse und sie kannten sich alle. Danach haben sie die Sehenswürdigkeiten am Hafen angeschaut. Sie hat sich mit Nicole aus Frankreich

10　unterhalten. Sie haben beide die gleichen Haustiere. Am Donnerstag besucht die Klasse ein Museum über die Geschichte Neuseelands und die Maori. Am Freitag steigen sie auf den Vulkan Rangitoto, und am Samstag grillen sie mit den Gastfamilien am Strand. Am Sonntag besichtigt Sarah mit ihrer Gastfamilie Hobbiton, den Drehort von *Der Herr der Ringe*, da sie die Filme nicht kennt.

15　Nächsten Montag fängt der richtige Sprachunterricht an. Sie meinte, es wird Spaß machen, da sie noch nicht so richtig Englisch miteinander sprechen.

</blockquote>

Es sind noch 10 falsche Informationen im Text. Notiere sie in dein Heft und berichtige sie.

0. <u>Zeile 2: vier Stunden → zwei Stunden</u>

1.

That's the end of
Test practice 4!

Unit 1, page 13

○ **4 Work with adjectives from the text.** → M Bus stop, p.140

a) Read what people at Uluru said. Put in the words.

| disappointed | beautiful ✔ | modern | surprised | afraid | delicious |

1. "Look at the evening sun on Uluru! It's <u>beautiful</u>!"
2. "Later we can eat some kangaroo meat. It's ——!"
3. "Tourists aren't allowed to climb Uluru. I was —— when I found out. ☹"
4. "It was my friend's birthday yesterday. She was —— when the guide gave her a small present!"
5. "Aboriginal people have a lot of traditions. But many have a —— lifestyle."
6. "Uluru is a safe place. You needn't be ——!"

Unit 1, page 14

○ **6 Complete the story about Omeo, a tour guide at Uluru.** → M Peer correction, p.141

a) Put in the right words.

| visited ✔ | didn't play | went | tried | arrived | asked | was | sang |

Last week a group of tourists from Germany (1) <u>visited</u> Uluru. They (2) a—— at three o'clock on Monday afternoon and they (3) w—— on a helicopter flight around the rock. It (4) w—— very exciting! After that they (5) a—— Omeo a lot of questions. They (6) s—— songs with Omeo in the evening, but he (7) d—— —— the didgeridoo for them. Later the tourists (8) t—— some delicious Aboriginal food.

Unit 1, page 14

○ **7 Make the questions and find the right answers.** → M Bus stop, p.140

a) Match the questions with the answers.

Friend:
1. <u>When did you visit Uluru?</u>
2. How long did you stay there?
3. Did you go on a walk around Uluru?
4. What did you like best?
5. How did you travel to Uluru?
6. Did you go on a helicopter tour?

Koa:
a. We went by plane.
b. Yes, we did. We walked for three hours!
c. No, we didn't. The flights are expensive.
d. We stayed for five days.
e. <u>We went to the rock in September.</u>
f. I liked the didgeridoo music best!

Unit 1, page 17

4 Work with the words. → M Think – pair – share, p.143

a) Make a mind map with the words and phrases.

a headache ✔   take tablets ✔

ill ✔   a high temperature

drink tea   tired

stay in bed   the flu   a cold

ill

I feel   ill   I can ....   take tablets

I have ....

a headache

Unit 1, page 17

5 (SPEAKING) Make an appointment to see the doctor.

a) Put the phrases in the right order. Act the dialogue. The receptionist speaks first (3).
→ M Read and look up, p.142

Receptionist:

1 Can you come today at 2:30 p.m.?

2 No problem. Goodbye.

3 Hello. How can I help you?

4 Good. What was the name again?

5 OK, Mr Hogan. See you at 2:30 p.m.

Patient:

6 Thank you. Goodbye

7 Yes, I can.

8 Hogan. That's H-O-G-A-N.

9 Hello. My name is Mr Hogan. I would like to make an appointment. I think I have a high temperature.

Unit 1, page 18

8 Write sentences about Penny. → M Bus stop, p.140

a) Complete the sentences.

1. If Penny goes to school on Monday, she —— —— cricket (play)
   If Penny goes to school on Monday, she <u>will play</u> cricket.
2. If she wants to talk, she —— —— her friends. (call)
3. They will have a barbecue too if they —— longer. (stay)
4. Penny will work with her best friend if she —— a project at school. (do)
5. If her dad isn't too busy, they —— —— surfing in a few weeks. (go)
6. She will take photos if she —— her cousin in Sydney next month. (visit)
7. Her cousin will come to Canberra in December if she —— time. (have)

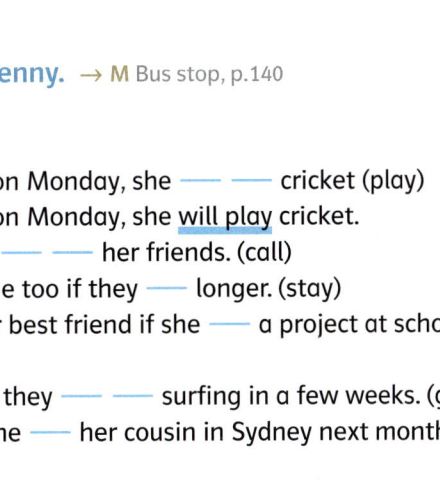

Unit 2, page 39

○ 5 Work with words for jobs. → M Peer correction, p.141

a) Match the sentence parts to say what the people do.

1. A computer programmer writes
2. A farmer produces
3. A tour guide shows
4. A virtual assistant does
5. A chef makes
6. A factory worker makes
7. A nurse looks after

a. meals in a restaurant.
b. car parts, for example.
c. food and keeps animals.
d. interesting sights to tourists.
e. office work for different people.
f. people who are ill.
g. computer programs.

Unit 2, page 40

○ 7 Complete what Manjit says about his work.

a) Complete the sentences. Where do you need the -s? The underlined words can help you.

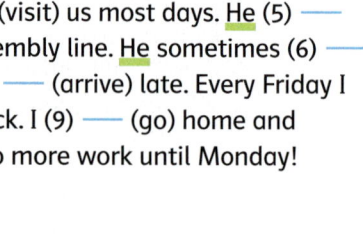

Manjit: I (1) work (work) between 40 and 65 hours every week. But I (2) —— (like) my job. I often (3) —— (listen) to music on the assembly line. Our boss (4) —— (visit) us most days. He (5) —— (work) in an office near the assembly line. He sometimes (6) —— (shout) at people when they (7) —— (arrive) late. Every Friday I (8) —— (finish) work at six o'clock. I (9) —— (go) home and the weekend (10) —— (start). No more work until Monday!

Unit 2, page 40

○ 8 Complete the sentences about the others.

a) Choose the right answers.

1. Prisha: My father **lives** • live with me.
2. My father **don't work** • **doesn't work** any more.
3. Vibhu **works** • **work** for an IT company.
4. He **write** • **writes** programs with other workers.
5. They **don't repair** • **doesn't repair** computers.
6. Kashida **shows** • **show** tourists the Taj Mahal.
7. She **don't sell** • **doesn't sell** souvenirs.

Language → G 5, p.131
She likes … ☺
She doesn't like … ☹

_____ Unit 2, page 43

○ **3** **Work with the text.**

1,16

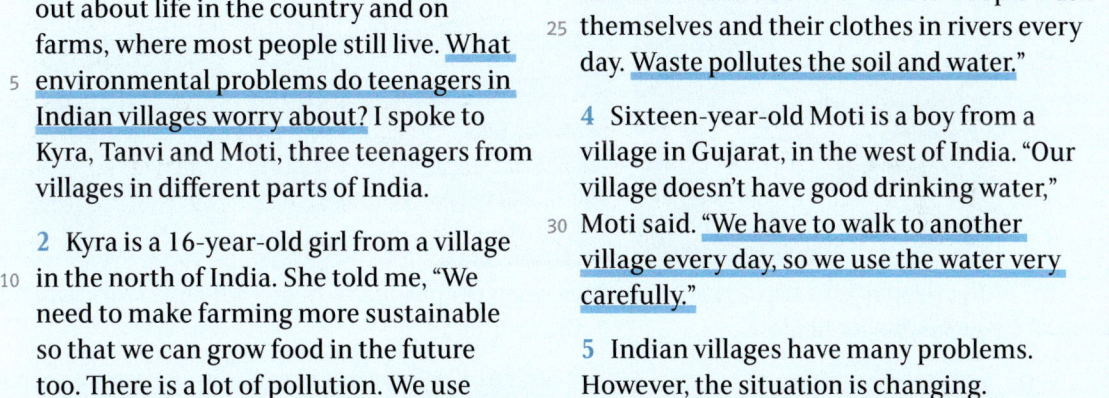

Deepali Chandra

What do Indian teenagers think?

By Deepali Chandra   *20th August 2021*

1 **1** The economy is growing fast in the big cities of India. But I wanted to find out about life in the country and on farms, where most people still live. What
5 environmental problems do teenagers in Indian villages worry about? I spoke to Kyra, Tanvi and Moti, three teenagers from villages in different parts of India.

2 Kyra is a 16-year-old girl from a village
10 in the north of India. She told me, "We need to make farming more sustainable so that we can grow food in the future too. There is a lot of pollution. We use fertilisers that help the crops to grow. But
15 they are slowly damaging the soil. Another problem is that there are more people, so we need more food for them. We grow two or three different crops in the same field every year. This is not good for the soil. The
20 crops don't grow well here."

3 I also spoke to Tanvi (15), from the east of the country. She said, "Villages in India don't have good sanitation. Many houses don't have bathrooms or toilets. People wash
25 themselves and their clothes in rivers every day. Waste pollutes the soil and water."

4 Sixteen-year-old Moti is a boy from a village in Gujarat, in the west of India. "Our village doesn't have good drinking water,"
30 Moti said. "We have to walk to another village every day, so we use the water very carefully."

5 Indian villages have many problems. However, the situation is changing.
35 Sustainable living is important for the young people there. Some villages have changed their crops, and this has helped the soil. Others have raised money for better sanitation and drinking water. What about
40 where you live? What can you do to help the environment?

a) Answer the questions. You can use short answers.

1. What kind of problems did Deepali ask about?
2. What is the problem with fertilisers?
3. What can happen when there are two or three crops in the same year?
4. Why is bad sanitation a problem?
5. Why do they use water carefully in Moti's village?
6. What have some villages done to get better sanitation and drinking water?

Unit 2, page 43

○ **4** **Work with words from the text.**

a) What is it? Choose the right answers.

1. People who are between 13 and 19 are **teenagers** · **teachers**.
2. A **village** · **valley** is a group of houses and other buildings in the country.
3. Farmers use **fertilisers** · **fields** to help plants to grow.
4. Water that is safe to drink is called **saving** · **drinking** water.
5. If farming is **sustainable** · **slow**, we will have food in the future too.
6. The **environment** · **economy** is another word for the world around us.

Unit 2, page 44

○ **7** **Write sentences about village life in India.**

a) Use the words to write a sentence for each photo. Put the parts of the sentences in the right order.

1. The people have breakfast at home every day.

The people have breakfast **every day** · **at home**

They wash clothes **in the river** · **in the morning**

People work **very hard** · **every day**

They walk **to get drinking water** · **a long way**

Moti feeds the goats **on the farm** · **every evening**

Crops don't grow **in the soil** · **very well**

Unit 2, page 45

○ **8 Deepali's blog** → M Bus stop, p.140

a) Choose the right answers.

> **BLOG**
>
> Hi everyone!
> Village life in India **is** • **are** (1) very different from in Europe. Most houses have chickens, so the people can get eggs **easy** • **easily** (2). They know each other **good** • **well** (3) and chat with **their** • **they** (4) neighbours.
> Most people in villages **work** • **works** (5) on farms. Many **don't have** • **doesn't have** (6) drinking water so they have to **get** • **gets** (7) it from another village. Tomorrow **I talk** • **I'll talk** (8) to two other teenagers in Gujarat.
> What do you like about where you live?
> Bye,
> Deepali

Unit 3, page 64

○ **3 Work with the texts.**

2,3 ⊙

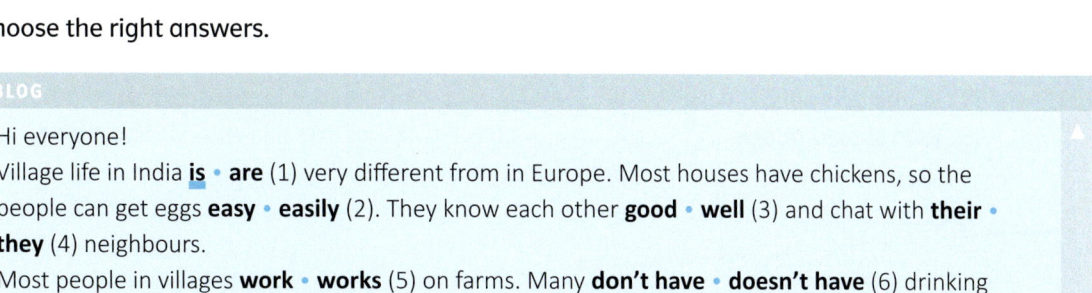

A INTERNET

Daily News | **News** | **Sports** | **Lifestyle**

1 **Accident in Durban**
10 Jan – A car hit a school bus with students yesterday. The accident happened in Umlazi, Durban, at about 1 p.m.
5 The bus driver was seriously injured. A student, Piet Jansen (16), and the car driver, Lunga Sekibo (23), a man from Cape Town, also had to go to hospital.
Police officer Riah Nkosi told us, "We don't
10 know what caused the accident yet. The car was going very fast. The driver didn't have a driving licence," she added.
Phil Davidson, a tourist from the USA, saw the accident. "The car was going fast when it
15 happened," Phil said. "The driver braked and the car skidded. It crashed into the bus."
The police are looking for more information about the accident.

B

Nicole: Jade. It's Nicole here. There's
20 just been an accident and Piet has gone to hospital! I really hope he's OK! A car hit our bus while we were travelling to the cricket match. We were really looking forward to it. Cebile was
25 showing me her new wallet when we heard an awful noise and then, bang! I still can't believe it! I really want to see you, Jade, but we have to go to the police station now. The police want all
30 the details. Call me later, OK?

S.120

a) Match the parts of the sentences.

1. **Text A:** Piet and the two drivers were
2. Phil Davidson saw
3. Riah Nkosi is looking for
4. **Text B:** Nicole tells
5. Nicole and Cebile were
6. Jade should phone

a. more information.
b. Jade about the accident.
c. the car hit the bus.
d. Nicole later.
e. injured in the accident.
f. on the bus when it happened.

_____ Unit 3, page 65

○ **4** Work with words from the text. → **M** Bus stop, p.140

a) Complete the online comment about the report.

| phones | accidents ✓ | brake | driving licence | skid | fast |

Why are there so many car (1) <u>accidents</u> 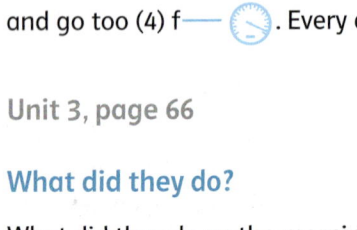 on South Africa's roads? We often read

about people who drive without a (2) d—l— . Many drivers look at their (3) p—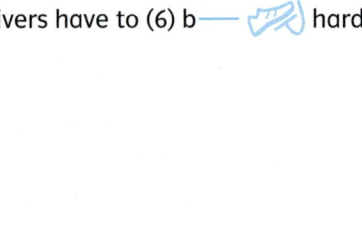

and go too (4) f— 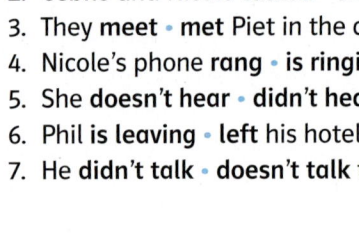. Every day cars (5) s—  and drivers have to (6) b— 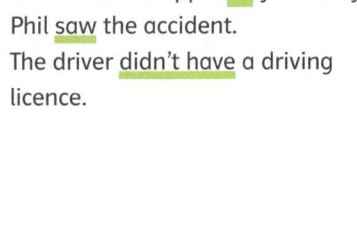 hard.

_____ Unit 3, page 66

○ **7** What did they do?

a) What did they do on the morning of the accident?

1. Piet **walks** · <u>**walked**</u> to school after breakfast. (walk)
2. Cebile and Nicole **talked** · **talk** at break. (talk)
3. They **meet** · **met** Piet in the cafeteria at lunchtime. (meet)
4. Nicole's phone **rang** · **is ringing** at 12:22 p.m. (ring)
5. She **doesn't hear** · **didn't hear** it. (not hear)
6. Phil **is leaving** · **left** his hotel at about 11:30 a.m. (leave)
7. He **didn't talk** · **doesn't talk** to his friend in the USA. (not talk)

Language → G1, p.127
The accident happen<u>ed</u> yesterday.
Phil <u>saw</u> the accident.
The driver <u>didn't have</u> a driving
licence.

_____ Unit 3, page 67

○ **10** Nicole is telling a friend about the accident. Complete her sentences.

a) Choose the right answers.

1. We were going to the cricket match when a car <u>**crashed**</u> · **was crashing** into the bus.
2. Cebile was showing me her new wallet when we **heard** · **were hearing** a loud bang.
3. The car driver was talking on his phone when the police **arrived** · **were arriving**.
4. While the police officer **talked** · **was talking** to the car driver, the witness came to help.
5. While I **sat** · **was sitting** in the police car, I sent a message to Jade.
6. While I **waited** · **was waiting** at the police station, my parents arrived.

D

Unit 3, page 69

2 Complete the sentences.

2,6

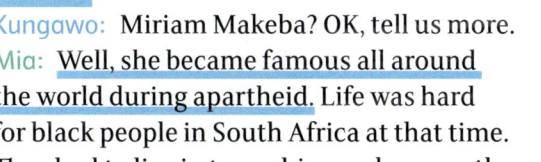

Miriam Makeba

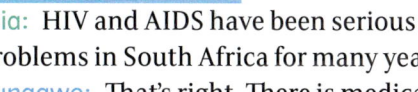

Zackie Achmat

1 **Kungawo:** Hi everyone and welcome to our podcast about inspiring South Africans. With me now is Mia, who is going to tell us about her very special South African role model.

5 **Mia:** Yes, Kungawo. We've already talked about music on the show. My role model is the South African singer and songwriter Miriam Makeba.

Kungawo: Miriam Makeba? OK, tell us more.

10 **Mia:** Well, she became famous all around the world during apartheid. Life was hard for black people in South Africa at that time. They had to live in townships and many other places were for white people only. I admire

15 Miriam Makeba because she fought against apartheid. The government took away her passport when she left South Africa. She couldn't go home.

Kungawo: That sounds awful!

20 **Mia:** Yes, it was. Her life has been an inspiration for a long time. She achieved a lot. What about you? Who do you admire?

Kungawo: My role model is Zackie Achmat.

Mia: Who's he?

25 **Kungawo:** Zackie Achmat is a South African film director. He fought against apartheid and has fought for gay and lesbian rights too. He has helped many South Africans with HIV and AIDS. He has made films about people

30 who have the diseases.

Mia: HIV and AIDS have been serious problems in South Africa for many years.

Kungawo: That's right. There is medication for HIV, but at first it was very expensive.

35 Zackie Achmat has been HIV-positive since 1990 but he didn't take medication right away. He fought for cheaper drugs. He only took medication in August 2003, when it was cheaper, and poorer people could pay for it

40 too.

Mia: He was really brave. South Africans have achieved a lot since 1994 and before that.

Kungawo: Yes, there's a lot that this country can be proud of.

1. Mia's role model is a South African singer and songwriter.
2. During apartheid Miriam Makeba became famous —— .
3. Miriam Makeba couldn't go back to her country when the government —— .
4. Zackie Achmat's films are about —— .
5. At first medication for HIV —— .
6. Zackie Achmat was brave because he only took medication when —— .

one hundred and twenty-one 121

Unit 3, page 69

○ **3 Work with words from the text.** → M Bus stop, p.140

a) Put the words into the right groups (nouns, verbs or adjectives).

brave   achieve   inspiration   sing   admire   proud

role model   singer   inspiring

Du kannst manchmal eine Silbe an den Anfang oder an das Ende eines Wortes stellen, um neue Wörter zu bilden.

Unit 3, page 70

○ **7 How long have they done it?** → M Peer correction, p.141

a) Make sentences with <u>for</u> or <u>since</u>.

1. Mia has been in Cape Town —— two days.
   Mia has been in Cape Town <u>for</u> two days.
2. She has lived in her flat —— January.
3. She has worked at a hairdressing salon —— two years.
4. Her parents have been on holiday in Durban —— last Friday.
5. Kungawo has shared a flat with his friend —— six months.
6. He has worked at a large supermarket —— November last year.
7. Kungawo and Mia have made podcasts together —— they met.
8. Mia has been interested in music —— a long time.

Mia, 18

Kungawo, 19

Unit 3, page 71

○ **8 (SPEAKING) Ask a partner.**

a) Ask your partner questions. → M Milling around, p.141

listen to South African music   meet a famous person

see a lion   organize a flea market   work with …   …

Language → G 8, p.134
<u>Have</u> you ever <u>seen</u> this film?
<u>Yes, I have.</u> / <u>No, I haven't.</u>

A: Have you ever listened to …?   B: Yes, I have. / No, I haven't. Have you ever met …?
A: Yes, I have. / No, I haven't. Have you ever seen …? …

Unit 4, page 91

○ **4 Work with words from the text.**

a) Choose the right words to complete Liam's e-mail about his interview.

E-MAIL

Hi Ella,
I wanted to get some **advice** • **news** (1) about my career so I talked to Ms Waaka, the careers advisor. First I **completed** • **looked at** (2) a job suitability test. Ms Waaka thinks I should study for a **qualification** • **quiz** (3) in tourism. Then I could work as an **assistant** • **artist** (4) in a tourist information **building** • **centre** (5). They're going to have a **jobs** • **careers** (6) day at the school in July. There will be a lot of **companies** • **schools** (7) with information about jobs.
What about you? How did your interview go?
Bye,
Liam

Unit 4, page 92

○ **7 Talk about plans.** → M Bus stop, p.140

a) Choose the right forms of 'to be' and complete the sentences about Ella and Liam's job plans.

1. Ella —— going to find out about jobs as a hairdresser.
   Ella is going to find out about jobs as a hairdresser.
2. Liam —— going to talk to different employers next week.
3. Liam: I —— going to apply for jobs in tourism.
4. Liam —— (not) going to work with his dad.
5. Ella: I —— going to train in a hairdressing salon.
6. Ella and Liam —— going to look for jobs on the internet.
7. Ella and Liam —— (not) going to leave school next year.
8. Ella and Liam: We —— going to visit a careers day soon.

Remember the forms of 'to be'?
I am ....
He/She is ....
We are ....
They are ....

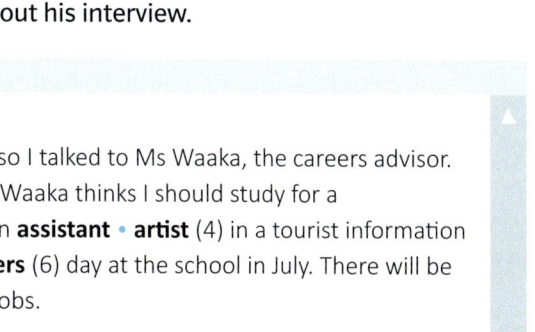

Unit 4, page 93

○ **9 Write questions and find the answers.**

a) Complete the questions about job plans.

1. Where —— you —— —— find out about jobs?
   Where are you going to find out about jobs?
2. What —— Liam —— —— do next year?
3. When —— you —— —— leave school?
4. Who —— Liam —— —— meet at the careers day?
5. When —— you —— —— write your CV?
6. Who —— you —— —— ask about your career?

Language → G 9, p.135
What are you going to do next year?

Unit 4, page 95

3 What do they do?

2,18

1 Some students from Newlands College are talking to the store manager of a supermarket in Wellington. They want to find out what it's like to work there. Later they are going to
5 write a report.

Mr Roberts: Welcome everyone. My name is John Roberts. I'm going to talk to you about the exciting jobs in retail today. We offer jobs and apprenticeships in customer service,
10 communication and IT. But before we start our tour, are there any questions?
Rose: Yes, I have a question. What do shop assistants do in their job?
Mr Roberts: Shop assistants do many
15 different things. They help customers find the right products in the store and they work at the checkouts. Shop assistants also fill the shelves and help present the products.
Nikau: Can you tell us how a supermarket
20 works?
Mr Roberts: Well, supermarkets buy their products from other local companies. These companies are called suppliers. Stores order large numbers of products from suppliers so
25 that the prices are cheaper. Then the products are sold to customers.
Nikau: When did this store open?
Mr Roberts: It opened in 2008. It's one of the largest stores in Wellington. We have over
30 60,000 products – not only food, but also clothes and many other goods. But we work in the community too. We donate food to local charities to reduce food waste, for example.

Oliver: That's cool! How much food did you
35 donate last year?
Mr Roberts: Well, last year we donated over NZ$3 million's worth of food.
Rose: Do you sell bread here?
Mr Roberts: Yes, we do. All our bread is made
40 in the store.
Grace: Do you offer internships?
Mr Roberts: Yes, internships are offered here. You can apply for one in our office or you can visit us at the job fair next month.
45 We're always looking for interns to help our fantastic team. We also offer summer jobs for students. You get a good salary and training is included.
Grace: Did you start your career here as a
50 shop assistant?
Mr Roberts: Yes, I did. Although I've been at this company for ten years, I'll never forget what I learned in my first six months. Let's start our tour now.

a) Match the parts of the sentences.

1. The store manager is talking to students
2. Stores order products
3. The suppliers deliver products
4. Shop assistants fill the shelves
5. Customers pay for products
6. The company donates food

a. at the checkouts.
b. to local charities.
c. from suppliers.
d. to the store.
e. about jobs in retail.
f. every day.

_____ **Unit 4, page 96**

○ **7** **Complete the questions about Grace's internship.** → **M** Peer correction, p.141

a) Ask the questions with the right form.

1. What —— you —— first? (do)
   What did you do first?
2. When did you —— ? (start)
3. How did you —— to work? (travel)
4. Did you —— with a computer? (work)
5. What —— you —— at lunchtime? (do)
6. When —— you —— the internship? (apply for)
7. —— you —— your internship? (enjoy)

_____ **Unit 4, page 97**

○ **9** **A report about a job fair**

a) Read Oliver's report. Choose the right answer.

Last week I (1) **visited** · visit a job fair at the Adelphi Hotel in Auckland. There (2) **were** · was many companies at the fair. There were also a lot of young people who were (3) **interesting** · **interested** in the companies. I wrote a list of questions before I (4) **went** · go to the fair. I also (5) **have taken** · **took** my CV with me. I talked to three employers and I want to apply for an (6) **intern** · **internship** with one of them. I stayed at the fair for about two (7) **hour** · **hours**. It's the (8) **best** · **better** way to find out about jobs.

Grammar

Mit **G** sind die Grammatikkapitel gekennzeichnet und der Reihe nach durchnummeriert. Eine Übersicht über alle Themen findest du unten auf dieser Seite.

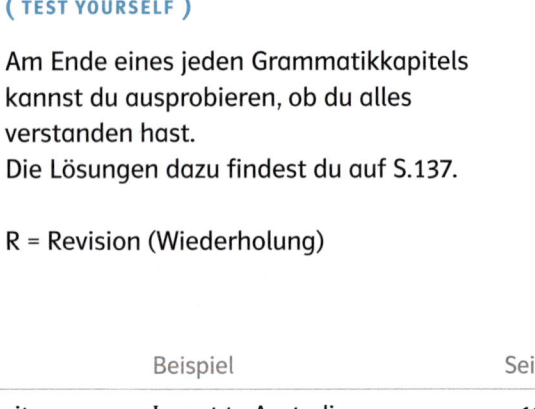 Beim Lupen-Symbol findest du Besonderheiten und Tipps.

(TEST YOURSELF)

Am Ende eines jeden Grammatikkapitels kannst du ausprobieren, ob du alles verstanden hast.
Die Lösungen dazu findest du auf S.137.

R = Revision (Wiederholung)

	Englisch	Deutsch	Beispiel	Seite
G1	**R:** simple past	einfache Vergangenheit	I went to Australia last year.	127
G2	**R:** will-future	Zukunft mit will	I hope we'll meet again.	128
G3	If-clauses I – with will-future – with can – with commands – with simple present	Bedingungssätze Typ I – mit will-future – mit can – mit Aufforderungen – mit simple present	If you stay in bed, you'll feel better soon.	129
G4	**R:** present progressive	Verlaufsform der Gegenwart	What are you doing?	130
G5	**R:** simple present	einfache Gegenwart	I don't work on Sundays.	131
G6	**R:** word order	Satzstellung	We work in the fields every day.	132
G7	past progressive – while and when	Verlaufsform der Vergangenheit – while und when	While I was talking to Sue, we heard a terrible noise.	133
G8	**R:** present perfect – for and since	Perfekt – for und since	Have you ever been to a charity concert? – I haven't been to a concert for years.	134
G9	**R:** going to-future	Zukunft mit going to	I'm not going to be a mechanic.	135
G10	**R:** passive voice – simple present – simple past	Passiv – einfache Gegenwart – einfache Vergangenheit	The island was hit by an earthquake.	136

Unit 1

G1 R: Die einfache Vergangenheit

Revision: The simple past

Um über Ereignisse zu sprechen, die in der Vergangenheit passiert und vorbei sind, verwendest du das **simple past.**

Das **simple past** bildest du so:
Hänge die Endung **-ed** an das Verb.
Achte auf unregelmäßige Verben, z. B. do → **did**, get → **got**, go → **went**.
Eine Liste der unregelmäßigen Verben findest du auf den Seiten 138–139.

Signalwörter	
yesterday	gestern
last year	letztes Jahr
a week ago	vor einer Woche
in 2016	(im Jahr) 2016

I **visited** Uluru last week.	Ich **habe** letzte Woche den Uluru **besucht.**
We **heard** some great music there.	Wir **haben** dort tolle Musik **gehört.**

Um zu sagen, was nicht passiert ist, setzt du **didn't** (= did not) vor das Verb.

I **didn't see** any tourists.	Ich **habe keine** Touristen **gesehen.**
Joe **didn't eat** kangaroo meat.	Joe **hat kein** Kängurufleisch **gegessen.**

Aussagen und Verneinungen mit **be** bildest du so:

I **was** in Sydney. I **wasn't** in Perth.	Ich **war** in Sydney. Ich **war nicht** in Perth.
The tour **was** fantastic.	Die Reise **war** fantastisch.
It **wasn't** dangerous at all.	Es **war** überhaupt **nicht** gefährlich.
The tourists **were** impressed.	Die Touristen **waren** beeindruckt.
They **weren't** disappointed.	Sie **waren nicht** enttäuscht.

Und so kannst du im **simple past** Fragen stellen und beantworten:

Did you **have** a good time in the outback?	Yes, I **did.**	No, I **didn't.**
When **did** you **meet** the Aboriginal people?	I **met** them last Saturday.	
Were you in Sydney too?	Yes, I **was.**	No, I **wasn't.**
Was the guide nice?	Yes, he **was.**	No, he **wasn't.**
Were the stories interesting?	Yes, they **were.**	No, they **weren't.**

(TEST YOURSELF) **Choose the right verbs for the simple past. Give short answers to the questions in 3. and 7. (☺ = Yes. ☹ = No.)**

1. Our family **has** • **had** a great time in Australia last summer.
2. We **don't climb** • **didn't climb** Uluru.
3. **Do** you **see** • **Did** you **see** any paintings? (☺)
4. What **ate** you • **did** you **eat** in the outback?
5. How long **do** you **stay** • **did** you **stay** at Uluru?
6. The weather **was** • **were** dry and hot.
7. **Was** • **Were** it dangerous? (☹)

G2 R: Die Zukunft mit will

Revision: The will-future

Mit dem **will-future** sprichst du über die Zukunft. Oft drückst du damit Hoffnungen, Wünsche und Vorhersagen aus. Dann beginnen diese Sätze mit **I hope**, **I think**, **I'm sure** oder **Maybe.**

Du bildest das will-future mit **will** oder **won't** und der **Grundform des Verbs**.

Häufig wird die Kurzform verwendet:

I will go   ⟶   I ~~will~~ go   **'ll**   ⟶ *I'll go*

I ~~will not~~ go   **won't**   ⟶ *I won't go*

Achtung! Im Deutschen kann man über Zukünftiges mit der Zukunft oder der Gegenwart sprechen. Vergleiche: Ich rufe dich morgen an. / Ich werde dich morgen anrufen.

The weather **will be** fine next week.	Das Wetter **wird** nächste Woche gut (**werden**).
Maybe I'**ll go** to a lake with Pete.	Vielleicht **fahre** ich mit Pete an einen See.
I hope I'**ll get** a job quickly.	Ich hoffe, dass ich schnell einen Job **bekomme**.
Will the interview **be** outside?	**Wird** das Interview draußen **stattfinden**?
Yes, it **will**. / No, it **won't**.	Ja. / Nein.
I'm sure it **won't rain**.	Ich bin sicher, dass es **nicht regnen wird**.

 Achtung! Verwechsle **will** (werden) nicht mit **want to** (wollen):

I **will buy** some souvenirs.	Ich **werde** ein paar Souvenirs **kaufen**.
I **want to buy** some souvenirs.	Ich **will** ein paar Souvenirs **kaufen**.

(TEST YOURSELF) **Put the verbs in the will-future. Give short answers to the questions in 4. and 5. (☺ = Yes. ☹ = No.)**

1. I hope I — (travel) to many countries.
2. Maybe I — (spend) a year in Australia after school.
3. I think I — (not start) working in July.
4. — the weather — (be) bad? (☹)
5. — your parents — (accept) your plans? (☺)
6. Where — you — (be) in ten years' time?
7. I'm sure I — (not become) a tour guide.
8. Where — you — (sleep) in the outback?

G3 Bedingungssätze Typ I

If-clauses I

If you see a sign like this in Australia, drive slowly.

If-Sätze benutzt man, um Bedingungen und Folgen auszudrücken. Im if-Satz steht das **simple present**, im Hauptsatz steht das **will-future**. Steht der **if**-Satz vorne, wird am Ende des **if**-Satzes ein Komma gesetzt. Steht der **if**-Satz hinter dem Hauptsatz, entfällt das Komma.

If I **feel** OK,	I'**ll come** with you.	Wenn es mir gut geht, komme ich mit.
If I **don't feel** better soon,	I'**ll go** to the doctor's.	Wenn es mir nicht bald besser geht, werde ich zum Arzt gehen.
If you **wear** warm clothes,	you **won't feel** cold.	Wenn du warme Sachen anziehst, wird dir nicht kalt werden.
I'**ll call** you	if I **have** time.	Ich rufe dich an, wenn ich Zeit habe.
We **won't come**	if you **are** ill.	Wir kommen nicht, wenn du krank bist.

Im Hauptsatz kann auch **can** oder **eine Aufforderung** stehen.
Sprichst du über **Fakten** oder **Tatsachen**, steht **simple present** im **if**-Satz <u>und</u> im Hauptsatz.

If you ask me, I **can help** you.	Wenn du mich fragst, **kann** ich dir **helfen**.
If you are not better by Monday, **go** to the doctor's!	Wenn es dir bis Montag nicht besser geht, **geh** zum Arzt! (Aufforderung)
If you want to buy special medicine, you **need** a prescription first.	Wenn du spezielle Medizin kaufen willst, **brauchst** du zuerst ein Rezept. (Fakt)

Diese Zeitenmuster sind in **if**-Sätzen Typ I möglich:

If-Satz: +   **Hauptsatz:**
simple present   will-future oder can/can't
                                           Befehlsform
                                           simple present

(TEST YOURSELF) **Complete the sentences.**

1. If I meet Julia, I —— (talk) to her.
2. If you ask the doctor, she —— (can give) you a prescription.
3. If you don't feel well, —— (stay) at home!
4. You —— (not be) late if you leave now.
5. If Liz calls the doctor, she —— (can make) an appointment for tomorrow.
6. Don't go swimming if you still —— (feel) tired.

G4 R: Die Verlaufsform der Gegenwart

Revision: The present progressive

Mit dem **present progressive** kannst du sagen, was jemand gerade tut oder was im Augenblick passiert.

Aussagen im present progressive bildest du so: **am/are/is + Verb + ing**.

<table>
<tr><td>**Signalwörter**
at the moment
now
Look, …
Listen, …</td><td>im Moment
jetzt
Schau mal, …
Hör mal, …</td></tr>
</table>

I'm **working** at the moment. I'll call you later.	Ich **arbeite** (gerade). Ich rufe dich später an.
The party is great. Everybody **is having** fun.	Die Party ist klasse. Jeder **hat** Spaß.

Achte auf die Schreibweise: writ**e** – writ**ing**, ru**n** – ru**nn**ing, si**t** – si**tt**ing, swi**m** – swi**mm**ing

So verneinst du Sätze: **am not / are not / is not + Verb + -ing**.

Come in. I'm **not sleeping**.	Komm' herein. Ich **schlafe nicht**.
Lisa **isn't wearing** her new shoes today.	Lisa **trägt** heute **nicht** ihre neuen Schuhe.

Bei Fragen stellst du **am/are/is** an den Satzanfang. Ein Fragewort steht noch davor.

Are you **listening**?	**Hörst** du **zu**?
Yes, I **am**. / No, I'm **not**.	Ja. / Nein.
What are you **doing** right now?	**Was machst** du (gerade)?
I'm **reading**.	Ich **lese** (gerade).
Who are you **talking to**?	**Mit wem sprichst** du (gerade)?

Du benutzt das **present progressive** auch, um ein Bild zu beschreiben. Zunächst beschreibst du, wen oder was du siehst ("I can see a/some/a lot of …" oder: "There is/are …"). Dann beschreibst du, was jemand tut. Du benutzt das **present progressive** für alle Handlungen, die im Bild zu sehen sind und für alles, was jemand **tut**.

Some people **are standing** around the fire.	Einige Leute **stehen** um ein Feuer herum.
They **are wearing** sports clothes.	Sie **tragen** Sportkleidung.
One woman **is talking** to another woman.	Eine Frau **spricht** mit einer anderen Frau.
It **is** cloudy, but it **isn't raining**.	Es **ist** bewölkt, aber es **regnet nicht**.

(TEST YOURSELF) **Use the present progressive.**

1. Where is Kate? – She —— (sleep).
2. I —— (make) lunch at the moment.
3. My parents —— (not work) today.
4. —— you —— (have) fun?
5. Why —— you —— (not listen)?
6. Who —— you —— (write) to right now?

Unit 2

G5 R: Die einfache Gegenwart

Revision: The simple present

Du kennst schon das **simple present**. Du benutzt es, um einen Zustand zu beschreiben oder um zu sagen, dass etwas gewohnheitsmäßig, regelmäßig oder häufig geschieht. Du verwendest es auch für feste Termine in der Zukunft, z.B. bei Programmen, Fahrplänen, Stundenplänen usw.

Signalwörter	
every day	jeden Tag
always	immer
usually	normalerweise
often	oft
sometimes	manchmal
never	nie

 He she, it, das **s** muss mit!

So bildest du das **simple present** mit **Vollverben**:

Aussagen	I **live** in Bavaria.	Ich **lebe** in Bayern.
	My train **arrives** at 9 p.m.	Mein Zug **kommt** um 21 Uhr **an**.
Verneinte Aussagen	I **don't live** in the country.	Ich **wohne nicht** auf dem Land.
	Ann **doesn't have** time.	Ann **hat keine** Zeit.
	Some people **don't like** fish.	Manche Leute **mögen keinen** Fisch.
Fragen	**Do** you **work** on an assembly line?	**Arbeitest** du an einem Fließband?
	Yes, I **do**. / No, I **don't**.	Ja. / Nein.
	Does the company **have** a café?	**Hat** die Firma ein Café?
	Yes, it **does**. / No, it **doesn't**.	Ja. / Nein.
	Where do you **live**?	**Wo** wohnst du?

So bildest du das **simple present** mit **be**, z.B.:

Aussagen	I'**m** a vegetarian.	Ich **bin** Vegetarier/in.
	Our customers **are** in Europe.	Unsere Kunden **sind** in Europa.
Verneinte Aussagen	I'**m not** a vegetarian.	Ich **bin nicht** Vegetarier/in.
	My job **isn't** boring.	Meine Arbeit **ist nicht** langweilig.
Fragen	**Are** you happy?	**Bist** du / **Seid** ihr glücklich?
	Yes, I **am**. / No, I'**m not**.	Ja. / Nein.
	Where is my bag?	**Wo ist** meine Tasche?

(TEST YOURSELF) **Choose the right verb. Write correct sentences.**

1. I always **are** • **travel** • **live** to work by bus.
2. Sam never **work** • **works** • **likes** at home.
3. I **aren't** • **don't** • **am not** start work at 6 a.m.
4. My boss **is** • **are** • **don't** never late.
5. **Do** • **Does** • **Is** • he speak English?
6. Where **do** • **does** • **is** you work?

G6 R: Die Satzstellung mit Angaben des Ortes, der Zeit und der Art und Weise

Revision: Word order

Die wichtigste Satzstellungsregel im Englischen lautet: **Subjekt – Verb – Objekt**
Bei 2 Objekten steht das indirekte Objekt (Wem?) vor dem direkten Objekt (Wen? Was?).

Subjekt	Verb	Indirektes Objekt (Wem?)	Direktes Objekt (Wen? Was?)	
We	need		clean drinking water.	Wir brauchen sauberes Trinkwasser.
They	showed	us	their village.	Sie haben uns ihr Dorf gezeigt.

Eine weitere Satzstellungsregel lautet: **Ort vor Zeit** (place before time).

Subjekt	Verb	Objekt	Ort	Zeit	
I	can eat	lunch	at home	every day.	Ich kann jeden Tag zu Hause zu Mittag essen.

I want to work **on a farm** **next summer.**
Ortsangabe Zeitangabe

Die Regel **Ort vor Zeit** ist deshalb so wichtig, weil die Reihenfolge im Deutschen oft genau anders herum üblich ist. Vergleiche:
Ich möchte im nächsten Sommer (Zeit) auf einer Farm (Ort) arbeiten.

Adverbien der Art und Weise stehen meistens **am Ende** des Satzes, aber oft **vor** einer **Orts-** oder einer **Zeitangabe**. Das gilt auch für **Fragen**.

Kyra **told** her story **quietly**.	Kyra **hat** ihre Geschichte **ruhig erzählt**.
We **can get** fresh eggs **easily** every day.	Wir **können** jeden Tag **leicht** frische Eier **bekommen**.
She **drove** the van **carefully** yesterday.	Sie **hat** den Lieferwagen gestern **vorsichtig gefahren**.
Some crops **don't grow well** here.	Einige Feldfrüchte **wachsen** hier **nicht gut**.
Did you **sleep well** last night?	**Hast** du letzte Nacht **gut geschlafen**?

(TEST YOURSELF) **Put the words in the right order.**

1. need • in their houses • people • good sanitation
2. they • differently • crops • grow • in this soil
3. safely • the water • carried • Louisa • to her home
4. villagers in India • fresh milk • can get at home • and eggs • easily
5. your friend • speak • does • well • English • ?
6. can we • the problem • easily • how • solve • ?

Unit 3

G7 Die Verlaufsform der Vergangenheit

The past progressive

While we were visiting the national park, we saw two elephants at a lake.

Mit dem **past progressive** drückst du aus, dass etwas in der Vergangenheit über einen **längeren Zeitraum** passierte. Im Deutschen sagt man etwa: Ich/Sie/Wir … war/waren (gerade) dabei, etwas zu tun. So bildest du Aussagen im **past progressive**: **was/were + Verb + -ing**

Yesterday I **was cleaning** my bike.	Gestern **habe** ich mein Rad **geputzt.**/ … **war** ich **dabei**, mein Rad **zu putzen.**

Das **past progressive** beschreibt auch eine Handlung, die andauerte, als plötzlich eine neue eintrat (**simple past**). Solche Sätze bildest du mit **while** (= während) und **when** (= als).

While I **was walking**, my wallet **fell** out of my pocket.	**Während** ich (gerade) **gelaufen bin, ist** mein Geldbeutel aus der Tasche **gefallen.**
She **was working** at her desk **when** the accident **happened.**	Sie **hat** (gerade) an ihrem Schreibtisch **gearbeitet, als** der Unfall **passiert ist.**

While I was walking, (andauernde Handlung)

↑

my wallet fell out of my pocket. (neues Ereignis)

 Liefen in der Vergangenheit zwei Handlungen zur gleichen Zeit und gleich lange, wird für beide Handlungen das **past progressive** benutzt.

While I **was working** in the garden, Nick **was preparing** some food.	**Während** ich im Garten **gearbeitet habe, hat** Nick etwas zum Essen **vorbereitet.**

(TEST YOURSELF) **Use the simple past or the past progressive.**

1. I ⎯⎯ (wait) for the train when I got Dad's message.
2. What ⎯⎯ you ⎯⎯ (do) between 8 a.m and 10 a.m. yesterday?
3. Joe was running in the park when he suddenly ⎯⎯ (see) a rainbow.
4. While we ⎯⎯ (have) our garden party, it started (start) to rain heavily.

G8 R: Das Perfekt mit for und since

Revision: The present perfect with for and since

Wenn eine Handlung in der Vergangenheit beginnt und in der Gegenwart zu einem Ergebnis führt, verwendest du das **present perfect**:
have/haven't oder **has/hasn't** (bei he, she, it) + **3. Form** des Verbs (past participle).
Bei den meisten Verben hängst du für die 3. Form ein **-ed** an das Verb, z.B. help → help**ed**

Signalwörter	
already	schon
just	gerade
not … yet	noch nicht
never	noch nie
ever (in Fragen)	jemals (in Fragen)
since	seit (Zeitpunkt)
for	seit (Zeitspanne)

Einige Verben haben unregelmäßige 3. Formen, z.B. be → **been**; write → **written**
Eine Liste der unregelmäßigen Verben findest du auf den Seiten 138–139.

I **have** just **tidied** my room.	Ich **habe** gerade mein Zimmer **aufgeräumt**.
The star **has** already **sung** in South Africa.	Der Star **hat** schon in Südafrika **gesungen**.
I **haven't been** to South Africa yet.	Ich **war** noch **nicht** in Südafrika.

Have you ever **met** a famous person?	Yes, I **have**.	No, I **haven't**.
Has your friend ever **been** on TV?	Yes, she **has**.	No, she **hasn't**.

Present perfect mit **for** (seit) und **since** (seit):
since verwendest du vor einem Zeitpunkt, z.B. **since** 6:00 a.m., **since** May, **since** I was young etc.
for verwendest du vor einer Zeitspanne, z.B. **for** one hour, **for** two years, **for** a long time etc.

I haven't seen Mia **since** Sunday.	Ich habe Mia **seit** Sonntag nicht gesehen.
I haven't seen Mia **for** a week.	Ich habe Mia **seit** einer Woche nicht gesehen.

for a week (Zeitspanne) → today

since Monday (Zeitpunkt)

(**TEST YOURSELF**) **Put the verbs in the present perfect. Choose for or since where necessary.**

1. I —— already —— (be) to South Africa a few times.
2. There —— (be) serious problems with AIDS **since • for** many years.
3. Mia —— (live) in South Africa **since • for** she was young.
4. South African people —— (achieve) a lot **since • for** 1994.
5. —— you ever —— (listen) to South African music?
6. I —— (not visit) the zoo **since • for** two years.

Unit 4

G9 R: Die Zukunft mit going to

Revision: The going to-future

Mit dem **going to-future** sagst du, was du in der Zukunft vorhast, planst, beabsichtigst zu tun.
Aussagen im **going to-future** bildest du so: **am/are/is + going to + Verb**

I **am** (I'm) **going to apply** for a job.	Ich **werde** mich für einen Job **bewerben**.
You **are** (You're) **going to work** at a café.	Du **wirst** in einem Café **arbeiten**.
She **is** (She's) **going to fly** to New Zealand.	Sie **hat vor**, nach Neuseeland **zu fliegen**.
We **are** (We're) **going to meet** Luke.	Wir **werden** Luke **treffen**.
They **are** (They're) **going to see** a film.	Sie **planen**, sich einen Film **anzusehen**.

So bildest du verneinte Sätze im **going to-future**:

I **am** (I'm) **not going to fly** anywhere.	Ich **beabsichtige nicht**, irgendwo **hinzufliegen**.
He **is** (He's) **not going to work** as a vet.	Er **hat nicht vor**, als Tierarzt **zu arbeiten**.
They **are** (They're) **not going to meet**.	Sie **werden sich nicht treffen**.

Fragen im going to-future bildest du, indem du **am**, **are** oder **is an den Satzanfang** stellst.
Fragewörter stehen noch davor am Satzanfang.

Are you **going to look for** a job on the internet?	**Wirst** du im Internet nach einem Job **suchen**?
Yes, I **am**./No, I'm **not**.	Ja./Nein.
Is Nora **going to leave** Germany?	**Plant** Nora Deutschland **zu verlassen**?
Yes, she **is**./No, she **isn't**.	Ja./Nein.
What are they **going to do** after school?	**Was werden** sie nach der Schule **tun**?
When are you **going to come back**?	**Wann planst** du **zurückzukommen**?

 Aufgepasst bei Sätzen und Fragen mit dem Verb go!

I'm **going to go** to New Zealand.	Ich **habe vor**, nach Neuseeland **zu fahren**.
Are you **going to go** to New Zealand?	**Hast** du **vor**, nach Neuseeland **zu fahren**?
Yes, I **am**./No, I'm **not**.	Ja./Nein.

(**TEST YOURSELF**) **Put the verbs in the going to-future. Give short answers to the questions in 5. and 6.** (= Yes. ☹ = No.).

1. Both Sue and I —— (write) our CVs soon.
2. We —— (apply for) jobs in tourism.
3. I —— (not work) in Germany.
4. What —— you —— (do) next summer?
5. —— you —— (go) to the next job fair? (☺)
6. —— you —— (visit) another country? (☹)

G10 R: Das Passiv

Revision: The passive voice (simple present and simple past)

Mit dem **Passiv** kannst du über eine Handlung Auskunft geben, ohne zu sagen, wer die Handlung ausführt. Im Vordergrund steht die Handlung.
Passivsätze gibt es wie Aktivsätze in allen Zeiten!

So bildest du das **Passiv** im **simple present**: am/are/is + **3. Form** des Verbs (past participle)
Eine Liste der unregelmäßigen Verben findest du auf den Seiten 138–139.

Fish **is delivered** every day.	Fisch **wird** jeden Tag **geliefert**.
These goods **are sold** in Bavaria.	Diese Waren **werden** in Bayern **verkauft**.
The products **are presented** in a nice way.	Die Produkte **werden** schön **präsentiert**.

So bildest du das **Passiv** im **simple past**: was/were + **3. Form** des Verbs (past participle)

The flight **was cancelled** ten minutes ago.	Der Flug **wurde** vor zehn Minuten **gestrichen**.
This T-shirt **was made** in Auckland.	Dieses T-Shirt **wurde** in Auckland **hergestellt**.
A lot of photos **were taken**.	Es **wurden** viele Fotos **gemacht**.
I **was born** in New Zealand.	Ich **wurde** in Neuseeland **geboren**.

Willst du in einem Passivsatz sagen, **wer** oder **was** die Handlung ausführt, ergänzt du sie, ihn oder es mit **by**.

My wallet **was found by** a young woman.	Mein Geldbeutel **wurde von** einer jungen Frau **gefunden**.
The island **was hit by** an earthquake.	Die Insel **wurde von** einem Erdbeben **getroffen**.

Aus vielen Aktivsätzen kannst du Passivsätze bilden.

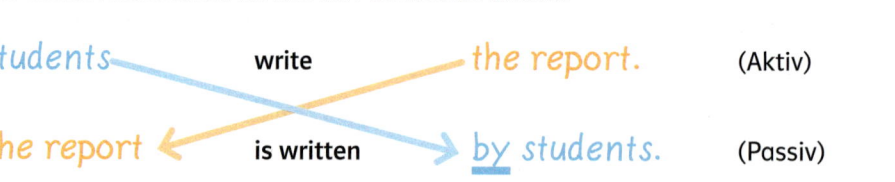

| Students | write | the report. | (Aktiv) |
| The report | is written | by students. | (Passiv) |

(TEST YOURSELF) **Choose the right words for the passive voice.**

1. Food and drinks **is offered · are offered** on the train.
2. Fresh fruit **is bought · are bought** every day.
3. People who buy things **is called · are called** customers.
4. Fresh products **is often sold · were often sold** at markets.
5. Lots of goods **are delivered · were delivered** to Europe in 2019.
6. How much money **is donated · was donated** by the company last year?

Lösungen

G1
1. had
2. didn't climb
3. Did … see; Yes, I did.
4. did … eat
5. did … stay
6. was
7. Was; No, it wasn't.

G2
1. 'll/will travel
2. 'll/will spend
3. won't/will not start
4. Will … be; No, it won't.
5. Will … accept; Yes, they will.
6. will … be
7. won't/will not become
8. will … sleep

G3
1. 'll/will talk
2. can give
3. stay
4. won't/will not be
5. can make
6. feel

G4
1. 's/is sleeping
2. 'm/am making
3. aren't/are not working
4. Are … having
5. are … not/aren't … listening
6. are … writing

G5
1. travel
2. works
3. don't
4. is
5. Does
6. do

G6
1. People need good sanitation in their houses.
2. They grow crops differently in this soil.
3. Louisa carried the water to her home safely./ Louisa carried the water safely to her home.
4. Villagers in India can get fresh milk and eggs easily at home.
5. Does your friend speak English well?
6. How can we solve the problem easily?/ How easily can we solve the problem?

G7
1. was waiting
2. were … doing
3. saw
4. were having

G8
1. 've/have … been
2. have been, for
3. has lived, since
4. have achieved, since
5. Have … listened
6. haven't/have not visited, for

G9
1. are going to write
2. 're/are going to apply for
3. 'm/am not going to work
4. are … going to do
5. Are … going to go; Yes, I am.
6. Are … going to visit; No, I'm not.

G10
1. are offered
2. is bought
3. are called
4. were often sold
5. were delivered
6. was donated

List of irregular verbs

Hier findest du alle unregelmäßigen Verben, die im Buch vorkommen. Die Liste enthält jeweils alle drei Formen, auch wenn sie noch nicht alle in den Units vorgekommen sind.

infinitive	simple past	past participle	German
to be [biː]	was, were [wɒz, wɜː]	been [biːn]	sein
to become [bɪˈkʌm]	became [bɪˈkeɪm]	become [bɪˈkʌm]	werden
to begin [bɪˈgɪn]	began [bɪˈgæn]	begun [bɪˈgʌn]	beginnen; anfangen
to break [breɪk]	broke [brəʊk]	broken [ˈbrəʊkn]	brechen
to bring [brɪŋ]	brought [brɔːt]	brought [brɔːt]	bringen; mitbringen
to build [bɪld]	built [bɪlt]	built [bɪlt]	bauen
to buy [baɪ]	bought [bɔːt]	bought [bɔːt]	kaufen
to catch [kætʃ]	caught [kɔːt]	caught [kɔːt]	fangen
to choose [tʃuːz]	chose [tʃəʊz]	chosen [ˈtʃəʊzn]	wählen; auswählen
to come [kʌm]	came [keɪm]	come [kʌm]	kommen
to cost [kɒst]	cost [kɒst]	cost [kɒst]	kosten
to cut [kʌt]	cut [kʌt]	cut [kʌt]	schneiden
to cut down [ˌkʌt ˈdaʊn]	cut down [ˌkʌt ˈdaʊn]	cut down [ˌkʌt ˈdaʊn]	fällen
to do [duː]	did [dɪd]	done [dʌn]	machen; tun
to drink [drɪŋk]	drank [dræŋk]	drunk [drʌŋk]	trinken
to drive [draɪv]	drove [drəʊv]	driven [ˈdrɪvn]	fahren; treiben
to eat [iːt]	ate [eɪt]	eaten [ˈiːtn]	essen
to fall [fɔːl]	fell [fel]	fallen [ˈfɔːln]	fallen
to feed [fiːd]	fed [fed]	fed [fed]	füttern
to feel [fiːl]	felt [felt]	felt [felt]	fühlen; sich fühlen
to fight [faɪt]	fought [fɔːt]	fought [fɔːt]	kämpfen
to find [faɪnd]	found [faʊnd]	found [faʊnd]	finden
to fly [flaɪ]	flew [fluː]	flown [fləʊn]	fliegen
to forget [fəˈget]	forgot [fəˈgɒt]	forgotten [fəˈgɒtn]	vergessen
to get [get]	got [gɒt]	got [gɒt]	bekommen; werden
to give [gɪv]	gave [geɪv]	given [ˈgɪvn]	geben; schenken
to go [gəʊ]	went [went]	gone [gɒn]	gehen; fahren
to grow [grəʊ]	grew [gruː]	grown [grəʊn]	wachsen
to have [hæv]	had [hæd]	had [hæd]	haben; besitzen
to hear [hɪə]	heard [hɜːd]	heard [hɜːd]	hören
to hit [hɪt]	hit [hɪt]	hit [hɪt]	treffen; schlagen; anfahren
to hold [həʊld]	held [held]	held [held]	halten; festhalten
to hurt [hɜːt]	hurt [hɜːt]	hurt [hɜːt]	verletzen; wehtun
to keep [kiːp]	kept [kept]	kept [kept]	halten; behalten
to know [nəʊ]	knew [njuː]	known [nəʊn]	kennen; wissen
to lead [liːd]	led [led]	led [led]	anführen; führen; leiten
to leave [liːv]	left [left]	left [left]	lassen; verlassen
to lose [luːz]	lost [lɒst]	lost [lɒst]	verlieren

infinitive	simple past	past participle	German
to make [meɪk]	made [meɪd]	made [meɪd]	machen; tun; erstellen; herstellen
to mean [miːn]	meant [ment]	meant [ment]	bedeuten; meinen
to meet [miːt]	met [met]	met [met]	kennenlernen; treffen
to pay [peɪ]	paid [peɪd]	paid [peɪd]	bezahlen
to put [pʊt]	put [pʊt]	put [pʊt]	setzen; legen; stellen
to read [riːd]	read [red]	read [red]	lesen; vorlesen
to ride [raɪd]	rode [rəʊd]	ridden ['rɪdn]	fahren; reiten
to ring [rɪŋ]	rang [ræŋ]	rung [rʌŋ]	klingeln; läuten
to run [rʌn]	ran [ræn]	run [rʌn]	laufen; rennen
to say [seɪ]	said [sed]	said [sed]	sagen; sprechen
to see [siː]	saw [sɔː]	seen [siːn]	sehen
to sell [sel]	sold [səʊld]	sold [səʊld]	verkaufen
to send [send]	sent [sent]	sent [sent]	schicken; senden
to shake [ʃeɪk]	shook [ʃʊk]	shaken ['ʃeɪkn]	beben; zittern; schütteln
to shoot [ʃuːt]	shot [ʃɒt]	shot [ʃɒt]	erschießen; schießen
to sing [sɪŋ]	sang [sæŋ]	sung [sʌŋ]	singen
to sit [sɪt]	sat [sæt]	sat [sæt]	sitzen
to sleep [sliːp]	slept [slept]	slept [slept]	schlafen
to speak [spiːk]	spoke [spəʊk]	spoken ['spəʊkn]	sprechen
to spend [spend]	spent [spent]	spent [spent]	verbringen; ausgeben
to stand [stænd]	stood [stʊd]	stood [stʊd]	stehen
to swim [swɪm]	swam [swæm]	swum [swʌm]	schwimmen
to swing [swɪŋ]	swung [swʌŋ]	swung [swʌŋ]	schwingen; schwenken
to take [teɪk]	took [tʊk]	taken ['teɪkn]	nehmen; mitnehmen; dauern; brauchen
to teach [tiːtʃ]	taught [tɔːt]	taught [tɔːt]	unterrichten
to tell [tel]	told [təʊld]	told [təʊld]	erzählen; sagen
to think [θɪŋk]	thought [θɔːt]	thought [θɔːt]	denken; glauben
to throw [θrəʊ]	threw [θruː]	thrown [θrəʊn]	werfen
to understand [ˌʌndəˈstænd]	understood [ˌʌndəˈstʊd]	understood [ˌʌndəˈstʊd]	verstehen
to wake up [ˌweɪkˈʌp]	woke up [ˌwəʊkˈʌp]	woken up [ˌwəʊknˈʌp]	aufwachen; aufwecken
to wear [weə]	wore [wɔː]	worn [wɔːn]	anhaben; tragen
to win [wɪn]	won [wʌn]	won [wʌn]	gewinnen
to write [raɪt]	wrote [rəʊt]	written ['rɪtn]	schreiben

1-minute-presentation

Step 1

Nimm ein Blatt Papier im DIN-A4-Format quer und falte es so, dass das untere Drittel nach hinten wegknickt.

Step 2

Schreibe den Vortragstext auf die oberen zwei Drittel.

Step 3

Streiche nun die wichtigsten Stichpunkte im Text an. Notiere sie noch einmal auf dem unteren Drittel. Das ist dein Spickzettel.

Step 4

In deiner Präsentation verwendest du nur den Spickzettel. Wenn du steckenbleibst, darfst du ihn umknicken und kurz auf den Text oben schauen.

Bus stop

(Lerntempoduett)

Step 1

Bearbeite die Aufgabe zunächst allein.
Schreibe deine Lösungen auf.

Step 2

Wenn du fertig bist, gehe zum „bus stop". Entweder wartet dort schon jemand oder du wartest dort auf die nächste Person. Vergleicht und korrigiert eure Ergebnisse zu zweit.

Step 3

Gehe danach wieder zu deinem Platz zurück.
Bearbeite die nächste Aufgabe.

Dramatic reading

(Szenisches Lesen)

Step 1

Verteilt die Rollen innerhalb eurer Gruppe.

Step 2

Lies dir deinen Text lautlos oder ganz leise immer wieder vor, bis du ihn gut kennst.

Step 3

Übt euren Text in der Gruppe mit der Methode „Read and look up" (Seite 142).

Step 4

Überlegt euch, wie ihr euch in der Rolle fühlt und wie ihr euch bewegen würdet. Tragt euren Text so frei wie möglich vor.

Gallery walk
(Galerierundgang)

Step 1
Hängt nach eurer Gruppenarbeit eure Produkte gut sichtbar im Klassenzimmer auf.

Step 2
Eine „Expertin" oder ein „Experte" aus jeder Gruppe bleibt bei dem Produkt stehen und erklärt es den anderen. Der Rest der Gruppe geht im Klassenzimmer herum. Nach jedem Durchgang wechselt die Expertin oder der Experte.

Step 3
Seht euch die Produkte der anderen an und bewertet sie.

Step 4
Wertet im Anschluss eure Ergebnisse in der Klasse aus.

Milling around
(Marktplatz)

Step 1
Bearbeite die Aufgabe zunächst allein.

Step 2
Auf ein Zeichen von eurer Lehrerin oder eurem Lehrer steht ihr auf und geht durch den Raum. Vergesst nicht, die Aufgabe und einen Stift mitzunehmen.

Step 3
Wenn ein Signal ertönt, bleibt ihr stehen. Besprecht die Aufgabe mit der Person, die euch am nächsten steht.

Step 4
Beim nächsten Signal trennt ihr euch und geht weiter durch den Raum. Wiederholt den Vorgang.

Peer correction
(Partnerkontrolle)

Step 1
Bearbeite die Aufgabe zunächst allein.

Step 2
Tausche deine Lösungen mit einer Partnerin oder einem Partner. Kontrolliere seine oder ihre Lösungen.

Step 3
Vergleicht eure Lösungen und korrigiert sie dann gemeinsam.

Placemat

(Platzdeckchen)

Step 1

Bildet Vierergruppen.

Step 2

Teilt ein großes Blatt Papier in fünf Bereiche ein.

Step 3

Setzt euch so hin, dass alle jeweils in eine Ecke des Blattes schreiben können.

Step 4

Jedes Gruppenmitglied denkt allein über das Thema nach und schreibt Ideen auf seinen Teil des Blattes.

Step 5

Tauscht euch über die Ideen aus. Einigt euch auf die besten Ideen und schreibt diese in die Mitte des Blattes.

Read and look up

(Lesen und Aufschauen)

Step 1

Schaue auf deinen Text und präge dir die erste Zeile oder den ersten Satz ein. Schaue hoch und sprich deine Zeile / deinen Satz lautlos oder leise vor dich hin. Nimm dir die nächste Zeile / den nächsten Satz vor.

Step 2

Übe nun mit einer Partnerin oder einem Partner. Erzähle deinen Text, Zeile für Zeile oder Satz für Satz. Dazwischen schaust du immer wieder nach unten auf deinen Text.

Step 3

Wiederhole alles, bis es gut klappt. Überlege dir, wo du stehen und wie du dich bewegen willst.

Round robin

(Blitzlicht)

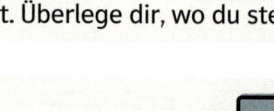

Step 1

Bildet Gruppen und setzt euch in einen Kreis.

Step 2

Jedes Gruppenmitglied überlegt sich kurz einen Satz, der seine persönliche Meinung zum Thema ausdrückt.

Step 3

Wenn alle bereit sind, sagen die Gruppenmitglieder der Reihe nach ihre Meinung. Die anderen Gruppenmitglieder dürfen die Sätze nicht kommentieren.

Think – pair – share

Step 1
Schreibe deine Ideen, Gedanken oder Lösungen zur Aufgabe auf.

Step 2
Tauscht euch zu zweit aus und besprecht eure Notizen.

Step 3
Präsentiert euer Ergebnis anderen Paaren oder der gesamten Klasse.

Tip top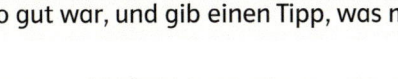

Step 1
Sage zunächst, was dir gut gefallen hat – was „top" war.

Step 2
Sage nun, was noch nicht so gut war, und gib einen Tipp, was man noch verbessern könnte.

Writers' conference
(Schreibwerkstatt)

Step 1
Bildet Vierergruppen.

Step 2
Lest euch eure Sätze/Texte gegenseitig vor.

Step 3
Die Zuhörerinnen und Zuhörer sagen, was ihnen gefallen hat, und können Verbesserungsvorschläge machen.

Step 4
Jede Gruppe wählt den besten Text aus und liest ihn der Klasse vor.

Vocabulary tips

Du kennst schon einige Tipps und Tricks zum Vokabellernen.
Erinnerst du dich? Hier gibt es noch mehr Tipps.

Lerntipp: Wortfamilien

Beim ersten Anschauen eines neuen Wortes solltest du dir überlegen, ob es einen
Anknüpfungspunkt an Wörter gibt, die du bereits kennst. Oft kann dir ein Wort aus der gleichen
Wortfamilie helfen, die Bedeutung des neuen Wortes zu erschließen. Hier zwei Beispiele:

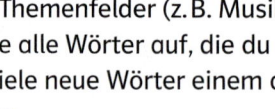

communication

to communicate
(kommunizieren)

communicator

communicative

to produce

product
(Produkt, Erzeugnis)

production

producer

productive

Lerntipp: Themenfelder

Lege dir zunächst verschiedene Themenfelder (z. B. Musik, Essen und Trinken, Umwelt) in deinem
Heft oder digital an und schreibe alle Wörter auf, die du zum jeweiligen Themenfeld schon kennst.
Versuche in Zukunft möglichst viele neue Wörter einem dieser Themenfelder zuzuordnen. Füge
auch weitere Themenfelder hinzu.

Lerntipp: Die richtige Übersetzung im Wörterbuch finden

Wenn du ein Wort im Wörterbuch nachschlägst, findest du oft viele verschiedene Übersetzungen.
Achte darauf, ob der Zusammenhang (z. B. Sport, Computer, Schule) im Eintrag mit angegeben ist.
Dies kann dir helfen zu entscheiden, welche Übersetzung am besten passt. Bei jedem Eintrag im
Wörterbuch findest du auch eine Angabe zur Wortart. Nomen werden mit n. (*noun*), Verben mit v.
(*verb*) und Adjektive mit adj. (*adjective*) abgekürzt.

Lerntipp: Auf „falsche Freunde" („false friends") achten

Bei diesen Wörtern musst du aufpassen. Man kann sie leicht verwechseln.

German	English	English	German
also	so	also	auch
arm	poor	arm	Arm
Chef; Chefin	boss	chef	Koch; Küchenchef
Karte; Plan	map	card	Karte
Kunst (als Schulfach)	Art	type	Art; Sorte; Typ
Rock	skirt	rock	Fels; Stein
stehen	to stand	to stay	bleiben; übernachten
(zu etw.) werden	to become	to get	bekommen

Diese Checkliste kann dir helfen, Fehler zu vermeiden. Prüfe alle deine Texte damit. Du kannst auch ein „Fehlertagebuch" führen, in dem du deine eigenen häufigen Fehler aufschreibst. So bist du beim nächsten Mal sicherer.

- **Schreibung:**
  - ☐ *gh* wird meist nicht gesprochen. Vergiss es beim Schreiben nicht: z. B. hi**gh**, ei**gh**t
  - ☐ *k* kommt vor *t* so gut wie nie vor: z. B. activity – A**k**tivität, O**c**tober – O**k**tober
  - ☐ *sh* kommt viel häufiger vor als *sch*: z. B. **sh**ip, **sh**oot

- **Gleiche Aussprache, unterschiedliche Schreibung:**
  - ☐ [iː] z. B. thr**ee**, t**ea**, th**e**se, p**eo**ple, f**ie**ld
  - ☐ [uː] z. B. f**oo**d, fr**ui**t, to d**o**, fl**ew**, s**u**permarket, barbec**ue**, b**eau**tiful
  - ☐ [eə] z. B. sh**are**, f**air**, c**are**ful
  - ☐ [aɪ] z. B. wh**i**te, s**igh**t, r**i**de

- **Achtung bei Kurzformen von *to be* und den Possessivpronomen:**
  - ☐ th**ey're** (Kurzform von *they are*) [ðeə] th**eir** (ihr, ihre) [ðeə]
  - ☐ **it's** (Kurzform von *it is*) [ɪts] **its** (sein) [ɪts]
  - ☐ **you're** (Kurzform von *you are*) [jɔː] **your** (dein; deine) [jɔː]

- **Gleiche Aussprache, unterschiedliche Schreibung und Bedeutung:**
  - ☐ [iː] z. B. to s**ee** – sehen, s**ea** – Meer
  - ☐ [uː] z. B. tw**o** – zwei, t**oo** – auch

- **Verdoppelung des Endkonsonanten:**
  - ☐ to sto**p** – sto**pp**ing, sto**pp**ed
  - ☐ to wi**n** – wi**nn**ing, wi**nn**er

- **y wird zu ie:**
  - ☐ in der 3. Person Singular und in der Vergangenheitsform: z. B. to worr**y** – he worr**ies** – he worr**ied** aber: to buy – she bu**ys**
  - ☐ im Plural: z. B. cit**y** – cit**ies**, part**y** – part**ies**; aber: boy – boy**s**
  - ☐ bei der Steigerung von Adjektiven: z. B. happ**y** – happ**ier** – (the) happ**iest**

- **Ähnlichkeiten in Schreibung und Aussprache zu deutschen Wörtern:**
  - ☐ **who** – wer; **where** – wo

- **Ähnlich und doch anders:**
  - ☐ Wortendung *-le*: z. B. tit**le** – Tite**l**; midd**le** – Mitte**l**-
  - ☐ *ph* statt *f*: z. B. **ph**one – Telefon; **ph**oto – **F**oto

- **Großschreibung:**
  - ☐ Monatsnamen und Wochentage: z. B. January, Monday
  - ☐ Eigennamen und geografische Namen: z. B. Koa, Penny, the Brooks, the Taj Mahal, Cape Town, South Africa, Australia

- **Plural:**
  - ☐ Der Plural bekommt normalerweise ein *s*: z. B. friend – friend**s**, chair – chair**s**, film – film**s**
  - ☐ Endet ein Wort auf *s* oder *x*, wird *es* angehängt: z. B. bus – bus**es**, box – box**es**
  - ☐ Manche Wörter haben einen unregelmäßigen Plural: z. B. man – men, child – children, shelf – shelves, mouse – mice

- **Apostroph:**
  - ☐ bei Kurzformen: z. B. she is → she's; they are → they're
  - ☐ beim Genitiv-s: z. B. Matt's friend, Emma's family, the Jacksons' house, the children's games

- **Wörterbuch:**
  - ☐ Prüfe die Schreibung aller Wörter, bei denen du dir nicht ganz sicher bist, indem du sie im Wörterbuch nachschlägst.

Word bank: **Talking about experiences** → 🌐 Find more online: mn28pj

Where I went

museum	concert	town/city	zoo	cathedral
gallery	theme park	airport	stadium	mountains

Useful phrases

Impressions **I had**
The building looked/was really . . .
The . . . was crowded/empty/busy/**quiet/**
cheap/expensive.
I was surprised that . . .
It was great/exciting/interesting to see . . .
The journey was really long/short/
interesting/boring.
Maybe I'll go again one day.
I won't go again.

Things **I found out**
. . . **was built in . . .**
. . . is the oldest/smallest/largest . . .
I found out that . . . came from/was born in/
died in/visited . . . in . . .
. . . takes place **every year/month/week/day.**
I learned that . . .
The guide told us about . . .
Did you know that . . . ?

Word bank: Talking about being ill → ⊕ Find more online: mn28pj

Being ill

I feel ...
ill.
sick.
weak.
tired.
a bit hot.

I have ...
a bad headache.
a high temperature.
a cold.
stomach ache.
a sore throat.
backache.

My head/foot/back/
throat/arm/leg/stomach/
ankle ... really hurts.

Giving advice

You should ...
go to the doctor's.
take some medicine/tablets.
go to the pharmacy.
stay in bed.
drink lots of water/tea.
do as the doctor says.
go back to the doctor if you don't feel better.

You shouldn't ...
do any sport for a week.
go to the party on Friday.
meet everyone in the snack bar.
stay up late.

Useful phrases

If you drink lots of water, you'll feel better.
If you take your medicine, you'll get better quicker.
If you stay in bed, you'll get more sleep.
You'll feel better if you sleep a lot.
Why don't you call me, and I'll come around and visit you?
Maybe you could call your mum and she could pick you up?
If you don't get better, you'll have to go back to the doctor.

Word bank: **Presenting a company** → 🌐 Find more online: mn28pj

snack bar

supermarket

clothes

plumber

electrician

carpenter

skilled tradespeople

baker

shops and catering

hairdressing salon

café

tax advisor

types of company

testing

hotline

IT

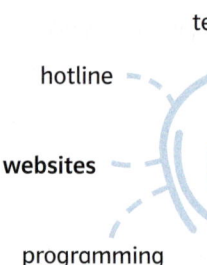

websites

programming

computing devices

finance

sports equipment

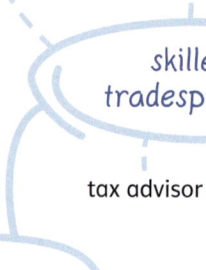
medicine

logistics

energy

international companies

clothes

cars

food

machines

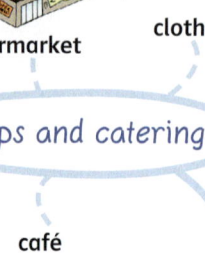

for schools

machines

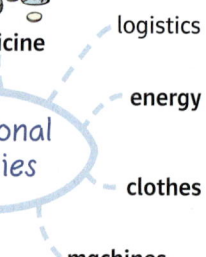

cars

in Europe

cooks meals

produces / manufactures

all over the world

sells

jewellery

products

for old people

for hospitals

containers

delivers

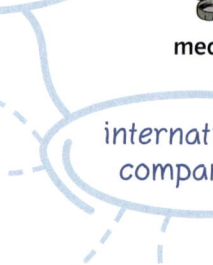

services for tourists

The company ...

packages

offers

websites

help

gives

designs

clothes

plans

advice

products

events

Word bank: **Sustainable living** → 🌐 Find more online: mn28pj

eat more vegetarian **food and less meat**

install solar panels **on the** roof

reduce consumption

What I can do

take my own bags when **I go shopping**

buy products **that aren't in lots of** packaging

recycle **as much as** possible

use public transport or my bike more often

turn off electrical **devices when I don't need them**

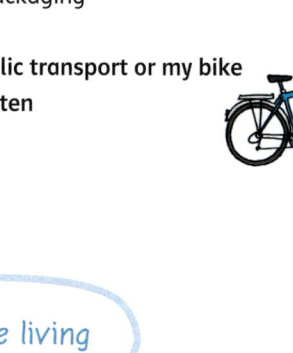

sustainable living

advise ⓘ **people about saving energy**

build more wind farms

increase **the price of flights**

What governments can do

research **new ways** of recycling

REDUCE RECYCLE REUSE

make public transport cheaper

improve **public transport**

Word bank: Talking about an accident → 🌐 Find more online: mn28pj

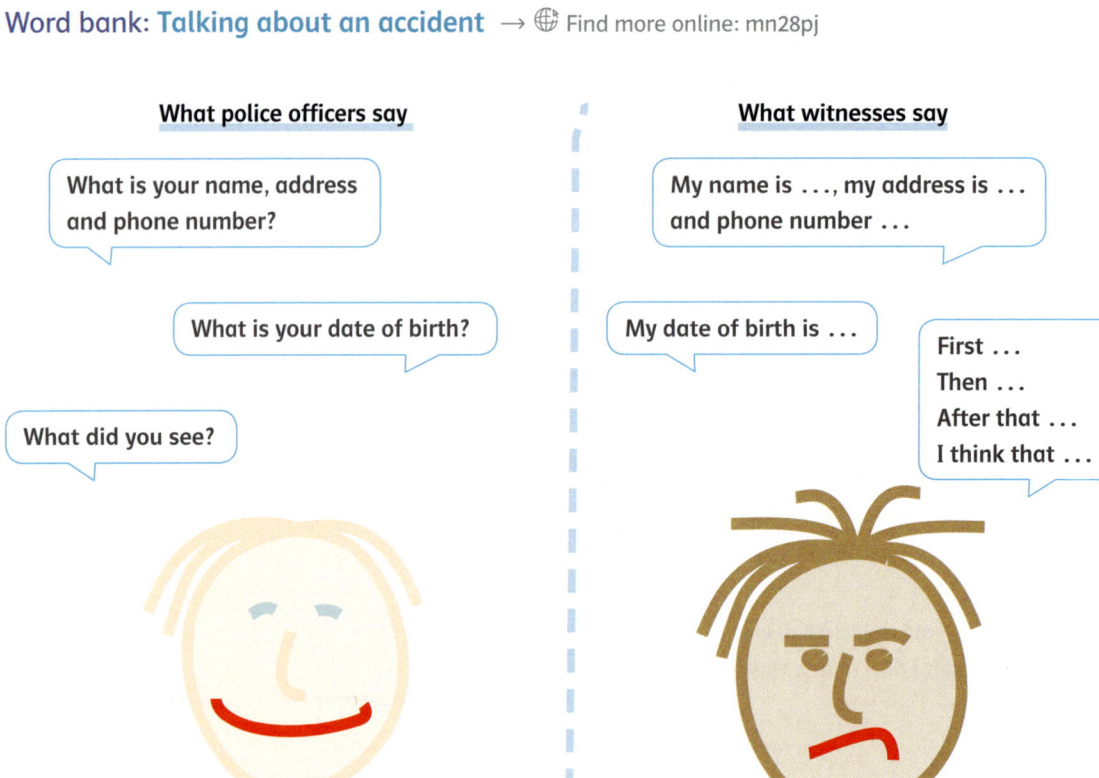

What police officers say

What is your name, address and phone number?

What is your date of birth?

What did you see?

What time did the accident happen?

Who was involved?
How many cars / people were in the accident?
What happened (next)?

Can you explain that in more detail, please?

What witnesses say

My name is …, my address is … and phone number …

My date of birth is …

First …
Then …
After that …
I think that …

I arrived at …
I think the accident happened …
minutes before I arrived.

There was (a car) and (three) people in the accident.

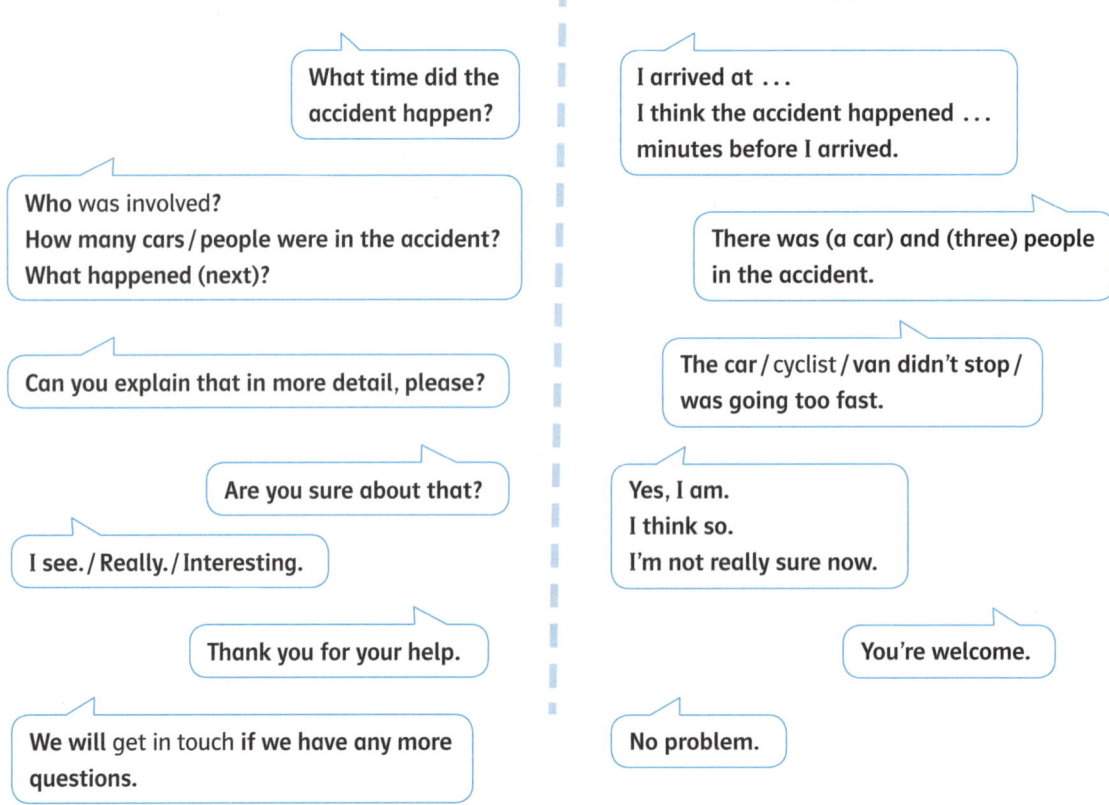

Are you sure about that?

I see. / Really. / Interesting.

Thank you for your help.

We will get in touch if we have any more questions.

The car / cyclist / van didn't stop / was going too fast.

Yes, I am.
I think so.
I'm not really sure now.

You're welcome.

No problem.

Word bank: **Describing a role model** → 🌐 Find more online: mn28pj

Personal qualities

confident	I admire people who are confident in front of others.
considerate	People who put others first are considerate.
determined	Someone who gets what they want is determined.
enthusiastic	If you are enthusiastic you can get lots of people to help you.
generous	Generous people do a lot to help charities.
happy	It makes people happy to help others.
helpful	If you ask a helpful person, they will always help you.
honest	Honest people tell the truth.
kind	Kind people always have time for other people.
nervous	He is nervous but doesn't show it.
polite	You are polite if you say please and thank you to others.
proud	She is very proud of who she is.
reliable	Reliable people are known for being there when you need them.
respectful	I look up to people who are respectful to everyone.
tolerant	I admire people who are tolerant.
self-confident	Self-confident people post pictures on social media.
strong	In hard situations you have to be strong.

Useful phrases

I admire ... because he/she ...
I follow ... because he/she ...
I read that ...
I saw pictures of ...

... is known for ...
... helps homeless/sick/... people/animals.
... raised lots of money for charities.
... always has time for ...

Word bank: **Jobs and qualities** → 🌐 Find more online: mn28pj

Jobs

with customers
baker Bäcker/-in
butcher Fleischer/-in; Metzger/-in
hairdresser Friseur/-in
salesperson Verkäufer/-in

working outside
animal keeper Tierpfleger/-in
bricklayer Maurer/-in
firefighter Feuerwehrmann/-frau
(landscape) gardener (Landschafts)Gärtner/-in

helping people
dentist's **assistant** Zahnarzthelfer/-in
nursery teacher Erzieher/-in
police officer Polizist/-in
speech therapist Logopäde/Logopädin

working with hands
carpenter Schreiner/-in; Tischler/-in
mechanic Mechaniker/-in
metalworker Metallbauer/-in
vehicle painter Fahrzeuglackierer/-in

being creative
chef Koch/Köchin
florist Florist/-in
media designer Mediengestalter/-in

working with computers
computer programmer Programmierer/-in
engineer Ingenieur/-in
office worker Büroarbeiter/-in

Qualities needed

creative
patient
flexible
well-organized
responsible
confident

good at listening to others
stay calm in difficult situations
like working outside
prefer **working in an office/inside**
can work in a team
good with one's hands

V

Word bank: Talking about an internship → 🌐 Find more online: mn28pj

prepare

order food and drinks

meetings

take notes

clear up

answer questions

help

customers

explain things

What did I do?

see a warehouse

sort stock

deliveries

prepare **deliveries**

check goods

plant **flowers/trees**

outside

build new fences

mow the lawn

talking about an internship

work in different departments

speak to customers

how to ...

organize a meeting

I learned ...

bored tired excited

How did I feel?

sad

nervous

welcome

happy confident

happens when things are delivered

work outside is like (hot/cold)

what ...

working conditions are like

a big/small company is like

when ...

people start and finish work

people have breaks

Useful phrases

The thing I liked best was . . .
I'd like to try . . . in the future.
I'd like to learn about . . .
I don't think I'll . . . again.

It helped me decide (not) to . . .
I was surprised that . . .
I didn't know that . . .

Vocabulary

Das Vocabulary enthält alle neuen Wörter und Wendungen. Die Reihenfolge ist wie im Buch.

Die Wortliste ist in drei Spalten aufgeteilt:

Links findest du das englische Wort mit der Lautschrift in Klammern. (Die Lautschrift wird ganz unten auf jeder Seite im *Dictionary* erklärt.)

In der mittleren Spalte steht die deutsche Übersetzung.

Rechts findest du Beispielsätze, Hinweise und Tipps, die dir beim Lernen helfen.

Die **fett** gedruckten Wörter musst du lernen.

Symbole und Abkürzungen:

⇔	Achtung Aussprache!	sth	something
✎	Achtung Schreibweise!	sb	somebody
↔	ist das Gegenteil von	*(sg)*	Einzahl (Singular)
→	ist verwandt mit	*(pl)*	Mehrzahl (Plural)
=	entspricht	R	ähnlich wie im Russischen
		T	ähnlich wie im Türkischen

Die *Word bank*-Seiten (S.146 bis 153) helfen dir, die *Task*-Aufgaben in den *Units* zu bearbeiten. Du findest dort nützlichen individuellen Wortschatz zum Thema der *Unit*, der dir hilft, über deine eigene Situation zu sprechen oder zu schreiben. Diese Wörter findest du auch im *Dictionary*.

Wenn du ein Wort nicht weißt und im Wörterbuch nachschlagen willst, schau auf den *Dictionary*-Seiten ab S.172 nach. Oder bei den *Instructions* auf S.221.

Zoom in – A world language

p. 8	**billion** [ˈbɪlɪən]	Milliarde	R биллион
	official language [əˌfɪʃl ˈlæŋgwɪdʒ]	Amtssprache	There are 22 **official languages** in India.
	majority [məˈdʒɒrəti]	Mehrheit; Mehrzahl	The **majority** of people speak English.
	speaker [ˈspiːkə]	Sprecher; Sprecherin; Redner; Rednerin	**speaker** → to speak
	(software) program [(ˌsɒfweə) ˈprəʊgræm]	(Software)Programm	His team writes **software programs**.
	half *(sg)* [hɑːf], **halves** *(pl)* [hɑːvz]	(die) Hälfte	**Half** of the population speaks English.
	competition [ˌkɒmpəˈtɪʃn]	Wettbewerb	James won the **competition**.
p. 9	**to communicate** [kəˈmjuːnɪkeɪt]	kommunizieren; sich verständigen	I can **communicate** in English.

English-speaking [ˌɪŋglɪʃˈspiːkɪŋ]	englischsprachig	The UK is an **English-speaking** country.
international [ˌɪntəˈnæʃnl]	international	⟺ Achtung Aussprache!
business [ˈbɪznɪs]	Geschäftswelt; Geschäft	English is the language of international **business**.
to **give** [gɪv]	halten	I have to **give** a presentation next week.
task [tɑːsk]	Aufgabe; Auftrag	They have to do these **tasks** in English.

Unit 1 Around Australia

p. 10 **around** [əˈraʊnd]	unterwegs (in)	This book is called '**Around** Australia'.

Intro

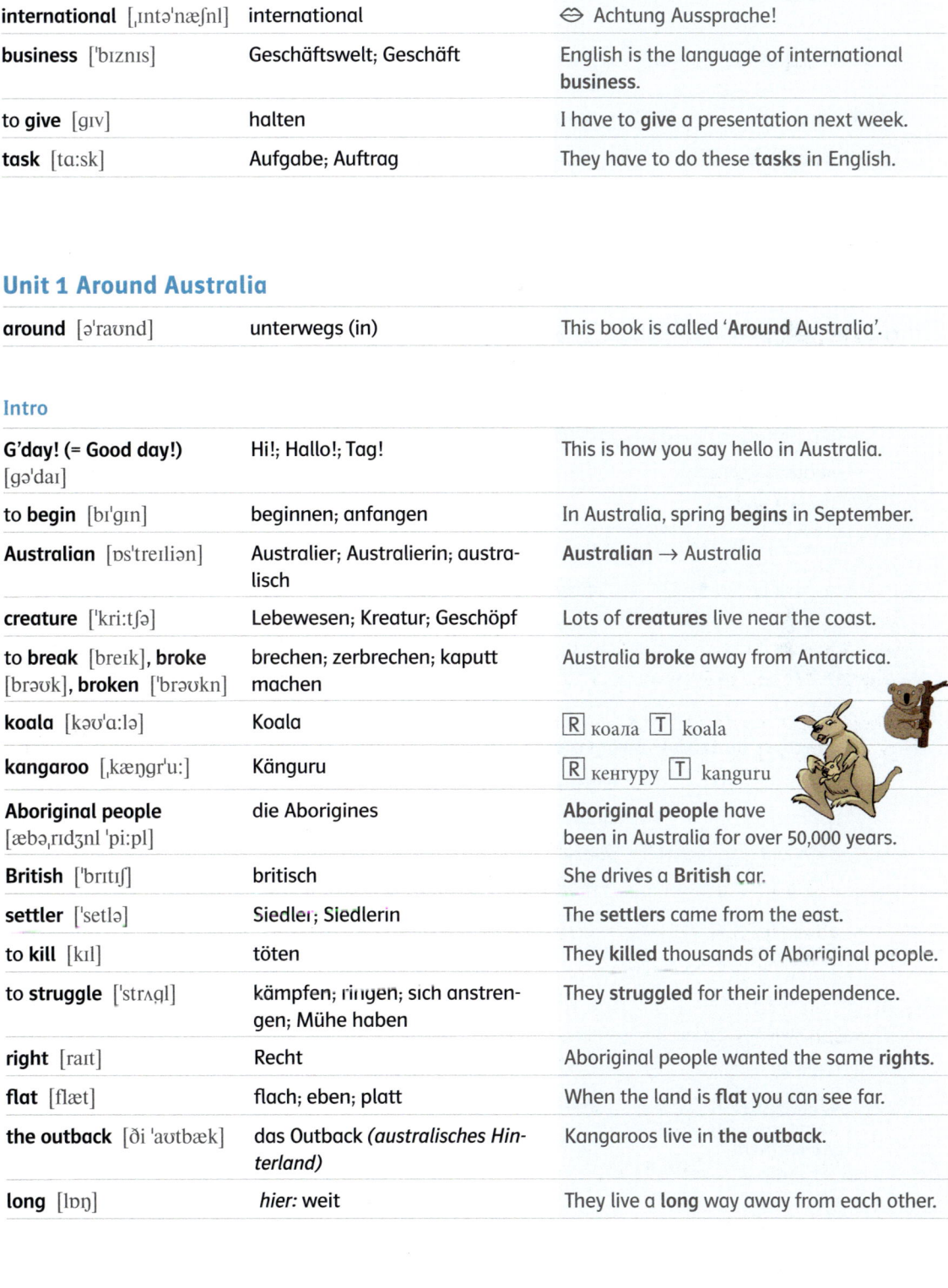

G'day! (= Good day!) [gəˈdaɪ]	Hi!; Hallo!; Tag!	This is how you say hello in Australia.
to **begin** [bɪˈgɪn]	beginnen; anfangen	In Australia, spring **begins** in September.
Australian [ɒsˈtreɪliən]	Australier; Australierin; australisch	**Australian** → Australia
creature [ˈkriːtʃə]	Lebewesen; Kreatur; Geschöpf	Lots of **creatures** live near the coast.
p. 11 to **break** [breɪk], **broke** [brəʊk], **broken** [ˈbrəʊkn]	brechen; zerbrechen; kaputt machen	Australia **broke** away from Antarctica.
koala [kəʊˈɑːlə]	Koala	R коала T koala
kangaroo [ˌkæŋgrˈuː]	Känguru	R кенгуру T kanguru
Aboriginal people [æbəˌrɪdʒnl ˈpiːpl]	die Aborigines	**Aboriginal people** have been in Australia for over 50,000 years.
British [ˈbrɪtɪʃ]	britisch	She drives a **British** car.
settler [ˈsetlə]	Siedler; Siedlerin	The **settlers** came from the east.
to **kill** [kɪl]	töten	They **killed** thousands of Aboriginal people.
to **struggle** [ˈstrʌgl]	kämpfen; ringen; sich anstrengen; Mühe haben	They **struggled** for their independence.
right [raɪt]	Recht	Aboriginal people wanted the same **rights**.
flat [flæt]	flach; eben; platt	When the land is **flat** you can see far.
the outback [ði ˈaʊtbæk]	das Outback (*australisches Hinterland*)	Kangaroos live in **the outback**.
long [lɒŋ]	*hier:* weit	They live a **long** way away from each other.

Topic 1

p. 12 **rock** [rɒk]	Fels; Stein	
Aboriginal [ˌæbəˈrɪdʒnl]	Aborigine-; zur Aborigine-Kultur gehörend	Koa saw some **Aboriginal** dances.
tribe [traɪb]	Stamm; Volksstamm	Koa's father is from an Aboriginal **tribe**.
lifestyle [ˈlaɪfstaɪl]	Lebensstil; Lebensart; Lebensweise	the way you live your life
disappointed [ˌdɪsəˈpɔɪntɪd]	enttäuscht	Some tourists were **disappointed**.
helicopter [ˈhelɪkɒptə]	Helikopter; Hubschrauber	There are **helicopter** flights over Uluru.
didgeridoo [ˌdɪdʒriˈduː]	Didgeridoo (australisches Musikinstrument)	Many Aboriginal people play the **didgeridoo**.
colourful [ˈkʌləfl]	bunt	colourful
dot [dɒt]	Punkt	There is a **dot** in the website address.
painting [ˈpeɪntɪŋ]	Gemälde	There were lots of **paintings** on the wall.
afraid [əˈfreɪd]	ängstlich	A star is never **afraid**.
giant [dʒaɪənt]	Riesen-; riesig	We saw **giant** creatures in the zoo.
to **think of** [ˈθɪŋk ˌəv]	davon halten	So what did you **think of** it?
delicious [dɪˈlɪʃəs]	lecker; köstlich	Achtung Aussprache!
to **learn** [lɜːn]	erfahren; herausfinden	They **learned** that a boy died in the fire.

— Das kenne ich schon

adjectives for talking about experiences

afraid [əˈfreɪd]	ängstlich		**excited** [ɪkˈsaɪtɪd]	aufgeregt; begeistert
boring [ˈbɔːrɪŋ]	langweilig		**exciting** [ɪkˈsaɪtɪŋ]	spannend; aufregend
confident [ˈkɒnfɪdnt]	selbstsicher; selbstbewusst; sicher		**happy** [ˈhæpi]	glücklich
			interesting [ˈɪntrəstɪŋ]	interessant
delicious [dɪˈlɪʃəs]	lecker; köstlich		**sad** [sæd]	traurig
disappointed [ˌdɪsəˈpɔɪntɪd]	enttäuscht		**surprised** [səˈpraɪzd]	überrascht
			worried [ˈwʌrid]	beunruhigt; besorgt

Topic 2

p. 16 **receptionist** [rɪˈsepʃnɪst]	Arzthelfer; Arzthelferin	I told the **receptionist** my name.
appointment [əˈpɔɪntmənt]	Termin	I've got an **appointment** at 9 o'clock.
list [lɪst]	Liste	I can't find you in our **list** of patients.
patient [ˈpeɪʃnt]	Patient; Patientin	The **patient** said he had a bad cold.

to **register** [ˈredʒɪstə]	sich registrieren lassen; sich eintragen; sich anmelden	You will have to **register** with us.
medical record [ˌmedɪkl ˈrekɔːd]	Krankenakte	We need your **medical records**.
ill [ɪl]	krank; schlecht	I feel really **ill** today.
Oh dear. [əʊ ˈdɪə]	Oje.	**Oh dear.** What happened?
What's the matter? [ˌwɒts ðə ˈmætə]	Was ist los?; Was hast du?	You look ill. **What's the matter?**
high temperature [ˌhaɪ ˈtemprətʃə]	Fieber	Penny has a **high temperature**.
to **catch sth** [kætʃ]	*hier:* sich etw. einfangen *(medizinisch)*	Penny has **caught a cold**.
flu [fluː]	Grippe	A lot of people have had the **flu**.
to **be afraid** [biː əˈfreɪd]	befürchten	I'm **afraid** you've caught the flu.
to **get better** [ˌget ˈbetə]	sich wieder besser fühlen; sich verbessern	You'll **get better** soon.
prescription [prɪˈskrɪpʃn]	Rezept *(für Arzneimittel)*	Here is a **prescription** for some tablets.
medicine [ˈmedsn]	Medikamente; Medizin	This **medicine** will help you.
to **take** [teɪk]	*hier:* einnehmen	Don't forget to **take** your medicine.
tablet [ˈtæblət]	Tablette	Have you got any headache **tablets**, please?
pharmacy [ˈfɑːməsi]	Apotheke	Take the prescription to the **pharmacy**.
You're welcome. [jɔː ˈwelkəm]	Gern geschehen.	Thanks. – **You're welcome.**
Get well soon! [ˌget wel ˈsuːn]	Gute Besserung!	Goodbye and **get well soon**!

═ Das kenne ich schon ═

at the doctor's

receptionist [rɪˈsepʃnɪst]	Arzthelfer; Arzthelferin	tired [ˈtaɪəd]	müde
patient [ˈpeɪʃnt]	Patient; Patientin	high temperature [ˌhaɪ ˈtemprətʃə]	Fieber
doctor [ˈdɒktə]	Arzt; Ärztin	headache [ˈhedeɪk]	Kopfweh; Kopfschmerzen
nurse [nɜːs]	Krankenpfleger; Krankenschwester	to be sick [bi: ˈsɪk]	sich übergeben
appointment [əˈpɔɪntmənt]	Termin	to take [teɪk], took [tʊk], taken [ˈteɪkn]	*hier:* einnehmen
medical record [ˌmedɪkl ˈrekɔːd]	Krankenakte	to catch sth [kætʃ]	*hier:* sich etw. einfangen (medizinisch)
prescription [prɪˈskrɪpʃn]	Rezept *(für Arzneimittel)*	to hurt [hɜːt], hurt [hɜːt], hurt [hɜːt]	verletzen; wehtun
medicine [ˈmedsn]	Medikamente; Medizin	to register [ˈredʒɪstə]	sich registrieren lassen; sich eintragen; sich anmelden
tablet [ˈtæblət]	Tablette	Get well soon! [ˌget wel ˈsuːn]	Gute Besserung!
pharmacy [ˈfɑːməsi]	Apotheke		
ill [ɪl]	krank; schlecht		
flu [fluː]	Grippe		
cold [kəʊld]	Erkältung		

Text

p. 20	**danger** [ˈdeɪndʒə]	Gefahr	**danger** → dangerous
	reef [riːf]	Riff	R риф T resif
	coral [ˈkɒrəl]	Koralle	R коралл
	climate change [ˈklaɪmət ˌtʃeɪndʒ]	Klimawandel	**Climate change** is dangerous.
	bleaching [ˈbliːtʃɪŋ]	Bleichen; Ausbleichen	Coral **bleaching** is a problem.
	temperature [ˈtemprətʃə]	Temperatur	R температура
	alga *(sg)* [ˈælgə], **algae** *(pl)* [ˈældʒiː]	Alge	Warm water kills the **algae** on the coral.
	area [ˈeəriə]	Fläche; Bereich	Large **areas** of the reef have already died.
	oil spill [ˈɔɪl ˌspɪl]	Ölteppich; Ölpest	**Oil spills** cause a lot of damage.
	to recover [rɪˈkʌvə]	sich erholen	It will take years for the reef to **recover**.
	government [ˈgʌvnmənt]	Regierung	✏ Achtung Schreibweise! gove**rn**ment
	law [lɔː]	Gesetz	The government has made new **laws**.
	however [haʊˈevə]	jedoch	**However**, I still don't like him.
	alone [əˈləʊn]	allein	**alone** ↔ together
	may [meɪ]	können; dürfen	The reef **may** die soon.

completely [kəmˈpliːtli]	völlig	That's **completely** wrong!
p. 21 **department** [dɪˈpɑːtmənt]	Abteilung	Let's go to the shoe **department**.
energy [ˈenədʒi]	Energie; Kraft	We have to save more **energy**.
GPO [ˌdʒiː piː ˈəʊ]	Hauptpostamt	Sydney's **GPO** building is very beautiful.
to **protest** [prəˈtest]	protestieren	I **protested** against the new law.
destruction [dɪˈstrʌkʃn]	Zerstörung	Can we stop the **destruction** of the reef?

Film

wide [waɪd]	breit; groß	**manta ray** [ˈmæntə ˌreɪ]	Teufelsrochen
whale shark [ˈweɪl ˌʃɑːk]	Walhai	**full of** [ˈfʊl ˌəv]	voller
saltwater crocodile [ˈsɔːltˌwɔːtə ˈkrɒkədaɪl]	Salzwasserkrokodil	**as much as** [əz ˈmʌtʃ ˌəz]	bis zu
		real [rɪəl]	echt; richtig; wirklich
dolphin [ˈdɒlfɪn]	Delfin		

Speaking skills

p. 28 **corner** [ˈkɔːnə]	Ecke	There's a TV in the **corner** of the room.
at the bottom [æt ðə ˈbɒtəm]	unten	The sea is **at the bottom** of the picture.
at the top [æt ðə ˈtɒp]	oben	The sky is **at the top**.

Unit 2 Exploring India

Intro

p. 36 **slum** [slʌm]	Slum; Elendsviertel	Millions of poor people live in **slums**.
Indian [ˈɪndiən]	Inder; Inderin; indisch	Most **Indians** speak English.
p. 37 to **lead** [liːd], **led** [led], **led** [led]	anführen; führen; leiten	A president **leads** a country.
protest [ˈprəʊtest]	Protest; Demonstration	**protest** → to protest
the British [ðə ˈbrɪtɪʃ]	die Briten	There were protests against **the British**.
independent [ˌɪndɪˈpendənt]	unabhängig	India is an **independent** country now.
environmental [ɪnˌvaɪrnˈmentl]	Umwelt-	**environmental** → environment
pollution [pəˈluːʃn]	Verschmutzung	There are problems with **pollution**.
waste [weɪst]	Abfall	**waste** = rubbish
arranged marriage [əˌreɪndʒd ˈmærɪdʒ]	arrangierte Hochzeit	There are many **arranged marriages** in India.
wedding [ˈwedɪŋ]	Hochzeit	There was a big party after the **wedding**.

several ['sevrl]	mehrere; einige; verschiedene	**several** = three or more, but not many

Topic 1

p. 38	**computer programmer** [kəm,pju:tə 'prəʊgræmə]	Programmierer; Programmiererin	My sister is a **computer programmer**.
	IT (Information Technology) [,aɪ'ti: (ɪnfə,meɪʃn tek'nɒlədʒi)]	Informatik; Informationstechnik	Vibhu works for a big **IT** company.
	to **solve** [sɒlv]	lösen	I like **solving** difficult problems.
	to **enjoy** + **-ing** [ɪn'dʒɔɪ … ɪŋ]	mögen; Gefallen finden an; genießen; genießen, … zu tun	I **enjoy** listening to music.
	tour guide ['tʊə ,gaɪd]	Reiseleiter; Reiseleiterin	Our **tour guide** knew a lot about India.
	prince [prɪns]	Prinz	⌀ Achtung Schreibweise! prin**ce**
	assembly line [ə'sembli ,laɪn]	Fließband	Manjit works on the **assembly line**.
	to **make** [meɪk]	*hier:* herstellen	The company **makes** car parts.
	goods *(pl only)* [gʊdz]	Waren; Güter	My parents sell **goods** in a small shop.
	machine [mə'ʃi:n]	Maschine; Automat	The **machines** were very loud.
	true [tru:]	wahr; richtig	It is **true** that he is leaving her.
	virtual ['vɜ:tʃuəl]	virtuell	I'm a **virtual** assistant and work online.
	office ['ɒfɪs]	Büro	My dad works in an **office** in London.

=== Das kenne ich schon ===

world of work

to communicate [kə'mju:nɪkeɪt]	kommunizieren; sich verständigen	office ['ɒfɪs]	Büro
to finish ['fɪnɪʃ]	beenden; fertig machen; erledigen; enden; aufhören	assembly line [ə'sembli ,laɪn]	Fließband
		machine [mə'ʃi:n]	Maschine; Automat
to help [help]	helfen	working hours *(pl)* ['wɜ:kɪŋ ,aʊəz]	Arbeitszeit
to organize ['ɔ:gənaɪz]	organisieren		
to sell [sel], sold [səʊld], sold [səʊld]	verkaufen	customer ['kʌstəmə]	Kunde; Kundin
		phone call ['fəʊn ,kɔ:l]	Telefonanruf; Anruf
to solve [sɒlv]	lösen	reservation [,rezə'veɪʃn]	Reservierung
to start [stɑ:t]	anfangen; beginnen; starten	(software) program [(,sɒfweə) 'prəʊgræm]	(Software)Programm
outside [,aʊt'saɪd]	außen; draußen; im Freien	e-mail ['i:meɪl]	E-Mail

Das kenne ich schon

phrases with -ing

to be good at + -ing [bi: 'gʊd ət ...ɪŋ]	gut sein in; gut sein bei	to hate + -ing [ˌheɪt '...ɪŋ]	hassen; nicht mögen
can't stand + -ing [ˌkɑ:nt 'stænd ...ɪŋ]	nicht ausstehen können; nicht ertragen	to like + -ing [ˌlaɪk '...ɪŋ]	mögen; gerne tun
to enjoy + -ing [ɪnˈdʒɔɪ '...ɪŋ]	mögen; Gefallen finden an; genießen; genießen, ... zu tun	to look forward to + -ing [ˌlʊk 'fɔ:wəd tə ...ɪŋ]	sich freuen auf

Topic 2

p. 42	teenager ['ti:nˌeɪdʒə]	Teenager; Jugendlicher; Jugendliche	Teenagers in India must work hard.
	economy [ɪˈkɒnəmi]	Wirtschaft	R экономия
	to grow [grəʊ], grew [gru:], grown [grəʊn]	wachsen; anbauen; züchten; ziehen	The economy is growing very fast.
	year-old [jɪərˌˈəʊld]	-jährig; Jahre alt	My 2-year-old sister sleeps a lot.
	farming ['fɑ:mɪŋ]	Landwirtschaft; Ackerbau	farming → farm, farmer
	sustainable [səˈsteɪnəbl]	nachhaltig	Farming needs to be more sustainable.
	fertiliser ['fɜ:tɪlaɪzə]	Dünger	Fertilisers cause pollution of the fields.
	crop [krɒp]	Feldfrucht; Ernte	Crops are the plants that farmers grow.
	to damage ['dæmɪdʒ]	beschädigen; schaden	The fire damaged a lot of houses.
	soil [sɔɪl]	Boden; Erde	Fertilisers pollute the soil.
	sanitation [ˌsænɪˈteɪʃn]	sanitäre Anlagen	Some villages don't have good sanitation.
	toilet ['tɔɪlət]	Toilette	
	to pollute [pəˈluːt]	verschmutzen; verunreinigen	to pollute → pollution
	drinking ['drɪŋkɪŋ]	Trink-	Everyone needs clean drinking water.
	living ['lɪvɪŋ]	Lebensweise; Wohnen; Leben	living → to live

Das kenne ich schon

living in the country

animal ['ænɪml]	Tier	crop [krɒp]	Feldfrucht; Ernte
farm [fɑ:m]	Bauernhof	plant [plɑ:nt]	Pflanze
farmer [fɑ:mə]	Bauer; Bäuerin; Landwirt; Landwirtin	to grow [grəʊ], grew [gru:], grown [grəʊn]	wachsen; anbauen; züchten; ziehen
farming ['fɑ:mɪŋ]	Landwirtschaft; Ackerbau	to feed [fi:d], fed [fed], fed [fed]	füttern
village ['vɪlɪdʒ]	Dorf	fertiliser ['fɜ:tɪlaɪzə]	Dünger
field [fi:ld]	Feld	pollution [pəˈluːʃn]	Verschmutzung
soil [sɔɪl]	Erde; Boden		

Text

p. 46	**certainly** ['sɜːtnli]	auf jeden Fall; offensichtlich; sicher	He **certainly** likes her.
	lawyer ['lɔɪə]	Anwalt; Anwältin; Jurist; Juristin	Gandhi became a **lawyer**.
	non-violent [ˌnɒn'vaɪələnt]	friedlich; gewaltfrei	Gandhi believed in **non-violent** protest.
	to break the law [ˌbreɪk ðə 'lɔː]	gegen das Gesetz verstoßen	Gandhi wasn't afraid to **break the law**.
	prison ['prɪzn]	Gefängnis	He's in **prison**.
	soul [səʊl]	Seele	Mahatma means 'great **soul**'.
p. 47	**salt** [sɔːlt]	Salz	I like **salt** on my chips.
	peaceful ['piːsfl]	friedlich	Gandhi was a **peaceful** man.
	to join [dʒɔɪn]	sich anschließen; beitreten	Come and **join** our team.
	march [maːtʃ]	Marsch; Kundgebung	Gandhi organized non-violent **marches**.
	unfortunately [ʌn'fɔːtʃnətli]	leider; unglücklicherweise	**Unfortunately**, there was a lot of violence.
	Hindu ['hɪnduː]	Hindu; hinduistisch	Gandhi was a **Hindu**.
	to respect [rɪ'spekt]	respektieren	I love and **respect** animals.
	religion [rɪ'lɪdʒn]	Religion	Gandhi respected other **religions**.
	extremist [ɪk'striːmɪst]	Extremist; Extremistin	⬯ Achtung Aussprache!

Das kenne ich schon

protests

march [maːtʃ]	Marsch; Kundgebung	to lead [liːd], led [led], led [led]	anführen; führen; leiten
non-violent [ˌnɒn'vaɪələnt]	friedlich; gewaltfrei		
protest ['prəʊtest]	Protest; Demonstration	violence (no pl) ['vaɪələns]	Gewalt
to protest [prə'test]	protestieren	prison ['prɪzn]	Gefängnis
to fight [faɪt]	kämpfen; (sich) streiten		

Film

feed [fiːd]	ernähren	delivery service [dɪ'lɪvri ˌsɜːvɪs]	Lieferdienst

Writing skills

p. 54	**in time** [ɪn 'taɪm]	rechtzeitig; pünktlich	I hope we'll be there **in time**.
	crazy ['kreɪzi]	verrückt	Look at her! She is **crazy**!
	sacred ['seɪkrɪd]	heilig	In India cows are **sacred**.

Unit 3 Discover South Africa

| p. 62 | to **discover** [dɪˈskʌvə] | entdecken | Let's **discover** the world. |
| | **South Africa** [ˌsaʊθˈæfrɪkə] | Südafrika | **South Africa** is a beautiful country. |

Intro

	parliament [ˈpɑːləmənt]	Parlament	∅ Achtung Schreibweise! parli<u>a</u>ment
	African [ˈæfrɪkən]	afrikanisch; aus Afrika; Afrikaner; Afrikanerin	T Afrikalı
	apartheid (no pl) [əˈpɑːtaɪt]	Apartheid	**Apartheid** started in the early 1940s.
	to **separate** [ˈsepreɪt]	trennen	∅ Achtung Schreibweise! sep<u>a</u>rate
	township [ˈtaʊnʃɪp]	Township (ehemalige Wohnsiedlungen für die schwarze Bevölkerung in Südafrika); Armutsviertel	Poor people live in **townships**.
	to **end** [end]	enden; beenden; aufhören	Classes **ended** at 2:30 p.m. on Friday.
p. 63	**South African** [ˌsaʊθˈæfrɪkən]	Südafrikaner; Südafrikanerin; südafrikanisch; aus Südafrika	**South African** → South Africa
	high school [ˈhaɪ ˌskuːl]	High School (weiterführende Schule, Oberstufe)	He didn't finish **high school**.
	rich [rɪtʃ]	reich	Some people in South Africa are very **rich**.
	electricity [ˌelɪkˈtrɪsəti]	Strom; Elektrizität	A lot of houses don't have **electricity**.
	safari [səˈfɑːri]	Safari	👄 Achtung Aussprache!
	lion [ˈlaɪən]	Löwe	
	elephant [ˈelɪfənt]	Elefant	
	buffalo (sg) [ˈbʌfləʊ], **buffaloes** (pl) [ˈbʌfləʊz]	Büffel	We saw **buffaloes** at the zoo.
	square [skweə]	Quadrat-	It has an area of 1,100 **square** kilometres.

Topic 1

p. 64	to **hit** [hɪt]	hier: anfahren; rammen	The car **hit** the bus.
	to **injure** [ˈɪndʒə]	verletzen	Piet was **injured** in the accident.
	driving licence [ˈdraɪvɪŋ ˌlaɪsns]	Führerschein	You need a **driving licence** to drive a car.
	to **add** [æd]	hinzufügen	"I'll come back later", she **added**.

to **brake** [breɪk]	bremsen	The car **braked** but it was too late.
to **skid** [skɪd]	schleudern; schlittern	The car **skidded** and hit the bus.
to **crash** [kræʃ]	krachen	The car **crashed** into the bus.
wallet ['wɒlɪt]	Brieftasche; Geldbeutel; Geldbörse	Oh no! I forgot my **wallet**!
bang [bæŋ]	peng; Knall	There was a noise and then, **bang**!
police station [pə'li:s ˌsteɪʃn]	Polizeirevier; Polizeiwache	We all had to go to the **police station**.
detail ['di:teɪl]	Detail; Einzelheit	T detay

Das kenne ich schon

road accidents

road accident ['rəʊd ˌæksɪdnt]	Verkehrsunfall		detail ['di:teɪl]	Detail; Einzelheit
accident ['æksɪdnt]	Unfall		hospital ['hɒspɪtl]	Krankenhaus
fast [fɑ:st]	schnell		to injure ['ɪndʒə]	verletzen
to hit [hɪt], hit [hɪt], hit [hɪt]	anfahren; rammen		to drive [draɪv], drove [drəʊv], driven ['drɪvn]	fahren
to brake [breɪk]	bremsen		driver ['draɪvə]	Fahrer; Fahrerin
to skid [skɪd]	schleudern; schlittern		driving licence ['draɪvɪŋ ˌlaɪsns]	Führerschein
to crash [kræʃ]	krachen			
witness ['wɪtnəs]	Zeuge; Zeugin		damage ['dæmɪdʒ]	Schäden; Schaden; Beschädigung
bang [bæŋ]	peng; Knall			
police station [pə'li:s ˌsteɪʃn]	Polizeirevier; Polizeiwache		to damage ['dæmɪdʒ]	schaden; beschädigen
police officer [pə'li:s ˌɒfɪsə]	Polizeibeamter; Polizeibeamtin		news [nju:z]	Nachricht(en)
			newspaper ['nju:sˌpeɪpə]	Zeitung

Topic 2

p. 68	**role model** ['rəʊl ˌmɒdl]	Vorbild	Miriam Makeba is Mia's **role model**.
	podcast ['pɒdkɑ:st]	Podcast	I got the new **podcast** last night.
	inspiring [ɪn'spaɪərɪŋ]	inspirierend; anregend	The programme is about **inspiring** people.
	songwriter ['sɒŋˌraɪtə]	Songschreiber; Songschreiberin; Liedermacher; Liedermacherin	She's a **songwriter** – she writes songs.
	to **admire** [əd'maɪə]	bewundern	I don't know who I **admire** most.
	inspiration [ˌɪnspɪ'reɪʃn]	Inspiration; Eingebung	⇔ Achtung Aussprache!
	to **achieve** [ə'tʃi:v]	erreichen; erfolgreich sein; leisten; vollbringen	Miriam Makeba **achieved** a lot.
	director [dɪ'rektə]	Regisseur; Regisseurin	Zackie Achmat is a famous film **director**.
	gay [geɪ]	homosexuell; schwul; Schwuler	He's **gay**. He loves men.

lesbian ['lezbiən]	homosexuell; lesbisch; Lesbe	She is **lesbian** and loves women.
HIV [ˌeɪtʃaɪ'vi:]	HIV; HI-Virus; HIV-	There is more information about **HIV** today.
AIDS [eɪdz]	Aids *(erworbene Immunabwehr- schwäche)*	He has helped many people with **AIDS**.
disease [dɪ'zi:z]	Krankheit	This new **disease** is very dangerous.
medication [ˌmedɪ'keɪʃn]	Medikament; Arznei; Arzneimit- tel	Medicine and tablets are **medication**.
at first [ət 'fɜ:st]	zuerst; zunächst	I wasn't happy **at first**, then it was OK.
right away [ˌraɪt ə'weɪ]	sofort; gleich	He didn't take medication **right away**.
drug [drʌg]	Medikament; Arznei; Arzneimit- tel	He fought for cheaper **drugs**.
only ['əʊnli]	*hier:* erst	He **only** took medication much later.
to pay [peɪ]	bezahlen	Poorer people couldn't **pay** for it.

━━━ Das kenne ich schon ━━━

for – since

for [fɔ:]		seit	since [sɪns]		seit
for two years [fə 'tu: ˌjɪəz]		seit zwei Jahren	since 2020 [sɪns 'twentitwenti]		seit 2020
for three hours [fə 'θri: ˌaʊəz]		seit drei Stunden	since last year [ˌsɪns 'la:st jɪə]		seit letztem Jahr
for a long time [fər ə 'lɒŋ taɪm]		seit Langem	since I was born [sɪns ˌaɪ wəz 'bɔ:n]		seit meiner Geburt
for many years [fə 'mæni ˌjɪəz]		seit vielen Jahren	since 3 o'clock [sɪns ˌθri: ə'klɒk]		seit 3 Uhr

---

Text

p. 72	unemployed [ˌʌnɪm'plɔɪd]	arbeitslos	**unemployed** → employee
	organization [ˌɔ:gnaɪ'zeɪʃn]	Organisation	**organization** → organize
	to cut down [ˌkʌt 'daʊn]	fällen	Our workers **cut down** trees.
	to control [kən'trəʊl]	kontrollieren	The workers **control** the area.
	to be in charge (of) [bi: ˌɪn 'tʃɑ:dʒ (əv)]	leiten; zuständig sein (für); die Verantwortung tragen (für)	Shaka would like to **be in charge of** the office.
	guitar [gɪ'tɑ:]	Gitarre	
	a bit [ə 'bɪt]	ein bisschen	At first, I was **a bit** worried.
	fortunately ['fɔ:tʃnətli]	zum Glück	**fortunately** ↔ unfortunately
	Afrikaans [ˌæfrɪ'kɑ:ns]	Afrikaans *(Sprache in Südafrika)*	Keeya speaks English and **Afrikaans**.
p. 73	Sesotho [sɪ'su:tu:]	Sesotho *(Sprache in Südafrika)*	I speak the **Sesotho** language at home.
	kindergarten ['kɪndəˌgɑ:tn]	Kindergarten	✐ Achtung Schreibweise: <u>k</u>indergarten

preschool [priːˈskuːl]	Vorschul-; Vorschule	Do you remember your **preschool** teacher?
to **do handicrafts** [ˌduː ˈhændɪkrɑːfts]	basteln	I **do handicrafts** in my free time.
a week [ə ˈwiːk]	in der Woche; pro Woche	I have school five days **a week**.
medical insurance [ˌmedɪkl ɪnˈʃʊərns]	Krankenversicherung	My family doesn't have **medical insurance**.
hope [həʊp]	Hoffnung	**hope** → to hope

Film

baboon [bəˈbuːn]	Pavian	flower [ˈflaʊə]	Blume

Mediation skills

p. 80	**distance** [ˈdɪstns]	Entfernung; Distanz	Find out the **distance** from A to B.
	gate [geɪt]	Tor	
	emergency [ɪˈmɜːdʒnsi]	Notfall	Help! It's an **emergency**.
	to **disturb** [dɪˈstɜːb]	stören; belästigen	Never **disturb** the animals.
	as long as [əz ˈlɒŋ əz]	solange; sofern	**As long as** we're together, we'll be safe.
	to **follow** [ˈfɒləʊ]	befolgen; folgen	**to follow** → follower
	rule [ruːl]	Regel	We must follow the **rules**.
	situation [ˌsɪtjuˈeɪʃn]	Situation	This was a very dangerous **situation**.
p. 81	**nature** [ˈneɪtʃə]	Natur	The ranger likes **nature** very much.
	could [kʊd]	könnte	**Could** you open the window, please?
	to **repeat** [rɪˈpiːt]	wiederholen	Could you **repeat** it, please?
	to **explain** [ɪkˈspleɪn]	erklären	Could you **explain** that again, please?

Unit 4 News from New Zealand

p. 88	**New Zealand** [ˌnjuːˈziːlənd]	Neuseeland	**New Zealand** is near Australia.

Intro

careers [kəˈrɪəz]	Berufs-	**careers** → career
advisor [ədˈvaɪzə]	Berater; Beraterin	**advisor** → advice
a third [ə ˈθɜːd]	ein Drittel	**A third** of my class is boys.
industry [ˈɪndəstri]	Industriezweig; Gewerbe	⇔ Achtung Aussprache!

p. 89	**volunteer** [ˌvɒlənˈtɪə]	Freiwilliger; Freiwillige; ehren-amtlicher Helfer; ehrenamtliche Helferin	**Volunteers** help people and don't get any money.
	member [ˈmembə]	Mitglied	The **members** of my family live together.
	club [klʌb]	Verein	R клуб
	free-time [ˌfriːˈtaɪm]	Freizeit-	Rugby is a popular **free-time** activity.
	Maori [ˈmaʊri]	Maori-; maorisch; Maori	R маори T Maori
	people [ˈpiːpl]	*hier:* Volk	What do you know about the Maori **people**?
	landscape [ˈlændskeɪp]	Landschaft	New Zealand has amazing **landscapes**.
	volcano *(sg)* [vɒlˈkeɪnəʊ], **volcanoes** *(pl)* [vɒlˈkeɪnəʊz]	Vulkan	R вулкан T volkan

Topic 1

p. 90	**form** [fɔːm]	Formular	The careers advisor looked at Liam's **form**.
	future [ˈfjuːtʃə]	zukünftig; Zukunfts-	Liam isn't sure about his **future** career.
	Ms [mɪz]	Frau *(Anrede)*	Our teacher is called **Ms** Miller.
	to **complete** [kəmˈpliːt]	ausfüllen; machen	He **completed** the form online.
	suitability [ˌsuːtəˈbɪləti]	Eignungs-; Eignung; Tauglichkeit	The **suitability** test was useful.
	test [test]	Test; Klassenarbeit	Who likes class **tests**?
	result [rɪˈzʌlt]	Ergebnis	You can find the **results** here.
	work experience [ˈwɜːk ɪkˌspɪəriəns]	Berufserfahrung; Praktikum	Liam wants to get some **work experience**.
	mechanic [mɪˈkænɪk]	Mechaniker; Mechanikerin	Liam doesn't want to become a **mechanic**.
	garage [ˈgærɑːʒ]	Kfz-Werkstatt; Tankstelle; Garage	Mechanics work in **garages**.
	to **go wrong** [ˌgəʊ ˈrɒŋ]	schiefgehen	When things **go wrong**, I don't get angry.
	calm [kɑːm]	ruhig; friedlich	I was **calm** when I spoke to the police.
	support [səˈpɔːt]	Unterstützung; Hilfe	My parents give me lots of **support**.
	communication [kəˌmjuːnɪˈkeɪʃn]	Kommunikation	**communication** → to communicate
	might [maɪt]	könnte	We **might** see a wild animal.
	tourist information centre [ˌtʊərɪst ɪnfəˈmeɪʃn ˌsentə]	Touristeninformation	Where's the **Tourist Information Centre**?
	to **study (for)** sth [ˈstʌdi (fə)]	(auf einen Abschluss) studieren; (für) etw. lernen	You can **study for a certificate** at school.
	certificate [səˈtɪfɪkət]	Zertifikat; Bescheinigung; Urkunde; Zeugnis	⚠ Achtung Schreibweise! certifi<u>ca</u>te

to **take an exam** [ˌteɪk ˌən ɪɡˈzæm]	eine Prüfung schreiben; ein Examen schreiben	You'll have to **take an exam** at the end.
careers day [kəˈrɪəz ˌdeɪ]	Berufsinformationstag	There's a **careers day** at school next week.
employer [ɪmˈplɔɪə]	Arbeitgeber; Arbeitgeberin	**employer** → employee
to **count on sb** [ˌkaʊnt ˈɒn]	sich auf jmdn. verlassen	You can **count on us**.
to **mind sth** [maɪnd]	etwas gegen etw. haben; einem etwas ausmachen	I don't **mind** hard work.
tool [tuːl]	Werkzeug; Gerät	

=== **Das kenne ich schon** ===

careers advice

career [kəˈrɪə]	Laufbahn; Karriere; Beruf	to take an exam [ˌteɪk ˌən ɪɡˈzæm]	eine Prüfung schreiben; ein Examen schreiben
careers [kəˈrɪəz]	Berufs-	certificate [səˈtɪfɪkət]	Zertifikat; Bescheinigung; Urkunde; Zeugnis
advice [ədˈvaɪs]	Rat; Ratschlag		
advisor [ədˈvaɪzə]	Berater; Beraterin	qualification [ˌkwɒlɪfɪˈkeɪʃn]	Ausbildung; Qualifikation; Abschluss; Schulabschluss
careers day [kəˈrɪəz ˌdeɪ]	Berufsinformationstag	future [ˈfjuːtʃə]	Zukunft
to complete [kəmˈpliːt]	ausfüllen; machen	company [ˈkʌmpəni]	Unternehmen; Firma; Gesellschaft
suitability [ˌsuːtəˈbɪləti]	Eignungs-, Eignung; Tauglichkeit		
		employer [ɪmˈplɔɪə]	Arbeitgeber; Arbeitgeberin
test [test]	Test; Klassenarbeit	training [ˈtreɪnɪŋ]	Ausbildung; Training
result [rɪˈzʌlt]	Ergebnis		

Topic 2

p. 94	**retail** [ˈriːteɪl]	Einzelhandel	Would you like a job in **retail**?
	report [rɪˈpɔːt]	Bericht	The students are going to write a **report**.
	apprenticeship [əˈprentɪʃɪp]	Ausbildung; Lehre	I will do an **apprenticeship** after school.
	shop assistant [ˈʃɒp əˌsɪstnt]	Verkäufer; Verkäuferin	The **shop assistant** gave me my things.
	product [ˈprɒdʌkt]	Produkt; Erzeugnis	⇔ Achtung Aussprache!
	checkout [ˈtʃekaʊt]	Kasse	Please pay at the **checkouts**.
	to **fill** [fɪl]	füllen; befüllen	I **fill** the shelves and make them look nice.
	to **present** [prɪˈzent]	präsentieren	**to present** → presentation
	to **work** [wɜːk]	funktionieren	I can't call you, my phone doesn't **work**.
	supplier [səˈplaɪə]	Zulieferer; Anbieter	We get our products from local **suppliers**.
	to **order** [ˈɔːdə]	bestellen	The supermarket **ordered** more fish.
	to **open** [ˈəʊpn]	eröffnen	The supermarket **opened** in 2008.

community [kə'mju:nəti]	Gemeinde; Gemeinschaft	Many **communities** don't have enough money.
to **donate** [də'neɪt]	spenden; stiften	We **donate** food to local charities.
to **reduce** [rɪ'dju:s]	reduzieren; vermindern; verringern	We must **reduce** the rubbish in our cities.
worth of ['wɜ:θˌɒv]	im Wert von	We gave NZ$3 million's **worth of** food.
intern ['ɪntɜ:n]	Praktikant; Praktikantin	**intern** → internship
to **be included** [bi: ɪn'klu:dɪd]	mit enthalten sein; inbegriffen sein	A picnic lunch **is included** in the trip.
although [ɔ:l'ðəʊ]	obwohl	**Although** she was slow, she wasn't late.

Das kenne ich schon

in a supermarket

to **sell** [sel], **sold** [səʊld], **sold** [səʊld]	verkaufen	**checkout** ['tʃekaʊt]	Kasse
retail ['ri:teɪl]	Einzelhandel	**customer service** [ˌkʌstəmə 'sɜ:vɪs]	Kundenbetreuung; Kundendienst; Kundenservice
shop [ʃɒp]	Laden; Geschäft		
shop assistant ['ʃɒpəˌsɪstnt]	Verkäufer; Verkäuferin	**supplier** [sə'plaɪə]	Zulieferer; Anbieter
		to **deliver** [dɪ'lɪvə]	liefern; ausliefern
to **fill** [fɪl]	füllen; befüllen	**product** ['prɒdʌkt]	Produkt; Erzeugnis
shelf (sg) [ʃelf], **shelves** (pl) [ʃelvz]	Regal; Regalbrett	**customer** ['kʌstəmə]	Kunde; Kundin
to **pack** [pæk]	einpacken; packen	to **buy** [baɪ], **bought** [bɔ:t], **bought** [bɔ:t]	kaufen
bag [bæg]	Tasche; Tüte		

Text

p. 98 **rider** ['raɪdə]	Reiter; Reiterin	**rider** → to ride
great- [greɪt]	Ur-	My **great-**grandfather ist very old.
grandmother ['grænˌmʌðə]	Großmutter	**grandmother** = grandma
chief [tʃi:f]	Häuptling	The leader of a group or tribe.
to **found** [faʊnd]	gründen; begründen	The city was **founded** in 1718.
bay [beɪ]	Bucht	
prayer [preə]	Gebet	Say a **prayer** for me on Sunday.
deep [di:p]	tief	The stone was too **deep**.
to **try hard** [ˌtraɪ 'ha:d]	sich anstrengen	I always **try hard** in my class tests.
to **get back** [ˌget 'bæk]	zurückkommen; zurückgehen	When he **got back** home, he felt very sad.

to **lament** [lə'ment]	klagen	Paka **lamented** very loudly in his room.
because of [bɪ'kɒz‿əv]	wegen	I was late **because of** the weather.
to **wish** [wɪʃ]	wünschen	I **wish** every day was Saturday.
out [aʊt]	hinaus	And then we went **out** into the sea.
wonder ['wʌndə]	Wunder	No **wonder** the boys couldn't get it.
to **stand up** [ˌstænd‿'ʌp]	aufstehen	He **stood up** and left the room.
mask [mɑ:sk]	Maske	Ⓡ маска Ⓣ maske
to **point** [pɔɪnt]	zeigen	**Point** to the cake you would like.
dolphin ['dɒlfɪn]	Delfin	Ⓡ дельфин
towards [tə'wɔ:dz]	auf … zu; in Richtung	We were walking **towards** the station.
to **seem** [si:m]	scheinen	Kahu **seemed** to talk to the dolphins.
to **nod** [nɒd]	nicken	The dolphins seemed to **nod**.
to **pick up** [ˌpɪk‿'ʌp]	aufheben	The man **picked up** something.
to **kiss** [kɪs]	küssen	I would never **kiss** him.
crayfish ['kreɪfɪʃ]	Languste; Flusskrebs	
close [kləʊs]	fest	They held each other **close**.
carving ['kɑ:vɪŋ]	Schnitzerei	The king got a **carving** as a present.

p. 99 (marginal note next to **wonder**)

— Das kenne ich schon

conjunctions

after ['ɑ:ftə]	nachdem	if [ɪf]	wenn; falls; ob
although [ɔ:l'ðəʊ]	obwohl	since [sɪns]	seit; seitdem
and [ænd]	und	so [səʊ]	also; deshalb
because [bɪ'kɒz]	weil; da	so that [səʊ 'ðæt]	damit; sodass
before [bɪ'fɔ:]	bevor; vorher; zuvor	until [ʌn'tɪl]	bis
but [bʌt]	aber	when [wen]	als; wenn
however [haʊ'evə]	jedoch	while [waɪl]	während

Das kenne ich schon

phrasal verbs

to ask about [ˌɑːsk əˈbaʊt]	fragen nach; sich erkundigen nach	to get out [ˌgetˈaʊt]	aussteigen; herauskommen
to cut down [ˌkʌt ˈdaʊn]	fällen	to get up [ˌgetˈʌp]	aufstehen
to drive off [ˌdraɪvˈɒf]	wegfahren	to look after [ˌlʊkˈɑːftə]	aufpassen auf; hüten; sich kümmern um
to fall off [ˌfɔːlˈɒf]	stürzen von; herunterfallen; hinunterfallen	to look at [ˈlʊkˌət]	anschauen
		to rely on [rɪˈlaɪ ɒn]	sich verlassen auf; vertrauen auf
to find out [ˌfaɪndˈaʊt]	herausfinden		
to get in [ˌgetˈɪn]	einsteigen	to stand for [ˈstænd fə]	stehen für
		to take out [ˌteɪkˈaʊt]	hinausbringen

Film

natural [ˈnætʃrl]	Natur-; natürlich	pool [puːl]	Tümpel

Writing skills

p. 106	Kiwi [ˈkiːwiː]	Kiwi (Kosename für Neuseeländer)	People from New Zealand are also called **Kiwis**.
	enquiry [ɪnˈkwaɪəri]	Anfrage	How do I write an **enquiry**?
	c/o [siːˈəʊ]	bei	**c/o** Ms Miller
	RE [riː]	Betr.	**RE**: Your ad for shop assistants
	qualified [ˈkwɒlɪfaɪd]	qualifiziert	**qualified** → qualification
	enclosed [ɪnˈkləʊzd]	beigefügt; anbei	My certificates and CV are **enclosed**.

Dictionary

Die Abkürzungen geben an, wo das Wort zum ersten Mal vorkommt.
Verwendete Abkürzungen und Zeichen:

U = Unit
* = unregelmäßige Verben

I = Band 1   II = Band 2   III = Band 3   IV = Band 4
V U1, 27 = Band 5, Unit 1, S.27
<V U1, 19> = nur zum Nachschlagen, gehört nicht zum Lernwortschatz

A

a [ə] ein; eine I
  a bit [ə ˈbɪt] ein bisschen V U3, 72
  a few [ə ˈfjuː] ein paar; einige; wenige IV
  a little (bit) [ə ˈlɪtl (bɪt)] ein (kleines) bisschen; ein (klein) wenig II
  a lot [ə ˈlɒt] viel; sehr I
  a lot of [ə ˈlɒt ˌəv] viel; viele; eine Menge I
  a week [ə ˈwiːk] in der Woche; pro Woche V U3, 73
  a year [ə ˈjɪə] pro Jahr; im Jahr IV
  a/one hundred [ˈhʌndrəd] hundert; einhundert I
  a/one thousand [ˈθaʊznd] tausend; eintausend II
a.m. [ˌeɪˈem] vormittags *(Uhrzeit)* III
***to be able to (do sth)** [biː ˈeɪbl tə] (etw. tun) können; (zu etw.) fähig sein *(Ersatzform für can)* IV
Aboriginal [ˌæbəˈrɪdʒnl] Aborigine-; zur Aborigine-Kultur gehörend V U1, 12
  Aboriginal people [ˌæbəˌrɪdʒnl ˈpiːpl] die Aborigines V U1, 11
about [əˈbaʊt] über I; ungefähr; circa; etwa II; an III; wegen IV
  to hang about [ˌhæŋ əˈbaʊt] herumhängen I
  out and about [ˌaʊt ən əˈbaʊt] unterwegs III
above [əˈbʌv] über; oberhalb II
accent [ˈæksnt] Akzent III
accident [ˈæksɪdnt] Unfall I
  road accident [ˈrəʊd ˌæksɪdnt] Verkehrsunfall <V U3, 64>

to achieve [əˈtʃiːv] erreichen; erfolgreich sein; leisten; vollbringen V U3, 68
across [əˈkrɒs] über II
to act [ækt] spielen; mitspielen III
  acting workshop [ˈæktɪŋ ˌwɜːkʃɒp] Schauspielworkshop III
activity [ækˈtɪvəti] Aktivität I
actor [ˈæktə] Schauspieler; Schauspielerin; Darsteller; Darstellerin III
to add [æd] hinzufügen V U3, 64
address [əˈdres] Adresse IV
adjective [ˈædʒɪktɪv] Adjektiv; Eigenschaftswort <III>
to admire [ədˈmaɪə] bewundern V U3, 68
adventure [ədˈventʃə] Abenteuer; Erlebnis III
adverb [ˈædvɜːb] Adverb <IV>
  adverb of manner [ˌædvɜːb əv ˈmænə] Adverb der Art und Weise <IV>
ad(vert) (= advertisement) [ˈæd(vɜːt) (ədˈvɜːtɪsmənt)] Werbung; Anzeige III
advice [ədˈvaɪs] Rat; Ratschlag III
to advise sb [ədˈvaɪz] jmdn. beraten; jmdm. (etw.) raten <V U2, 149>
advisor [ədˈvaɪzə] Berater; Beraterin V U4, 88
  tax advisor [ˈtæks ədˌvaɪzə] Steuerberater; Steuerberaterin <V U2, 148>
afraid [əˈfreɪd] ängstlich V U1, 12
  to be afraid [biː əˈfreɪd] befürchten V U1, 16
  I'm afraid [aɪm əˈfreɪd] leider IV

African [ˈæfrɪkən] afrikanisch; aus Afrika; Afrikaner; Afrikanerin V U3, 62
  African American [ˌæfrɪkən əˈmerɪkən] Afroamerikaner; Afroamerikanerin IV
  South African [ˌsaʊθ ˈæfrɪkən] Südafrikaner; Südafrikanerin; südafrikanisch; aus Südafrika V U3, 63
Afrikaans [ˌæfrɪˈkɑːns] Afrikaans *(Sprache in Südafrika)* V U3, 72
after [ˈɑːftə] nach I; nachdem IV
  after that [ˌɑːftə ˈðæt] danach I
afternoon [ˌɑːftəˈnuːn] Nachmittag I
again [əˈgen] noch einmal; wieder I
against [əˈgenst] gegen III
check-in agent [ˌtʃekɪn ˈeɪdʒnt] Check-in-Mitarbeiter; Check-in-Mitarbeiterin IV
travel agent [ˈtrævl ˌeɪdʒnt] Reisebürokaufmann; Reisebürokauffrau IV
travel agent's [ˈtrævl ˌeɪdʒnts] Reisebüro IV
ago [əˈgəʊ] vor II
to agree (on) [əˈgriː (ɒn)] sich einigen (auf) <V U4, 103>
to agree (with) [əˈgriː (wɪð)] zustimmen; einer Meinung sein (mit) II
AIDS [eɪdz] Aids *(erworbene Immunabwehrschwäche)* V U3, 68
air [eə] Luft III
airport [ˈeəpɔːt] Flughafen IV
Alaskan [əˈlæskən] alaskisch; Alaska- IV
alga *(sg)* [ˈælgə], **algae** *(pl)* [ˈældʒiː] Alge V U1, 20
all [ɔːl] alle; ganz I
  all of [ˈɔːl ˌəv] ganz II

all over [ˌɔːl ˈəʊvə] in ganz; überall II

all around the world [ɔːl əˌraʊnd ðə ˈwɜːld] in aller Welt II

All the best, [ˌɔːl ðə ˈbest] Alles Gute II

of all the states [əvˌɔːl ðə ˌsteɪts] von allen Staaten IV

all-day [ˈɔːldeɪ] Ganztages- III

allergy [ˈælədʒi] Allergie <V U3, 74>

alligator [ˈælɪɡeɪtə] Alligator II

*to be **allowed** to (do sth) [bi: əˈlaʊd tə] (etw. tun) dürfen IV

almost [ˈɔːlməʊst] fast; beinahe <V U3, 76>

alone [əˈləʊn] allein V U1, 20

alphabet [ˈælfəbet] Alphabet <I>

alphabetical [ˌælfəˈbetɪkl] alphabetisch <II>

already [ɔːlˈredi] schon; bereits III

also [ˈɔːlsəʊ] auch I

although [ɔːlˈðəʊ] obwohl V U4, 94

always [ˈɔːlweɪz] immer I; schon immer III

amazing [əˈmeɪzɪŋ] erstaunlich; unglaublich; toll II

American [əˈmerɪkən] amerikanisch; Amerikanisch; aus Amerika; Amerikaner; Amerikanerin II

African American [ˌæfrɪkən əˈmerɪkən] Afroamerikaner; Afroamerikanerin IV

American football [əˌmerɪkən ˈfʊtbɔːl] American Football II

Native American [ˌneɪtɪv əˈmerɪkən] Ureinwohner Amerikas; Ureinwohnerin Amerikas; Indianer; Indianerin; indianisch III

an [æn] ein; eine I

and [ænd] und I

angry [ˈæŋgri] wütend; zornig; verärgert; böse II

animal [ˈænɪml] Tier I

animal rescue shelter [ˈænɪml ˈreskjuː ˌʃeltə] Tierheim I

ankle [ˈæŋkl] Fußgelenk; Fußknöchel <V U1, 147>

announcement [əˈnaʊnsmənt] Durchsage; Ankündigung <II>

annoyed [əˈnɔɪd] verärgert IV

another [əˈnʌðə] ein anderer; noch ein; andere IV

answer [ˈɑːnsə] Antwort II

to **answer** [ˈɑːnsə] antworten; beantworten II

any [ˈeni] irgendwelche; irgendeine I

not … any more [ˌnɒt … eni ˈmɔː] nicht mehr III

not … any [ˌnɒt … eni] kein; keine III

anybody [ˈeniˌbɒdi] irgendjemand; jemand; jeder III

anyone [ˈeniwʌn] irgendjemand; irgendeiner IV

anything [ˈeniθɪŋ] etwas; irgendetwas III

not … anything [nɒt … ˈeniθɪŋ] nichts III

Anything else? [ˌeniθɪŋ ˈels] Darf es sonst noch etwas sein? I

apartheid (no pl) [əˈpɑːtaɪt] Apartheid V U3, 62

apartment (AE) [əˈpɑːtmənt] Wohnung; Apartment IV

app [æp] App IV

apple [ˈæpl] Apfel I

applicant [ˈæplɪkənt] Bewerber; Bewerberin <V U4, 103>

application [ˌæplɪˈkeɪʃn] Bewerbung IV

letter of application [ˌletər əv ˌæplɪˈkeɪʃn] Bewerbungsschreiben IV

to **apply** (for) [əˈplaɪ (fə)] sich bewerben (für/um) IV

appointment [əˈpɔɪntmənt] Termin V U1, 16

apprenticeship [əˈprentɪʃɪp] Ausbildung; Lehre V U4, 94

April [ˈeɪprl] April I

area [ˈeəriə] Gebiet; Gegend; Areal IV; Fläche; Bereich V U1, 20

argument [ˈɑːgjəmənt] Auseinandersetzung; Streit II

arm [ɑːm] Arm II

around [əˈraʊnd] um … herum II; durch; um III ; unterwegs (in) V U1, 10; vorbei <V U1, 147>

to walk around [ˌwɔːk əˈraʊnd] umherlaufen; herumlaufen <I>

arranged marriage [əˌreɪndʒd ˈmærɪdʒ] arrangierte Hochzeit V U2, 37

arrival [əˈraɪvl] Ankömmling IV

to **arrive** [əˈraɪv] ankommen I

Art [ɑːt] Kunst I

article [ˈɑːtɪkl] Artikel; Bericht (in einer Zeitung) <V U1, 20>

artist [ˈɑːtɪst] Künstler; Künstlerin III

as [æz] wie; als II

… as well as … [əz ˈwel əz] sowohl … als auch … II

as … as [əz … əz] so … wie III

as long as [əz ˈlɒŋ əz] solange; sofern V U3, 80

as much as [əz ˈmʌtʃ əz] bis zu <V U1, 23>

to **ask** [ɑːsk] fragen I

to ask about [ˈɑːsk əˌbaʊt] fragen nach; sich erkundigen nach II

to ask for [ˈɑːsk fɔː] bitten um <III>

to ask the way [ɑːsk ðə ˈweɪ] nach dem Weg fragen <II>

aspect [ˈæspekt] Aspekt; Gesichtspunkt; Blickwinkel <IV>

assembly line [əˈsembli ˌlaɪn] Fließband V U2, 38

assistant [əˈsɪstnt] Verkäufer; Verkäuferin I; Helfer; Helferin; Assistent; Assistentin; Mitarbeiter; Mitarbeiterin IV

shop assistant [ˈʃɒp əˌsɪstnt] Verkäufer; Verkäuferin V U4, 94

at [æt] zu; in; an; auf; um; bei I

at first [ət ˈfɜːst] zuerst; zunächst V U3, 68

at home [ət ˈhəʊm] zu Hause; daheim I

at night [ət ˈnaɪt] nachts IV

at school [ət ˈskuːl] in der Schule I

at the back (of) [ət ðə ˈbæk (ɒv)] hinten (in) <III>

at the bottom [æt ðə ˈbɒtəm] unten V U1, 28

at the doctor's [ət ðə ˈdɒktəz] beim Arzt II

at the end [ət ði ˈend] am Ende II

at the moment [ət ðə ˈməʊmənt] im Moment; momentan II

at the same time [ət ðə seɪm ˈtaɪm] gleichzeitig; nebenher II

at

s six • **z** zoo • **ʃ** she • **ʒ** revision • **h** her • **m** me • **n** no • **ŋ** sing • **iə** hear • **l** let • **r** red • **j** yes　　173

at the seaside [ət ðə 'siːsaɪd] am Meer I

at the top [æt ðə 'tɒp] oben V U1, 28

ate [eɪt] simple past von *to eat* II

attic ['ætɪk] Dachboden I

August ['ɔːgəst] August I

aunt [aːnt] Tante I

Australian [ɒsˈtreɪliən] Australier; Australierin; australisch V U1, 10

autumn ['ɔːtəm] Herbst II

available [əˈveɪləbl] erhältlich; verfügbar IV

to avoid [əˈvɔɪd] aus dem Weg gehen; vermeiden; meiden; ausweichen IV

away [əˈweɪ] weg; entfernt II

to be a long way away [biː ə 'lɒŋ ˌweɪ əˈweɪ] weit weg sein II

right away [raɪt əˈweɪ] sofort; gleich V U3, 68

awesome ['ɔːsəm] großartig; toll; beeindruckend III

awful ['ɔːfl] schrecklich; furchtbar I

B

baboon [bəˈbuːn] Pavian <V U3, 75>

back [bæk] Rücken <V U1, 147>

at the back (of) [ət ðə 'bæk (ɒv)] hinten (in) <III>

back [bæk] zurück II

to get back [get 'bæk] zurückkommen; zurückgehen V U4, 98

backache ['bækeɪk] Rückenschmerzen <V U1, 147>

background ['bækgraʊnd] Hintergrund III

bacon ['beɪkn] Speck I

bad [bæd] schlecht I; schlimm II

That's too bad. [ˌðæts tuː 'bæd] Schade! II

bag [bæg] Tasche; Tüte; Sack I

bagpipes (pl) ['bægpaɪps] Dudelsack III

baker ['beɪkə] Bäcker; Bäckerin <V U2, 148>

balcony ['bælkəni] Balkon I

ball [bɔːl] Ball I; Kugel III

cannon ball ['kænən ˌbɔːl] Kanonenkugel III

banana [bəˈnaːnə] Banane I

band [bænd] Band; Musikgruppe II

bang [bæŋ] peng; Knall V U3, 64

snack bar ['snæk ˌbaː] Imbissstube; Café I

barbecue ['baːbɪkjuː] Grill; Grillfest I

to bark [baːk] bellen II

base [beɪs] Base; Mal III

baseball ['beɪsbɔːl] Baseball III

basic ['beɪsɪk] grundlegend <III>

basket ['baːskɪt] Basketballkorb; Korb III

basketball ['baːskɪtbɔːl] Basketball II

bat [bæt] Fledermaus I

bathroom ['baːθrʊm] Bad(ezimmer) II

batter ['bætə] Schlagmann; Schlagfrau III

bay [beɪ] Bucht V U4, 98

*to be [biː] sein I

to be a long way away [biː ə 'lɒŋ ˌweɪ əˈweɪ] weit weg sein II

to be able to (do sth) [biː 'eɪbl tə] (etw. tun) können; (zu etw.) fähig sein (Ersatzform für can) IV

to be afraid [biː əˈfreɪd] befürchten V U1, 16

to be allowed to (do sth) [biː əˈlaʊd tə] (etw. tun) dürfen IV

to be born [biː 'bɔːn] geboren werden IV

to be fed up (with) [biː ˌfed 'ʌp (wɪð)] die Nase voll haben (von) III

to be fun [biː 'fʌn] Spaß machen; witzig sein II

to be going to do sth [biː ˌgəʊɪŋ tə 'duː] etw. tun werden III

to be good at [biː 'gʊd ˌət] gut sein in; gut sein bei I

to be homesick [biː 'həʊmsɪk] Heimweh haben IV

to be in charge (of) [biː ˌɪn 'tʃaːdʒ (ɒv)] leiten; zuständig sein (für); die Verantwortung tragen (für) V U3, 72

to be included [biː ɪnˈkluːdɪd] mit enthalten sein; inbegriffen sein V U4, 94

to be interested in [biː 'ɪntrəstɪd ˌɪn] interessiert sein an; sich interessieren für III

to be involved [biː ɪnˈvɒlvd] sich beteiligen; sich engagieren <V U3, 150>

to be known [biː 'nəʊn] bekannt sein <V U3, 151>

to be late [biː 'leɪt] zu spät kommen II

to be lucky [biː ˈlʌki] Glück haben II

to be scared [biː 'skeəd] Angst haben I

to be sick [biː 'sɪk] sich übergeben I

beach [biːtʃ] Strand I

bear [beə] Bär II

grizzly bear ['grɪzli ˌbeə] Grizzlybär IV

beautiful ['bjuːtɪfl] schön; hübsch; wunderschön III

became [bɪˈkeɪm] simple past von *to become* II

because [bɪˈkɒz] weil; da I

because of [bɪˈkɒz ˌɒv] wegen V U4, 98

*to become [bɪˈkʌm] (zu etw.) werden II

bed [bed] Bett I

bed and breakfast (B & B) [ˌbed ən 'brekfəst] Frühstückspension III

to go to bed [ˌgəʊ tə 'bed] ins Bett gehen I

bedroom ['bedrʊm] Kinderzimmer; Schlafzimmer II

been [biːn] past participle von *to be* III

before [bɪˈfɔː] vor; bevor II; vorher; zuvor III

before [bɪˈfɔː] bevor <I>

began [bɪˈgæn] simple past von *to begin* V U4, 98

*to begin [bɪˈgɪn] beginnen; anfangen V U1, 10

beginning [bɪˈgɪnɪŋ] Anfang; Beginn II

behind [bɪˈhaɪnd] hinter I

to believe [bɪˈliːv] glauben II

bell [bel] Glocke II

below [bɪˈləʊ] unten <IV>

best [best] am besten; beste; am liebsten II

All the best, [ˌɔːl ðə 'best] Alles Gute II

p pen • b bed • t ten • d dad • k cat • g grey • tʃ chair • dʒ joke • f fan • v very • θ three • ð the

Best wishes, [ˌbest ˈwɪʃɪz] Viele Grüße; Alles Gute! I

better [ˈbetə] besser II
to get better [ˌget ˈbetə] sich wieder besser fühlen; sich verbessern V U1, 16

between [bɪˈtwiːn] zwischen III

big [bɪg] groß I
big wheel [ˌbɪg ˈwiːl] Riesenrad II

bike [baɪk] Fahrrad I
to go bike riding [ˌgəʊ ˈbaɪk ˌraɪdɪŋ] Fahrrad fahren II

billion [ˈbɪliən] Milliarde V ZI, 8

Biology [baɪˈɒlədʒi] Biologie I

bird [bɜːd] Vogel IV
early bird [ˈɜːli ˌbɜːd] Frühaufsteher; Frühaufsteherin <V U3, 76>

date of **birth** [ˌdeɪt əv ˈbɜːθ] Geburtsdatum IV

birthday [ˈbɜːθdeɪ] Geburtstag I

biscuit [ˈbɪskɪt] Keks III

a **bit** [ə ˈbɪt] ein bisschen V U3, 72

black [blæk] schwarz I

blackboard [ˈblækbɔːd] Tafel I

blanket [ˈblæŋkɪt] Decke; Bettdecke; Wolldecke IV

bleaching [ˈbliːtʃɪŋ] Bleichen; Ausbleichen V U1, 20

blog [blɒg] Blog; Internettagebuch I

blue [bluː] blau I

boarding card [ˈbɔːdɪŋ ˌkaːd] Bordkarte IV

boarding time [ˈbɔːdɪŋ ˌtaɪm] Einsteigezeit IV

boat [bəʊt] Boot; Schiff IV

body [ˈbɒdi] Leiche; Körper IV

book [bʊk] Buch; Heft I
exercise book [ˈeksəsaɪz ˌbʊk] Übungsheft I

to **book** [bʊk] buchen; reservieren III

boom [buːm] Donner; Boom IV

Boom! [buːm] Bum! IV

border [ˈbɔːdə] Grenze IV

bored [bɔːd] gelangweilt <V U4, 153>

boring [ˈbɔːrɪŋ] langweilig I

*to be **born** [bi: ˈbɔːn] geboren werden IV

borough [ˈbʌrə] Stadtteil; Bezirk IV

to **borrow** [ˈbɒrəʊ] (sich) ausleihen II

boss [bɒs] Boss; Chef; Chefin III

both [bəʊθ] beide IV

a **bottle** of [ə ˈbɒtl̩ əv] eine Flasche … II

at the **bottom** [æt ðə ˈbɒtəm] unten V U1, 28

bought [bɔːt] simple past von *to buy* I; past participle von *to buy* III

to **bounce** [baʊns] prellen; hüpfen III

box [bɒks] Box; Kiste; Schachtel I
telephone box [ˈtelɪfəʊn ˌbɒks] Telefonzelle II

boy [bɔɪ] Junge; Bub I

bracket [ˈbrækɪt] Klammer <V U1, 14>

to **brake** [breɪk] bremsen V U3, 64

brave [breɪv] mutig; tapfer III

bread [bred] Brot I

break [breɪk] Pause I

*to **break** [breɪk] brechen; zerbrechen; kaputt machen V U1, 11
to break the law [ˌbreɪk ðə ˈlɔː] gegen das Gesetz verstoßen V U2, 46

breakfast [ˈbrekfəst] Frühstück I
bed and breakfast (B & B) [ˌbed ən ˈbrekfəst] Frühstückspension III
to have breakfast [ˌhæv ˈbrekfəst] frühstücken I

bricklayer [ˈbrɪkleɪə] Maurer; Maurerin <V U4, 152>

bridge [brɪdʒ] Brücke II

*to **bring** [brɪŋ] mitbringen; bringen II

British [ˈbrɪtɪʃ] britisch V U1, 11
the British [ðə ˈbrɪtɪʃ] die Briten V U2, 37

brochure [ˈbrəʊʃə] Broschüre; Prospekt III

broke [brəʊk] simple past von *to break* V U1, 11

broken [ˈbrəʊkn] past participle von *to break* V U1, 11

brother [ˈbrʌðə] Bruder I

brought [brɔːt] simple past von *to bring* II

brown [braʊn] braun I

buffalo *(sg)* [ˈbʌfləʊ], **buffaloes** *(pl)* [ˈbʌfləʊz] Büffel V U3, 63

*to **build** [bɪld] bauen II

building [ˈbɪldɪŋ] Gebäude; Bauwerk II

built [bɪlt] simple past von *to build* II

burger [ˈbɜːgə] Hamburger I

bus [bʌs] Bus I

on the bus [ˌɒn ðə ˈbʌs] im Bus II

business [ˈbɪznɪs] Geschäftswelt; Geschäft V ZI, 9

busy [ˈbɪzi] beschäftigt I; belebt; voller Menschen <V U1, 146>
a busy day [ə ˌbɪzi ˈdeɪ] ein ausgefüllter Tag II

but [bʌt] aber I

butcher [ˈbʊtʃə] Fleischer; Fleischerin; Metzger; Metzgerin <V U4, 152>

butter [ˈbʌtə] Butter I

*to **buy** [baɪ] kaufen I

by [baɪ] von; an; neben III; bis <V U4, 100>
by (train) [baɪ (treɪn)] mit (dem Zug) I

Bye. [baɪ] Tschüss. I

C

c/o [siːˈəʊ] bei V U4, 106

caber [ˈkeɪbə] Baumstamm III
caber toss [ˈkeɪbə ˌtɒs] Baumstammwerfen III

cable car [ˈkeɪbl̩ ˌkaː] seilgezogene Straßenbahn; Seilbahn IV

café [ˈkæfeɪ] Café III

cafeteria [kæfəˈtɪəriə] Cafeteria; Mensa I

cage [keɪdʒ] Käfig II

cake [keɪk] Kuchen I

calculator [ˈkælkjəleɪtə] Taschenrechner I

phone **call** [ˈfəʊn ˌkɔːl] Telefonanruf; Anruf I

to **call** [kɔːl] anrufen; rufen; nennen III

caller [ˈkɔːlə] Anrufer; Anruferin <II>

calm [kaːm] ruhig; friedlich V U4, 90

came [keɪm] simple past von *to come* I

camp [kæmp] Camp; Lager III

*to go **camping** [ˌgəʊ ˈkæmpɪŋ] campen gehen; zelten gehen III

campsite [ˈkæmpsaɪt] Campingplatz; Zeltplatz III

can [kæn] können I; Dose IV

can't [kaːnt] nicht können I
I can't wait [aɪ ˌkaːnt ˈweɪt] ich kann es kaum erwarten III

Canadian

Canadian [kəˈneɪdiən] Kanadier; Kanadierin; kanadisch; aus Kanada IV

canal [kəˈnæl] Kanal III

cannon [ˈkænən] Kanone III
  cannon ball [ˈkænən ˌbɔːl] Kanonenkugel III

canoe [kəˈnuː] Kanu IV

canoeing [kəˈnuːɪŋ] Kanufahren I

capital (city) [ˈkæpɪtl (ˌsɪti)] Hauptstadt I

captain [ˈkæptɪn] Kapitän; Kapitänin; Mannschaftsführer; Mannschaftsführerin II

caption [ˈkæpʃn] Bildunterschrift; Untertitel <III>

car [kɑː] Auto I

card [kɑːd] Karte III
  boarding card [ˈbɔːdɪŋ ˌkɑːd] Bordkarte IV

*to take **care** of [teɪk ˈkeər əv] sich kümmern um; sorgen für <V U2, 48>

career [kəˈrɪə] Laufbahn; Karriere; Beruf IV

careers [kəˈrɪəz] Berufs- V U4, 88
  careers day [kəˈrɪəz ˌdeɪ] Berufsinformationstag V U4, 90

careful [ˈkeəfl] vorsichtig; sorgfältig III

caretaker [ˈkeəˌteɪkə] Hausmeister; Hausmeisterin I

Caribbean [ˌkærɪˈbiːən] Karibe; Karibin; karibisch IV

carnival [ˈkɑːnɪvl] Karneval; Fasching I

carpenter [ˈkɑːpntə] Schreiner; Schreinerin; Tischler; Tischlerin <V U2, 148>

carpet [ˈkɑːpɪt] Teppich II

carving [ˈkɑːvɪŋ] Schnitzerei V U4, 99

castle [ˈkɑːsl] Burg; Schloss III

cat [kæt] Katze I

*to **catch** [kætʃ] fangen II
  to catch (bus/train) [kætʃ (bʌs/treɪn)] nehmen (Bus/Zug); bekommen (Bus/Zug) III
  to catch sth [kætʃ] sich etw. einfangen (medizinisch) V U1, 16

catering [ˈkeɪtrɪŋ] Gastronomie; Verpflegung <V U2, 148>

cathedral [kəˈθiːdrl] Kathedrale; Dom <V U1, 146>

caught [kɔːt] simple past von to catch II; past participle von to catch V U1, 16

to **cause** [kɔːz] verursachen; auslösen IV

cave [keɪv] Höhle IV

to **celebrate** [ˈseləbreɪt] feiern III

cent [sent] Cent (Währung) III

center (AE) [ˈsentə] Zentrum; Mitte; Center III

centre [ˈsentə] Zentrum; Mitte; Center III
  city centre [ˌsɪti ˈsentə] Stadtzentrum; Stadtmitte II
  shopping centre [ˈʃɒpɪŋ ˌsentə] Einkaufszentrum I
  sports centre [ˈspɔːts ˌsentə] Sportzentrum I

century [ˈsenʃri] Jahrhundert IV

certainly [ˈsɜːtnli] auf jeden Fall; offensichtlich; sicher V U2, 46

certificate [səˈtɪfɪkət] Zertifikat; Bescheinigung; Urkunde; Zeugnis V U4, 90
  secondary school leaving certificate [ˈsekndri skuːl ˌliːvɪŋ səˈtɪfɪkət] mittlerer Schulabschluss; Realschulabschluss IV

chain [tʃeɪn] Kette III

chair [tʃeə] Stuhl I

champion [ˈtʃæmpiən] Gewinner; Gewinnerin; Sieger; Siegerin <I>

chance [tʃɑːns] Möglichkeit; Chance; Gelegenheit III

change [tʃeɪndʒ] Wechselgeld I
  climate change [ˈklaɪmət ˌtʃeɪndʒ] Klimawandel V U1, 20

to **change** [tʃeɪndʒ] verändern; ändern; wechseln II; umsteigen III

chant [tʃɑːnt] Sprechgesang <I>

charades [ʃəˈrɑːdz] Scharaden <II>

*to be in **charge** (of) [biː ˌɪn ˈtʃɑːdʒ (əv)] leiten; zuständig sein (für); die Verantwortung tragen (für) V U3, 72

charity [ˈtʃæriti] Wohltätigkeitsorganisation; Stiftung; wohltätige Zwecke; Wohltätigkeits- II

chart [tʃɑːt] Tabelle; Diagramm <I>

to **chat** [tʃæt] chatten; plaudern II

cheap [tʃiːp] günstig; billig II

to **check** [tʃek] überprüfen; kontrollieren II

check-in agent [ˌtʃekɪn ˈeɪdʒnt] Check-in-Mitarbeiter; Check-in-Mitarbeiterin IV

checklist [ˈtʃeklɪst] Checkliste <I>

checkout [ˈtʃekaʊt] Kontrolle <I>; Kasse V U4, 94

cheerleader [ˈtʃɪəˌliːdə] Cheerleader; Cheerleaderin III

cheerleading [ˈtʃɪəˌliːdɪŋ] Cheerleading III

cheese [tʃiːz] Käse I

chef [ʃef] Koch; Küchenchef II

chicken [ˈtʃɪkɪn] Hähnchen; Huhn I
  chicken fried rice [ˈtʃɪkɪn ˌfraɪd ˈraɪs] gebratener Reis mit Hühnerfleisch II

chief [tʃiːf] Häuptling V U4, 98

children (pl) [ˈtʃɪldrn] Kinder I

chimpanzee [ˌtʃɪmpnˈziː] Schimpanse II

Chinese [tʃaɪˈniːz] chinesisch; Chinesisch; aus China; Chinese; Chinesin II

chips (pl) [tʃɪps] Pommes frites I

chocolate [ˈtʃɒklət] Schokolade I

*to **choose** [tʃuːz] wählen; auswählen III

chorus [ˈkɔːrəs] Refrain <I>

chose [tʃəʊz] simple past von to choose III

chosen [ˈtʃəʊzn] past participle von to choose III

Christmas [ˈkrɪsməs] Weihnachten I
  Merry Christmas! [ˌmeri ˈkrɪsməs] Frohe Weihnachten! I

church [tʃɜːtʃ] Kirche II

cinema [ˈsɪnəmə] Kino I

citizen [ˈsɪtɪzn] Staatsbürger; Staatsbürgerin; Staatsangehöriger; Staatsangehörige IV

city [ˈsɪti] Stadt; Großstadt I
  city centre [ˌsɪti ˈsentə] Stadtzentrum; Stadtmitte II

class [klɑːs] Klasse I; Unterricht; Unterrichtsstunde; Kurs IV

classmate [ˈklɑːsmeɪt] Klassenkame-
rad; Klassenkameradin; Mitschü-
ler; Mitschülerin <IV>

classroom [ˈklɑːsrʊm] Klassenzimmer I

to **clean** [kliːn] sauber machen;
putzen II

to **clear** up [ˌklɪərˈʌp] aufräumen
<V U4, 153>

clear [klɪə] klar; deutlich III

climate [ˈklaɪmət] Klima IV
climate change [ˈklaɪmət ˌtʃeɪndʒ]
Klimawandel V U1, 20

to **climb** [klaɪm] besteigen; klettern;
erklettern; steigen II

clock [klɒk] Uhr II
o'clock [əˈklɒk] Uhr (Zeitangabe bei
vollen Stunden) I

to **close** [kləʊz] zumachen; schließen I

close [kləʊs] fest V U4, 99

closed [kləʊzd] geschlossen I

clothes (pl only) [kləʊðz] Kleider;
Kleidung I

cloud [klaʊd] Wolke II

cloudy [ˈklaʊdi] bewölkt; wolkig II

club [klʌb] Klub; Treff; Schul-AG I;
Verein V U4, 89

clue [kluː] Hinweis; Spur I

coal mine [ˈkəʊl ˌmaɪn] Kohlenbergwerk; Kohlengrube III

coast [kəʊst] Küste III

coat [kəʊt] Jacke I

cola [ˈkəʊlə] Cola I

cold [kəʊld] kalt I; Erkältung; Kälte II

collar [ˈkɒlə] Halsband I

to **collect** [kəˈlekt] sammeln <I>

collection [kəˈlekʃn] Sammlung III

colony [ˈkɒləni] Kolonie IV

color (AE) [ˈkʌlə] Farbe III

colour [ˈkʌlə] Farbe I
colourful [ˈkʌləfl] bunt V U1, 12

*to **come** [kʌm] kommen I

come [kʌm] past participle von to
come <IV>

comic [ˈkɒmɪk] Comic(heft) II

comment [ˈkɒment] Kommentar IV

to **comment** (on) [ˈkɒment (ɒn)]
kommentieren IV

to **communicate** [kəˈmjuːnɪkeɪt]
kommunizieren; sich verständigen
V ZI, 9

communication [kəˌmjuːnɪˈkeɪʃn]
Kommunikation V U4, 90

community [kəˈmjuːnəti] Gemeinde;
Gemeinschaft V U4, 94

company [ˈkʌmpəni] Unternehmen;
Firma; Gesellschaft II

comparative [kəmˈpærətɪv] Kompa-
rativ <IV>

to **compare** [kəmˈpeə] vergleichen <I>

comparison [kəmˈpærɪsn] Vergleich
<IV>

competition [ˌkɒmpəˈtɪʃn] Wettbewerb V ZI, 8

to **complain** [kəmˈpleɪn] sich
beschweren; sich beklagen IV

to **complete** [kəmˈpliːt] vervollständigen <I>; ausfüllen; machen V U4, 90

completely [kəmˈpliːtli] völlig V U1, 20

computer [kəmˈpjuːtə] Computer I
computer programmer [kəmˌpjuːtə
ˈprəʊgræmə] Programmierer;
Programmiererin V U2, 38

computing [kəmˈpjuːtɪŋ] Computer-
<V U2, 148>

concert [ˈkɒnsət] Konzert I

working **conditions** (pl only) [ˈwɜːkɪŋ
kənˌdɪʃnz] Arbeitsbedingungen
<V U4, 153>

confident [ˈkɒnfɪdnt] selbstsicher;
selbstbewusst; sicher IV

Congratulations! [kənˌgrætʃəˈleɪʃnz]
Glückwunsch! II

staying **connected** [ˌsteɪɪŋ kəˈnektɪd]
in Verbindung bleiben III

considerate [kənˈsɪdrət] rücksichts-
voll; aufmerksam <V U3, 151>

consumption [kənˈsʌmpʃn] Ver-
brauch; Konsum <V U2, 149>

contact [ˈkɒntækt] Kontakt I

to **contact** [ˈkɒntækt] kontaktieren; sich in Verbindung setzen
<V U2, 50>

container [kənˈteɪnə] Container;
Behälter; Behältnis <V U2, 148>

content [ˈkɒntent] Inhalt <V U2, 51>

continent [ˈkɒntɪnənt] Kontinent;
Erdteil II

to **control** [kənˈtrəʊl] kontrollieren
V U3, 72

cook [kʊk] Koch; Köchin <V U2, 48>

to **cook** [kʊk] kochen II

cookie (AE) [ˈkʊki] Keks III

cooking [ˈkʊkɪŋ] Kochen; Koch- II

cool [kuːl] cool; super I

to **copy** [ˈkɒpi] abschreiben; kopieren
<III>

copyright [ˈkɒpiraɪt] Copyright; Urheberrecht IV

coral [ˈkɒrəl] Koralle V U1, 20

corn [kɔːn] Mais; Korn; Getreide IV

corner [ˈkɔːnə] Ecke V U1, 28

to **correct** [kəˈrekt] verbessern; richtigstellen; korrigieren II

correct [kəˈrekt] richtig; korrekt <I>

*to **cost** [kɒst] kosten III

cost [kɒst] simple past, past participle von to cost III

costume [ˈkɒstjuːm] Kostüm I

could [kʊd] könnte V U3, 81; konnte III

to **count on sb** [kaʊntˈɒn] sich auf
jmdn. verlassen V U4, 90

country [ˈkʌntri] Land; ländliche
Gegend I
home country [ˌhəʊm ˈkʌntri]
Heimat; Heimatland IV

of **course** [əv ˈkɔːs] natürlich; selbstverständlich II

cousin [ˈkʌzn] Cousin; Cousine II

cow [kaʊ] Kuh III

to **crash** [kræʃ] krachen V U3, 64

crayfish [ˈkreɪfɪʃ] Languste; Flusskrebs V U4, 99

crazy [ˈkreɪzi] verrückt V U2, 54

creative [kriˈeɪtɪv] kreativ <V U4, 152>

creature [ˈkriːtʃə] Lebewesen; Kreatur; Geschöpf V U1, 10

cricket [ˈkrɪkɪt] Kricket II

saltwater **crocodile** [sɔːltˌwɔːtə
ˈkrɒkədaɪl] Salzwasserkrokodil
<V U1, 23>

crop [krɒp] Feldfrucht; Ernte V U2, 42

crowded [ˈkraʊdɪd] überfüllt
<V U1, 146>
crowded with people [ˌkraʊdɪd wɪð
ˈpiːpl] voller Leute <V U3, 76>

crown jewels (pl) [ˌkraʊn ˈdʒuːəlz]
Kronjuwelen II

crust [krʌst] Kruste; Rinde IV

culture ['kʌltʃə] Kultur III

a cup of [ə 'kʌp ̩əv] eine Tasse … II

current ['kʌrnt] Strömung III

customer ['kʌstəmə] Kunde; Kundin I
customer service [ˌkʌstəmə 'sɜːvɪs] Kundenbetreuung; Kundendienst; Kundenservice IV

***to cut down** [ˌkʌt 'daʊn] fällen V U3, 72

CV (curriculum vitae) [ˌsiː'viː: (kəˌrɪkjələm'viːtaɪ)] Lebenslauf IV

cyclist ['saɪklɪst] Radfahrer; Radfahrerin <V U3, 150>

D

dad [dæd] Papa; Vati I

daily routine [ˌdeɪli ruː'tiːn] Alltag <V U2, 40>

damage ['dæmɪdʒ] Schäden; Schaden; Beschädigung IV

to **damage** ['dæmɪdʒ] beschädigen; schaden V U2, 42

dance [dɑːns] Tanz III
square dance ['skweə ˌdɑːns] Squaredance *(amerikanischer Volkstanz)* II

to **dance** [dɑːns] tanzen I

dancer ['dɑːnsə] Tänzer; Tänzerin I

dancing ['dɑːnsɪŋ] Tanz; Tanzen III

danger ['deɪndʒə] Gefahr V U1, 20

dangerous ['deɪndʒrəs] gefährlich III

dark [dɑːk] dunkel I

date [deɪt] Datum; Zeitpunkt IV
date of birth [ˌdeɪt ̩əv 'bɜːθ] Geburtsdatum IV

daughter ['dɔːtə] Tochter I

day [deɪ] Tag I
a busy day [ə ˌbɪzi 'deɪ] ein ausgefüllter Tag II
careers day [kə'rɪəz ˌdeɪ] Berufsinformationstag V U4, 90
lucky day [ˌlʌki 'deɪ] Glückstag II
one day ['wʌn deɪ] eines Tages I
sports day ['spɔːts ˌdeɪ] Sportfest II

dead [ded] tot IV

Oh dear. [əʊ 'dɪə] Oje. V U1, 16

Dear …, [dɪə] Liebe(r) …, *(Anrede in Briefen)* I; Sehr geehrte(r) …, IV

December [dɪ'sembə] Dezember I

to **decide** [dɪ'saɪd] (sich) entscheiden; beschließen III

decision [dɪ'sɪʒn] Entscheidung IV

decoration [dek'reɪʃn] Dekoration; Schmuck <V U1, 25>

deep [diːp] tief V U4, 98

defining relative clause [dɪˌfaɪnɪŋ 'relətɪv ˌklɔːz] notwendiger Relativsatz <IV>

definition [ˌdefɪ'nɪʃn] Definition <V U2, 43>

delayed [dɪ'leɪd] verspätet IV

delicious [dɪ'lɪʃəs] lecker; köstlich V U1, 12

to **deliver** [dɪ'lɪvə] liefern; ausliefern IV

delivery [dɪ'lɪvri] Lieferung; Auslieferung; Zustellung <V U4, 153>
delivery service [dɪ'lɪvri ˌsɜːvɪs] Lieferdienst <V U2, 49>

dentist ['dentɪst] Zahnarzt; Zahnärztin <V U4, 152>

to **depart** [dɪ'pɑːt] abfliegen; abfahren IV

department [dɪ'pɑːtmənt] Abteilung V U1, 21

to **describe** [dɪ'skraɪb] beschreiben <III>

design [dɪ'zaɪn] Design; Gestaltung; Entwurf II
DT (Design Technology) [ˌdiː'tiː: (dɪˌzaɪn tek'nɒlədʒi)] Technik I

to **design** [dɪ'zaɪn] konstruieren; entwerfen; gestalten; entwickeln IV

desk [desk] Schreibtisch; Tisch II

to **destroy** [dɪ'strɔɪ] zerstören IV

destruction [dɪ'strʌkʃn] Zerstörung V U1, 21

detail ['diːteɪl] Detail; Einzelheit V U3, 64

detective [dɪ'tektɪv] Detektiv; Detektivin I

determined [dɪ'tɜːmɪnd] entschlossen; entschieden; zielstrebig <V U3, 151>

device [dɪ'vaɪs] Gerät; Vorrichtung <V U2, 148>

dialogue ['daɪəlɒg] Dialog; Gespräch II

diameter [daɪ'æmɪtə] Durchmesser II

diamond ['daɪəmənd] Diamant <II>

diary ['daɪəri] Tagebuch I

dictionary ['dɪkʃnri] Wörterbuch <II>

did [dɪd] simple past von *to do* I

didgeridoo [ˌdɪdʒri'duː:] Didgeridoo *(australisches Musikinstrument)* V U1, 12

to **die** [daɪ] sterben III

difference ['dɪfrns] Unterschied <IV>

different ['dɪfrnt] verschieden; unterschiedlich; anders I; andere III

difficult ['dɪfɪklt] schwierig; schwer; kompliziert III

dinner ['dɪnə] Mittagessen; Abendessen I

direct speech [dɪˌrekt 'spiːtʃ] direkte Rede <V U3, 76>

directions *(pl)* [dɪ'rekʃnz] Wegbeschreibung; Anweisungen <III>
giving directions [ˌgɪvɪŋ dɪ'rekʃnz] eine Wegbeschreibung geben; Anweisungen geben <II>

director [dɪ'rektə] Regisseur; Regisseurin V U3, 68

dirty ['dɜːti] dreckig; schmutzig I

to **disagree** [ˌdɪsə'griː:] anderer Meinung sein; nicht einverstanden sein IV

disappointed [ˌdɪsə'pɔɪntɪd] enttäuscht V U1, 12

to **discover** [dɪ'skʌvə] entdecken V U3, 62

disease [dɪ'ziːz] Krankheit V U3, 68

to empty the dishwasher [ˌemti ðə 'dɪʃwɒʃə] die Spülmaschine ausräumen II

to load the dishwasher [ˌləʊd ðə 'dɪʃwɒʃə] die Spülmaschine einräumen II

distance ['dɪstns] Entfernung; Distanz V U3, 80

to **disturb** [dɪ'stɜːb] stören; belästigen V U3, 80

***to do** [duː:] machen; tun I
to do handicrafts [ˌduː: 'hændikrɑːfts] basteln V U3, 73
to do homework [ˌduː: 'həʊmwɜːk] Hausaufgabe(n) machen I
to do magic [ˌduː: 'mædʒɪk] zaubern II

doctor ['dɒktə] Arzt; Ärztin II

at the doctor's [ət ðə 'dɒktəz] beim Arzt II

dog [dɒg] Hund I

dollar ($) ['dɒlə] Dollar (amer. Währungseinheit) IV

dolphin ['dɒlfɪn] Delfin V U4, 99

don't sing [dəʊnt 'sɪŋ] singe nicht; singt nicht I

to donate [də'neɪt] spenden; stiften V U4, 94

done [dʌn] past participle von to do III

door [dɔ:] Tür II

doorbell ['dɔ:bel] Türklingel I

dot [dɒt] Punkt V U1, 12

down [daʊn] hinunter; herunter III

draft [drɑ:ft] Entwurf <II>

drama ['drɑ:mə] Theater-; Drama; Schauspielerei III

drank [dræŋk] simple past von to drink II

*****to draw** [drɔ:] zeichnen <I>

dream [dri:m] Traum I

dress [dres] Kleid I

fancy dress [ˌfænsi 'dres] Kostüm; Verkleidung I

drink [drɪŋk] Getränk I

*****to drink** [drɪŋk] trinken II

drinking ['drɪŋkɪŋ] Trink- V U2, 42

*****to drive** [draɪv] fahren; treiben IV

to drive off [ˌdraɪv 'ɒf] wegfahren IV

driving licence ['draɪvɪŋ ˌlaɪsns] Führerschein V U3, 64

driven ['drɪvn] past participle von to drive IV

driver ['draɪvə] Fahrer; Fahrerin IV

drove [drəʊv] simple past von to drive IV

drug [drʌg] Droge IV; Medikament; Arznei; Arzneimittel V U3, 68

dry [draɪ] trocken II

DT (Design Technology) [ˌdi:'ti: (dɪˌzaɪn tek'nɒlədʒi)] Technik I

due [dju:] fällig <V U4, 100>

during ['dʒʊərɪŋ] bei; während IV

DVD [ˌdi:vi:'di:] DVD I

E

e.g. (= for example) [ˌi:'dʒi:] z. B. (= zum Beispiel) <II>

each [i:tʃ] jede <I>

each one [ˌi:tʃ 'wʌn] jedes <IV>

each other [ˌi:tʃ'ʌðə] einander; sich; gegenseitig III

early ['ɜ:li] früh II

early bird ['ɜ:li ˌbɜ:d] Frühaufsteher; Frühaufsteherin <V U3, 76>

earth [ɜ:θ] Welt; Erde III

earthquake ['ɜ:θkweɪk] Erdbeben IV

east [i:st] Ost-; Osten III

easy ['i:zi] einfach; leicht I

*****to eat** [i:t] essen I

economy [ɪ'kɒnəmi] Wirtschaft V U2, 42

education [ˌedʒʊ'keɪʃn] Ausbildung; Erziehung; Bildung IV

efficient [ɪ'fɪʃnt] effizient; leistungsfähig IV

egg [eg] Ei I

Eid [i:d] muslimisches Fest I

eight [eɪt] acht I

eighteen [ˌeɪ'ti:n] achtzehn I

eighty ['eɪti] achtzig I

not … either [nɒt … 'aɪðə] auch nicht III

electrical [ɪ'lektrɪkl] Elektro- <V U2, 149>

electrician [ˌelɪk'trɪʃn] Elektriker; Elektrikerin <V U2, 148>

electricity [ˌelɪk'trɪsəti] Strom; Elektrizität V U3, 63

elephant ['elɪfənt] Elefant V U3, 63

eleven [ɪ'levn] elf I

e-mail ['i:meɪl] E-Mail II

emergency [ɪ'mɜ:dʒnsi] Notfall V U3, 80

emotion [ɪ'məʊʃn] Gefühl; Emotion <V U3, 76>

employee [ɪm'plɔɪi:] Mitarbeiter; Mitarbeiterin; Arbeitnehmer; Arbeitnehmerin; Angestellter; Angestellte IV

employer [ɪm'plɔɪə] Arbeitgeber; Arbeitgeberin V U4, 90

to empty the dishwasher [ˌemti ðə 'dɪʃwɒʃə] die Spülmaschine ausräumen II

empty ['emti] leer <V U1, 146>

enclosed [ɪn'kləʊzd] beigefügt; anbei V U4, 112

end [end] Ende; Schluss II

at the end [ˌət ði 'end] am Ende II

end-of-term [ˌend əv 'tɜ:m] Schuljahresabschluss <I>

to end [end] enden; beenden; aufhören V U3, 62

ending ['endɪŋ] Ende; Schluss <III>

energy ['enədʒi] Energie; Kraft V U1, 21

search engine ['sɜ:tʃ ˌendʒɪn] Suchmaschine <IV>

engineer [ˌendʒɪ'nɪə] Ingenieur; Ingenieurin; Techniker; Technikerin II

English ['ɪŋglɪʃ] Englisch I; englisch; aus England III

English-speaking [ˌɪŋglɪʃ'spi:kɪŋ] englischsprachig V ZI, 9

the English [ðɪ 'ɪŋglɪʃ] die Engländer III

to enjoy [ɪn'dʒɔɪ] genießen; Gefallen finden an IV

to enjoy + -ing [ɪn'dʒɔɪ …ɪŋ] mögen; Gefallen finden an; genießen; genießen, … zu tun V U2, 38

to enjoy oneself [ɪn'dʒɔɪ wʌnˌself] Spaß haben; sich amüsieren IV

enough [ɪ'nʌf] genug; genügend III

enquiry [ɪn'kwaɪəri] Anfrage V U4, 106

enthusiastic [ɪnˌθju:zi'æstɪk] enthusiastisch; begeistert <V U3, 151>

entry ['entri] Eintrag; Eintritt <II>

environment [ɪn'vaɪrənmənt] Umwelt; Umgebung II

environmental [ɪnˌvaɪrn'mentl] Umwelt- V U2, 37

episode ['epɪsəʊd] Folge; Episode IV

equipment [ɪ'kwɪpmənt] Ausrüstung; Zubehör; Ausstattung <III>

to escape [ɪ'skeɪp] entkommen; fliehen; entfliehen; flüchten IV

euro ['jʊərəʊ] Euro (Währung) III

European [ˌjʊərə'pi:ən] Europäer; Europäerin; europäisch; aus Europa III

evening ['i:vnɪŋ] Abend I

in the evening [ɪn ði 'i:vnɪŋ] abends I

event [ɪ'vent] Veranstaltung; Ereignis II

ever ['evə] schon einmal; jemals; überhaupt III

every ['evri] jede I; alle II

everyone ['evriwʌn] alle; jeder; zusammen II

everything ['evriθɪŋ] alles II

everywhere ['evriweə] überallhin; überall II

exam [ɪg'zæm] Prüfung; Examen V U4, 90

to take an exam [ˌteɪk ən ɪg'zæm] eine Prüfung schreiben; ein Examen schreiben V U4, 90

example [ɪg'zɑːmpl] Beispiel III

for example [fər ɪg'zɑːmpl] zum Beispiel III

excited [ɪk'saɪtɪd] aufgeregt; begeistert II

exciting [ɪk'saɪtɪŋ] spannend; aufregend I

Excuse me. [ɪk'skjuːz mi] Entschuldigung. II

exercise ['eksəsaɪz] Übung I

exercise book ['eksəsaɪz ˌbʊk] Übungsheft I

exhibition [ˌeksɪ'bɪʃn] Ausstellung III

expensive [ɪk'spensɪv] teuer I

experience [ɪk'spɪəriəns] Erfahrung; Erlebnis IV

work experience ['wɜːk ɪkˌspɪəriəns] Berufserfahrung; Praktikum V U4, 90

experiment [ɪk'sperɪmənt] Versuch; Experiment II

to **explain** [ɪk'spleɪn] erklären V U3, 81

to **explore** [ɪk'splɔː] erkunden; erforschen IV

expression [ɪk'spreʃn] Ausdruck; Wendung; Äußerung <IV>

extra ['ekstrə] zusätzlich <IV>

extremist [ɪk'striːmɪst] Extremist; Extremistin V U2, 47

eye [aɪ] Auge I

F

face [feɪs] Gesicht I

face painting ['feɪs ˌpeɪntɪŋ] Schminken II

fact [fækt] Fakt; Tatsache II

factory ['fæktri] Fabrik; Werk III

fair [feə] Fest; Messe; Jahrmarkt II; fair; gerecht IV

fall *(AE)* [fɔːl] Herbst III

*to **fall** [fɔːl] fallen; hinfallen I

to fall off [ˌfɔːlˈɒf] von etw. stürzen; herunterfallen; hinunterfallen II

to fall out [ˌfɔːlˈaʊt] herausfallen III

fallen ['fɔːlən] past participle von *to fall* III

family ['fæmli] Familie I

family tree [ˌfæmli 'triː] Familienstammbaum <I>

famous ['feɪməs] berühmt I

fan [fæn] Fan I

fancy dress [ˌfænsi 'dres] Kostüm; Verkleidung I

fantastic [fæn'tæstɪk] fantastisch; großartig II

far [fɑː] weit II

farm [fɑːm] Bauernhof I

wind farm ['wɪnd ˌfɑːm] Windpark <V U2, 149>

farmer ['fɑːmə] Bauer; Bäuerin; Landwirt; Landwirtin I

farming ['fɑːmɪŋ] Landwirtschaft; Ackerbau V U2, 42

fashion ['fæʃn] Mode IV

fast [fɑːst] schnell II

father ['fɑːðə] Vater I

favorite *(AE)* ['feɪvrɪt] Lieblings- III

favourite ['feɪvrɪt] Lieblings- I

feature story ['fiːtʃə ˌstɔːri] Leitartikel; Sonderbericht <V U3, 76>

February ['februri] Februar I

fed [fed] simple past von *to feed* I

*to be **fed** up (with) [biː ˌfedˈʌp (wɪð)] die Nase voll haben (von) III

fee [fiː] Gebühr <V U4, 100>

*to **feed** [fiːd] füttern I; ernähren <V U2, 49>

feedback ['fiːdbæk] Rückmeldung; Feedback <I>

*to **feel** [fiːl] (sich) fühlen II; sich anfühlen III

feeling ['fiːlɪŋ] Gefühl <II>

fell [fel] simple past von *to fall* I

felt [felt] simple past von *to feel* II; past participle von *to feel* III

fence [fens] Zaun <V U4, 153>

fertiliser ['fɜːtɪlaɪzə] Dünger V U2, 42

festival ['festɪvl] Festival; Fest III

fete [feɪt] Fest <V U4, 100>

a **few** [ə 'fjuː] ein paar; einige; wenige IV

science fiction [ˌsaɪəns 'fɪkʃn] Science-Fiction I

field ['fiːld] Spielfeld; Feld; Gebiet III

playing field ['pleɪɪŋ ˌfiːld] Sportplatz II

fifteen [ˌfɪf'tiːn] fünfzehn I

fifty ['fɪfti] fünfzig I

*to **fight** [faɪt] kämpfen; (sich) streiten II

figure ['fɪgə] Figur; Gestalt II

to **fill** [fɪl] füllen; befüllen V U4, 94

to fill in [ˌfɪlˈɪn] eintragen; ausfüllen <II>

film [fɪlm] Film I

finance ['faɪnæns] Finanzen <V U2, 148>

*to **find** [faɪnd] finden; herausfinden I

to find out [ˌfaɪndˈaʊt] herausfinden IV; erkundigen <I>

fine [faɪn] gut; in Ordnung; schön I

I'm fine. [ˌaɪm 'faɪn] Mir geht es gut. I

to **finish** ['fɪnɪʃ] fertigstellen; vervollständigen I; beenden; fertig machen; erledigen; enden; aufhören II

fire [faɪə] Feuer III

firefighter ['faɪəˌfaɪtə] Feuerwehrmann; Feuerwehrfrau <V U4, 152>

first ['fɜːst] zuerst; als Erstes II; erste I

at first [ət 'fɜːst] zuerst; zunächst V U3, 68

the first time [ðə fɜːst 'taɪm] das erste Mal I

first-aid [ˌfɜːst'eɪd] Erste-Hilfe- IV

fish *(sg)* [fɪʃ], **fish** *(pl)* [fɪʃ] Fisch I

*to go **fishing** [ˌgəʊ 'fɪʃɪŋ] angeln gehen; fischen gehen IV

fit [fɪt] fit III

five [faɪv] fünf I

flag [flæg] Flagge; Fahne IV

flat [flæt] Wohnung I; flach; eben; platt V U1, 11

flea [fliː] Floh I

flea market ['fliː ˌmɑːkɪt] Flohmarkt I

flew [fluː] simple past von *to fly* II

flexible ['fleksɪbl] flexibel IV

flight [flaɪt] Flug IV
　Have a good flight! [ˌhæv‿ə ɡʊd ˈflaɪt] Guten Flug! IV
floor [flɔː] Stockwerk; Etage II
florist [ˈflɒrɪst] Florist; Floristin <V U4, 152>
flower [ˈflaʊə] Blume <V U3, 75>
flu [fluː] Grippe V U1, 16
*to **fly** [flaɪ] fliegen II
flyer [ˈflaɪə] Flyer; Faltblatt <III>
flying [ˈflaɪɪŋ] Fliegen III
to **follow** [ˈfɒləʊ] befolgen; folgen V U3, 80
follower [ˈfɒləʊə] Follower; Followerin; Anhänger; Anhängerin IV
food [fuːd] Essen; Lebensmittel I
foot (sg) [fʊt], **feet** (pl) [fiːt] Fuß II
　on foot [ɒn ˈfʊt] zu Fuß I
football [ˈfʊtbɔːl] Fußball I
　American football [əˈmerɪkən ˈfʊtbɔːl] American Football II
for [fɔː] für I; seit IV
　for example [fər ɪɡˈzaːmpl] zum Beispiel III
　for the 200th time [fə ðə ˈtuː hʌndrədθ ˌtaɪm] zum 200. Mal III
foreground [ˈfɔːɡraʊnd] Vordergrund III
forever [fəˈrevə] für immer; ewig IV
*to **forget** [fəˈɡet] vergessen II
forgot [fəˈɡɒt] simple past von to forget II
form [fɔːm] Form <I>; Formular V U4, 90
fortunately [ˈfɔːtʃnətli] zum Glück V U3, 72
forty [ˈfɔːti] vierzig I
to look **forward** to (+ ing) [ˌlʊk ˈfɔːwəd tə] sich freuen auf IV
fought [fɔːt] simple past von to fight II
to **found** [faʊnd] gründen; begründen V U4, 98
found [faʊnd] simple past von to find II; past participle von to find III
　lost and found notice [ˌlɒst ən ˈfaʊnd ˌnəʊtɪs] Suchplakat; Aushang III
four [fɔː] vier I
fourteen [ˌfɔːˈtiːn] vierzehn I
free [friː] kostenlos; frei III

free time [ˌfriː ˈtaɪm] Freizeit I
free-time [ˌfriːˈtaɪm] Freizeit- V U4, 89
freeze frame [ˈfriːz ˌfreɪm] Standbild <II>
French [frenʃ] französisch; Französisch; aus Frankreich IV
Friday [ˈfraɪdeɪ] Freitag I
chicken **fried** rice [ˈtʃɪkɪn ˌfraɪd ˈraɪs] gebratener Reis mit Hühnerfleisch II
friend [frend] Freund; Freundin I
　to make friends [ˌmeɪk ˈfrendz] Freundschaft(en) schließen II
friendly [ˈfrendli] freundlich; sympathisch IV
frisbee [ˈfrɪzbi] Frisbee; Frisbeescheibe I
from [frɒm] aus; von I
in **front** [ɪn ˈfrʌnt] vorn II
in **front** of [ɪn ˈfrʌnt əv] vor; davor I
fruit [fruːt] Obst; Frucht I
full of [ˈfʊl əv] voller <V U1, 23>
fun [fʌn] Spaß; Freude I; lustig; spaßig; amüsant I
　to be fun [bi ˈfʌn] Spaß machen; witzig sein II
funny [ˈfʌni] merkwürdig; komisch; lustig I
future [ˈfjuːtʃə] Zukunft IV; zukünftig; Zukunfts- V U4, 90

G

G'day! (= Good day!) [ɡəˈdaɪ] Hi!; Hallo!; Tag! V U1, 10
gallery [ˈɡæləri] Galerie <V U1, 146>
game [ɡeɪm] Spiel I
gap [ɡæp] Lücke; Spalt <II>
garage [ˈɡærɑːʒ] Kfz-Werkstatt; Tankstelle; Garage V U4, 90
garden [ˈɡɑːdn] Garten I
gardener [ˈɡɑːdnə] Gärtner; Gärtnerin <V U2, 48>
gate [ɡeɪt] Gate; Flugsteig IV; Tor V U3, 80
gave [ɡeɪv] simple past von to give I
gay [ɡeɪ] homosexuell; schwul; Schwuler V U3, 68
generous [ˈdʒenrəs] großzügig <V U3, 151>

German [ˈdʒɜːmən] Deutsch I; Deutscher; Deutsche; deutsch; aus Deutschland II
*to **get** [ɡet] bekommen; werden; kommen I; holen; bringen IV
　to get back [ˌɡet ˈbæk] zurückkommen; zurückgehen V U4, 98
　to get better [ˌɡet ˈbetə] sich wieder besser fühlen; sich verbessern V U1, 16
　to get in [ˌɡet ˈɪn] einsteigen IV
　to get in touch [ˌɡet ɪn ˈtʌtʃ] in Verbindung treten (mit); kontaktieren <V U3, 150>
　to get into [ˌɡet ˈɪntə] bilden <I>
　to get lost [ˌɡet ˈlɒst] verloren gehen; sich verirren IV
　to get off [ˌɡet ˈɒf] aussteigen II
　to get on sth [ˌɡet ˈɒn] in etw. steigen; in etw. einsteigen IV
　to get out [ˌɡet ˈaʊt] aussteigen; herauskommen IV
　to get up [ˌɡet ˈʌp] aufstehen I
　to get used to (sth) [ˌɡet ˈjuːst tə] sich gewöhnen an (etw.) IV
　Get well soon! [ˌɡet wel ˈsuːn] Gute Besserung! V U1, 16
ghost [ɡəʊst] Geist; Gespenst IV
giant [ˈdʒaɪənt] Riesen-; riesig V U1, 12
girl [ɡɜːl] Mädchen I
*to **give** [ɡɪv] geben; schenken I; halten V ZI, 9
　giving directions [ˌɡɪvɪŋ dɪˈrekʃnz] eine Wegbeschreibung geben; Anweisungen geben <II>
given [ˈɡɪvn] past participle von to give IV
glove [ɡlʌv] Handschuh II
*to **go** [ɡəʊ] gehen; fahren I; hinkommen <IV>
　to go bike riding [ˌɡəʊ ˈbaɪk ˌraɪdɪŋ] Fahrrad fahren II
　to go camping [ˌɡəʊ ˈkæmpɪŋ] campen gehen; zelten gehen III
　to go fishing [ˌɡəʊ ˈfɪʃɪŋ] angeln gehen; fischen gehen IV
　to go on [ˌɡəʊ ˈɒn] weitergehen <III>
　to go rafting [ˌɡəʊ ˈrɑːftɪŋ] raften gehen III

go

goal

to go skating [ˌɡəʊ 'skeɪtɪŋ] inline-skaten gehen; Schlittschuhlaufen gehen II

to go surfing [ˌɡəʊ 'sɜːfɪŋ] surfen gehen III

to go swimming [ˌɡəʊ 'swɪmɪŋ] schwimmen gehen I

to go tandem bike riding [ˌɡəʊ 'tændəm ˌbaɪk raɪdɪŋ] Tandem fahren II

to go to bed [ˌɡəʊ tə 'bed] ins Bett gehen I

to go together [ˌɡəʊ tə'ɡeðə] zusammenpassen <III>

to go wrong [ˌɡəʊ 'rɒŋ] schiefgehen V U4, 90

goal [ɡəʊl] Tor; Treffer; Ziel III

goalpost ['ɡəʊlpəʊst] Torpfosten; Torstange III

goat [ɡəʊt] Ziege III

gold [ɡəʊld] Gold; golden; Gold- III

gone [ɡɒn] past participle von *to go* III

good [ɡʊd] gut I

to be good at [bi: 'ɡʊdˌət] gut sein in; gut sein bei I

Good luck! [ˌɡʊd 'lʌk] Alles Gute!; Viel Glück! IV

Have a good flight! [ˌhævˌə ɡʊd 'flaɪt] Guten Flug! IV

Goodbye. [ɡʊd'baɪ] Auf Wiedersehen.; Servus. I

goods *(pl only)* [ɡʊdz] Waren; Güter V U2, 38

got [ɡɒt] simple past von *to get* I; past participle von *to get* IV

government ['ɡʌvnmənt] Regierung V U1, 20

GPO [ˌdʒiː piː 'əʊ] Hauptpostamt V U1, 21

GPS (Global Positioning System) [ˌdʒiːpiː'es] GPS *(ein satellitengestütztes System zur weltweiten Positionsbestimmung)* I

grade *(AE)* [ɡreɪd] Klasse; Jahrgangsstufe; Note II

grammar ['ɡræmə] Grammatik <I>

grandfather ['ɡrænˌfaːðə] Großvater II

grandma ['ɡrænmaː] Oma I

grandmother ['ɡrænˌmʌðə] Großmutter V U4, 98

grandparents *(pl)* ['ɡrænˌpeərnts] Großeltern II

great [ɡreɪt] großartig; toll I; groß; riesig III

great- [ɡreɪt] Ur- V U4, 98

great-great-grandad [ˌɡreɪtɡreɪt 'ɡrændæd] Ururopa I

green [ɡriːn] grün I

greenhouse ['ɡriːnhaʊs] Gewächshaus; Treibhaus <V U2, 48>

to **greet** [ɡriːt] begrüßen; grüßen <V U3, 71>

grew [ɡruː] simple past von *to grow* V U2, 42

grey [ɡreɪ] grau I

grizzly bear ['ɡrɪzli ˌbeə] Grizzlybär IV

group [ɡruːp] Gruppe IV

***to grow** [ɡrəʊ] wachsen; anbauen; züchten; ziehen V U2, 42

grown [ɡrəʊn] past participle von *to grow* V U2, 42

to **guess** [ɡes] überlegen; raten; erraten I

Guess what? [ɡes 'wɒt] Stellt euch vor!; Stell dir vor! II

guest [ɡest] Gast IV

guide [ɡaɪd] Führer; Führerin IV

tour guide ['tʊə ˌɡaɪd] Reiseleiter; Reiseleiterin V U2, 38

guinea pig ['ɡɪni ˌpɪɡ] Meerschweinchen II

guitar [ɡɪ'taː] Gitarre V U3, 72

gun [ɡʌn] Pistole; Schusswaffe; Waffe IV

H

had [hæd] simple past von *to have* I; past participle von *to have* IV

hairdresser ['heəˌdresə] Friseur; Friseurin IV

hairdressing salon ['heədresɪŋ ˌsælɒn] Friseursalon IV

half *(sg)* [haːf], **halves** *(pl)* [haːvz] (die) Hälfte V ZI, 8

half [haːf] halb III

half past (seven) [haːf 'paːst (ˌsevn)] halb (acht) II

half a million [ˌhaːfˌə 'mɪljən] eine halbe Million III

Halloween [ˌhæləʊ'iːn] Halloween I

hammer ['hæmə] Hammer III

hammer throwing ['hæmə ˌθrəʊɪŋ] Hammerwerfen III

hamster ['hæmstə] Hamster I

hand [hænd] Hand II

*to do **handicrafts** [ˌduː 'hændɪkraːfts] basteln V U3, 73

*to **hang** about [ˌhænˌə'baʊt] herumhängen I

to **happen** ['hæpn] passieren; geschehen II; vorkommen; sich ereignen IV

That's what happened. [ˌðæts wɒt 'hæpnd] Das ist passiert. II

happy ['hæpi] glücklich I; froh; fröhlich IV

hard [haːd] hart; schwer; schwierig II

to try hard [ˌtraɪ 'haːd] sich anstrengen V U4, 98

hat [hæt] Mütze; Hut II

to **hate** [heɪt] hassen; nicht mögen I

*to **have** [hæv] haben; besitzen; essen; trinken I

to have (got) to ['hæv (ɡɒt) tə] müssen II

to have a party [ˌhævˌə 'paːti] eine Party feiern I

to have breakfast [ˌhæv 'brekfəst] frühstücken I

to have got [hæv 'ɡɒt] haben; besitzen II

to have to ['hæv tə] müssen II

Have a good flight! [ˌhævˌə ɡʊd 'flaɪt] Guten Flug! IV

he [hiː] er I

head [hed] Kopf II

headache ['hedeɪk] Kopfweh; Kopfschmerzen II

heading ['hedɪŋ] Überschrift <I>

headline ['hedlaɪn] Überschrift <V U3, 76>

healthy ['helθi] gesund III

*to **hear** [hɪə] hören II

to hear about [ˌhɪərˌə'baʊt] erfahren von; hören von IV

heard [hɜːd] simple past von *to hear* II; past participle von *to hear* IV

hearing ['hɪərɪŋ] Gehör II

heavy ['hevi] schwer; stark; schwierig III

height [haɪt] Höhe II

held [held] simple past von *to hold* II

helicopter ['helɪkɒptə] Helikopter; Hubschrauber V U1, 12

Hello. [hə'ləʊ] Hallo. I

helmet ['helmət] Helm I

help [help] Hilfe I

helpful ['helpfl] hilfreich; hilfsbereit <V U3, 151>

to **help** [help] helfen I

helper ['helpə] Helfer; Helferin <V U4, 102>

her [hɜ:] ihr I; sie II

here [hɪə] hier I; hierhin; hierher III

Here you are. [ˌhɪə juˈɑ:] Bitte schön. I

hers [hɜ:z] ihre III

herself [hə'self] sich selbst; sich; selbst IV

Hi. [haɪ] Hi.; Hallo. I

high [haɪ] hoch; groß II

high school ['haɪ ˌsku:l] High School *(weiterführende Schule, Oberstufe)* V U3, 63

high temperature [ˌhaɪ 'temprətʃə] Fieber V U1, 16

junior high school [ˌdʒu:niə 'haɪ sku:l] Junior Highschool *(Mittelschule in den USA, in der Regel Klassenstufe 7–9)* II

hill [hɪl] Berg; Hügel IV

him [hɪm] ihm; ihn II

himself [hɪm'self] sich; selbst; sich selbst IV

Hindi ['hɪndi:] Hindi *(Sprache in Indien)* <V ZI, 8>

Hindu ['hɪndu:] Hindu; hinduistisch V U2, 47

his [hɪz] sein I; seine III

Hispanic [hɪ'spænɪk] Hispanoamerikaner; Hispanoamerikanerin; hispanisch IV

history ['hɪstri] Geschichte <V U4, 100>

*to **hit** [hɪt] schlagen; treffen III; anfahren; rammen V U3, 64

hit [hɪt] simple past, past participle von *to hit* III

HIV [ˌeɪtʃaɪ'vi:] HIV; HI-Virus; HIV- V U3, 68

hobby ['hɒbi] Hobby II

hockey ['hɒki] Eishockey; Hockey IV

ice hockey ['aɪs ˌhɒki] Eishockey IV

*to **hold** [həʊld] halten; festhalten II; abhalten <V U1, 25>

hole [həʊl] Loch I

holiday ['hɒlədeɪ] Ferien; Urlaub II

holiday *(AE)* ['hɒlədeɪ] Feiertag IV

home [həʊm] Zuhause; Heim; nach Hause I; Startseite <V U4, 100>

at home [ət 'həʊm] zu Hause; daheim I

home country [ˌhəʊm 'kʌntri] Heimat; Heimatland IV

homeless ['həʊmləs] obdachlos <V U3, 151>

*to be **homesick** [bi: 'həʊmsɪk] Heimweh haben IV

homework ['həʊmwɜ:k] Hausaufgabe(n) I

to do homework [ˌdu: 'həʊmwɜ:k] Hausaufgabe(n) machen I

honest ['ɒnɪst] ehrlich <V U3, 151>

to **hoover** ['hu:və] staubsaugen II

hope [həʊp] Hoffnung V U3, 73

to **hope (for)** [həʊp (fə)] hoffen (auf) II

horse [hɔ:s] Pferd I

horse riding ['hɔ:s ˌraɪdɪŋ] Reiten I

hospital ['hɒspɪtl] Krankenhaus II

hostel ['hɒstl] Herberge; Hostel II

hot [hɒt] heiß I

hot dog ['hɒt ˌdɒg] Hotdog II

hotel [hə'tel] Hotel IV

hotline ['hɒtlaɪn] Hotline <V U2, 148>

hour [aʊə] Stunde II

hours *(pl)* ['aʊəz] Zeiten IV

working hours *(pl)* ['wɜ:kɪŋ ˌaʊəz] Arbeitszeit IV

visiting hours *(pl)* ['vɪzɪtɪŋ ˌaʊəz] Besuchszeiten <V U3, 74>

house [haʊs] Haus I

how [haʊ] wie I

How are you? [ˌhaʊ'ɑ: jə] Wie geht es dir? I

How can I help you? [ˌhaʊ kæn aɪ 'help ju:] Was kann ich für euch/dich tun? I

How much (is/are) …? [ˌhaʊ 'mʌtʃ (ɪz/ɑ:)] Wie viel (kostet/kosten) …? I

How old are you? [haʊ 'əʊld ə ju:] Wie alt bist du? I

how to … ['haʊ tə] wie man … IV

however [haʊ'evə] jedoch V U1, 20

a/one **hundred** ['hʌndrəd] hundert; einhundert I

hungry ['hʌŋgri] hungrig I

treasure **hunt** ['treʒə ˌhʌnt] Schnitzeljagd; Schatzsuche II

hurling ['hɜ:lɪŋ] Hurling *(ähnliche Sportart wie Hockey)* III

hurricane ['hʌrɪkən] Hurrikan; Orkan; Wirbelsturm IV

*to **hurt** [hɜ:t] verletzen; wehtun II

hurt [hɜ:t] simple past von *to hurt* II; verletzt III; past participle von *to hurt* <V U3, 74>

husky ['hʌski] Husky *(Schlittenhunderasse)* IV

I

I [aɪ] ich I

I can't find … [aɪ ka:nt 'faɪnd] ich kann … nicht finden I

I can't wait [aɪ ˌka:nt 'weɪt] ich kann es kaum erwarten III

I don't mind. [aɪ ˌdəʊnt 'maɪnd] Es macht nichts. IV

I don't know. [ˌaɪ dəʊnt 'nəʊ] Ich weiß (es) nicht! I

I wouldn't like (to) … [aɪ 'wʊdnt laɪk (tə)] ich möchte nicht …; ich würde nicht gerne … I

I'm afraid [aɪm ə'freɪd] leider IV

I'm sorry. [aɪm 'sɒri] Es tut mir leid.; Entschuldigung. II

I'd (= I would) [aɪd] ich würde; ich hätte gern I

I'd like (to) … (= I would like to) [aɪd 'laɪk (tə)] ich möchte …; ich würde gerne … I

I'd love (to) … (= I would love to) [aɪd 'lʌv (tə)] ich würde sehr gern …; ich hätte gern … IV

I'm fine. [aɪm 'faɪn] Mir geht es gut. I

ice cream [aɪs 'kri:m] Eis; Eiscreme II

ice hockey ['aɪs ˌhɒki] Eishockey IV

idea [aɪ'dɪə] Idee I

if [ɪf] wenn; falls; ob IV

if

ill [ɪl] krank; schlecht V U1, 16

to imagine [ɪ'mædʒɪn] sich vorstellen <II>

immigrant ['ɪmɪɡrənt] Einwanderer; Einwanderin; Immigrant; Immigrantin IV

important [ɪm'pɔːtnt] wichtig III

impossible [ɪm'pɒsəbl] unmöglich IV

impression [ɪm'preʃn] Eindruck <V U1, 146>

to improve [ɪm'pruːv] verbessern <V U2, 149>

in [ɪn] im; in; auf; am I; bei; an IV

in front [ɪn 'frʌnt] vorn II

in the middle of [ɪn ðə 'mɪdl̩ əv] mitten in II

in a park [ɪn ə 'pɑːk] im Park I

in front of [ɪn 'frʌnt əv] vor; davor I

in the evening [ɪn ði̩ 'iːvnɪŋ] abends I

in the north of [ɪn ðə 'nɔːθ əv] im Norden von III

in time [ɪn 'taɪm] rechtzeitig; pünktlich V U2, 54

*to be included [bi: ɪn'kluːdɪd] mit enthalten sein; inbegriffen sein V U4, 94

to increase [ɪn'kriːs] erhöhen <V U2, 149>

independence [ˌɪndɪ'pendəns] Unabhängigkeit IV

independent [ˌɪndɪ'pendənt] unabhängig V U2, 37

Indian ['ɪndiən] Inder; Inderin; indisch V U2, 36

indoor [ˌɪn'dɔː] Hallen-; Innen- III

industry ['ɪndəstri] Industrie III; Industriezweig; Gewerbe V U4, 88

tourist industry ['tʊərɪst ˌɪndəstri] Tourismus IV

information [ˌɪnfə'meɪʃn] Information(en) II

to injure ['ɪndʒə] verletzen V U3, 64

inside cover [ˌɪnsaɪd 'kʌvə] Umschlaginnenseite <II>

inspiration [ˌɪnspɪ'reɪʃn] Inspiration; Eingebung V U3, 68

inspiring [ɪn'spaɪərɪŋ] inspirierend; anregend V U3, 68

to install [ɪn'stɔːl] installieren <V U2, 149>

medical insurance [ˌmedɪkl̩ ɪn'ʃʊərns] Krankenversicherung V U3, 73

interest ['ɪntrəst] Interesse IV

*to be interested in [bi: 'ɪntrəstɪd ɪn] interessiert sein an; sich interessieren für III

interesting ['ɪntrəstɪŋ] interessant I

intern ['ɪntɜːn] Praktikant; Praktikantin V U4, 94

international [ˌɪntə'næʃnl̩] international V ZI, 9

internet ['ɪntənet] Internet I

to surf the internet [ˌsɜːf ði 'ɪntənet] im Internet surfen <III>

internship ['ɪntɜːnʃɪp] Praktikum; Berufspraktikum IV

interview ['ɪntəvjuː] Interview; Befragung; Gespräch IV

job interview ['dʒɒb ˌɪntəvjuː] Vorstellungsgespräch <IV>

to interview ['ɪntəvjuː] befragen; interviewen <II>

interviewer ['ɪntəvjuːə] Interviewer; Interviewerin; Befrager; Befragerin IV

into ['ɪntu] in; in … hinein II

intro ['ɪntrəʊ] Auftakt; Einführung <I>

to introduce sb to sb [ˌɪntrə'djuːs] jmdn. jmdm. vorstellen III

introduction [ˌɪntrə'dʌkʃn] Einleitung; Einführung <III>; Vorstellung <V U1, 24>

Inuit ['ɪnuɪt] Inuit *(Ureinwohner Kanadas)* IV

invitation [ˌɪnvɪ'teɪʃn] Einladung I

to invite [ɪn'vaɪt] einladen II

*to be involved [bi: ɪn'vɒlvd] sich beteiligen; sich engagieren <V U3, 150>

Irish ['aɪrɪʃ] irisch; Irisch; aus Irland III

is [ɪz] ist I

Is something wrong? [ɪz 'sʌmθɪŋ rɒŋ] Stimmt etwas nicht? II

island ['aɪlənd] Insel IV

it [ɪt] es; er; sie I; ihn; ihm II

it's (= it is) [ɪts] es ist I

It's ten pounds. [ɪts ˌten 'paʊndz] Es kostet zehn Pfund. I

IT (Information Technology) [ˌaɪ'tiː (ˌɪnfəˌmeɪʃn tek'nɒlədʒi)] Informatik; Informationstechnik V U2, 38

Italian [ɪ'tæliən] italienisch; Italienisch; Italiener; Italienerin IV

item ['aɪtəm] Ding; Artikel; Gegenstand IV

its [ɪts] sein; ihr I

J

January ['dʒænjuri] Januar I

Japanese [ˌdʒæpn'iːz] japanisch; Japanisch; aus Japan; Japaner; Japanerin IV

jeans *(pl)* [dʒiːnz] Jeans I

crown jewels *(pl)* [ˌkraʊn 'dʒuːəlz] Kronjuwelen II

jewellery ['dʒuːəlri] Schmuck <V U2, 148>

job [dʒɒb] Job I; Aufgabe; Tätigkeit III

job ad ['dʒɒb æd] Stellenanzeige <IV>

job interview ['dʒɒb ˌɪntəvjuː] Vorstellungsgespräch <IV>

to join [dʒɔɪn] sich anschließen; beitreten V U2, 47

journey ['dʒɜːni] Fahrt; Reise III

juice [dʒuːs] Saft I

July [dʒʊ'laɪ] Juli I

long jump ['lɒŋ ˌdʒʌmp] Weitsprung II

to jump [dʒʌmp] springen III

June [dʒuːn] Juni I

junior ['dʒuːniə] Nachwuchs- <V U4, 100>

junior high school [ˌdʒuːniə 'haɪ skuːl] Junior Highschool *(Mittelschule in den USA, in der Regel Klassenstufe 7–9)* II

just [dʒʌst] gerade (eben); soeben; einfach; nur III

just for fun [ˌdʒʌst fə 'fʌn] nur (so) zum Spaß <I>

K

kangaroo [ˌkæŋɡr'uː] Känguru V U1, 11

kayak ['kaɪæk] Kajak IV

kayaking ['kaɪækɪŋ] Kajakfahren IV

*to keep [kiːp] halten II

to keep away [ˌkiːp ə'weɪ] fernhalten IV

to keep in touch [ˌkiːp ɪn 'tʌtʃ] in Kontakt bleiben II

to keep sb prisoner [ˌkiːp ˈprɪznə] jmdn. gefangen halten IV

keeper [ˈkiːpə] Pfleger; Pflegerin <V U4, 152>

kept [kept] simple past von *to keep* II; past participle von *to keep* IV

key [kiː] Schlüssel III

to kick [kɪk] schießen; treten III

kid [kɪd] Kind I

to kill [kɪl] töten V U1, 11

kilo (kg, kilogram) [ˈkɪləʊ] Kilo (kg, Kilogramm) I

kilometre (km) [kɪˈlɒmɪtə] Kilometer (km) IV

kilt [kɪlt] Kilt; Schottenrock III

kind [kaɪnd] Art; Sorte II; freundlich; nett <V U3, 151>

kindergarten [ˈkɪndəˌgaːtn] Kindergarten V U3, 73

king [kɪŋ] König II

newspaper kiosk [ˈnjuːspeɪpə ˌkiːɒsk] Zeitungsstand II

to kiss [kɪs] küssen V U4, 99

kitchen [ˈkɪtʃɪn] Küche II

Kiwi [ˈkiːwiː] Kiwi *(Kosename für Neuseeländer)* V U4, 106

knew [njuː] simple past von *to know* IV

to knock sb off sth [ˌnɒk … ˈɒf] jmdn. von etw. stoßen IV

*to know [nəʊ] wissen; kennen I
I don't know. [ˌaɪ dəʊnt ˈnəʊ] Ich weiß (es) nicht! I

*to be known [bi: ˈnəʊn] bekannt sein <V U3, 151>

koala [kəʊˈaːlə] Koala V U1, 11

L

to label [ˈleɪbl] beschriften <II>

ladder [ˈlædə] Leiter I

lady [ˈleɪdi] Frau; Dame IV

lake [leɪk] See IV

to lament [ləˈment] klagen V U4, 98

lamp [læmp] Lampe II

to land [lænd] landen IV

landmark [ˈlænmaːk] Wahrzeichen IV

landscape [ˈlændskeɪp] Landschaft V U4, 89

language [ˈlæŋgwɪdʒ] Grammatik <I>; Sprache IV

official language [əˌfɪʃl ˈlæŋgwɪdʒ] Amtssprache V ZI, 8

lantern [ˈlæntən] Laterne II

laptop [ˈlæptɒp] Laptop I

large [laːdʒ] groß II

to last [laːst] dauern; andauern II

last [laːst] letzte I

late [leɪt] (zu) spät II
to be late [bi: ˈleɪt] zu spät kommen II

later [ˈleɪtə] später I

to laugh [laːf] lachen II

law [lɔː] Gesetz V U1, 20
to break the law [ˌbreɪk ðə ˈlɔː] gegen das Gesetz verstoßen V U2, 46
to mow the lawn [ˌməʊ ðə ˈlɔːn] den Rasen mähen <V U4, 153>

lawyer [ˈlɔːə] Anwalt; Anwältin; Jurist; Juristin V U2, 46

*to lead [liːd] anführen; führen; leiten V U2, 37

leader [ˈliːdə] Leiter; Leiterin III

to learn [lɜːn] lernen II; erfahren; herausfinden V U1, 12

*to leave [liːv] verlassen; lassen; abfahren; weggehen II; vergessen; hinterlassen III; abfliegen; gehen IV

leaving [ˈliːvɪŋ] Abschieds- II

led [led] simple past, past participle von *to lead* V U2, 37

left [left] links; simple past von *to leave* II; übrig; past participle von *to leave* III
on the left [ɒn ðə ˈleft] links; auf der linken Seite II

leg [leg] Bein II

lesbian [ˈlezbiən] homosexuell; lesbisch; Lesbe V U3, 68

less [les] weniger III

lesson [ˈlesn] Schulstunde; Unterricht I

let's (= let us) [lets] lass(t) uns I

letter [ˈletə] Buchstabe; Brief; Schreiben IV
letter of application [ˌletər əv ˌæplɪˈkeɪʃn] Bewerbungsschreiben IV

driving licence [ˈdraɪvɪŋ ˌlaɪsns] Führerschein V U3, 64

to lie [laɪ] lügen IV

life *(sg)* [laɪf], lives *(pl)* [laɪvz] Leben II

lifestyle [ˈlaɪfstaɪl] Lebensstil; Lebensart; Lebensweise V U1, 12

lift [lɪft] Aufzug II

to like [laɪk] mögen; gernhaben I
like + -ing [ˌlaɪk ˈ…ɪŋ] … gerne I

like [laɪk] wie I; als ob IV
like this [ˌlaɪk ˈðɪs] so; auf diese Weise <I>

line [laɪn] Linie III; Zeile <IV>
assembly line [əˈsembli ˌlaɪn] Fließband V U2, 38
zip line [ˈzɪp ˌlaɪn] Seilrutsche III

link [lɪŋk] Link; Verbindung <V U4, 100>

lion [ˈlaɪən] Löwe V U3, 63
mountain lion [ˈmaʊntɪn ˌlaɪən] Puma II

list [lɪst] Liste V U1, 16
shopping list [ˈʃɒpɪŋ ˌlɪst] Einkaufszettel I

to listen (to) [ˈlɪsn (tə)] anhören; hören; zuhören I

listening [ˈlɪsnɪŋ] Hörverstehen <I>
listening skills [ˈlɪsnɪŋ ˌskɪlz] Fertigkeit Hören <I>

little [ˈlɪtl] klein I
a little (bit) [ə ˈlɪtl (bɪt)] ein (kleines) bisschen; ein (klein) wenig II

to live [lɪv] wohnen; leben I

living [ˈlɪvɪŋ] Lebensweise; Wohnen; Leben V U2, 42
living room [ˈlɪvɪŋ ˌrʊm] Wohnzimmer II

to load the dishwasher [ˌləʊd ðə ˈdɪʃwɒʃə] die Spülmaschine einräumen II

local [ˈləʊkl] örtlich; lokal; hiesig II

location [ləʊˈkeɪʃn] Ort <V U1, 24>

locked [lɒkt] abgeschlossen I

logistics [ləˈdʒɪstɪks] Logistik <V U2, 148>

lonely [ˈləʊnli] einsam III

long [lɒŋ] lang III; weit V U1, 11
as long as [əz ˈlɒŋ əz] solange; sofern V U3, 80
to be a long way away [bi: ə ˈlɒŋ ˌweɪ əˈweɪ] weit weg sein II
long jump [ˈlɒŋ ˌdʒʌmp] Weitsprung II

longer

longer ['lɒŋɡə] länger I

to **look** [lʊk] schauen; aussehen; sehen; nachschauen I

to look after [lʊk ˈɑːftə] aufpassen auf; hüten; sich kümmern um II

to look at [ˈlʊk ət] anschauen I

to look for [ˈlʊk fə] suchen (nach) IV

to look forward to (+ -ing) [lʊk ˈfɔːwəd tə] sich freuen auf IV

to look to do sth [ˈlʊk tə] etw. planen <V U4, 100>

to look up to sb [lʊk ˈʌp tə] zu jmdm. aufschauen; jmdn. bewundern <V U3, 151>

*to **lose** [luːz] verlieren II

lost [lɒst] simple past von to lose II; past participle von to lose III

to get lost [ɡet ˈlɒst] verloren gehen; sich verirren IV

lost and found notice [ˌlɒst ən ˈfaʊnd ˌnəʊtɪs] Suchplakat; Aushang III

a **lot** [ə ˈlɒt] viel; sehr I

a **lot** of [ə ˈlɒt əv] viel; viele; eine Menge I

lots of [ˈlɒts əv] jede Menge; viel; viele I

loud [laʊd] laut I

Love, [lʌv] Liebe Grüße; Herzliche Grüße I

to **love** [lʌv] lieben; gern mögen I

I'd love (to) … (= I would love to) [aɪd ˈlʌv (tə)] ich würde sehr gern …; ich hätte gern … IV

Good **luck!** [ɡʊd ˈlʌk] Alles Gute!; Viel Glück! IV

lucky [ˈlʌki] glücklich; Glück bringend II

to be lucky [bi ˈlʌki] Glück haben II

lucky day [ˌlʌki ˈdeɪ] Glückstag II

lunch [lʌnʃ] Mittagessen I

lunchtime [ˈlʌnʃtaɪm] Mittagspause; Mittagszeit I

M

machine [məˈʃiːn] Maschine; Automat V U2, 38

made [meɪd] simple past von to make II; past participle von to make III

magazine [ˌmæɡəˈziːn] Zeitschrift IV

*to do **magic** [ˌduː ˈmædʒɪk] zaubern II

magician [məˈdʒɪʃn] Zauberkünstler; Zauberkünstlerin II

main [meɪn] wichtigste <III>

majority [məˈdʒɒrəti] Mehrheit; Mehrzahl V ZI, 8

*to **make** [meɪk] erstellen; basteln; machen; tun I; bilden; ausmachen <II>; herstellen V U2, 38

to make friends [ˌmeɪk ˈfrendz] Freundschaft(en) schließen II

to make reservations [ˌmeɪk rezəˈveɪʃnz] reservieren IV

to make up [ˌmeɪk ˈʌp] erfinden; sich ausdenken <V U2, 41>

mall [mɔːl] Einkaufspassage; Einkaufszentrum II

man (sg) [mæn], **men** (pl) [men] Mann I

manager [ˈmænɪdʒə] Manager; Managerin; Geschäftsführer; Geschäftsführerin IV

manta ray [ˈmæntə ˌreɪ] Teufelsrochen <V U1, 23>

to **manufacture** [ˌmænjəˈfæktʃə] fertigen; herstellen <V U2, 148>

many [ˈmeni] viele I

Maori [ˈmaʊri] Maori-; maorisch; Maori V U4, 89

map [mæp] Karte; Plan II

March [mɑːtʃ] März I

march [mɑːtʃ] Marsch; Kundgebung V U2, 47

market [ˈmɑːkɪt] Markt I

flea market [ˈfliː ˌmɑːkɪt] Flohmarkt I

arranged **marriage** [əˌreɪndʒd ˈmærɪdʒ] arrangierte Hochzeit V U2, 37

mask [mɑːsk] Maske V U4, 99

match [mætʃ] Spiel; Match I

to **match** [mætʃ] zuordnen <I>

to match sth [mætʃ] zu etw. passen <V U2, 50>

Math (AE) [mæθ] Mathe; Mathematik III

Maths [mæθs] Mathe I

What's the **matter?** [ˌwɒts ðə ˈmætə] Was ist los?; Was hast du? V U1, 16

May [meɪ] Mai I

may [meɪ] können; dürfen V U1, 20

maybe [ˈmeɪbi] vielleicht II

me [miː] ich; mich; mir I

meal [miːl] Essen; Mahlzeit II

*to **mean** [miːn] bedeuten; meinen IV

meaning [ˈmiːnɪŋ] Bedeutung <III>

meant [ment] simple past, past participle von to mean IV

meat [miːt] Fleisch IV

mechanic [mɪˈkænɪk] Mechaniker; Mechanikerin V U4, 90

medal [ˈmedl] Medaille II

media [ˈmiːdiə] Medien <II>

media designer [ˈmiːdiə dɪˌzaɪnə] Mediengestalter; Mediengestalterin <V U4, 152>

social media [ˌsəʊʃl ˈmiːdiə] soziale Medien III

mediation [ˌmiːdiˈeɪʃn] Sprachmittlung <I>

mediation skills [ˌmiːdiˈeɪʃn ˌskɪlz] Fertigkeit Sprachmittlung <I>

medical insurance [ˌmedɪkl ɪnˈʃʊərns] Krankenversicherung V U3, 73

medical record [ˌmedɪkl ˈrekɔːd] Krankenakte V U1, 16

medication [ˌmedɪˈkeɪʃn] Medikament; Arznei; Arzneimittel V U3, 68

medicine [ˈmedsn] Medikamente; Medizin V U1, 16

*to **meet** [miːt] kennenlernen; treffen I; (sich) treffen II

meeting [ˈmiːtɪŋ] Besprechung; Meeting <V U4, 153>

member [ˈmembə] Mitglied V U4, 89

menu [ˈmenjuː] Menu; Speisekarte <V U2, 48>

Merry Christmas! [ˌmeri ˈkrɪsməs] Frohe Weihnachten! I

mess [mes] Durcheinander; Unordnung I

message [ˈmesɪdʒ] Nachricht; SMS II

messenger [ˈmesɪndʒə] Kurier; Kurierin; Bote; Botin IV

met [met] simple past von to meet II

metal [ˈmetl] Metall-; metallen III

metalworker ['metlwɜ:kə] Metall-
bauer; Metallbauerin <V U4, 152>

meter *(AE)* ['mi:tə] Meter III

metre ['mi:tə] Meter II

middle ['mɪdl] Mitte III
in the middle of [ɪn ðə 'mɪdl̩ əv]
mitten in II

might [maɪt] könnte V U4, 90

mild [maɪld] mild II

mile [maɪl] Meile III

million ['mɪljən] Million I
half a million [ˌha:f ə 'mɪljən] eine
halbe Million III

mind map ['maɪnd ˌmæp] Wörternetz
<I>

to **mind** sth [maɪnd] etwas gegen
etw. haben; einem etwas ausmachen V U4, 90
Never mind. [ˌnevə 'maɪnd] Macht
nichts.; Schon gut.; Mach dir nichts
draus. II

coal **mine** ['kəʊl ˌmaɪn] Kohlenbergwerk; Kohlengrube III

mine [maɪn] meine III

minute ['mɪnɪt] Minute I

to **miss** [mɪs] verpassen; vermissen II

Miss [mɪs] Frau *(Anrede)* IV

missing ['mɪsɪŋ] fehlend; verschwun-
den <V U2, 37>

mistake [mɪ'steɪk] Fehler <V U1, 11>

model ['mɒdl] Vorlage; Muster <I>
role model ['rəʊl ˌmɒdl] Vorbild
V U3, 68

modern ['mɒdn] modern I

mom *(AE)* [mɒm] Mama III

at the **moment** [ət ðə 'məʊmənt] im
Moment; momentan II

Monday ['mʌndeɪ] Montag I

money ['mʌni] Geld I
to raise money [ˌreɪz 'mʌni] Geld
sammeln; Geld aufbringen II

month [mʌnθ] Monat II

moose *(sg)* [mu:s], **moose** *(pl)* [mu:s]
Elch IV

more [mɔ:] mehr; weitere II
more often [mɔ:r ˌɒfn] häufiger;
öfter IV

morning ['mɔ:nɪŋ] Morgen; Vormittag I
this morning [ðɪs 'mɔ:nɪŋ] heute
Morgen II

most [məʊst] die meisten; die Mehrheit; am meisten III

mother ['mʌðə] Mutter I

to **motivate** ['məʊtɪveɪt] anspornen;
motivieren III

mountain ['maʊntɪn] Berg II
mountain lion ['maʊntɪn ˌlaɪən]
Puma II

mouse *(sg)* [maʊs], **mice** *(pl)* [maɪs]
Maus I

mouth [maʊθ] Mund II

mouthguard ['maʊθɡa:d] Mundschutz <V U4, 100>

to **move** [mu:v] umziehen II; (sich)
bewegen; ziehen IV

movement ['mu:vmənt] Bewegung IV

movie *(AE)* ['mu:vi] Film III

to **mow the lawn** [ˌməʊ ðə 'lɔ:n] den
Rasen mähen <V U4, 153>

Mr ['mɪstə] Herr *(Anrede)* I

Mrs ['mɪsɪz] Frau *(Anrede)* I

Ms [mɪz] Frau *(Anrede)* V U4, 90

much [mʌtʃ] viel I
as much as [əz 'mʌtʃ əz] bis zu
<V U1, 23>

mud [mʌd] Schlamm; Matsch I

muffin ['mʌfɪn] Muffin II

multicultural [ˌmʌltɪ'kʌltʃrl] multikulturell IV

mum [mʌm] Mama; Mutti I

museum [mju:'zi:əm] Museum II

music ['mju:zɪk] Musik I

Muslim ['mʊzlɪm] Muslim; Muslimin I

must [mʌst] müssen II

my [maɪ] mein I
My name is … [maɪ 'neɪm ɪz] Ich
heiße … I

myself [maɪ'self] mich; selbst III; mir;
mich selbst IV

N

name [neɪm] Name I

to **name** [neɪm] benennen <I>

narrator [nə'reɪtə] Erzähler; Erzählerin I

nation ['neɪʃn] Volk; Nation; Land;
Staat III

national ['næʃnl] National-; national
III

national park [ˌnæʃnl 'pa:k] Nationalpark III

nationality [ˌnæʃn'æləti] Nationalität;
Staatsangehörigkeit IV

native ['neɪtɪv] eingeboren; einhei-
misch <V ZI, 8>
Native American [ˌneɪtɪv ə'merɪkən]
Ureinwohner Amerikas; Urein-
wohnerin Amerikas; Indianer;
Indianerin; indianisch III

natural ['nætʃrl] Natur-; natürlich
<V U4, 101>

nature ['neɪtʃə] Natur V U3, 81

near [nɪə] in der Nähe von I; nah II

nearly ['nɪəli] fast; beinahe II

neck [nek] Hals; Nacken II

to **need** [ni:d] brauchen I
to need to ['ni:d ˌtə] müssen III

negative ['neɡətɪv] negativ <IV>

neighbour ['neɪbə] Nachbar; Nachbarin I

nervous ['nɜ:vəs] nervös; aufgeregt
<V U3, 151>

netball ['netbɔ:l] Korbball I

never ['nevə] nie; niemals II
Never mind. [ˌnevə 'maɪnd] Macht
nichts.; Schon gut.; Mach dir nichts
draus. II

new [nju:] neu I

news [nju:z] Nachricht(en);
Neuigkeit(en) II

newspaper ['nju:sˌpeɪpə] Zeitung III
newspaper kiosk ['nju:speɪpə
ˌki:ɒsk] Zeitungsstand II

next [nekst] nächste I; als Nächstes II
next to ['nekst tə] neben I

nice [naɪs] schön; nett I
Nice to meet you. [ˌnaɪs tə 'mi:t ju:]
Schön, dich kennenzulernen. I

night [naɪt] Nacht I
at night [ət 'naɪt] nachts IV

nine [naɪn] neun I

nineteen [ˌnaɪn'ti:n] neunzehn I

ninety ['naɪnti] neunzig I

no [nəʊ] kein; keine; nein I
no one ['nəʊ wʌn] niemand I

nobody ['nəʊbədi] niemand II

to **nod** [nɒd] nicken V U4, 99

noise [nɔɪz] Geräusch I

noisy ['nɔɪzi] laut III

non- [nɒn] nicht- <V ZI, 8>

non-violent [ˌnɒnˈvaɪələnt] friedlich; gewaltfrei V U2, 46

north [nɔːθ] Norden; Nord- III
in the north of [ˌɪn ðə ˈnɔːθ ˌəv] im Norden von III

nose [nəʊz] Nase II

not [nɒt] nicht I
not … any [ˌnɒt … eni] kein; keine III
not … any more [ˌnɒt … eni ˈmɔː] nicht mehr III
not … anything [ˌnɒt … ˈeniθɪŋ] nichts III
not … either [ˌnɒt … ˈaɪðə] auch nicht III
not … yet [ˌnɒt … ˈjet] noch nicht III

note [nəʊt] Notiz; Zettel; Nachricht <V U1, 13>

notes (pl) [nəʊts] Notizen <I>
to take notes [teɪk ˈnəʊts] sich Notizen machen <I>

nothing [ˈnʌθɪŋ] nichts II

lost and found **notice** [ˌlɒst ən ˈfaʊnd ˌnəʊtɪs] Suchplakat; Aushang III

noun [naʊn] Nomen; Hauptwort <V U3, 69>

November [nəˈvembə] November I

now [naʊ] jetzt; nun I

number [ˈnʌmbə] Zahl; Nummer I; Anzahl <V ZI, 8>

nurse [nɜːs] Krankenpfleger; Krankenschwester IV

nursery teacher [ˈnɜːsri ˌtiːtʃə] Erzieher; Erzieherin <V U4, 152>

O

o'clock [əˈklɒk] Uhr (Zeitangabe bei vollen Stunden) I

occasionally [əˈkeɪʒnli] gelegentlich III

ocean [ˈəʊʃn] Ozean <V U3, 78>

October [ɒkˈtəʊbə] Oktober I

odd one out [ˌɒd wʌnˈaʊt] das Wort, das nicht in die Gruppe passt <I>

of [ɒv] von I; mit; vor; aus III
of course [əv ˈkɔːs] natürlich; selbstverständlich II
of all the states [əv ˈɔːl ðə ˌsteɪts] von allen Staaten IV

to turn **off** [tɜːn ˈɒf] abschalten; ausschalten <V U2, 149>

to knock sb **off** sth [ˌnɒk … ˈɒf] jmdn. von etw. stoßen IV

to **offer** [ˈɒfə] bieten; anbieten IV

office [ˈɒfɪs] Büro V U2, 38

police **officer** [pəˈliːs ˌɒfɪsə] Polizeibeamter; Polizeibeamtin I

official [əˈfɪʃl] offiziell <IV>
official language [əˌfɪʃl ˈlæŋgwɪdʒ] Amtssprache V ZI, 8

often [ˈɒfn] oft; häufig II
more often [mɔːr ˈɒfn] häufiger; öfter IV

oh [əʊ] Null (bei Uhrzeiten und Telefonnummern) III
Oh dear. [ˌəʊ ˈdɪə] Oje. V U1, 16

oil [ɔɪl] Öl II
oil spill [ˈɔɪl ˌspɪl] Ölteppich; Ölpest V U1, 20

OK (okay) [əʊˈkeɪ] okay I

old [əʊld] alt I

on [ɒn] auf; an; am I; mit II
to put on [ˌpʊt ˈɒn] anziehen II
to try on [traɪ ˈɒn] anprobieren II
on foot [ɒn ˈfʊt] zu Fuß I
on Saturdays [ɒn ˈsætədeɪz] samstags I
on the bus [ɒn ðə ˈbʌs] im Bus II
on the left [ɒn ðə ˈleft] links; auf der linken Seite II
on the right [ɒn ðə ˈraɪt] rechts; auf der rechten Seite II
on TV [ɒn ˌtiːˈviː] im Fernsehen III

once [wʌns] einmal; einst II
once upon a time [ˌwʌns əpɒn ə ˈtaɪm] es war einmal II

one [wʌn] eins; ein I
a/one hundred [ˈhʌndrəd] hundert; einhundert I
a/one thousand [ˈθaʊznd] tausend; eintausend II
each one [ˌiːtʃ ˈwʌn] jedes <IV>
no one [ˈnəʊ wʌn] niemand I
one day [ˈwʌn deɪ] eines Tages I
one(s) [wʌn(z)] Platzhalter für ein Nomen III

online [ɒnˈlaɪn] online; Online- II

only [ˈəʊnli] nur I; erst V U3, 68

to **open** [ˈəʊpn] öffnen; aufmachen I; eröffnen V U4, 94

open [ˈəʊpn] geöffnet I; offen <V U4, 100>

opportunity [ˌɒpəˈtjuːnəti] Chance; Möglichkeit; Gelegenheit IV

opposite [ˈɒpəzɪt] Gegenteil <I>; gegenüber II

or [ɔː] oder I

orange [ˈɒrɪndʒ] orange; Orange I

order [ˈɔːdə] Reihenfolge <I>
word order [ˈwɜːd ˌɔːdə] Wortstellung; Satzstellung <II>

to **order** [ˈɔːdə] bestellen V U4, 94

organization [ˌɔːgnaɪˈzeɪʃn] Organisation V U3, 72

to **organize** [ˈɔːgnaɪz] organisieren I

other [ˈʌðə] andere II
each other [ˌiːtʃ ˈʌðə] einander; sich; gegenseitig III

others [ˈʌðəz] anderen II

our [aʊə] unser I

ours [aʊəz] unsere III

ourselves [ˌaʊəˈselvz] uns; selbst; uns selbst IV

out [aʊt] hinaus V U4, 98
out and about [ˌaʊt ən əˈbaʊt] unterwegs III
out of … [ˈaʊt ˌəv] aus … heraus I

the **outback** [ðɪ ˈaʊtbæk] das Outback (australisches Hinterland) V U1, 11

outdoors [ˌaʊtˈdɔːz] im Freien <V U2, 48>

outside [ˌaʊtˈsaɪd] außerhalb; außen; draußen; im Freien II

oval [ˈəʊvl] oval; eiförmig III

over [ˈəʊvə] vorbei <II>; über; herüber; drüben III
all over [ɔːl ˈəʊvə] in ganz; überall II
to turn over [ˌtɜːn ˈəʊvə] umkippen; (sich) umdrehen III

to **own** [əʊn] besitzen III

own [əʊn] eigene II

P

p.m. [ˌpiːˈem] nachmittags (Uhrzeit) III

to **pack** [pæk] packen; einpacken III

package [ˈpækɪdʒ] Paket IV

packaging [ˈpækɪdʒɪŋ] Verpackung <V U2, 149>

page [peɪdʒ] Seite <I>

to **paint** [peɪnt] bemalen; malen; streichen II

painting [ˈpeɪntɪŋ] Gemälde V U1, 12
face painting [ˈfeɪs peɪntɪŋ] Schminken II
wall painting [ˈwɔːl peɪntɪŋ] Wandmalerei II

pair [peə] Paar <II>

solar **panel** [ˌsəʊlə ˈpænl] Sonnenkollektor <V U2, 149>

paper [ˈpeɪpə] Papier III

parade [pəˈreɪd] Parade; Umzug; Prozession IV

parents (pl) [ˈpeərnts] Eltern I

park [pɑːk] Park I
national park [ˌnæʃnl ˈpɑːk] Nationalpark III
theme park [ˈθiːm ˌpɑːk] Freizeitpark II

parliament [ˈpɑːləmənt] Parlament V U3, 62

part [pɑːt] Teil; Rolle II
to take part (in) [ˌteɪk ˈpɑːt (ɪn)] mitmachen (bei); teilnehmen (an) II

partner [ˈpɑːtnə] Partner; Partnerin I

party [ˈpɑːti] Party; Feier I
to have a party [ˌhæv ə ˈpɑːti] eine Party feiern I

to **pass** on [ˌpɑːs ˈɒn] weitergeben <V U3, 81>

passenger [ˈpæsndʒə] Passagier; Passagierin IV

passive voice [ˈpæsɪv ˌvɔɪs] Passiv <IV>

passport [ˈpɑːspɔːt] Pass; Reisepass IV

past [pɑːst] vorbei (an) I; nach (bei Uhrzeitangaben) II; Vergangenheit III
half past (seven) [ˌhɑːf ˈpɑːst (ˌsevn)] halb (acht) II
quarter to/past [ˈkwɔːtə tə/pɑːst] Viertel vor/nach II

patient [ˈpeɪʃnt] Patient; Patientin V U1, 16; geduldig <V U2, 51>

*to **pay** [peɪ] bezahlen V U3, 68

PE (Physical Education) [ˌpiːˈiː (ˌfɪzɪkl edʒʊˈkeɪʃn)] Sportunterricht I

peaceful [ˈpiːsfl] friedlich V U2, 47

pen [pen] Stift; Füller I

pencil [ˈpensl] Bleistift I

penfriend [ˈpenfrend] Brieffreund; Brieffreundin III

people [ˈpiːpl] Leute; Menschen I; Volk V U4, 89
Aboriginal people [ˌæbəˌrɪdʒnl ˈpiːpl] die Aborigines V U1, 11

per [pɜː] pro <V U4, 100>

percent (%) [pəˈsent] Prozent III

present **perfect** [ˌpreznt ˈpɜːfɪkt] das Perfekt <III>

person (sg) [ˈpɜːsn] Mensch; Person II

persons (pl) [ˈpɜːsns] Leute; Menschen II

pet [pet] Haustier I

pharmacist [ˈfɑːməsɪst] Apotheker; Apothekerin <V U1, 22>

pharmacy [ˈfɑːməsi] Apotheke V U1, 16

phone [fəʊn] Telefon; Handy I
phone call [ˈfəʊn ˌkɔːl] Telefonanruf; Anruf I

to **phone** [fəʊn] anrufen; telefonieren II

photo [ˈfəʊtəʊ] Foto I
to take photos (of) [ˌteɪk ˈfəʊtəʊz (əv)] Fotos machen; fotografieren II

phrase [freɪz] Wortverbindung; Satzteil; Satz; Redewendung <III>

to **pick** up [ˌpɪk ˈʌp] abholen <V U1, 147>; aufheben V U4, 99

picnic [ˈpɪknɪk] Picknick I

picture [ˈpɪktʃə] Bild I

picture-based [ˈpɪktʃəbeɪst] bildbezogen <III>

a **piece** of [ə ˈpiːs əv] ein Stück … II

pier [pɪə] Pier II

pink [pɪŋk] pink; rosa I

pizza [ˈpiːtsə] Pizza I

place [pleɪs] Platz; Stelle; Ort I
to take place [ˌteɪk ˈpleɪs] stattfinden <V U1, 146>

plan [plæn] Plan IV

to **plan** [plæn] planen IV

plane [pleɪn] Flugzeug IV

planner [ˈplænə] Kalender; Planer II

plant [plɑːnt] Pflanze III

to **plant** [plɑːnt] pflanzen <V U4, 153>

plate [pleɪt] Teller; (Kontinental-) Platte IV

play [pleɪ] Theaterstück III

to **play** [pleɪ] spielen I

player [ˈpleɪə] Spieler; Spielerin II

playground [ˈpleɪgraʊnd] Schulhof; Pausenhof; Spielplatz I

playing field [ˈpleɪŋ ˌfiːld] Sportplatz II

please [pliːz] bitte I

plum [plʌm] Pflaume I

plumber [ˈplʌmə] Installateur; Installateurin; Klempner; Klempnerin <V U2, 148>

podcast [ˈpɒdkɑːst] Podcast V U3, 68

poem [ˈpəʊɪm] Gedicht III

point [pɔɪnt] Punkt III

to **point** [pɔɪnt] zeigen V U4, 99

police [pəˈliːs] Polizei IV
police officer [pəˈliːs ˌɒfɪsə] Polizeibeamter; Polizeibeamtin I
police station [pəˈliːs ˌsteɪʃn] Polizeirevier; Polizeiwache V U3, 64

polite [pəˈlaɪt] höflich <V U3, 151>

to **pollute** [pəˈluːt] verschmutzen; verunreinigen V U2, 42

pollution [pəˈluːʃn] Verschmutzung V U2, 37

pool [puːl] Tümpel <V U4, 101>
swimming pool [ˈswɪmɪŋ ˌpuːl] Schwimmbad I

poor [pɔː] arm IV

pop [pɒp] Pop (Musik) II

popular [ˈpɒpjələ] beliebt III

population (no pl) [ˌpɒpjəˈleɪʃn] Bevölkerung; Einwohner; Einwohnerzahl IV

positive [ˈpɒzətɪv] positiv III

possible [ˈpɒsəbl] möglich <V U2, 149>

post [pəʊst] Post; Beitrag <V U1, 12>

to **post** [pəʊst] posten; online stellen III

postcard [ˈpəʊskɑːd] Postkarte I

poster [ˈpəʊstə] Poster II

pot [pɒt] Topf III

potato (sg) [pəˈteɪtəʊ], **potatoes** (pl) [pəˈteɪtəʊz] Kartoffel IV

pound (£) [paʊnd] Pfund (brit. Währungseinheit) I

practice [ˈpræktɪs] Training; Übung I

to **practise** [ˈpræktɪs] üben; trainieren <II>

prayer [preə] Gebet V U4, 98

s six • **z** zoo • **ʃ** she • **ʒ** revision • **h** her • **m** me • **n** no • **ŋ** sing • **iə** hear • **l** let • **r** red • **j** yes

prayer

189

to **prefer** [prɪ'fɜ:] bevorzugen; vorziehen <V U4, 152>

to **prepare** [prɪ'peə] vorbereiten <IV>

preschool [pri:'sku:l] Vorschul-; Vorschule V U3, 73

prescription [prɪ'skrɪpʃn] Rezept *(für Arzneimittel)* V U1, 16

present ['preznt] Geschenk I

present perfect [ˌpreznt 'pɜ:fɪkt] das Perfekt <III>

present progressive [ˌpreznt prə'gresɪv] Verlaufsform der Gegenwart <II>

to **present** [prɪ'zent] präsentieren V U4, 94

presentation [ˌprezn'teɪʃn] Präsentation; Referat; Vortrag III
   presentation skills [ˌprezn'teɪʃn ˌskɪlz] Fertigkeit Präsentieren <III>

presenter [prɪ'zentə] Moderator; Moderatorin <V U1, 25>

president ['prezɪdnt] Präsident; Präsidentin III

pretty ['prɪti] hübsch II

price [praɪs] Preis I

primary school ['praɪmri ˌsku:l] Grundschule IV

prince [prɪns] Prinz V U2, 38

prison ['prɪzn] Gefängnis V U2, 46

prisoner ['prɪznə] Gefangener; Gefangene IV
   to **keep sb prisoner** [ki:p 'prɪznə] jmdn. gefangen halten IV

prize [praɪz] Preis; Gewinn II

probably ['prɒbəbli] wahrscheinlich IV

problem ['prɒbləm] Problem I

procession [prə'seʃn] Umzug; Festzug II

to **produce** [prə'dju:s] erzeugen; herstellen; anbauen IV

product ['prɒdʌkt] Produkt; Erzeugnis V U4, 94

profile ['prəʊfaɪl] Profil; Steckbrief III

(software) program [(ˌsɒfweə) 'prəʊgræm] (Software)Programm V ZI, 8

programme ['prəʊgræm] Sendung; Programm III

computer programmer [kəmˌpju:tə 'prəʊgræmə] Programmierer; Programmiererin V U2, 38

programming ['prəʊgræmɪŋ] Programmieren <V U2, 148>

present progressive [ˌpreznt prə'gresɪv] Verlaufsform der Gegenwart <II>

project ['prɒdʒekt] Projekt II

to **protect** [prə'tekt] schützen III

protest ['prəʊtest] Protest; Demonstration V U2, 37

to **protest** [prə'test] protestieren V U1, 21

proud (of) [praʊd (əv)] stolz (auf) IV

to **prove** [pru:v] beweisen IV

to **provide** [prə'vaɪd] bereitstellen; bieten; versorgen <V U4, 100>

public transport [ˌpʌblɪk 'trænspɔ:t] öffentliche Verkehrsmittel III

to **pull** [pʊl] ziehen I

pullover ['pʊləʊvə] Pullover I

to **push** [pʊʃ] schieben I

stone put ['stəʊn ˌpʊt] Steinstoßen III

*to **put** [pʊt] setzen; legen; stellen I; bringen; stecken II
   to **put in** [pʊt 'ɪn] einsetzen <I>
   to **put into** [ˌpʊt 'ɪntə] eingeben (in) <IV>
   to **put on** [pʊt 'ɒn] anziehen II

put [pʊt] simple past von *to put* I

Q

qualification [ˌkwɒlɪfɪ'keɪʃn] Ausbildung; Qualifikation; Abschluss; Schulabschluss IV

qualified ['kwɒlɪfaɪd] qualifiziert V U4, 112

quality ['kwɒləti] Eigenschaft; Qualität; Merkmal <V U4, 93>

quantity ['kwɒntəti] Menge <IV>

quarter to/past ['kwɔ:tə tə/pɑ:st] Viertel vor/nach II

queen [kwi:n] Königin II

question ['kwestʃən] Frage I

queue [kju:] Warteschlange II

quick [kwɪk] schnell IV

quiet ['kwaɪət] leise; ruhig; still II

quite [kwaɪt] ziemlich; ganz; völlig II

quiz [kwɪz] Rätsel <I>; Quiz; Ratespiel IV

R

rabbit ['ræbɪt] Kaninchen I

raccoon [rə'ku:n] Waschbär I

race [reɪs] Wettrennen; Rennen; Wettlauf II
   sack race ['sæk ˌreɪs] Sackhüpfen II

radio ['reɪdiəʊ] Radio III

raffle ['ræfl] Gewinnspiel; Tombola II

raft [rɑ:ft] Raft; Floß III

rafting ['rɑ:ftɪŋ] Rafting III
   to **go rafting** [ˌgəʊ 'rɑ:ftɪŋ] raften gehen III

railway ['reɪlweɪ] Eisenbahn; Bahn IV
   railway station ['reɪlweɪ ˌsteɪʃn] Bahnhof IV

to **rain** [reɪn] regnen I

rainbow ['reɪnbəʊ] Regenbogen III

rainy ['reɪni] regnerisch II

to **raise** [reɪz] sammeln; aufbringen <V U4, 100>
   to **raise money** [ˌreɪz 'mʌni] Geld sammeln; Geld aufbringen II

ran [ræn] simple past von *to run* II

rang [ræŋ] simple past von *to ring* II

ranger *(AE)* ['reɪndʒə] Ranger; Rangerin IV

rap [ræp] Rap I

rapid ['ræpɪd] Stromschnelle III

rarely ['reəli] selten III

RE [ri:] Betr. V U4, 106

*to **read** [ri:d] lesen; vorlesen II

read [red] simple past von *to read* II

reading ['ri:dɪŋ] Lesen <I>; Lesung <V U1, 24>
   reading skills ['ri:dɪŋ ˌskɪlz] Fertigkeit Lesen <I>

ready ['redi] bereit; fertig I

real [rɪəl] echt; richtig; wirklich <V U1, 23>

really ['rɪəli] wirklich; eigentlich I

reason ['ri:zn] Grund <V U3, 71>

*to **rebuild** [ˌri:'bɪld] wiederaufbauen IV

receptionist [rɪ'sepʃnɪst] Empfangschef; Empfangsdame IV; Arzthelfer; Arzthelferin V U1, 16 medical **record** [ˌmedɪkl ˈrekɔːd] Krankenakte V U1, 16

to **record** [rɪˈkɔːd] aufnehmen; aufzeichnen <I>

to **recover** [rɪˈkʌvə] sich erholen V U1, 20

to **recycle** [ˌriːˈsaɪkl] recyceln; wiederverwerten <V U2, 149>

recycling [ˌriːˈsaɪklɪŋ] Recycling; Wiederaufbereitung <V U2, 149>

red [red] rot I

to **reduce** [rɪˈdjuːs] reduzieren; vermindern; verringern V U4, 94

reef [riːf] Riff V U1, 20

reference [ˈrefrns] Referenz; Arbeitszeugnis; Empfehlung IV

reflexive pronoun [rɪˌfleksɪv ˈprəʊnaʊn] Reflexivpronomen <IV>

reggae [ˈregeɪ] Reggae (Musik) IV

to **register** [ˈredʒɪstə] sich registrieren lassen; sich eintragen; sich anmelden V U1, 16

registration [ˌredʒɪˈstreɪʃn] Überprüfung der Anwesenheit I

reliable [rɪˈlaɪəbl] verlässlich; zuverlässig; vertrauenswürdig IV

religion [rɪˈlɪdʒn] Religion V U2, 47

to **rely** (on) [rɪˈlaɪ (ɒn)] sich verlassen (auf); vertrauen (auf) IV

to **remember** [rɪˈmembə] sich erinnern (an); sich merken III

to **repair** [rɪˈpeə] reparieren IV

to **repeat** [rɪˈpiːt] wiederholen V U3, 81

report [rɪˈpɔːt] Bericht V U4, 94

to **report** [rɪˈpɔːt] berichten <III>

request [rɪˈkwest] Anfrage IV

animal **rescue** shelter [ˈænɪml ˈreskjuːˌʃeltə] Tierheim I

research [rɪˈsɜːtʃ] Recherche; Forschung <IV>

to **research** [rɪˈsɜːtʃ] recherchieren; erforschen; untersuchen <V U4, 99>

reservation [ˌrezəˈveɪʃn] Reservat; Reservierung III
   to make reservations [ˌmeɪk rezəˈveɪʃnz] reservieren IV

respectful [rɪˈspektfl] respektvoll <V U3, 151>

to **respect** [rɪˈspekt] respektieren V U2, 47

responsible [rɪsˈpɒnsəbl] verantwortungsvoll; verantwortlich <V U4, 152>

rest [rest] Rest II

restaurant [ˈrestrɒnt] Restaurant II

result [rɪˈzʌlt] Ergebnis V U4, 90

retail [ˈriːteɪl] Einzelhandel V U4, 94

return ticket [rɪˈtɜːn ˌtɪkɪt] Hin- und Rückfahrkarte III

rhyme [raɪm] Reim <III>

to **rhyme** [raɪm] (sich) reimen <III>

rice [raɪs] Reis II
   chicken fried rice [ˈtʃɪkɪn ˌfraɪd ˈraɪs] gebratener Reis mit Hühnerfleisch II

rich [rɪtʃ] reich V U3, 63

Richter scale (no pl) [ˈrɪktə ˌskeɪl] Richterskala IV

ride [raɪd] Fahrt; Fahrgeschäft; Ritt II

*to **ride** [raɪd] fahren; reiten I

rider [ˈraɪdə] Reiter; Reiterin V U4, 98

horse **riding** [ˈhɔːs ˌraɪdɪŋ] Reiten I

right [raɪt] Recht V U1, 11

right [raɪt] richtig; korrekt I; rechts; rechte II; okay <V U3, 74>
   right away [ˌraɪt əˈweɪ] sofort; gleich V U3, 68
   on the right [ɒn ðə ˈraɪt] rechts; auf der rechten Seite II
   You're right. [jɔː ˈraɪt] Du hast recht. I

*to **ring** [rɪŋ] klingeln; läuten I

river [ˈrɪvə] Fluss I

road [rəʊd] Straße I
   road accident [ˈrəʊd ˌæksɪdnt] Verkehrsunfall <V U3, 64>
   road train [ˈrəʊd ˌtreɪn] Fernlastzug <V U1, 26>

rock [rɒk] Fels; Stein V U1, 12
   rock climbing [ˈrɒk ˌklaɪmɪŋ] Klettern I

rocket [ˈrɒkɪt] Rakete III

role [rəʊl] Rolle <V U1, 19>
   role model [ˈrəʊl ˌmɒdl] Vorbild V U3, 68
   role play [ˈrəʊl ˌpleɪ] Rollenspiel <I>

roller coaster [ˈrəʊlə ˌkəʊstə] Achterbahn II

roof [ruːf] Dach III

room [ruːm] Zimmer; Raum I

root word [ˌruːt ˈwɜːd] Grundwort; Stammwort <IV>

daily **routine** [ˌdeɪli ruːˈtiːn] Alltag <V U2, 40>

rubber [ˈrʌbə] Radiergummi I

rubbish [ˈrʌbɪʃ] Müll; Abfall I

rugby [ˈrʌgbi] Rugby III

rule [ruːl] Regel V U3, 80

ruler [ˈruːlə] Lineal I

*to **run** [rʌn] laufen; rennen; fahren II
   to run away [ˌrʌn əˈweɪ] weglaufen II

Russian [ˈrʌʃn] Russisch; russisch; aus Russland; Russe; Russin IV

S

sack race [ˈsæk ˌreɪs] Sackhüpfen II

sacred [ˈseɪkrɪd] heilig V U2, 54

sad [sæd] traurig I

safari [səˈfɑːri] Safari V U3, 63

safe [seɪf] sicher; ungefährlich; in Sicherheit; unversehrt IV

said [sed] simple past von to say I; past participle von to say III

salad [ˈsæləd] Salat I

salary [ˈsælri] Gehalt IV

salesperson [ˈseɪlzˌpɜːsn] Verkäufer; Verkäuferin <V U4, 152>

hairdressing **salon** [ˈheədresɪŋ ˌsælɒn] Friseursalon IV

salt [sɔːlt] Salz V U2, 47

saltwater crocodile [ˈsɔːltˌwɔːtə ˈkrɒkədaɪl] Salzwasserkrokodil <V U1, 23>

the **same** [ðə ˈseɪm] der gleiche; derselbe; gleich; genauso II
   at the same time [ət ðə seɪm ˈtaɪm] gleichzeitig; nebenher II

sandwich [ˈsænwɪdʒ] Sandwich; belegtes Brot I

sang [sæŋ] simple past von to sing II

sanitation [ˌsænɪˈteɪʃn] sanitäre Anlagen V U2, 42

sat [sæt] simple past, past participle von to sit IV

Saturday [ˈsætədeɪ] Samstag I
   on Saturdays [ɒn ˈsætədeɪz] samstags I

to **save** [seɪv] retten; sparen II

saw [sɔː] simple past von to see I

s six • **z** zoo • **ʃ** she • **ʒ** revision • **h** her • **m** me • **n** no • **ŋ** sing • **iə** hear • **l** let • **r** red • **j** yes

191

saw

saxophone ['sæksəfəʊn] Saxofon I

*to **say** [seɪ] nennen; sagen; nachsprechen; sprechen I; aussprechen III

Richter **scale** (no pl) ['rɪktə ˌskeɪl] Richterskala IV

to **scan** [skæn] nach Details durchsuchen; scannen <III>

to **scare** [skeə] erschrecken <II>

*to be **scared** [bi: 'skeəd] Angst haben I

scarf (sg) [skɑ:f], **scarves** (pl) [skɑ:vz] Schal; Tuch II

scary ['skeəri] unheimlich; gruselig; beängstigend I

scene [si:n] Szene <II>

scenery ['si:nri] Kulissen; Bühnenbild III

school [sku:l] Schule I

at **school** [ət 'sku:l] in der Schule I

high **school** ['haɪ ˌsku:l] High School (weiterführende Schule, Oberstufe) V U3, 63

junior high **school** [ˌdʒu:niə 'haɪ sku:l] Junior Highschool (Mittelschule in den USA, in der Regel Klassenstufe 7–9) II

primary **school** ['praɪmri ˌsku:l] Grundschule IV

school trip [ˌsku:l 'trɪp] Klassenfahrt; Schulausflug II

secondary **school** ['sekndri ˌsku:l] weiterführende Schule; Mittelschule IV

science ['saɪəns] Naturwissenschaft; Wissenschaft III

science fiction [ˌsaɪəns 'fɪkʃn] Science-Fiction I

to **score** [skɔ:] erzielen III

Scottish ['skɒtɪʃ] schottisch; aus Schottland III

scratch [skrætʃ] Kratzer IV

screenshot ['skri:nʃɒt] Bildschirmfoto <IV>

sea [si:] Meer I

search [sɜ:tʃ] Recherche; Suche <IV>

search engine ['sɜ:tʃ ˌendʒɪn] Suchmaschine <IV>

to **search** [sɜ:tʃ] suchen <V U2, 41>

at the **seaside** [ət ðə 'si:saɪd] am Meer I

season ['si:zn] Jahreszeit; Saison II

seat [si:t] Sitzplatz; Sitz III

Take a **seat**. [ˌteɪk ə 'si:t] Setz dich.; Setzen Sie sich.; Nimm Platz.; Nehmen Sie Platz. IV

second ['seknd] Sekunde <I>; zweite II; zweit- IV

secondary school ['sekndri ˌsku:l] weiterführende Schule; Mittelschule IV

secondary school leaving certificate ['sekndri sku:l ˌli:vɪŋ sə'tɪfɪkət] mittlerer Schulabschluss; Realschulabschluss IV

second-hand [ˌsekn'hænd] gebraucht; secondhand; aus zweiter Hand I

*to **see** [si:] sehen I

See you. ['si: ju:] Wir sehen uns.; Bis bald.; Tschüss. II

See you soon. [ˌsi: ju: 'su:n] Bis bald. I

to **see** sb [si:] jmdn. empfangen <V U3, 74>

to **seem** [si:m] scheinen V U4, 99

seen [si:n] past participle von to see III

self-confident [ˌself'kɒnfɪdnt] selbstsicher; selbstbewusst <V U3, 151>

selfie ['selfi] Selfie IV

*to **sell** [sel] verkaufen I

*to **send** [send] schicken; senden I

sense [sens] Sinn; Bedeutung IV

sense of smell [ˌsens əv 'smel] Geruchssinn IV

sent [sent] simple past von to send I

sentence ['sentəns] Satz <I>

to **separate** ['sepreɪt] trennen V U3, 62

Sepedi [se'peədi] Nord-Sotho (Sprache in Südafrika) <V U3, 79>

September [sep'tembə] September I

series (no pl) ['sɪəri:z] Serie IV

serious ['sɪəriəs] ernst; schwer II

service ['sɜ:vɪs] Dienst; Service <V U2, 148>

customer **service** [ˌkʌstəmə 'sɜ:vɪs] Kundenbetreuung; Kundendienst; Kundenservice IV

delivery **service** [dɪ'lɪvri ˌsɜ:vɪs] Lieferdienst <V U2, 49>

Sesotho [sɪ'su:tu:] Sesotho (Sprache in Südafrika) V U3, 73

Setswana [se'tswa:nə] Setswana (Sprache in Südafrika) <V U3, 79>

settler ['setlə] Siedler; Siedlerin V U1, 11

seven ['sevn] sieben I

seventeen [ˌsevn'ti:n] siebzehn I

seventy ['sevnti] siebzig I

several ['sevrl] mehrere; einige; verschiedene V U2, 37

*to **shake** [ʃeɪk] beben; zittern; schütteln IV

shaken ['ʃeɪkn] past participle von to shake IV

shamrock ['ʃæmrɒk] Kleeblatt III

to **share** [ʃeə] teilen III

shark [ʃɑ:k] Hai I

whale **shark** ['weɪl ˌʃɑ:k] Walhai <V U1, 23>

she [ʃi:] sie I

sheep (sg) [ʃi:p], **sheep** (pl) [ʃi:p] Schaf I

shelf (sg) [ʃelf], **shelves** (pl) [ʃelvz] Regal; Regalbrett II

animal rescue **shelter** [ˌænɪml 'reskju: ˌʃeltə] Tierheim I

ship [ʃɪp] Schiff I

shirt [ʃɜ:t] Hemd; Shirt I

shoe [ʃu:] Schuh I

shook [ʃʊk] simple past von to shake IV

*to **shoot** [ʃu:t] schießen; erschießen IV

shop [ʃɒp] Geschäft; Laden I

shop assistant ['ʃɒp əˌsɪstnt] Verkäufer; Verkäuferin V U4, 94

sports **shop** ['spɔ:ts ˌʃɒp] Sportgeschäft II

shopping ['ʃɒpɪŋ] Einkaufen I

shopping centre ['ʃɒpɪŋ ˌsentə] Einkaufszentrum I

shopping list ['ʃɒpɪŋ ˌlɪst] Einkaufszettel I

short [ʃɔ:t] kurz II

shorts (pl) [ʃɔ:ts] Shorts; kurze Hose II

shot [ʃɒt] simple past, past participle von to shoot IV

should [ʃʊd] sollte III

to **shout** [ʃaʊt] rufen; schreien I

show [ʃəʊ] Show; Aufführung I

*to **show** [ʃəʊ] zeigen II

sick [sɪk] krank <V U1, 147>

to be sick [bi: 'sɪk] sich übergeben I

side [saɪd] Seite II

sight [saɪt] Sehenswürdigkeit II

sign [saɪn] Schild; Zeichen; Anzeichen IV

to sign [saɪn] unterschreiben; unterzeichnen <V U3, 74>

to signal ['sɪgnl] blinken IV

silly ['sɪli] albern II

simple past [ˌsɪmpl 'pɑ:st] einfache Vergangenheit <II>

simple present [ˌsɪmpl 'preznt] einfache Gegenwart; Präsens <II>

since [sɪns] seit; seitdem IV

Yours sincerely, [ˌjɔ:z sɪn'sɪəli] Mit freundlichen Grüßen IV

*to sing [sɪŋ] singen I

don't sing [ˌdəʊnt 'sɪŋ] singe nicht; singt nicht I

singer ['sɪŋə] Sänger; Sängerin I

single ticket [ˌsɪŋgl 'tɪkɪt] einfache Fahrkarte III

sister ['sɪstə] Schwester I

*to sit [sɪt] sitzen IV

to sit (down) [sɪt ('daʊn)] sich setzen; sich hinsetzen I

site [saɪt] Seite (im Internet) <IV>

situation [ˌsɪtjuˈeɪʃn] Situation V U3, 80

six [sɪks] sechs I

sixteen [ˌsɪk'sti:n] sechzehn I

sixty ['sɪksti] sechzig I

size [saɪz] Größe II

to skate [skeɪt] inlineskaten; Schlittschuh laufen II

skateboard ['skeɪtbɔ:d] Skateboard I

skater ['skeɪtə] Skater; Skaterin I

*to go skating [ˌgəʊ 'skeɪtɪŋ] inlineskaten gehen; Schlittschuhlaufen gehen II

to skid [skɪd] schleudern; schlittern V U3, 64

skill [skɪl] Fertigkeit; Geschick; Kenntnis; Fähigkeit IV

skilled [skɪld] qualifiziert; ausgebildet; Fach- <V U2, 148>

to skim [skɪm] überfliegen <III>

skirt [skɜ:t] Rock III

sky [skaɪ] Himmel IV

slave [sleɪv] Sklave; Sklavin IV

slave trader ['sleɪv ˌtreɪdə] Sklavenhändler; Menschenhändler IV

sled [sled] Schlitten IV

sleep [sli:p] Schlaf <V U1, 147>

*to sleep [sli:p] schlafen II

slept [slept] simple past von to sleep II

slow [sləʊ] langsam IV

slum [slʌm] Slum; Elendsviertel V U2, 36

small [smɔ:l] klein I

smell [smel] Geruch; Duft IV

sense of smell [ˌsens əv 'smel] Geruchssinn IV

*to smell [smel] riechen <V U3, 77>

smoke [sməʊk] Rauch IV

smurf [smɜ:f] Schlumpf I

snack bar ['snæk ˌbɑ:] Imbissstube; Café I

snow [snəʊ] Schnee II

snowboard ['snəʊbɔ:d] Snowboard I

snowy ['snəʊi] schneereich; verschneit II

so [səʊ] also; deshalb I; so; dermaßen II

so that [səʊ 'ðæt] damit; sodass IV

soccer (AE) ['sɒkə] Fußball II

social media [ˌsəʊʃl 'mi:diə] soziale Medien III

software ['sɒftweə] Software IV

soil [sɔɪl] Boden; Erde V U2, 42

solar panel [ˌsəʊlə 'pænl] Sonnenkollektor <V U2, 149>

sold [səʊld] simple past von to sell II; past participle von to sell V U4, 94

to solve [sɒlv] lösen V U2, 38

some [sʌm] etwas; einige; ein paar I

somebody ['sʌmbədi] jemand I

someone ['sʌmwʌn] jemand; irgendjemand III

something ['sʌmθɪŋ] etwas I

sometimes ['sʌmtaɪmz] manchmal I

son [sʌn] Sohn IV

song [sɒŋ] Lied I

songwriter ['sɒŋˌraɪtə] Songschreiber; Songschreiberin; Liedermacher; Liedermacherin V U3, 68

soon [su:n] bald II

See you soon. [ˌsi: ju: 'su:n] Bis bald. I

sore throat [ˌsɔ: 'θrəʊt] Halsschmerzen <V U1, 147>

Sorry. ['sɒri] Tut mir leid.; Entschuldigung. I

I'm sorry. [aɪm 'sɒri] Es tut mir leid.; Entschuldigung. II

to sort [sɔ:t] sortieren <IV>

soul [səʊl] Seele V U2, 46

sound [saʊnd] Laut; Geräusch; Ton <I>

to sound [saʊnd] klingen III

source [sɔ:s] Quelle <V ZI, 8>

South African [ˌsaʊθ 'æfrɪkən] Südafrikaner; Südafrikanerin; südafrikanisch; aus Südafrika V U3, 63

south [saʊθ] Süd-; Süden III

southern ['sʌðən] südlich; Süd-; Südstaaten- IV

souvenir [ˌsu:vn'ɪə] Souvenir; Andenken II

space [speɪs] Raumfahrt; Weltraum III

Spanish ['spænɪʃ] spanisch; Spanisch; aus Spanien IV

*to speak [spi:k] sprechen I

English-speaking [ˌɪŋglɪʃ'spi:kɪŋ] englischsprachig V ZI, 9

speaker ['spi:kə] Sprecher; Sprecherin; Redner; Rednerin V ZI, 8

speaking ['spi:kɪŋ] Sprechen <I>

speaking skills ['spi:kɪŋ ˌskɪlz] Fertigkeit Sprechen <I>

special ['speʃl] besonders; speziell I

direct speech [dɪˌrekt 'spi:tʃ] direkte Rede <V U3, 76>

speech therapist ['spi:tʃ ˌθerəpɪst] Logopäde; Logopädin <V U4, 152>

*to spell [spel] buchstabieren <V U3, 65>

spelling ['spelɪŋ] Rechtschreibung I

*to spend [spend] verbringen (Zeit); ausgeben (Geld) II

spent [spent] simple past von to spend II

oil spill ['ɔɪl ˌspɪl] Ölteppich; Ölpest V U1, 20

spoke [spəʊk] simple past von to speak V U2, 42

*to spoken ['spəʊkn] past participle von to speak <V U3, 79>

sport [spɔ:t] Sport III

sports (pl only) [spɔ:ts] Sportarten I

sports centre ['spɔːts ˌsentə] Sportzentrum I

sports day ['spɔːts ˌdeɪ] Sportfest II

sports shop ['spɔːts ˌʃɒp] Sportgeschäft II

spring [sprɪŋ] Frühling II

to **spy** [spaɪ] sehen I

square [skweə] Quadrat- V U3, 63

square dance ['skweə ˌdɑːns]
Squaredance (amerikanischer
Volkstanz) II

stadium ['steɪdiəm] Stadion I

stage [steɪdʒ] Bühne II

stall [stɔːl] Stand; Bude I

*to **stand** [stænd] stehen II

can't stand + -ing [ˌkɑːnt 'stænd …
ɪŋ] etw. nicht ausstehen können;
etw. nicht ertragen III

to stand for ['stænd fə] stehen für
III

to stand up [ˌstænd ˈʌp] aufstehen
V U4, 99

star [stɑː] Star I

start [stɑːt] Anfang; Beginn; Start <I>

to **start** [stɑːt] anfangen; beginnen;
starten I

state [steɪt] Bundesstaat; Staat III

of all the states [əvˈɔːl ðə ˌsteɪts]
von allen Staaten IV

statement ['steɪtmənt] Aussage <IV>

station ['steɪʃn] Station; Bahnhof;
Haltestelle III

police station [pəˈliːs ˌsteɪʃn] Polizeirevier; Polizeiwache V U3, 64

railway station ['reɪlweɪ ˌsteɪʃn]
Bahnhof IV

train station ['treɪn ˌsteɪʃn] Bahnhof
<III>

statue ['stætʃuː] Statue IV

to **stay** [steɪ] bleiben; übernachten I

to stay up [ˌsteɪ ˈʌp] aufbleiben
<V U1, 147>

staying connected [ˌsteɪɪŋ
kəˈnektɪd] in Verbindung bleiben III

steamboat ['stiːmbəʊt] Dampfer;
Dampfschiff IV

step [step] Schritt; Stufe II

stick [stɪk] Schläger; Stock III

still [stɪl] noch; immer noch II

stock [stɒk] Bestand <V U4, 153>

stomach ['stʌmək] Magen; Bauch
<V U1, 147>

stomachache ['stʌmək‚eɪk] Bauch-
weh; Bauchschmerzen <V U1, 147>

stone [stəʊn] Stein III

stone put ['stəʊn ˌpʊt] Steinstoßen
III

stood [stʊd] simple past von to stand
II

stop [stɒp] Haltestelle; Halt II

to **stop** [stɒp] beenden; aufhören;
anhalten II

store (AE) [stɔː] Laden; Geschäft III

storm [stɔːm] Sturm I

story ['stɔːri] Geschichte I

feature story ['fiːtʃə ˌstɔːri] Leitartikel; Sonderbericht <V U3, 76>

straight on [streɪt ˈɒn] geradeaus II

strawberry ['strɔːbri] Erdbeere I

street [striːt] Straße I

stress [stres] Betonung <V U1, 13>

strong [strɒŋ] stark III; stabil IV

to **struggle** ['strʌɡl] kämpfen; ringen;
sich anstrengen; Mühe haben
V U1, 11

*to be **stuck** [bi: ˈstʌk] feststecken;
stecken bleiben I

student ['stjuːdnt] Schüler; Schülerin I

study skills ['stʌdi ˈskɪlz] Fertigkeit
Lern- und Arbeitstechniken <I>

to **study** (for) sth ['stʌdi (fə)] (auf
einen Abschluss) studieren; (für)
etw. lernen V U4, 90

subject ['sʌbdʒɪkt] Schulfach I; Betreff
III

successful [səkˈsesfl] erfolgreich IV

suddenly ['sʌdnli] plötzlich; auf
einmal I

suitability [ˌsuːtəˈbɪləti] Eignungs-;
Eignung; Tauglichkeit V U4, 90

suitable ['suːtəbl] geeignet; passend
<V U3, 65>

suitcase ['suːtkeɪs] Koffer IV

summer ['sʌmə] Sommer II

sun [sʌn] Sonne II

Sunday ['sʌndeɪ] Sonntag I

sunny ['sʌni] sonnig II

superlative [suːˈpɜːlətɪv] Superlativ
<IV>

supermarket ['suːpəˌmɑːkɪt] Supermarkt I

supplier [səˈplaɪə] Zulieferer; Anbieter
V U4, 94

supplies (pl) [səˈplaɪz] Vorräte IV

support [səˈpɔːt] Unterstützung; Hilfe
V U4, 90

sure [ʃɔː] sicher II

to **surf** the internet [ˌsɜːf ði ˈɪntənet]
im Internet surfen <III>

surfing ['sɜːfɪŋ] Surfen; Wellenreiten;
Surf- IV

to go surfing [ˌgəʊ ˈsɜːfɪŋ] surfen
gehen III

surprise [səˈpraɪz] Überraschung III

surprised [səˈpraɪzd] überrascht II

survey ['sɜːveɪ] Umfrage <III>

sustainable [səˈsteɪnəbl] nachhaltig
V U2, 42

swam [swæm] simple past von to
swim IV

sweet [swiːt] Süßigkeit; Bonbon I

*to **swim** [swɪm] schwimmen I

*to go **swimming** [ˌgəʊ ˈswɪmɪŋ]
schwimmen gehen I

swimming pool ['swɪmɪŋ ˌpuːl]
Schwimmbad I

*to **swing** [swɪŋ] schwingen; schwenken III

sword [sɔːd] Schwert III

swung [swʌŋ] simple past, past participle von to swing III

symbol ['sɪmbl] Symbol III

T

table ['teɪbl] Tisch; Tabelle <I>

tablet ['tæblət] Tablette V U1, 16

tail [teɪl] Schwanz I

*to **take** [teɪk] mitnehmen; nehmen I;
hinbringen II; dauern; brauchen III;
einnehmen V U1, 16

to take an exam [ˌteɪk ən ɪgˈzæm]
eine Prüfung schreiben; ein Examen schreiben V U4, 90

to take care of [ˌteɪk ˈkeər əv] sich
kümmern um; sorgen für <V U2, 48>

to take notes [ˌteɪk ˈnəʊts] sich
Notizen machen <I>

to take out [ˌteɪk ˈaʊt] hinausbringen II

to take part (in) [teɪk 'pɑːt (ɪn)] mitmachen (bei); teilnehmen (an) II

to take photos (of) [teɪk 'fəʊtəʊz (əv)] Fotos machen; fotografieren II

to take place [teɪk 'pleɪs] stattfinden <V U1, 146>

to take the dog for a walk [teɪk ðə dɒg fɔːr ə 'wɔːk] den Hund ausführen I

to take turns [teɪk 'tɜːnz] sich abwechseln <I>

Take a seat. [teɪk ə 'siːt] Setz dich.; Setzen Sie sich.; Nimm Platz.; Nehmen Sie Platz. IV

taken ['teɪkn] past participle von *to take* III

talent ['tælənt] Talent; Begabung I

talk [tɔːk] Vortrag; Gespräch; Unterhaltung <III>

to talk (to) [tɔːk (tə)] reden (mit); sprechen (mit) I

tall [tɔːl] hoch; groß II

tandem ['tændəm] Tandem II

task [tɑːsk] Aufgabe; Auftrag V ZI, 9

to taste [teɪst] schmecken <V U2, 48>

taught [tɔːt] simple past, past participle von *to teach* IV

tax advisor ['tæks əd,vaɪzə] Steuerberater; Steuerberaterin <V U2, 148>

tea [tiː] Tee; Abendessen I

*to teach [tiːtʃ] lehren; beibringen; unterrichten IV

teacher ['tiːtʃə] Lehrer; Lehrerin I

team [tiːm] Mannschaft; Team; Gruppe I

technology [tek'nɒlədʒi] Technik; Technologie III
DT (Design Technology) [,diː'tiː (dɪˌzaɪn tek'nɒlədʒi)] Technik I

teddy ['tedi] Teddybär I

teen [tiːn] Jugend-; Teenager; Teenagerin; Jugendlicher; Jugendliche II

teenager ['tiːnˌeɪdʒə] Teenager; Jugendlicher; Jugendliche V U2, 42

telephone box ['telɪfəʊn ,bɒks] Telefonzelle II

television ['telɪvɪʒn] Fernsehen; Fernseher III

*to tell [tel] erzählen; sagen I

to tell sb to do sth ['tel tə ,duː] jmdm. etw. auftragen III

temperature ['temprətʃə] Temperatur V U1, 20
high temperature [,haɪ 'temprətʃə] Fieber V U1, 16

ten [ten] zehn I

tennis ['tenɪs] Tennis I

tent [tent] Zelt II

test [test] Test; Klassenarbeit V U4, 90

to test [test] testen; prüfen II

testing ['testɪŋ] Testen <V U2, 148>

text [tekst] Text <I>

than [ðæn] als II

thank you ['θæŋk ju] Dankeschön <V U1, 25>

Thank you. ['θæŋk ju] Danke. I

Thank you very much. [,θæŋk ju veri 'mʌtʃ] Vielen Dank.; Herzlichen Dank. <V U1, 22>

thankful ['θæŋkfl] dankbar IV

Thanks. [θæŋks] Danke. I

Thanksgiving [,θæŋks'gɪvɪŋ] Erntedankfest IV

that [ðæt] das; dieses; jene I; dass II; der; die III
after that [,ɑːftə 'ðæt] danach I
so that [səʊ 'ðæt] damit; sodass IV
that's why ['ðæts waɪ] deshalb; deswegen II
That's too bad. [,ðæts tuː 'bæd] Schade! II

the [ðə] die; der; das I

theater (AE) ['θɪətə] Theater III

theatre ['θɪətə] Theater III

their [ðeə] ihr I

theirs [ðeəz] ihre III

them [ðem] sie (Pl.) I; ihnen II

theme [θiːm] Thema; Motto <I>
theme park ['θiːm ,pɑːk] Freizeitpark II

themselves [ðəm'selvz] sich; selbst; sie selbst III; sich selbst IV

then [ðen] dann; danach I

there [ðeə] da; dort; dorthin; dahin I
there are [ðeər 'ɑː] da sind; es gibt I
there's (= there is) [ðeəz] da ist; dort ist; es gibt I

these [ðiːz] diese II

they [ðeɪ] sie (Pl.) I

thing [θɪŋ] Sache; Ding I

*to think [θɪŋk] denken; glauben II; überlegen <IV>
to think about [,θɪŋk ə'baʊt] nachdenken über; sich überlegen; denken an III
to think of ['θɪŋk əv] denken an/über; sich einfallen lassen; sich ausdenken III; davon halten V U1, 12

third [θɜːd] dritte II
a third [ə 'θɜːd] ein Drittel V U4, 88

thirteen [θɜː'tiːn] dreizehn I

thirty ['θɜːti] dreißig I

this [ðɪs] das; dies I
this morning [ðɪs 'mɔːnɪŋ] heute Morgen II
like this [laɪk 'ðɪs] so; auf diese Weise <I>

those [ðəʊz] jene II

thought [θɔːt] simple past von *to think* II; past participle von *to think* III

a/one thousand ['θaʊznd] tausend; eintausend II

three [θriː] drei I

threw [θruː] simple past von *to throw* II

throat [θrəʊt] Hals <V U1, 147>
sore throat [,sɔː 'θrəʊt] Halsschmerzen <V U1, 147>

through [θruː] durch III

*to throw [θrəʊ] werfen II

Thursday ['θɜːzdeɪ] Donnerstag I

ticket ['tɪkɪt] Ticket; Eintrittskarte; Fahrschein II
return ticket [rɪ'tɜːn ,tɪkɪt] Hin- und Rückfahrkarte III
single ticket [,sɪŋgl 'tɪkɪt] einfuche Fahrkarte III

to tidy ['taɪdi] aufräumen; in Ordnung bringen II

tidy ['taɪdi] ordentlich <II>

time [taɪm] Zeit; Uhrzeit; Mal I
at the same time [ət ðə seɪm 'taɪm] gleichzeitig; nebenher II
boarding time ['bɔːdɪŋ ,taɪm] Einsteigezeit IV
free time [,friː 'taɪm] Freizeit I
for the 200th time [fə ðə 'tuː hʌndrədθ ,taɪm] zum 200. Mal III

in time [ɪn 'taɪm] rechtzeitig; pünktlich V U2, 54

the first time [ðə fɜːst 'taɪm] das erste Mal I

timeline ['taɪm͵laɪn] Zeitstrahl <V U2, 47>

timetable ['taɪm͵teɪbl] Stundenplan I; Fahrplan III

tip [tɪp] Tipp; Ratschlag <I>

tired ['taɪəd] müde I

title ['taɪtl] Titel; Überschrift <I>

to [tuː] zu; nach; in I; um zu; an II; auf; bei; bis III; für IV

quarter to/past ['kwɔːtə tə/pɑːst] Viertel vor/nach II

today [tə'deɪ] heute I

together [tə'geðə] zusammen I

to go together [͵gəʊ tə'geðə] zusammenpassen <III>

toilet ['tɔɪlət] Toilette V U2, 42

told [təʊld] simple past von *to tell* I; past participle von *to tell* III

tolerant ['tɒlrnt] tolerant <V U3, 151>

tomato *(sg)* [tə'mɑːtəʊ], **tomatoes** *(pl)* [tə'mɑːtəʊz] Tomate I

tomorrow [tə'mɒrəʊ] morgen II

too [tuː] auch; zu I

took [tʊk] simple past von *to take* II

tool [tuːl] Werkzeug; Gerät V U4, 90

tooth *(sg)* [tuːθ], **teeth** *(pl)* [tiːθ] Zahn II

top [tɒp] Spitze; oberer Teil; oberes Ende II; Top- <V ZI, 8>

at the top [æt ðə 'tɒp] oben V U1, 28

topic ['tɒpɪk] Thema IV

topic-based ['tɒpɪkbeɪst] themenbezogen <IV>

torch [tɔːtʃ] Taschenlampe I

caber **toss** ['keɪbə ͵tɒs] Baumstammwerfen III

*to get in **touch** [͵get ɪn 'tʌtʃ] in Verbindung treten (mit); kontaktieren <V U3, 150>

*to keep in **touch** [͵kiːp ɪn 'tʌtʃ] in Kontakt bleiben II

tour [tʊə] Tour; Führung; Reise III

tour guide ['tʊə ͵gaɪd] Reiseleiter; Reiseleiterin V U2, 38

tourism ['tʊərɪzm] Tourismus IV

tourist ['tʊərɪst] Tourist; Touristin II

tourist industry ['tʊərɪst ͵ɪndəstri] Tourismus IV

tourist information centre [͵tʊərɪst ɪnfə'meɪʃn ͵sentə] Touristeninformation V U4, 90

towards [tə'wɔːdz] auf … zu; in Richtung V U4, 99

tower ['taʊə] Turm II

town [taʊn] Stadt I

twin town [͵twɪn 'taʊn] Partnerstadt III

townhouse ['taʊnhaʊs] Reihenhaus III

township ['taʊnʃɪp] Township *(ehemalige Wohnsiedlungen für die schwarze Bevölkerung in Südafrika)*; Armutsviertel V U3, 62

slave **trader** ['sleɪv ͵treɪdə] Sklavenhändler; Menschenhändler IV

tradespeople ['treɪdspiːpl] Handwerker *(Pl.)* <V U2, 148>

tradition [trə'dɪʃn] Tradition III

traffic ['træfɪk] Verkehr III

train [treɪn] Zug I

train station ['treɪn ͵steɪʃn] Bahnhof <III>

to **train** [treɪn] trainieren; eine Ausbildung machen; ausbilden IV

trainer ['treɪnə] Turnschuh II

training ['treɪnɪŋ] Ausbildung; Training IV

tram [træm] Straßenbahn I

transport ['trænspɔːt] Verkehr; Transport II

public transport [͵pʌblɪk 'trænspɔːt] öffentliche Verkehrsmittel III

to **transport** [træn'spɔːt] transportieren; befördern IV

travel agent ['trævl ͵eɪdʒnt] Reisebürokaufmann; Reisebürokauffrau IV

travel agent's ['trævl ͵eɪdʒnts] Reisebüro IV

to **travel** ['trævl] fahren; reisen II

treasure hunt ['treʒə ͵hʌnt] Schnitzeljagd; Schatzsuche II

tree [triː] Baum I

trial ['traɪəl] Probe; Probe- <V U4, 100>

tribe [traɪb] Stamm; Volksstamm V U1, 12

trick [trɪk] Kunststück; Trick I; Streich II

trip [trɪp] Ausflug; Fahrt; Reise I

school trip [͵skuːl 'trɪp] Klassenfahrt; Schulausflug II

true [truː] richtig; wahr V U2, 38

trumpet ['trʌmpɪt] Trompete II

truth [truːθ] Wahrheit IV

to **try** [traɪ] versuchen; probieren; ausprobieren III

to try hard [͵traɪ 'hɑːd] sich anstrengen V U4, 98

to try on [͵traɪ 'ɒn] anprobieren II

T-shirt ['tiːʃɜːt] T-Shirt II

tsunami [tsʊ'nɑːmi] Tsunami *(durch Seebeben ausgelöste Flutwelle)* IV

Tuesday ['tjuːzdeɪ] Dienstag I

turkey ['tɜːki] Truthahn; Pute IV

Turkish ['tɜːkɪʃ] türkisch; Türkisch; aus der Türkei IV

Your turn. [jɔː 'tɜːn] Du bist dran. <V U3, 81>

to **turn** [tɜːn] abbiegen II

to turn off [͵tɜːn 'ɒf] abschalten; ausschalten <V U2, 149>

to turn over [͵tɜːn 'əʊvə] umkippen; (sich) umdrehen III

Turn the music down. [͵tɜːn ðə mjuːzɪk 'daʊn] Mach die Musik leiser. I

*to take **turns** [͵teɪk 'tɜːnz] sich abwechseln <I>

tutorial [tjuː'tɔːriəl] Tutorial; Anleitung IV

TV [tiː'viː] Fernseher I; Fernseh-; Fernsehen IV

on TV [͵ɒn ͵tiː'viː] im Fernsehen III

to watch TV [͵wɒtʃ tiː'viː] fernsehen I

twelve [twelv] zwölf I

twenty ['twenti] zwanzig I

twenty-one [͵twenti'wʌn] einundzwanzig I

twin town [͵twɪn 'taʊn] Partnerstadt III

two [tuː] zwei I

type [taɪp] Sorte; Art; Typ <III>

typical ['tɪpɪkl] typisch; charakteristisch <I>

U

uncle ['ʌŋkl] Onkel I

under ['ʌndə] unter I

underground ['ʌndəgraʊnd] U-Bahn I

underlined [ˌʌndəˈlaɪnd] unterstrichen <III>

*to **understand** [ˌʌndəˈstænd] verstehen II

understood [ˌʌndəˈstʊd] simple past von to understand II

unemployed [ˌʌnɪmˈplɔɪd] arbeitslos V U3, 72

unfortunately [ʌnˈfɔːtʃnətli] leider; unglücklicherweise V U2, 47

unhappy [ʌnˈhæpi] unglücklich; traurig II

uniform [ˈjuːnɪfɔːm] Uniform I

unit [ˈjuːnɪt] Lektion; Kapitel <I>

until [ʌnˈtɪl] bis III

up [ʌp] hinauf; oben; hoch II
to stand up [ˌstænd ˈʌp] aufstehen V U4, 99

update [ˈʌpdeɪt] aktuelle Information; Update; Aktualisierung IV

to **upload** [ʌpˈləʊd] hochladen II

US [juːˈes] US-amerikanisch III

us [ʌs] uns; wir II

to **use** [juːz] benutzen; verwenden; nehmen; nutzen III
to get used to (sth) [ˌget ˈjuːst tə] sich gewöhnen an (etw.) IV

useful [ˈjuːsfl] nützlich; hilfreich; brauchbar III

usually [ˈjuːʒli] normalerweise; gewöhnlich II

V

vacation (AE) [vəˈkeɪʃn] Urlaub; Ferien III

valley [ˈvæli] Tal III

van [væn] Lieferwagen, Transporter IV

vegetable (veg) [ˈvedʒtəbl (vedʒ)] Gemüse IV

vegetarian [ˌvedʒɪˈteəriən] Vegetarier; Vegetarierin I; vegetarisch <V U2, 149>

vehicle painter [ˈvɪəkl ˌpeɪntə] Fahrzeuglackierer; Fahrzeuglackiererin <V U4, 152>

verb [vɜːb] Verb <II>

very [ˈveri] sehr I

vet [vet] Tierarzt; Tierärztin IV

video [ˈvɪdiəʊ] Video III

viewing [ˈvjuːɪŋ] Hör-/Sehverstehen <I>
viewing skills [ˈvjuːɪŋ ˌskɪlz] Fertigkeit Hör-/Sehverstehen <I>

village [ˈvɪlɪdʒ] Dorf I

violence (no pl) [ˈvaɪələns] Gewalt IV

virtual [ˈvɜːtʃuəl] virtuell V U2, 38

visit [ˈvɪzɪt] Besuch III

to **visit** [ˈvɪzɪt] besuchen I

visiting hours (pl) [ˈvɪzɪtɪŋ ˌaʊəz] Besuchszeiten <V U3, 74>

visitor [ˈvɪzɪtə] Besucher; Besucherin II

vocabulary [vəˈkæbjələri] Vokabular; Wortschatz <IV>

volcano (sg) [vɒlˈkeɪnəʊ], **volcanoes** (pl) [vɒlˈkeɪnəʊz] Vulkan V U4, 89

volunteer [ˌvɒlənˈtɪə] Freiwilliger; Freiwillige; ehrenamtlicher Helfer; ehrenamtliche Helferin V U4, 89

W

to **wait** (for) [weɪt (fə)] warten (auf) II

*to **wake** up [ˌweɪk ˈʌp] aufwachen; erwachen; aufwecken III

walk [wɔːk] Wanderung; Spaziergang I

to **walk** [wɔːk] laufen; gehen; zu Fuß gehen IV
to walk around [ˌwɔːk əˈraʊnd] umherlaufen; herumlaufen <I>

wall [wɔːl] Wand; Mauer II
wall painting [ˈwɔːl peɪntɪŋ] Wandmalerei II

wallet [ˈwɒlɪt] Brieftasche; Geldbeutel; Geldbörse V U3, 64

to **want** (to) [wɒnt (tə)] wollen; mögen I

wanted [ˈwɒntɪd] gesucht <V U4, 102>

wardrobe [ˈwɔːdrəʊb] Kleiderschrank II

warehouse [ˈweəhaʊs] Lager; Lagerhalle; Depot <V U4, 153>

warm [wɔːm] warm II

warm-up [ˈwɔːmʌp] Aufwärmtraining; Aufwärmen II

was [wɒz] simple past von to be I

wash [wɒʃ] Wäsche II

to **wash** [wɒʃ] (sich) waschen; spülen II

waste [weɪst] Abfall V U2, 37

to **watch** [wɒtʃ] anschauen; ansehen I; zuschauen; zusehen; beobachten II
to watch TV [ˌwɒtʃ tiːˈviː] fernsehen I

water [ˈwɔːtə] Wasser I

wave [weɪv] Welle III

wax [wæks] Wachs II

way [weɪ] Weg I; Art und Weise III
to ask the way [ˌɑːsk ðə ˈweɪ] nach dem Weg fragen <II>
to be a long **way** away [bi: ə ˌlɒŋ ˌweɪ əˈweɪ] weit weg sein II

we [wiː] wir I

weak [wiːk] schwach <V U1, 147>

*to **wear** [weə] tragen; anhaben I

weather [ˈweðə] Wetter; Witterung II

website [ˈwebsaɪt] Website; Internetseite III

wedding [ˈwedɪŋ] Hochzeit V U2, 37

Wednesday [ˈwenzdeɪ] Mittwoch I

week [wiːk] Woche I
a week [ə ˈwiːk] in der Woche; pro Woche V U3, 73

weekend [ˈwiːkend] Wochenende I

welcome (to) [ˈwelkəm (tə)] willkommen (bei/in) I
You're welcome. [jɔː ˈwelkəm] Gern geschehen. V U1, 16

well [wel] gut II
Well, ... [wel] Na ja, ...; Also ... II
... as well as ... [əz ˈwel əz] sowohl ... als auch ... II
Well done! [wel ˈdʌn] Gut gemacht! II

well-organized [ˈwelˌɔːgnaɪzd] gut organisiert <V U4, 152>

Welsh [welʃ] Walisisch; walisisch; aus Wales III

went [went] simple past von to go I

were [wɜː] simple past von to be I

west [west] Westen; West- III

wet [wet] nass I

whale [weɪl] Wal IV
whale shark [ˈweɪl ˌʃɑːk] Walhai <V U1, 23>
whale-watching [ˈweɪlˌwɒtʃɪŋ] Walbeobachtungs- IV

what [wɒt] was; welche I

what

wheel

What about …? [ˌwɒt ə'baʊt] Und …?; Was ist mit …? II

What colour is …? [ˌwɒt 'kʌlər ɪz] Welche Farbe hat …? I

What time is it? [ˌwɒt 'taɪm ɪz ɪt] Wie viel Uhr ist es?; Wie spät ist es? I

What's the matter? [ˌwɒts ðə 'mætə] Was ist los?; Was hast du? V U1, 16

What's the weather like? [ˌwɒts ðə 'weðə laɪk] Wie ist das Wetter? II

What's your name? [ˌwɒts jə 'neɪm] Wie heißt du? I

wheel [wiːl] Rad II

  big wheel [ˌbɪg 'wiːl] Riesenrad II

wheelchair ['wiːltʃeə] Rollstuhl I

when [wen] wann I; wenn; als II

where [weə] wo; wohin; woher I

  Where are you from? [ˌweər ə ju 'frɒm] Woher kommst du? I

which [wɪtʃ] welche; was II; das; der; die III

while [waɪl] während IV

white [waɪt] weiß I

who [huː] wer I; die; der; das III

whose [huːz] wessen <III>

why [waɪ] warum I

  that's why ['ðæts waɪ] deshalb; deswegen II

wide [waɪd] breit; groß <V U1, 23>

wild [waɪld] wild IV

wilderness ['wɪldənəs] Wildnis IV

will [wɪl] werden II

*to win [wɪn] siegen; gewinnen I

wind [wɪnd] Wind I

  wind farm ['wɪnd ˌfɑːm] Windpark <V U2, 149>

window ['wɪndəʊ] Fenster I

windy ['wɪndi] windig II

winner ['wɪnə] Sieger; Siegerin; Gewinner; Gewinnerin I

winter ['wɪntə] Winter I

Best wishes, [ˌbest 'wɪʃɪz] Viele Grüße; Alles Gute! I

to wish [wɪʃ] wünschen V U4, 98

with [wɪð] mit I; bei II

without [wɪ'ðaʊt] ohne II

witness ['wɪtnəs] Zeuge; Zeugin IV

wizard ['wɪzəd] Zauberer II

woke up [ˌwəʊk 'ʌp] simple past von to wake up III

woken up [ˌwəʊkn 'ʌp] past participle von to wake up III

wolf (sg) [wʊlf], **wolves** (pl) [wʊlvz] Wolf II

woman (sg) ['wʊmən], **women** (pl) ['wɪmɪn] Frau I

won [wʌn] simple past von to win II; past participle von to win III

won't (= will not) [wəʊnt] nicht werden II

wonder ['wʌndə] Wunder V U4, 99

wood [wʊd] Holz I; Wald IV

woof [wʊf] wau I

wool [wʊl] Wolle I

word [wɜːd] Wort II

  root word [ˌruːt 'wɜːd] Grundwort; Stammwort <IV>

  word order ['wɜːd ˌɔːdə] Wortstellung; Satzstellung <II>

wore [wɔː] simple past von to wear I

work [wɜːk] Arbeit II

  work experience ['wɜːk ɪkˌspɪəriəns] Berufserfahrung; Praktikum V U4, 90

  to work [wɜːk] arbeiten I; funktionieren V U4, 94

worker ['wɜːkə] Arbeiter; Arbeiterin; Angestellter; Angestellte IV

working conditions (pl) ['wɜːkɪŋ kənˌdɪʃnz] Arbeitsbedingungen <V U4, 153>

  working hours (pl) ['wɜːkɪŋ ˌaʊəz] Arbeitszeit IV

workshop ['wɜːkʃɒp] Workshop; Seminar III

  acting workshop ['æktɪŋ ˌwɜːkʃɒp] Schauspielworkshop III

world [wɜːld] Welt I

  all around the world [ɔːl əˌraʊnd ðə 'wɜːld] in aller Welt II

worried ['wʌrid] beunruhigt; besorgt II

to worry ['wʌri] sich Sorgen machen I

  Don't worry. [dəʊnt 'wʌri] Mach dir keine Sorgen. I

worse [wɜːs] schlechter; schlimmer II

worst [wɜːst] schlimmste; schlechteste II

worth [wɜːθ] wert V U4, 94

worth of ['wɜːθ əv] im Wert von V U4, 94

would [wʊd] würde(n) <IV>

  I wouldn't like (to) … [aɪ 'wʊdnt laɪk (tə)] ich möchte nicht …; ich würde nicht gerne … I

  I'd (= I would) [aɪd] ich würde; ich hätte gern I

  I'd love (to) … (= I would love to) [aɪd 'lʌv (tə)] ich würde sehr gern …; ich hätte gern … IV

  Would you like (to) …? [ˌwʊd jə 'laɪk (tə)] Möchtest du …?; Würdest du gern …? I

Wow! [waʊ] Wow!; Toll! I

wrecked [rekt] demoliert; zerstört; zertrümmert IV

*to write [raɪt] schreiben I

writer ['raɪtə] Verfasser; Verfasserin; Schriftsteller; Schriftstellerin <V U3, 76>

writing ['raɪtɪŋ] Schreiben <I>

  writing skills ['raɪtɪŋ ˌskɪlz] Fertigkeit Schreiben <II>

wrong [rɒŋ] falsch I

  to go wrong [gəʊ 'rɒŋ] schiefgehen V U4, 90

wrote [rəʊt] simple past von to write II

X

Xhosa ['kɔːsə] Xhosa (Sprache in Südafrika) <V U3, 79>

Xitsonga [ksi'tsɒŋgə] Xitsonga (Sprache in Südafrika) <V U3, 79>

Y

year [jɪə] Klasse; Jahrgangsstufe; Jahr I

year-old [ˌjɪər'əʊld] -jährig; Jahre alt V U2, 42

yellow ['jeləʊ] gelb I

yes [jes] ja I

yesterday ['jestədeɪ] gestern I

yet [jet] schon III

  not … yet [nɒt … 'jet] noch nicht III

you [juː] du; Sie; ihr; dich; euch; dir; Ihnen I

You're welcome. [jɔ: 'welkəm] Gern geschehen. V U1, 16

young [jʌŋ] jung II

your [jɔ:] dein; euer; Ihr I

yours [jɔ:z] deine; eure; Ihre III
Yours sincerely, [jɔ:z sɪn'sɪəli] Mit freundlichen Grüßen IV
Yours, [jɔ:z] Dein *(Grußformel in Briefen oder E-Mails)* II

yourself [jɔ:'self] dich; selbst III; dir; dir selbst; sich; sich selbst IV

yourselves [jɔ:'selvz] selbst; euch; euch selbst; sich; Sie sich; Sie sich selbst IV

youth [ju:θ] Jugend- I

Z

zero ['zɪərəʊ] null I

zip line ['zɪp ˌlaɪn] Seilrutsche III

zoo [zu:] Zoo; Tierpark IV

to **zoom in** ['zu:m ˌɪn] heranzoomen <I>

Zulu ['zu:lu:] Zulu *(Sprache in Südafrika)* <V U3, 79>

Boys' names

Daku [dɑ:'ku:] V U1, 15

John [dʒɒn] V U4, 94

Koa [kəʊ'ɑ:] V U1, 12

Koro ['kɒrəʊ] V U4, 98

Krish [krɪʃ] V U2, 37

Kungawo [kʌŋə'wəʊ] V U3, 68

Leo ['li:əʊ] <V U4, 100>

Liam ['li:əm] V U4, 88

Lunga ['lʌŋə] V U3, 64

Manjit [mæn'dʒɪt] V U2, 38

Mason ['meɪsn] V U4, 89

Matt [mæt] <V U4, 102>

Moti ['mɒti] V U2, 42

Nikau ['nɪkəʊ] V U4, 94

Oliver ['ɒlɪvə] V U4, 94

Omeo ['ɔ:miəʊ] V U1, 14

Paka ['pʌkə] V U4, 98

Peter ['pi:tə] V U1, 11

Phil [fɪl] V U3, 64

Piet [pit] V U3, 64

Rawiri [rə'wi:ri] V U4, 98

Robert ['rɒbət] V U1, 21

Sanjay ['sændʒeɪ] <V U2, 48>

Shaka ['ʃækə] V U3, 72

Tanvi ['tænvi] V U2, 42

Uuka ['ju:kə] V U3, 73

Vibhu [vɪb'hu:] V U2, 38

Girls' names

Amahle [ə'mɑ:lə] V U3, 73

Amita [ə'mi:tə] V U2, 37

Barbara ['bɑ:brə] V U1, 21

Bertha ['bɜ:θə] V U3, 72

Cathy ['kæθi] V U3, 65

Cebile ['sebɪlə] V U3, 64

Chandran ['tʃændrn] V U2, 54

Deepali ['di:pəli] V U2, 42

Ella ['elə] V U4, 91

Hazel ['heɪzl] V U4, 89

Jasmine ['dʒæzmɪn] <V U2, 48>

Joan [dʒəʊn] V U4, 106

Julia ['dʒu:liə] <V U1, 24>

Kahu [kə'hu:] V U4, 98

Kashida [kæ'ʃi:də] V U2, 38

Keeya ['ki:jə] V U3, 72

Kyra ['kaɪrə] V U2, 42

Nani ['nɑ:ni] V U4, 98

Nicole [nɪ'kəʊl] V U3, 64

Penny ['peni] V U1, 10

Prisha ['prɪʃə] V U2, 38

Riah ['ri:ə] V U3, 64

Rose [rəʊz] V U4, 94

Sophia [sə'fi:ə] V U3, 71

Surnames

Apirana [æpɪ'rɑ:nə] V U4, 98

Campbell ['kæmbl] <V U4, 102>

Chandra ['tʃændrə] V U2, 42

Davidson ['deɪvɪdsn] V U3, 64

Flowers ['flaʊəz] V U4, 98

Hogan ['həʊgn] V U1, 17

Jansen ['jansn] V U3, 64

Nkosi [nə'kɒsi] V U3, 64

Phillips ['fɪlɪps] V U1, 21

Robson ['rɒbsn] V U1, 16

Sekibo [sə'ki:bəʊ] V U3, 64

Singh [sɪŋ] V U2, 54

Thompson ['tɒmsn] V U1, 21

Waaka ['wækə] V U4, 90

Watkins ['wɒtkɪnz] V U1, 16

Place names

Africa ['æfrɪkə] Afrika II

Agra ['ɑ:grə] *Ort in Indien* V U2, 38

America [ə'merɪkə] Amerika III

Antarctica [æn'tɑ:ktɪkə] Antarktis II

Auckland ['ɔ:klənd] *Stadt in Neuseeland* V U4, 88

Australia [ɒs'treɪliə] Australien I

Bangalore [ˌbæŋgə'lɔ:] *Großstadt in Indien* V U2, 38

Bavaria [bə'veəriə] Bayern I

Bloemfontein ['blu:mfənteɪn] *Hauptstadt Südafrikas* V U3, 62

Brisbane ['brɪzbən] *Großstadt in Australien* V U1, 21

Britain ['brɪtn] Großbritannien II

The British Isles [ðə ˌbrɪtɪʃ 'aɪlz] die Britischen Inseln III

Cambridge ['keɪmbrɪdʒ] *Stadt in Ostengland* <V U2, 48>

Canada ['kænədə] Kanada I

Canberra ['kænbrə] *Hauptstadt von Australien* V U1, 10

The Cape of Good Hope [ðə ˌkeɪp əv gʊd 'həʊp] Kap der Guten Hoffnung <V U3, 78>

Cape Town ['keɪp ˌtaʊn] Kapstadt *(Hauptstadt Südafrikas)* V U3, 62

Christchurch ['kraɪsˌtʃɜ:tʃ] *Stadt in Neuseeland* V U4, 92

Cuba ['kju:bə] Kuba IV

Durban ['dɜ:bən] *Stadt in Südafrika* V U3, 64

Eastern Cape ['i:stn ˌkeɪp] Ostcap V U3, 73

England ['ɪŋglənd] England I

Europe ['jʊərəp] Europa II

France [frɑ:ns] Frankreich IV

Germany ['dʒɜ:məni] Deutschland I

Great Britain [ˌgreɪt 'brɪtn] Großbritannien I

Gujarat [ˌgʊdʒə'rɑ:t] *indischer Bundesstaat* V U2, 42

India ['ɪndiə] Indien I

Ireland ['aɪələnd] Irland III

Istanbul [ˌɪstæn'bʊl] *Großstadt in der Türkei* I

Italy ['ɪtli] Italien IV

Jamaica [dʒə'meɪkə] Jamaika II

Johannesburg [dʒə'hænɪsbɜ:g] *Großstadt in Südafrika* V U3, 73

Klerksdorp ['klerksdɔ:p] *Stadt in Südafrika* V U3, 72

London ['lʌndən] *Hauptstadt von England* I

Makhanda [məˈkændə] *Stadt in Südafrika* V U3, 73

Manchester ['mæntʃɪstə] *Stadt in Nordengland* II

Mexico ['meksɪkəʊ] Mexiko IV

Moscow ['mɒskəʊ] Moskau I

Mumbai [ˌmʌmˈbaɪ] *Großstadt in Indien* V U2, 36

New Delhi [ˌnjuː ˈdeli] Neu-Delhi V U2, 36

New Zealand [ˌnjuː ˈziːlənd] Neuseeland V U4, 88

North Shore [ˌnɔ:θ ˈʃɔ:] *Region in Neuseeland* <V U4, 100>

Northern Ireland [ˌnɔ:ðnˈaɪələnd] Nordirland III

Perth [pɜ:θ] *Stadt in Australien* V U1, 12

Poland ['pəʊlənd] Polen II

Porbandar ['pɔ:bəndɑ:] *Stadt in Indien* V U2, 46

Pretoria [prɪˈtɔ:riə] *Hauptstadt Südafrikas* V U3, 62

The Republic of Ireland [ðə rɪˌpʌblɪkˌəv ˈaɪələnd] Irland III

Russia ['rʌʃə] Russland I

Sanand ['sænənd] *Ort in Indien* V U2, 38

Scotland ['skɒtlənd] Schottland I

South Africa [ˌsaʊθˈæfrɪkə] Südafrika V U3, 62

Soweto [səʊˈwetəʊ] *Stadt in Südafrika* V U3, 73

Sydney ['sɪdni] *Stadt in Australien* V U1, 10

Thailand ['taɪlænd] **Thailand** I

Turkey ['tɜ:ki] Türkei I

UK (United Kingdom) [ˈjuːˈkeɪ (juːˌnaɪtɪd ˈkɪŋdəm)] Vereinigtes Königreich von Großbritannien und Nordirland II

Umlazi [ʊmˈlɑːzi] *Stadtteil von Durban* V U3, 64

United States [juːˌnaɪtɪdˈsteɪts] Vereinigte Staaten II

USA (United States of America) [juːesˈeɪ (juːˌnaɪtɪdˌsteɪtsˌəv əˈmerɪkə)] USA (Vereinigte Staaten von Amerika) I

Wales [weɪlz] Wales III

Wellington ['welɪŋtən] *Stadt in Neuseeland* V U4, 88

Whangara ['wɒngaːrə] *Ort in Neuseeland* V U4, 98

Other names

Zackie **Achmat** [ˌzæki ˈækmet] *südafrikanischer Regisseur* V U3, 68

ACT [eɪ siː ˈtiː] *Abkürzung für das Territorium um Canberra* V U1, 21

Adelphi Hotel [əˈdelfi ˌhətel] *Hotelname* V U4, 97

All Blacks [ˌɔːl ˈblæks] *neuseeländisches Rugby-Team* <V U4, 106>

Auckland Hockey Club [ˌɔːklənd ˈhɒki ˌklʌb] *Name eines Hockeyvereins* <V U4, 100>

Cape Town Cycle Tour [keɪp ˌtaʊn ˈsaɪkl ˌtʊə] *Name eines Radrennens* <V U3, 78>

Daily News [ˌdeɪli ˈnjuːz] *Zeitungsname* V U3, 64

Darwin Road [ˌdɑːwɪn ˈrəʊd] *Straßenname* V U1, 16

Mahatma **Gandhi** [məˌhaːtmə ˈgændi] *indischer Freiheitskämpfer* V U2, 37

Mohandas **Gandhi** [məˌhændəs ˈgændi] *Geburtsname von Mahatma Gandhi* V U2, 46

Great Barrier Reef [ˌgreɪt ˌbæriə ˈriːf] *Korallenriff vor der Küste Australiens* V U1, 10

Mika **Hensing** [ˌmaɪkə ˈhensɪŋ] *Verfasserin* <V U3, 76>

Holi ['hɒli] *Name eines indischen Festes* V U2, 37

Kakadu National Park [ˌkækəduː ˌnæʃnl ˈpaːk] *Nationalpark in Australien* <V U1, 23>

Kruger National Park [ˌkruːgə ˌnæʃnl ˈpaːk] *Nationalpark in Südafrika* V U3, 63

Miriam **Makeba** [ˌmɪriəm məˈkeɪbə] *südafrikanische Sängerin* V U3, 68

Martens Place [ˌmaːtnz ˈpleɪs] *Straßenname* V U1, 21

Mount Tongariro [maʊnt ˈtɒngəriːrəʊ] *Berg in Neuseeland* <V U4, 101>

National Certificate of Tourism [ˌnæʃnl səˌtɪfɪkətˌev ˈtʊərɪzm] *Zertifikat der neuseeländischen Tourismusbranche* V U4, 90

Nelson **Mandela** [ˌnelsn mænˈdelə] *Präsident von Südafrika (1994–1999)* V U3, 62

Newlands College [ˌnjuːlənz ˈkɒlɪdʒ] *Name einer Hochschule* V U4, 90

Ningaloo Reef [ˌnɪngəluːˈriːf] Ningaloo-Riff <V U1, 23>

North Island ['nɔːθ ˌaɪlənd] Nordinsel <V U4, 101>

Pacific Ocean [pəˌsɪfɪkˈəʊʃn] Pazifischer Ozean V U4, 89

Paikea ['paɪkjə] *Urahn von Neuseeland* V U4, 98

QLD [ˌkjuː el ˈdiː] *Abkürzung für Queensland* V U1, 21

Ring of Fire [ˌrɪŋˌəv ˈfaɪə] Pazifischer Feuerring *(Vulkangürtel und Erdbebengebiet bei Neuseeland)* V U4, 89

Salt March [ˌsɔːlt ˈmaːtʃ] Salzmarsch *(Protestmarsch)* V U2, 46

School of the Air [ˌskuːlˌəv ði ˈeə] *Fernunterricht in Australien* V U1, 11

South Island ['saʊθ ˌaɪlənd] Südinsel <V U4, 101>

Sydney Harbour Bridge [ˌsɪdni ˌhaːbə ˈbrɪdʒ] *ein Wahrzeichen von Sydney* <V U1, 26>

Table Mountain ['teɪbl ˌmaʊntɪn] Tafelberg V U3, 62

Taj Mahal [ˌtaːdʒ məˈhaːl] *Grabmoschee in Indien* V U2, 36

The Whale Rider [ðə ˌweɪl ˈraɪdə] Whalerider *(Roman über ein Maorimädchen)* V U4, 98

Tshepong Hospital [ˌʃiːpɒŋ ˈhɒspɪtl] *Krankenhaus in Südafrika* V U3, 72

Uluru [uːˈluːruː] Uluru = Ayers Rock *(heiliger Berg der Aborigines)* V U1, 12

Working for Water [ˌwɜːkɪŋ fə ˈwɔːtə] *südafrikanisches Umweltprogramm* V U3, 72

World Cup [wɜːld ˈkʌp] Weltmeisterschaft <V U3, 78>

Karen **Zoid** [ˌkærn ˈzɔɪd] *Sängerin* V U3, 71

p pen • b bed • t ten • d dad • k cat • g grey • tʃ chair • dʒ joke • f fan • v very • θ three • ð the

A

abbiegen to turn II
Abend evening I
Abendessen dinner; tea I
abends in the evening I
Abenteuer adventure III
aber but I
abfahren to leave II; to depart IV
Abfall rubbish I; waste V U2, 37
abfliegen to depart; to leave IV
abgeschlossen locked I
die Aborigines Aboriginal people
   V U1, 11
Aborigine- Aboriginal V U1, 12
   zur Aborigine-Kultur gehörend
   Aboriginal V U1, 12
Abschieds- leaving II
Abschluss qualification IV
Abteilung department V U1, 21
acht eight I
Achterbahn roller coaster II
achtzehn eighteen I
achtzig eighty I
Ackerbau farming V U2, 42
Adresse address IV
Afrikaans (Sprache in Südafrika)
   Afrikaans V U3, 72
Afrikaner African V U3, 62
Afrikanerin African V U3, 62
afrikanisch African V U3, 62
Afroamerikaner African American IV
Afroamerikanerin African American
   IV
Aids (erworbene Immunabwehr-
   schwäche) AIDS V U3, 68
Aktivität activity I
Aktualisierung update IV
aktuelle Information update IV
Akzent accent III
Alaska Alaskan IV
alaskisch Alaskan IV
albern silly II
alle all I; everyone; every II
   von allen Staaten of all the states
   IV
allein alone V U1, 20
alles everything II
   Alles Gute Best wishes, I; All the
   best, II
Alligator alligator II
als as; than; when II

als Nächstes next II
als ob like IV
also so I
Also … Well, … II
alt old I
am in; on I
   am Ende at the end II
Amerikaner American II
Amerikanerin American II
Amerikanisch American II
amerikanisch American II
Amtssprache official language V ZI, 8
amüsant fun III
sich amüsieren to enjoy oneself IV
an on; at I; to II; about; by III; in IV
anbauen to produce IV; to grow
   V U2, 42
anbei enclosed V U4, 112
anbieten to offer IV
Anbieter supplier V U4, 94
andauern to last II
Andenken souvenir II
andere other II; different III; another IV
   anderen others II
   ein anderer another IV
   anderer Meinung sein to disagree
   IV
ändern to change II
anders different I
anfahren to hit V U3, 64
Anfang beginning II
anfangen to start I
Anfrage request IV; enquiry V U4, 106
sich anfühlen to feel III
anführen to lead V U2, 37
angeln gehen to go fishing IV
Angestellte worker; employee IV
Angestellter worker; employee IV
Angst haben to be scared I
ängstlich afraid V U1, 12
anhaben to wear I
anhalten to stop II
Anhänger follower IV
Anhängerin follower IV
anhören to listen (to) I
ankommen to arrive I
Ankömmling arrival IV
sanitäre Anlagen sanitation V U2, 42
Anleitung tutorial IV
sich anmelden to register V U1, 16
anprobieren to try on II

anregend inspiring V U3, 68
Anruf phone call I
anrufen to phone II; to call III
anschauen to look at; to watch I
sich anschließen to join V U2, 47
ansehen to watch I
anspornen to motivate III
sich anstrengen to struggle V U1, 11;
   to try hard V U4, 98
Antwort answer II
antworten to answer II
Anwalt lawyer V U2, 46
Anwältin lawyer V U2, 46
Anzeichen sign IV
Anzeige ad(vert) (= advertisement) III
anziehen to put on II
Apartheid apartheid (no pl) V U3, 62
Apartment apartment (AE) IV
Apfel apple I
Apotheke pharmacy V U1, 16
App app IV
April April I
Arbeit work II
arbeiten to work I
Arbeiter worker IV
Arbeiterin worker IV
Arbeitgeber employer V U4, 90
Arbeitgeberin employer V U4, 90
Arbeitnehmer employee IV
Arbeitnehmerin employee IV
arbeitslos unemployed V U3, 72
Arbeitszeit working hours (pl) IV
Arbeitszeugnis reference IV
Areal area IV
Arm arm II
arm poor IV
Armutsviertel township V U3, 62
Art kind II
   Art und Weise way III
Artikel item IV
Arznei medication; drug V U3, 68
Arzneimittel medication; drug
   V U3, 68
Arzt doctor II
Arzthelfer receptionist V U1, 16
Arzthelferin receptionist V U1, 16
Ärztin doctor II
Assistent assistant IV
Assistentin assistant IV
auch too; also I
   auch nicht not … either III

auch

auf

auf in; on; at I; to III
  auf einmal suddenly I
  Auf Wiedersehen. Goodbye. I
  auf … zu towards V U4, 99
  auf der linken Seite on the left II
  auf der rechten Seite on the right II
  auf jeden Fall certainly V U2, 46
Geld **aufbringen** to raise money II
Aufführung show I
Aufgabe job III; task V ZI, 9
aufgeregt excited II
aufheben to pick up V U4, 99
aufhören to finish; to stop II; to end
  V U3, 62
aufmachen to open I
aufpassen auf to look after II
aufräumen to tidy II
aufregend exciting I
aufstehen to get up I; to stand up
  V U4, 99
Auftrag task V ZI, 9
jmdm. etw. **auftragen** to tell sb to do
  sth III
aufwachen to wake up III
Aufwärmen warm-up II
Aufwärmtraining warm-up II
aufwecken to wake up III
Aufzug lift II
Auge eye I
August August I
aus from I; of III
  aus dem Weg gehen to avoid IV
ausbilden to train IV
Ausbildung training; qualification;
  education IV; apprenticeship
  V U4, 94
  eine Ausbildung machen to train
  IV
Ausbleichen bleaching V U1, 20
sich **ausdenken** to think of III
Auseinandersetzung argument II
Ausflug trip I
den Hund **ausführen** to take the dog
  for a walk I
ausfüllen to complete V U4, 90
ausgeben (Geld) to spend II
ein **ausgefüllter** Tag a busy day II
Aushang lost and found notice III
(sich) **ausleihen** to borrow II
ausliefern to deliver IV
auslösen to cause IV

einem etwas **ausmachen** to mind sth
  V U4, 90
ausprobieren to try III
die Spülmaschine **ausräumen** to
  empty the dishwasher II
aussehen to look I
außen outside II
außerhalb outside II
aussprechen to say III
etw. nicht **ausstehen** können can't
  stand + -ing III
aussteigen to get off II; to get out IV
Ausstellung exhibition III
Australier Australian V U1, 10
Australierin Australian V U1, 10
australisch Australian V U1, 10
auswählen to choose III
ausweichen to avoid IV
Auto car I
Automat machine V U2, 38

B

Bad(ezimmer) bathroom II
Bahn railway IV
Bahnhof station III; railway station IV
bald soon II
Balkon balcony I
Ball ball I
Banane banana I
Band band II
Bär bear II
Base base III
Baseball baseball III
Basketball basketball II
Basketballkorb basket III
basteln to make II; to do handicrafts
  V U3, 73
bauen to build II
Bauer farmer I
Bäuerin farmer I
Bauernhof farm I
Baum tree I
Baumstamm caber III
Baumstammwerfen caber toss III
Bauwerk building II
beängstigend scary I
beantworten to answer II
beben to shake IV
bedeuten to mean IV
Bedeutung sense IV

beeindruckend awesome III
beenden to finish; to stop II; to end
  V U3, 62
befolgen to follow V U3, 80
befördern to transport IV
Befrager interviewer IV
Befragerin interviewer IV
Befragung interview IV
befüllen to fill V U4, 94
befürchten to be afraid V U1, 16
Begabung talent I
begeistert excited II
Beginn beginning II
beginnen to start I; to begin V U1, 10
begründen to found V U4, 98
bei at I; with II; to III; in; during IV;
  c/o V U4, 106
beibringen to teach IV
beide both IV
beigefügt enclosed V U4, 112
Bein leg II
beinahe nearly II
Beispiel example III
  zum Beispiel for example III
beitreten to join V U2, 47
sich **beklagen** to complain IV
bekommen to get I
bekommen (Bus/Zug) to catch (bus/
  train) III
belästigen to disturb V U3, 80
beliebt popular III
bellen to bark II
bemalen to paint II
benutzen to use III
beobachten to watch II
Berater advisor V U4, 88
Beraterin advisor V U4, 88
Bereich area V U1, 20
bereit ready I
bereits already III
Berg mountain II; hill IV
Bericht report V U4, 94
Beruf career IV
Berufs- careers V U4, 88
Berufserfahrung work experience
  V U4, 90
Berufsinformationstag careers day
  V U4, 90
Berufspraktikum internship IV
berühmt famous I
beschädigen to damage V U2, 42

Beschädigung damage IV
beschäftigt busy I
Bescheinigung certificate V U4, 90
beschließen to decide III
sich beschweren to complain IV
besitzen to have I; to have got II; to
   own III
besonders special I
besorgt worried II
besser better II
sich wieder besser fühlen to get
   better V U1, 16
Gute Besserung! Get well soon!
   V U1, 16
beste best II
   am besten best II
besteigen to climb II
bestellen to order V U4, 94
Besuch visit III
besuchen to visit I
Besucher visitor II
Besucherin visitor II
Betr. RE V U4, 106
Betreff subject III
Bett bed I
   ins Bett gehen to go to bed I
Bettdecke blanket IV
beunruhigt worried II
Bevölkerung population (no pl) IV
bevor before II
(sich) bewegen to move IV
Bewegung movement IV
beweisen to prove IV
sich bewerben (für/um) to apply
   (for) IV
Bewerbung application IV
Bewerbungsschreiben letter of
   application IV
bewölkt cloudy II
bewundern to admire V U3, 68
bezahlen to pay V U3, 68
Bezirk borough IV
bieten to offer IV
Bild picture I
Bildung education IV
billig cheap II
Biologie Biology I
bis until; to III
   Bis bald. See you soon. I; See you. II
ein bisschen a bit V U3, 72
ein (kleines) bisschen a little (bit) II

bitte please I
   Bitte schön. Here you are. I
blau blue I
bleiben to stay I
   in Verbindung bleiben staying
   connected III
   stecken bleiben to be stuck I
Bleichen bleaching V U1, 20
Bleistift pencil I
blinken to signal IV
Blog blog I
Boden soil V U2, 42
Bonbon sweet I
Boom boom IV
Boot boat IV
Bordkarte boarding card IV
böse angry II
Boss boss III
Bote messenger IV
Botin messenger IV
Box box I
brauchbar useful III
brauchen to need I; to take III
braun brown I
brechen to break V U1, 11
bremsen to brake V U3, 64
Brief letter IV
Brieffreund penfriend III
Brieffreundin penfriend III
Brieftasche wallet V U3, 64
bringen to bring II; to get IV
die Briten the British V U2, 37
britisch British V U1, 11
Broschüre brochure III
Brot bread I
   belegtes Brot sandwich I
Brücke bridge II
Bruder brother I
Bub boy I
Buch book I
buchen to book III
Buchstabe letter IV
Bucht bay V U4, 98
Bude stall I
Bühne stage II
Bühnenbild scenery III
Bundesstaat state III
bunt colourful V U1, 12
Burg castle III
Büro office V U2, 38
Bus bus I

Butter butter I

C

Café snack bar I; café III
Cafeteria cafeteria I
Camp camp III
campen gehen to go camping III
Campingplatz campsite III
Cent (Währung) cent III
Center centre; center (AE) III
Chance chance III; opportunity IV
chatten to chat II
Check-in-Mitarbeiter check-in agent
   IV
Check-in-Mitarbeiterin check-in
   agent IV
Cheerleader cheerleader III
Cheerleaderin cheerleader III
Cheerleading cheerleading III
Chef boss III
Chefin boss III
Chinese Chinese II
Chinesin Chinese II
Chinesisch Chinese II
chinesisch Chinese II
circa about II
Cola cola I
Comic(heft) comic II
Computer computer I
cool cool I
Copyright copyright IV
Cousin cousin II
Cousine cousin II

D

da there; because I
Dach roof III
Dachboden attic I
daheim at home I
dahin there I
Dame lady IV
damit so that IV
Dampfer steamboat IV
Dampfschiff steamboat IV
danach then; after that I
dankbar thankful IV
Danke. Thanks.; Thank you. I
dann then I
Darsteller actor III

Darstellerin

Darstellerin actor III
das the; this; that I; which; who III
dass that II
Datum date IV
dauern to last II; to take III
davor in front of I
Decke blanket IV
dein your I
    Dein *(Grußformel in Briefen oder E-Mails)* Yours, II
deine yours III
Delfin dolphin V U4, 99
demoliert wrecked IV
Demonstration protest V U2, 37
denken to think II
    denken an to think about III
    denken an/über to think of III
der the I; which; that; who III
dermaßen so II
derselbe the same II
deshalb so I
Design design II
Detail detail V U3, 64
Detektiv detective I
Detektivin detective I
deutlich clear III
Deutsch German I
deutsch German II
Deutsche German II
Deutscher German II
Dezember December I
Dialog dialogue II
dich you I; yourself III
Didgeridoo *(australisches Musikinstrument)* didgeridoo V U1, 12
die the I; which; that; who III
Dienstag Tuesday I
dies this I
diese these II
dieses that I
Ding thing I; item IV
dir you I; yourself IV
    dir selbst yourself IV
Distanz distance V U3, 80
Dollar *(amer. Währungseinheit)* dollar ($) IV
Donner boom IV
Donnerstag Thursday I
Dorf village I
dort there I
dorthin there I

Dose can IV
Drama drama III
draußen outside II
dreckig dirty I
drei three I
dreißig thirty I
dreizehn thirteen I
dritte third II
ein Drittel a third V U4, 88
Droge drug IV
drüben over III
du you I
Dudelsack bagpipes *(pl)* III
Duft smell IV
Dünger fertiliser V U2, 42
dunkel dark I
durch around; through III
Durcheinander mess I
Durchmesser diameter II
dürfen may V U1, 20
    (etw. tun) dürfen to be allowed to (do sth) IV

E

eben flat V U1, 11
Ecke corner V U1, 28
effizient efficient IV
ehrenamtliche Helferin volunteer V U4, 89
ehrenamtlicher Helfer volunteer V U4, 89
Ei egg I
eiförmig oval III
eigene own II
eigentlich really I
Eignung suitability V U4, 90
Eignungs- suitability V U4, 90
ein one; a; an I
    ein bisschen a bit V U3, 72
    ein paar a few IV
einander each other III
eine a; an I
einfach easy I; just III
    einfache Fahrkarte single ticket III
    die einfachste the least difficult III
sich **einfallen** lassen to think of III
sich etw. **einfangen** *(medizinisch)* to catch sth V U1, 16
Eingebung inspiration V U3, 68
einhundert a/one hundred I

einige some I; a few IV; several V U2, 37
Einkaufen shopping I
Einkaufspassage mall II
Einkaufszentrum shopping centre I; mall II
Einkaufszettel shopping list I
einladen to invite II
Einladung invitation I
einmal once II
    schon einmal ever III
einnehmen to take V U1, 16
einpacken to pack III
die Spülmaschine **einräumen** to load the dishwasher II
eins one I
einsam lonely III
einst once II
einsteigen to get in IV
    in etw. einsteigen to get on sth IV
Einsteigezeit boarding time IV
eintausend a/one thousand II
sich **eintragen** to register V U1, 16
Eintrittskarte ticket II
einundzwanzig twenty-one I
nicht **einverstanden** sein to disagree IV
Einwanderer immigrant IV
Einwanderin immigrant IV
Einwohner population *(no pl)* IV
Einwohnerzahl population *(no pl)* IV
Einzelhandel retail V U4, 94
Einzelheit detail V U3, 64
Eis ice cream II
Eiscreme ice cream II
Eisenbahn railway IV
Eishockey ice hockey; hockey IV
Elch moose IV
Elefant elephant V U3, 63
Elektrizität electricity V U3, 63
Elendsviertel slum V U2, 36
elf eleven I
Eltern parents *(pl)* I
E-Mail e-mail II
Empfangschef receptionist IV
Empfangsdame receptionist IV
Empfehlung reference IV
Ende end II
    am Ende at the end II
    oberes Ende top II
enden to finish II; to end V U3, 62

Energie energy V U1, 21

die **Engländer** the English III

Englisch English I

englisch English III

englischsprachig English-speaking V ZI, 9

entdecken to discover V U3, 62

entfernt away II

Entfernung distance V U3, 80

entfliehen to escape IV

mit **enthalten** sein to be included V U4, 94

entkommen to escape IV

(sich) **entscheiden** to decide III

Entscheidung decision IV

Entschuldigung. Sorry. I; I'm sorry.; Excuse me. II

enttäuscht disappointed V U1, 12

entwerfen to design IV

entwickeln to design IV

Entwurf design II

Episode episode IV

er it; he I

Erdbeben earthquake IV

Erdbeere strawberry I

Erde earth III; soil V U2, 42

Erdteil continent II

sich **ereignen** to happen IV

Ereignis event II

erfahren to learn V U1, 12

erfahren von to hear about IV

Erfahrung experience IV

erfolgreich successful IV

erfolgreich sein to achieve V U3, 68

erforschen to explore IV

Ergebnis result V U4, 90

erhältlich available IV

sich **erholen** to recover V U1, 20

sich **erinnern** (an) to remember III

Erkältung cold II

erklären to explain V U3, 81

erklettern to climb II

erkunden to explore IV

sich **erkundigen** nach to ask about II

Erlebnis adventure III; experience IV

erledigen to finish II

ernst serious II

Ernte crop V U2, 42

Erntedankfest Thanksgiving IV

eröffnen to open V U4, 94

erraten to guess I

erreichen to achieve V U3, 68

erschießen to shoot IV

erst only V U3, 68

erstaunlich amazing II

erste first I

das erste Mal the first time I

Erste-Hilfe- first-aid IV

als **Erstes** first II

etw. nicht **ertragen** can't stand + -ing III

erwachen to wake up III

erzählen to tell I

Erzähler narrator I

Erzählerin narrator I

erzeugen to produce IV

Erzeugnis product V U4, 94

Erziehung education IV

erzielen to score III

es it I

Es macht nichts. I don't mind. IV

Es tut mir leid. I'm sorry. II

es war einmal once upon a time II

Essen food I; meal II

essen to eat; to have I

Etage floor II

etwa about II

etwas something; some I; anything III

euch you I; yourselves IV

euch selbst yourselves IV

euer your I

eure yours III

Euro *(Währung)* euro III

Europäer European III

Europäerin European III

europäisch European III

ewig forever IV

Examen exam V U4, 90

ein Examen schreiben to take an exam V U4, 90

Experiment experiment II

Extremist extremist V U2, 47

Extremistin extremist V U2, 47

F

Fabrik factory III

(zu etw.) **fähig** sein *(Ersatzform für can)* to be able to (do sth) IV

Fähigkeit skill IV

fahren to go; to ride I; to run; to travel II; to drive IV

Fahrrad fahren to go bike riding II

Tandem fahren to go tandem bike riding II

Fahrer driver IV

Fahrerin driver IV

Fahrgeschäft ride II

einfache **Fahrkarte** single ticket III

Fahrplan timetable III

Fahrrad bike I

Fahrrad fahren to go bike riding II

Fahrschein ticket II

Fahrt trip I; ride II; journey III

fair fair IV

Fakt fact II

auf jeden **Fall** certainly V U2, 46

fallen to fall I

fällen to cut down V U3, 72

falls if IV

falsch wrong I

Familie family I

Fan fan I

fangen to catch II

fantastisch fantastic II

Farbe colour I; color *(AE)* III

Fasching carnival I

fast nearly II

Februar February I

Feier party I

feiern to celebrate III

eine Party feiern to have a party I

Feiertag holiday *(AE)* IV

Feld field III

Feldfrucht crop V U2, 42

Fels rock V U1, 12

Fenster window I

Ferien holiday II; vacation *(AE)* III

fernhalten to keep away IV

Fernseh- TV IV

Fernsehen television III; TV IV

im Fernsehen on TV III

fernsehen to watch TV I

Fernseher TV I; television III

fertig ready I

fertig machen to finish II

Fertigkeit skill IV

fertigstellen to finish I

Fest fair II; festival III

fest close V U4, 99

festhalten to hold II

Festival festival III
feststecken to be stuck I
Festzug procession II
Feuer fire III
Fieber high temperature V U1, 16
Figur figure II
Film film I; movie *(AE)* III
finden to find I
 Gefallen finden an to enjoy IV
 Gefallen finden an to enjoy + -ing
 V U2, 38
Firma company II
Fisch fish I
fischen gehen to go fishing IV
fit fit III
flach flat V U1, 11
Fläche area V U1, 20
Flagge flag IV
eine **Flasche** … a bottle of II
Fledermaus bat I
Fleisch meat IV
flexibel flexible IV
Fliegen flying III
fliegen to fly II
fliehen to escape IV
Fließband assembly line V U2, 38
Floh flea I
Flohmarkt flea market I
Floß raft III
flüchten to escape IV
Flug flight IV
 Guten Flug! Have a good flight! IV
Flughafen airport IV
Flugsteig gate IV
Flugzeug plane IV
Fluss river I
Flusskrebs crayfish V U4, 99
Folge episode IV
Follower follower IV
Followerin follower IV
Formular form V U4, 90
Foto photo I
 Fotos machen to take photos (of)
 II
fotografieren to take photos (of) II
Frage question I
fragen to ask I
 fragen nach to ask about II
Französisch French IV
französisch French IV
Frau woman I; lady IV

Frau *(Anrede)* Mrs I; Miss IV; Ms
 V U4, 90
frei free III
im **Freien** outside II
Freitag Friday I
Freiwillige volunteer V U4, 89
Freiwilliger volunteer V U4, 89
Freizeit free time I
Freizeit- free-time V U4, 89
Freizeitpark theme park II
Freude fun I
sich **freuen** auf to look forward to
 (+ -ing) IV
Freund friend I
Freundin friend I
freundlich friendly IV
Freundschaft(en) schließen to make
 friends II
friedlich non-violent V U2, 46; peace-
 ful V U2, 47; calm V U4, 90
Frisbee frisbee I
Frisbeescheibe frisbee I
Friseur hairdresser IV
Friseurin hairdresser IV
Friseursalon hairdressing salon IV
froh happy IV
 Frohe Weihnachten! Merry Christ-
 mas! I
fröhlich happy IV
Frucht fruit I
früh early II
Frühling spring II
Frühstück breakfast I
frühstücken to have breakfast I
Frühstückspension bed and breakfast (B & B) III
(sich) **fühlen** to feel II
 sich wieder besser fühlen to get
 better V U1, 16
führen to lead V U2, 37
Führer guide IV
Führerin guide IV
Führerschein driving licence V U3, 64
Führung tour III
füllen to fill V U4, 94
Füller pen I
fünf five I
fünfzehn fifteen I
fünfzig fifty I
funktionieren to work V U4, 94
für for I; to IV

 für immer forever IV
furchtbar awful I
Fuß foot II
 zu Fuß on foot I
 zu Fuß gehen to walk IV
Fußball football !; soccer *(AE)* II
füttern to feed I

G

ganz all I; all of; quite II
 in ganz all over II
Ganztages- all-day III
Garage garage V U4, 90
Garten garden I
Gast guest IV
Gate gate IV
Gebäude building II
geben to give I
Gebet prayer V U4, 98
Gebiet field III; area IV
geboren werden to be born IV
gebratener Reis mit Hühnerfleisch
 chicken fried rice II
gebraucht second-hand I
Geburtsdatum date of birth IV
Geburtstag birthday I
Gedicht poem III
Gefahr danger V U1, 20
gefährlich dangerous III
Gefallen finden an to enjoy IV
Gefallen finden an to enjoy + -ing
 V U2, 38
jmdn. **gefangen** halten to keep sb
 prisoner IV
Gefangene prisoner IV
Gefangener prisoner IV
Gefängnis prison V U2, 46
gegen against III
 etwas gegen etw. haben to mind
 sth V U4, 90
Gegend area IV
gegenseitig each other III
Gegenstand item IV
gegenüber opposite II
Gehalt salary IV
gehen to go I; to walk; to leave IV
 aus dem Weg gehen to avoid IV
 campen gehen to go camping III
 fischen gehen to go fishing IV
 inlineskaten gehen to go skating II

ins Bett gehen to go to bed I
raften gehen to go rafting III
Schlittschuhlaufen gehen to go skating II
zelten gehen to go camping III
Gehör hearing II
Geist ghost IV
gelb yellow I
Geld money I
Geld aufbringen to raise money II
Geld sammeln to raise money II
Geldbeutel wallet V U3, 64
Geldbörse wallet V U3, 64
Gelegenheit chance III; opportunity IV
gelegentlich occasionally III
Gemälde painting V U1, 12
Gemeinde community V U4, 94
Gemüse vegetable (veg) IV
genauso the same II
genießen to enjoy IV
genießen to enjoy + -ing V U2, 38
genießen, … zu tun to enjoy + -ing V U2, 38
genug enough III
genügend enough III
geöffnet open I
gerade (eben) just III
geradeaus straight on II
Gerät tool V U4, 90
Geräusch noise I
gerecht fair IV
Gern geschehen. You're welcome. V U1, 16
ich hätte **gern** … I'd love (to) … (= I would love to) IV
ich würde sehr **gern** … I'd love (to) … (= I would love to) IV
… **gerne** like + -ing I
gernhaben to like I
Geruch smell IV
Geruchssinn sense of smell IV
Geschäft shop I; store (AE) III; business V ZI, 9
Geschäftsführer manager IV
Geschäftsführerin manager IV
Geschäftswelt business V ZI, 9
geschehen to happen II
Geschenk present I
Geschichte story I
Geschick skill IV

geschlossen closed I
Geschöpf creature V U1, 10
Gesellschaft company II
Gesetz law V U1, 20
gegen das Gesetz verstoßen to break the law V U2, 46
Gesicht face I
Gespenst ghost IV
Gespräch dialogue II; interview IV
Gestalt figure II
gestalten to design IV
Gestaltung design II
gestern yesterday I
gesund healthy III
Getränk drink I
Getreide corn IV
Gewalt violence (no pl) IV
gewaltfrei non-violent V U2, 46
Gewerbe industry V U4, 88
Gewinn prize II
gewinnen to win I
Gewinner winner I
Gewinnerin winner I
Gewinnspiel raffle II
sich **gewöhnen** an (etw.) to get used to (sth) IV
gewöhnlich usually II
Gitarre guitar V U3, 72
glauben to think; to believe II
gleich the same II; right away V U3, 68
der **gleiche** the same II
gleichzeitig at the same time II
Glocke bell II
Glück bringend lucky II
Glück haben to be lucky II
Viel **Glück!** Good luck! IV
zum **Glück** fortunately V U3, 72
glücklich happy I; lucky II
Glückstag lucky day II
Glückwunsch! Congratulations! II
Gold gold III
Gold- gold III
golden gold III
grau grey I
Grenze border IV
Grill barbecue I
Grillfest barbecue I
Grippe flu V U1, 16
Grizzlybär grizzly bear IV
groß big I; large; high; tall II; great III

großartig great I; fantastic II; awesome III
Größe size II
Großeltern grandparents (pl) II
Großmutter grandmother V U4, 98
Großstadt city I
Großvater grandfather II
grün green I
gründen to found V U4, 98
Grundschule primary school IV
Gruppe team I; group IV
gruselig scary I
Viele **Grüße** Best wishes, I
Mit freundlichen **Grüßen** Yours sincerely, IV
günstig cheap II
gut fine; good I; well II
gut sein in to be good at I
Gut gemacht! Well done! II
gut sein bei to be good at I
Gute Besserung! Get well soon! V U1, 16
Guten Flug! Have a good flight! IV
Mir geht es gut. I'm fine. I
Alles **Gute!** Best wishes, I; All the best, II; Good luck! IV
Güter goods (pl only) V U2, 38

H

haben to have I; to have got II
Angst haben to be scared I
Glück haben to be lucky II
Hähnchen chicken I
Hai shark I
halb half III
halb (acht) half past (seven) II
eine halbe Million half a million III
(die) **Hälfte** half V ZI, 8
Hallen- indoor III
Hallo. Hello.; Hi. I
Hallo! G'day! (= Good day!) V U1, 10
Hals neck II
Halsband collar I
Halt stop II
halten to hold; to keep II; to give V ZI, 9
davon halten to think of V U1, 12
jmdn. gefangen halten to keep sb prisoner IV
Haltestelle stop II; station III

Hamburger burger I
Hammer hammer III
Hammerwerfen hammer throwing III
Hamster hamster I
Hand hand II
   aus zweiter Hand second-hand I
Handschuh glove II
Handy phone I
hart hard II
hassen to hate I
häufig often II
häufiger more often IV
Häuptling chief V U4, 98
Hauptpostamt GPO V U1, 21
Hauptstadt capital (city) I
Haus house I
   nach Hause home I
   zu Hause at home I
Hausaufgabe(n) homework I
   Hausaufgabe(n) machen to do
   homework I
Hausmeister caretaker I
Hausmeisterin caretaker I
Haustier pet I
Heft book I
heilig sacred V U2, 54
Heim home I
Heimat home country IV
Heimatland home country IV
Heimweh haben to be homesick IV
heiß hot I
Ich **heiße** … My name is … I
helfen to help I
Helfer assistant IV
Helferin assistant IV
Helikopter helicopter V U1, 12
Helm helmet I
Hemd shirt I
herausfallen to fall out III
herausfinden to find I; to find out IV;
   to learn V U1, 12
herauskommen to get out IV
Herberge hostel II
Herbst autumn II; fall (AE) III
Herr (Anrede) Mr I
herstellen to produce IV; to make
   V U2, 38
herüber over III
herumhängen to hang about I
herunter down III
herunterfallen to fall off II

Herzliche Grüße Love, I
heute today I
   heute Morgen this morning II
Hi! G'day! (= Good day!) V U1, 10
hier here I
hierher here III
hierhin here III
hiesig local II
High School (weiterführende Schule,
   Oberstufe) high school V U3, 63
Hilfe help I; support V U4, 90
hilfreich useful III
Himmel sky IV
Hin- und Rückfahrkarte return ticket
   III
hinauf up II
hinaus out V U4, 98
hinausbringen to take out II
hinbringen to take II
Hindu Hindu V U2, 47
hinduistisch Hindu V U2, 47
in … **hinein** into II
hinfallen to fall I
sich **hinsetzen** to sit (down) I
hinter behind I
Hintergrund background III
hinterlassen to leave III
hinunter down III
hinunterfallen to fall off II
Hinweis clue I
hinzufügen to add V U3, 64
hispanisch Hispanic IV
Hispanoamerikaner Hispanic IV
Hispanoamerikanerin Hispanic IV
HIV HIV V U3, 68
HIV- HIV V U3, 68
HI-Virus HIV V U3, 68
Hobby hobby II
hoch high; up; tall II
hochladen to upload II
Hochzeit wedding V U2, 37
   arrangierte Hochzeit arranged
   marriage V U2, 37
Hockey hockey IV
hoffen (auf) to hope (for) II
Hoffnung hope V U3, 73
Höhe height II
Höhle cave IV
holen to get IV
Holz wood I

homosexuell lesbian V U3, 68; gay
   V U3, 68
hören to listen (to) I; to hear II
   hören von to hear about IV
kurze **Hose** shorts (pl) II
Hostel hostel II
Hotdog hot dog II
Hotel hotel IV
hübsch pretty II; beautiful III
Hubschrauber helicopter V U1, 12
Hügel hill IV
Huhn chicken I
gebratener Reis mit **Hühnerfleisch**
   chicken fried rice II
Hund dog I
   den Hund ausführen to take the
   dog for a walk I
hundert a/one hundred I
hungrig hungry I
hüpfen to bounce III
Hurrikan hurricane IV
Husky (Schlittenhunderasse) husky IV
Hut hat I
hüten to look after II

I

ich I; me I
   ich hätte gern I'd (= I would) I
   ich hätte gern … I'd love (to)
   … (= I would love to) IV
   ich möchte … I'd like (to) …
   (= I would like to) I
   ich würde I'd (= I would) I
   ich würde gerne … I'd like (to) …
   (= I would like to) I
   ich würde nicht gerne … I
   wouldn't like (to) … I
   ich würde sehr gern … I'd love (to)
   … (= I would love to) IV
Idee idea I
ihm it; him II
ihn it; him II
Ihnen you I
ihnen them II
ihr you; her; their; its I
Ihr your I
Ihre yours III
ihre hers; theirs III
im in I
   im Fernsehen on TV III

im Freien outside II
im Jahr a year IV
im Moment at the moment II
im Norden von in the north of III
im Wert von worth of V U4, 94
Imbissstube snack bar I
immer always I
für immer forever IV
immer noch still II
schon immer always III
Immigrant immigrant IV
Immigrantin immigrant IV
in to; in; at I; into II
in der Schule at school I
in der Woche a week V U3, 73
in ganz all over II
in Ordnung fine I
in Richtung towards V U4, 99
inbegriffen sein to be included V U4, 94
Inder Indian V U2, 36
Inderin Indian V U2, 36
Indianer Native American III
Indianerin Native American III
indianisch Native American III
indisch Indian V U2, 36
Industrie industry III
Industriezweig industry V U4, 88
Informatik IT (Information Technology) V U2, 38
aktuelle **Information** update IV
Information(en) information II
Ingenieur engineer II
Ingenieurin engineer II
inlineskaten to skate II
inlineskaten gehen to go skating II
Innen- indoor III
Insel island IV
Inspiration inspiration V U3, 68
inspirierend inspiring V U3, 68
interessant interesting I
Interesse interest IV
sich **interessieren** für to be interested in III
interessiert sein an to be interested in III
international international V ZI, 9
Internetseite website III
Internettagebuch blog I
Interview interview IV
Interviewer interviewer IV

Interviewerin interviewer IV
irgendeine any I
irgendeiner anyone IV
irgendetwas anything III
irgendjemand someone; anybody III; anyone IV
irgendwelche any I
Irisch Irish III
irisch Irish III
Italiener Italian IV
Italienerin Italian IV
Italienisch Italian IV
italienisch Italian IV

J

ja yes I
Jacke coat I
Jahr year I
im Jahr a year IV
Jahre alt year-old V U2, 42
pro Jahr a year IV
Jahreszeit season II
Jahrgangsstufe year I; grade (AE) II
Jahrhundert century IV
-jährig year-old V U2, 42
Jahrmarkt fair II
Januar January I
Japaner Japanese IV
Japanerin Japanese IV
Japanisch Japanese IV
japanisch Japanese IV
jede every I
jeder everyone II; anybody III
jedoch however V U1, 20
jemals ever III
jemand somebody I; someone; anybody III
jene that I; those II
jetzt now I
Job job I
Jugend- youth I; teen II
Jugendliche teen II; teenager V U2, 42
Jugendlicher teen II; teenager V U2, 42
Juli July I
jung young II
Junge boy I
Juni June I
Jurist lawyer V U2, 46
Juristin lawyer V U2, 46

K

Käfig cage II
Kajak kayak IV
Kajakfahren kayaking IV
Kalender planner II
kalt cold I
Kälte cold II
kämpfen to fight II; to struggle V U1, 11
Kanadier Canadian IV
Kanadierin Canadian IV
kanadisch Canadian IV
Kanal canal III
Känguru kangaroo V U1, 11
Kaninchen rabbit I
Kanone cannon III
Kanonenkugel cannon ball III
Kanu canoe IV
Kanufahren canoeing I
Kapitän captain II
Kapitänin captain II
kaputt machen to break V U1, 11
Karibe Caribbean IV
Karibin Caribbean IV
karibisch Caribbean IV
Karneval carnival I
Karriere career IV
Karte map II; card III
Kartoffel potato IV
Käse cheese I
Kasse checkout V U4, 94
Katze cat I
kaufen to buy I
kein no I; not … any III
keine no I; not … any III
Keks biscuit; cookie (AE) III
kennen to know I
kennenlernen to meet I
Kenntnis skill IV
Kette chain III
Kfz-Werkstatt garage V U4, 90
Kilo (kg, Kilogramm) kilo (kg, kilogram) I
Kilometer (km) kilometre (km) IV
Kilt kilt III
Kind kid I
Kinder children (pl) I
Kindergarten kindergarten V U3, 73
Kinderzimmer bedroom II
Kino cinema I
Kirche church II

Kiste box I

Kiwi *(Kosename für Neuseeländer)* Kiwi V U4, 106
klagen to lament V U4, 98
klar clear III
Klasse year; class I; grade *(AE)* II
Klassenarbeit test V U4, 90
Klassenfahrt school trip II
Klassenzimmer classroom I
Kleeblatt shamrock III
Kleid dress I
Kleider clothes *(pl only)* I
Kleiderschrank wardrobe II
Kleidung clothes *(pl only)* I
klein little; small I
Klettern rock climbing I
klettern to climb II
Klima climate IV
Klimawandel climate change V U1, 20
klingeln to ring I
klingen to sound III
Klub club I
Knall bang V U3, 64
Koala koala V U1, 11
Koch chef II
Koch- cooking II
Kochen cooking II
kochen to cook II
Koffer suitcase IV
Kohlenbergwerk coal mine III
Kohlengrube coal mine III
Kolonie colony IV
komisch funny I
kommen to come; to get I
  zu spät kommen to be late II
Kommentar comment IV
kommentieren to comment (on) IV
Kommunikation communication V U4, 90
kommunizieren to communicate V ZI, 9
kompliziert difficult III
König king II
Königin queen II
können can I; may V U1, 20
  (etw. tun) können to be able to (do sth) IV
  nicht können can't I
konnte could III
könnte could V U3, 81; might V U4, 90
konstruieren to design IV

Kontakt contact I
  in Kontakt bleiben to keep in touch II
Kontinent continent II
kontrollieren to check II; to control V U3, 72
Konzert concert I
Kopf head II
Kopfschmerzen headache II
Kopfweh headache II
Koralle coral V U1, 20
Korb basket III
Korbball netball I
Korn corn IV
Körper body IV
korrekt right I
korrigieren to correct II
kosten to cost III
kostenlos free III
köstlich delicious V U1, 12
Kostüm costume; fancy dress I
krachen to crash V U3, 64
Kraft energy V U1, 21
krank ill V U1, 16
Krankenakte medical record V U1, 16
Krankenhaus hospital II
Krankenpfleger nurse IV
Krankenschwester nurse IV
Krankenversicherung medical insurance V U3, 73
Krankheit disease V U3, 68
Kratzer scratch IV
Kreatur creature V U1, 10
Kricket cricket II
Kronjuwelen crown jewels *(pl)* II
Kruste crust IV
Küche kitchen II
Kuchen cake I
Küchenchef chef II
Kugel ball III
Kuh cow III
Kulissen scenery III
Kultur culture III
sich **kümmern** um to look after II
Kunde customer I
Kundenbetreuung customer service IV
Kundendienst customer service IV
Kundenservice customer service IV
Kundgebung march V U2, 47
Kundin customer I

Kunst Art I
Künstler artist III
Künstlerin artist III
Kunststück trick I
Kurier messenger IV
Kurierin messenger IV
Kurs class IV
kurz short II
  kurze Hose shorts *(pl)* II
küssen to kiss V U4, 99
Küste coast III

L

lachen to laugh II
Laden shop I; store *(AE)* III
Lager camp III
Lampe lamp II
Land country I; nation III
landen to land IV
ländliche Gegend country I
Landschaft landscape V U4, 89
Landwirt farmer I
Landwirtin farmer I
Landwirtschaft farming V U2, 42
lang long III
länger longer I
langsam slow IV
Languste crayfish V U4, 99
langweilig boring I
Laptop laptop I
lassen to leave II
  lass(t) uns let's (= let us) I
Laterne lantern II
Laufbahn career IV
laufen to run II; to walk IV
  Schlittschuh laufen to skate II
laut loud I; noisy III
läuten to ring I
Leben life II; living V U2, 42
leben to live I
Lebensart lifestyle V U1, 12
Lebenslauf CV (curriculum vitae) IV
Lebensmittel food I
Lebensstil lifestyle V U1, 12
Lebensweise lifestyle V U1, 12; living V U2, 42
Lebewesen creature V U1, 10
lecker delicious V U1, 12
legen to put I
lehren to teach IV

Lehrer teacher I
Lehrerin teacher I
Leiche body IV
leicht easy I
Es tut mir **leid**. I'm sorry. II
Tut mir **leid**. Sorry. I
leider I'm afraid IV; unfortunately V U2, 47
leise quiet II
leisten to achieve V U3, 68
leistungsfähig efficient IV
leiten to lead V U2, 37; to be in charge (of) V U3, 72
Leiter ladder I; leader III
Leiterin leader III
(für) etw. **lernen** to study (for) sth V U4, 90
lernen to learn II
Lesbe lesbian V U3, 68
lesbisch lesbian V U3, 68
lesen to read II
letzte last I
Leute people I; persons (pl) II
Liebe(r) …, (Anrede in Briefen) Dear …, I
Liebe Grüße Love, I
lieben to love I
Lieblings- favourite I; favorite (AE) III
am **liebsten** best II
Lied song I
Liedermacher songwriter V U3, 68
Liedermacherin songwriter V U3, 68
liefern to deliver IV
Lieferwagen van IV
Lineal ruler I
Linie line III
links on the left; left II
Liste list V U1, 16
Loch hole I
lokal local II
lösen to solve V U2, 38
Löwe lion V U3, 63
Luft air III
lügen to lie IV
lustig funny I; fun III

M

machen to do; to make I; to complete V U4, 90
eine Ausbildung machen to train IV
Fotos machen to take photos (of) II
Hausaufgabe(n) machen to do homework I
kaputt machen to break V U1, 11
Mach die Musik leiser. Turn the music down. I
Mach dir keine Sorgen. Don't worry. I
Mach dir nichts draus. Never mind. II
Macht nichts. Never mind. II
Mädchen girl I
Mahlzeit meal II
Mai May I
Mais corn IV
Mal time I; base III
das erste Mal the first time I
zum 200. Mal for the 200th time III
malen to paint II
Mama mum I; mom (AE) III
Manager manager IV
Managerin manager IV
manchmal sometimes I
Mann man I
Mannschaft team I
Mannschaftsführer captain II
Mannschaftsführerin captain II
Maori Maori V U4, 89
Maori- Maori V U4, 89
maorisch Maori V U4, 89
Markt market I
Marsch march V U2, 47
März March I
Maschine machine V U2, 38
Maske mask V U4, 99
Match match I
Mathe Maths I; Math (AE) III
Mathematik Math (AE) III
Matsch mud I
Mauer wall II
Maus mouse I
Mechaniker mechanic V U4, 90
Mechanikerin mechanic V U4, 90
Medaille medal II
soziale **Medien** social media III
Medikament medication; drug V U3, 68
Medikamente medicine V U1, 16
Medizin medicine V U1, 16
Meer sea I
am Meer at the seaside I
Meerschweinchen guinea pig II
mehr more II
nicht mehr not … any more III
mehrere several V U2, 37
Mehrheit majority V ZI, 8
die Mehrheit most III
Mehrzahl majority V ZI, 8
meiden to avoid IV
Meile mile III
mein my I
meine mine III
meinen to mean IV
anderer **Meinung** sein to disagree IV
einer **Meinung** sein (mit) to agree (with) II
am **meisten** most III
die **meisten** most III
eine **Menge** a lot of I
Mensa cafeteria I
Mensch person (sg) II
Menschen people I; persons (pl) II
Menschenhändler slave trader IV
sich **merken** to remember III
merkwürdig funny I
Messe fair II
Metall- metal III
metallen metal III
Meter metre II; meter (AE) III
mich me I; myself III
mich selbst myself IV
mild mild II
Milliarde billion V ZI, 8
Million million I
eine halbe Million half a million III
Minute minute I
mir me I; myself IV
mit with I; on II; of III
mit (dem Zug) by (train) I
mit enthalten sein to be included V U4, 94
Mitarbeiter employee; assistant IV
Mitarbeiterin employee; assistant IV
mitbringen to bring II
Mitglied member V U4, 89
mitmachen (bei) to take part (in) II
mitnehmen to take I
mitspielen to act III
Mittagessen lunch; dinner I

Mittagspause lunchtime I
Mittagszeit lunchtime I
Mitte centre; middle; center *(AE)* III
Mittelschule secondary school IV
mitten in in the middle of II
mittlerer Schulabschluss secondary
 school leaving certificate IV
Mittwoch Wednesday I
Mode fashion IV
modern modern I
mögen to like; to want (to) I; to enjoy
 + -ing V U2, 38
 gern mögen to love I
 nicht mögen to hate I
 ich möchte nicht … I wouldn't like
 (to) … I
 ich möchte … I'd like (to) …
 (= I would like to) I
 Möchtest du …? Would you like
 (to) …? I
Möglichkeit chance III; opportunity
 IV
im **Moment** at the moment II
momentan at the moment II
Monat month II
Montag Monday I
Morgen morning I
 heute Morgen this morning II
morgen tomorrow II
motivieren to motivate III
müde tired I
Muffin muffin II
Mühe haben to struggle V U1, 11
Müll rubbish I
multikulturell multicultural IV
Mund mouth II
Museum museum II
Musik music I
Musikgruppe band II
Muslim Muslim I
Muslimin Muslim I
müssen to have to; must II; to need
 to III
mutig brave III
Mutter mother I
Mutti mum I
Mütze hat II

N

Na ja, … Well, … II

nach to; after I
 nach *(bei Uhrzeitangaben)* past II
 nach Hause home I
Nachbar neighbour I
Nachbarin neighbour I
nachdem after IV
nachdenken über to think about III
nachhaltig sustainable V U2, 42
Nachmittag afternoon I
nachmittags *(Uhrzeit)* p.m. III
Nachricht message II
Nachricht(en) news II
nachschauen to look I
nächste next I
 als Nächstes next II
Nacht night I
nachts at night IV
Nacken neck II
nah near II
in der **Nähe** von near I
Name name I
Nase nose II
 die Nase voll haben (von) to be fed
 up (with) III
nass wet I
Nation nation III
national national III
National- national III
Nationalität nationality IV
Nationalpark national park III
Natur nature V U3, 81
natürlich of course II
Naturwissenschaft science III
neben next to I; by III
nebenher at the same time II
nehmen to take I; to use III
 nehmen (Bus/Zug) to catch (bus/
 train) III
 Nehmen Sie Platz. Take a seat. IV
 Nimm Platz. Take a seat. IV
nein no I
nennen to call III
nett nice I
neu new I
Neuigkeit(en) news II
neun nine I
neunzehn nineteen I
neunzig ninety I
nicht not I
 auch nicht not … either III
 nicht können can't I

 nicht mögen to hate I
 nicht einverstanden sein to disagree IV
 nicht mehr not … any more III
nichts nothing II; not … anything III
nicken to nod V U4, 99
nie never II
niemals never II
niemand no one I; nobody II
noch still II
 immer noch still II
 noch ein another IV
 noch einmal again I
 noch nicht not … yet III
Nord- north III
Norden north III
 im Norden von in the north of III
normalerweise usually II
Note grade *(AE)* II
Notfall emergency V U3, 80
November November I
null zero I
Null *(bei Uhrzeiten und Telefonnummern)* oh III
Nummer number I
nun now I
nur only I; just III
nutzen to use III
nützlich useful III

O

ob if IV
 als ob like IV
oben up II; at the top V U1, 28
oberer Teil top II
oberes Ende top II
oberhalb above II
Obst fruit I
obwohl although V U4, 94
oder or I
offensichtlich certainly V U2, 46
öffentliche Verkehrsmittel public
 transport III
öffnen to open I
oft often II
öfter more often IV
ohne without II
Oje. Oh dear. V U1, 16
okay OK (okay) I
Oktober October I

Öl oil II
Ölpest oil spill V U1, 20
Ölteppich oil spill V U1, 20
Oma grandma I
Onkel uncle I
online online II
   online stellen to post III
Online- online II
Orange orange I
orange orange I
in Ordnung fine I
   in Ordnung bringen to tidy II
Organisation organization V U3, 72
organisieren to organize I
Orkan hurricane IV
Ort place I
örtlich local II
Ost- east III
Osten east III
das Outback (australisches Hinter-
   land) the outback V U1, 11
oval oval III

P

ein paar some I; a few IV
packen to pack III
Paket package IV
Papa dad I
Papier paper III
Parade parade IV
Park park I
Parlament parliament V U3, 62
Partner partner I
Partnerin partner I
Partnerstadt twin town III
Party party I
   eine Party feiern to have a party I
Pass passport IV
Passagier passenger IV
Passagierin passenger IV
passieren to happen II
   Das ist passiert. That's what hap-
   pened. II
Patient patient V U1, 16
Patientin patient V U1, 16
Pause break I
Pausenhof playground I
peng bang V U3, 64
Person person (sg) II
Pferd horse I

Pflanze plant III
Pflaume plum I
Pfund (brit. Währungseinheit) pound
   (£) I
Picknick picnic I
Pier pier II
pink pink I
Pistole gun IV
Pizza pizza I
Plan map II; plan IV
planen to plan IV
Planer planner II
platt flat V U1, 11
(Kontinental-)Platte plate IV
Platz place I
plaudern to chat II
plötzlich suddenly I
Podcast podcast V U3, 68
Polizei police IV
Polizeibeamter police officer I
Polizeibeamtin police officer I
Polizeirevier police station V U3, 64
Polizeiwache police station V U3, 64
Pommes frites chips (pl) I
Pop (Musik) pop II
positiv positive III
posten to post III
Poster poster II
Postkarte postcard I
Praktikant intern V U4, 94
Praktikantin intern V U4, 94
Praktikum internship IV
Präsentation presentation III
präsentieren to present V U4, 94
Präsident president III
Präsidentin president III
Preis price I; prize II
prellen to bounce III
Prinz prince V U2, 38
pro Jahr a year IV
pro Woche a week V U3, 73
probieren to try III
Problem problem I
Produkt product V U4, 94
Profil profile III
Programm programme III
(Software)Programm (software)
   program V ZI, 8
Programmierer computer program-
   mer V U2, 38

Programmiererin computer pro-
   grammer V U2, 38
Projekt project II
Prospekt brochure III
Protest protest V U2, 37
protestieren to protest V U1, 21
Prozent percent (%) III
Prozession parade IV
prüfen to test II
Prüfung exam V U4, 90
   eine Prüfung schreiben to take an
   exam V U4, 90
Pullover pullover I
Puma mountain lion II
Punkt point III; dot V U1, 12
pünktlich in time V U2, 54
Pute turkey IV
putzen to clean II

Q

Quadrat- square V U3, 63
Qualifikation qualification IV
qualifiziert qualified V U4, 112
Quiz quiz IV

R

Rad wheel II
Radiergummi rubber I
Radio radio III
Raft raft III
raften gehen to go rafting III
Rafting rafting III
Rakete rocket III
rammen to hit V U3, 64
Ranger ranger (AE) IV
Rangerin ranger (AE) IV
Rap rap I
Rat advice III
raten to guess I
Ratespiel quiz IV
Ratschlag advice III
Rauch smoke IV
Raum room I
Raumfahrt space III
Realschulabschluss secondary
   school leaving certificate IV
Du hast recht. You're right. I
Recht right V U1, 11
rechte right II

rechts on the right; right II
Rechtschreibung spelling I
rechtzeitig in time V U2, 54
reden (mit) to talk (to) I
Redner speaker V ZI, 8
Rednerin speaker V ZI, 8
reduzieren to reduce V U4, 94
Referat presentation III
Referenz reference IV
Regal shelf II
Regalbrett shelf II
Regel rule V U3, 80
Regenbogen rainbow III
Reggae (Musik) reggae IV
Regierung government V U1, 20
Regisseur director V U3, 68
Regisseurin director V U3, 68
sich **registrieren** lassen to register V U1, 16
regnen to rain I
regnerisch rainy II
reich rich V U3, 63
Reihenhaus townhouse III
Reis rice II
  gebratener Reis mit Hühnerfleisch chicken fried rice II
Reise trip I; tour; journey III
Reisebüro travel agent's IV
Reisebürokauffrau travel agent IV
Reisebürokaufmann travel agent IV
Reiseleiter tour guide V U2, 38
Reiseleiterin tour guide V U2, 38
reisen to travel II
Reisepass passport IV
Reiten horse riding I
reiten to ride I
Reiter rider V U4, 98
Reiterin rider V U4, 98
Religion religion V U2, 47
Rennen race II
rennen to run II
reparieren to repair IV
Reservat reservation III
reservieren to book III; to make reservations IV
Reservierung reservation III
respektieren to respect V U2, 47
Rest rest II
Restaurant restaurant II
retten to save II

Rezept (für Arzneimittel) prescription V U1, 16
Richterskala Richter scale (no pl) IV
richtig right I; true V U2, 38
richtigstellen to correct II
in **Richtung** towards V U4, 99
Riesen- giant V U1, 12
Riesenrad big wheel II
riesig great III; giant V U1, 12
Riff reef V U1, 20
Rinde crust IV
ringen to struggle V U1, 11
Ritt ride II
Rock skirt III
Rolle part II
Rollstuhl wheelchair I
rosa pink I
rot red I
Hin- und **Rückfahrkarte** return ticket III
rufen to shout I; to call III
Rugby rugby III
ruhig quiet II; calm V U4, 90
Russe Russian IV
Russin Russian IV
Russisch Russian IV
russisch Russian IV

S

Sache thing I
Sack bag I
Sackhüpfen sack race II
Safari safari V U3, 63
Saft juice I
sagen to say; to tell I
Saison season II
Salat salad I
Salz salt V U2, 47
Geld **sammeln** to raise money II
Sammlung collection III
Samstag Saturday I
samstags on Saturdays I
Sandwich sandwich I
Sänger singer I
Sängerin singer I
sanitäre Anlagen sanitation V U2, 42
sauber machen to clean II
Saxofon saxophone I
Schachtel box I
Schade! That's too bad. II

Schaden damage IV
schaden to damage V U2, 42
Schäden damage IV
Schaf sheep I
Schal scarf II
Schatzsuche treasure hunt II
schauen to look I
Schauspieler actor III
Schauspielerei drama III
Schauspielerin actor III
Schauspielworkshop acting workshop III
scheinen to seem V U4, 99
schenken to give I
schicken to send I
schieben to push I
schiefgehen to go wrong V U4, 90
schießen to kick III; to shoot IV
Schiff ship I; boat IV
Schild sign IV
Schimpanse chimpanzee II
schlafen to sleep II
Schlafzimmer bedroom II
schlagen to hit III
Schläger stick III
Schlagfrau batter III
Schlagmann batter III
Schlamm mud I
schlecht bad I; ill V U1, 16
schlechter worse II
schlechteste worst II
schleudern to skid V U3, 64
schließen to close I
  Freundschaft(en) schließen to make friends II
schlimm bad II
schlimmer worse II
schlimmste worst II
Schlitten sled IV
schlittern to skid V U3, 64
Schlittschuh laufen to skate II
Schlittschuhlaufen gehen to go skating II
Schloss castle III
Schlumpf smurf I
Schluss end II
Schlüssel key III
Schminken face painting II
schmutzig dirty I
Schnee snow II
schneereich snowy II

schnell fast II; quick IV

Schnitzeljagd treasure hunt II

Schnitzerei carving V U4, 99

Schokolade chocolate I

schon already; yet III

schon einmal ever III

schon immer always III

Schon gut. Never mind. II

schön fine; nice I; beautiful III

High **School** (*weiterführende Schule, Oberstufe*) high school V U3, 63

Schottenrock kilt III

schottisch Scottish III

schrecklich awful I

Schreiben letter IV

eine Prüfung **schreiben** to take an exam V U4, 90

ein Examen schreiben to take an exam V U4, 90

Schreibtisch desk II

schreien to shout I

Schritt step II

Schuh shoe I

Schulabschluss qualification IV

mittlerer Schulabschluss secondary school leaving certificate IV

Schul-AG club I

Schulausflug school trip II

Schule school I

in der Schule at school I

weiterführende Schule secondary school IV

Schüler student I

Schülerin student I

Schulfach subject I

Schulhof playground I

Schulstunde lesson I

Schusswaffe gun IV

schütteln to shake IV

schützen to protect III

Schwanz tail I

schwarz black I

schwenken to swing III

schwer hard; serious II; heavy; difficult III

Schwert sword III

Schwester sister I

schwierig hard II; heavy; difficult III

Schwimmbad swimming pool I

schwimmen to swim I

schwimmen gehen to go swimming I

schwingen to swing III

schwul gay V U3, 68

Schwuler gay V U3, 68

Science-Fiction science fiction I

sechs six I

sechzehn sixteen I

sechzig sixty I

secondhand second-hand I

See lake IV

Seele soul V U2, 46

sehen to spy; to see; to look I

Wir sehen uns. See you. II

Sehenswürdigkeit sight II

sehr very I

Sehr geehrte(r) …, Dear …, IV

Seilbahn cable car IV

seilgezogene Straßenbahn cable car IV

Seilrutsche zip line III

sein his; to be; its I

einer Meinung sein (mit) to agree (with) II

weit weg sein to be a long way away II

seine his III

seit for; since IV

seitdem since IV

Seite side II

selbst myself; themselves; yourself III; himself; ourselves; yourselves; herself IV

selbstbewusst confident IV

selbstsicher confident IV

selbstverständlich of course II

Selfie selfie IV

selten rarely III

Seminar workshop III

senden to send I

Sendung programme III

September September I

Serie series (*no pl*) IV

Servus. Goodbye. I

Sesotho (*Sprache in Südafrika*) Sesotho V U3, 73

setzen to put I

sich setzen to sit (down) I

Setz dich. Take a seat. IV

Setzen Sie sich. Take a seat. IV

Shirt shirt I

Shorts shorts (*pl*) II

Show show I

sich each other; themselves III; himself; yourselves; herself; yourself IV

sich selbst himself; herself; themselves; yourself IV

sicher sure II; safe; confident IV; certainly V U2, 46

in **Sicherheit** safe IV

sie it; she I; her II

Sie you I

Sie sich yourselves IV

Sie sich selbst yourselves IV

sie (*Pl.*) they; them I

sie selbst themselves III

sieben seven I

siebzehn seventeen I

siebzig seventy I

Siedler settler V U1, 11

Siedlerin settler V U1, 11

siegen to win I

Sieger winner I

Siegerin winner I

singen to sing I

singe nicht don't sing I

singt nicht don't sing I

Sinn sense IV

Situation situation V U3, 80

Sitz seat III

sitzen to sit IV

Sitzplatz seat III

Skateboard skateboard I

Skater skater I

Skaterin skater I

Sklave slave IV

Sklavenhändler slave trader IV

Sklavin slave IV

Slum slum V U2, 36

SMS message II

Snowboard snowboard I

so so II

so … wie as … as III

sodass so that IV

soeben just III

sofern as long as V U3, 80

sofort right away V U3, 68

Software software IV

Sohn son IV

solange as long as V U3, 80

sollte should III

Sommer summer II
Songschreiber songwriter V U3, 68
Songschreiberin songwriter V U3, 68
Sonne sun II
sonnig sunny II
Sonntag Sunday I
sich **Sorgen** machen to worry I
   Mach dir keine Sorgen. Don't worry. I
sorgfältig careful III
Sorte kind II
Souvenir souvenir II
sowohl … als auch … … as well as … II
soziale Medien social media III
Spanisch Spanish IV
spanisch Spanish IV
spannend exciting I
sparen to save II
Spaß fun I
   Spaß haben to enjoy oneself IV
   Spaß machen to be fun II
spaßig fun III
(zu) **spät** late II
   zu spät kommen to be late II
später later I
Spaziergang walk I
Speck bacon I
spenden to donate V U4, 94
speziell special I
Spiel game; match I
spielen to play I; to act III
Spieler player II
Spielerin player II
Spielfeld field III
Spielplatz playground I
Spitze top II
Sport sport III
Sportarten sports (pl only) I
Sportfest sports day II
Sportgeschäft sports shop II
Sportplatz playing field II
Sportunterricht PE (Physical Education) I
Sportzentrum sports centre I
Sprache language IV
sprechen to say; to speak I
   sprechen (mit) to talk (to) I
Sprecher speaker V ZI, 8
Sprecherin speaker V ZI, 8
springen to jump III

spülen to wash II
die **Spülmaschine** ausräumen to empty the dishwasher II
die **Spülmaschine** einräumen to load the dishwasher II
Spur clue I
Staat state; nation III
   von allen Staaten of all the states IV
Staatsangehörige citizen IV
Staatsangehöriger citizen IV
Staatsangehörigkeit nationality IV
Staatsbürger citizen IV
Staatsbürgerin citizen IV
stabil strong IV
Stadion stadium I
Stadt city; town I
Stadtmitte city centre II
Stadtteil borough IV
Stadtzentrum city centre II
Stamm tribe V U1, 12
Stand stall I
Star star I
stark heavy; strong III
starten to start I
Station station III
Statue statue IV
staubsaugen to hoover II
Steckbrief profile III
stecken to put II
   stecken bleiben to be stuck I
stehen to stand II
   stehen für to stand for III
steigen to climb II
   in etw. steigen to get on sth IV
Stein stone III; rock V U1, 12
Steinstoßen stone put III
Stell dir vor! Guess what? II
Stelle place I
stellen to put I
   online stellen to post III
Stellt euch vor! Guess what? II
sterben to die III
Stift pen I
stiften to donate V U4, 94
Stiftung charity II
still quiet II
Stimmt etwas nicht? Is something wrong? II
Stock stick III
Stockwerk floor II

stolz (auf) proud (of) IV
stören to disturb V U3, 80
jmdn. von etw. **stoßen** to knock sb off sth IV
Strand beach I
Straße street; road I
Straßenbahn tram I
   seilgezogene Straßenbahn cable car IV
Streich trick II
streichen to paint II
Streit argument II
(sich) **streiten** to fight II
Strom electricity V U3, 63
Stromschnelle rapid III
Strömung current III
ein **Stück** … a piece of II
(auf einen Abschluss) **studieren** to study (for) sth V U4, 90
Stufe step II
Stuhl chair I
Stunde hour II
Stundenplan timetable I
Sturm storm I
von etw. **stürzen** to fall off II
suchen (nach) to look for IV
Suchplakat lost and found notice III
Süd- south III; southern IV
Südafrikaner South African V U3, 63
Südafrikanerin South African V U3, 63
südafrikanisch South African V U3, 63
Süden south III
südlich southern IV
Südstaaten- southern IV
super cool I
Supermarkt supermarket I
Surf- surfing IV
Surfen surfing IV
surfen gehen to go surfing III
Süßigkeit sweet I
Symbol symbol III
sympathisch friendly IV

T

Tablette tablet V U1, 16
Tafel blackboard I
Tag day I
   ein ausgefüllter Tag a busy day II
   eines Tages one day I
   Tag! G'day! (= Good day!) V U1, 10

Tagebuch diary I

Tal valley III

Talent talent I

Talentwettbewerb talent show I

Tandem tandem II

    Tandem fahren to go tandem bike riding II

Tankstelle garage V U4, 90

Tante aunt I

Tanz dancing; dance III

Tanzen dancing III

tanzen to dance I

Tänzer dancer I

Tänzerin dancer I

tapfer brave III

Tasche bag I

Taschenlampe torch I

Taschenrechner calculator I

eine **Tasse** … a cup of II

Tätigkeit job III

Tatsache fact II

Tauglichkeit suitability V U4, 90

tausend a/one thousand II

Team team I

Technik DT (Design Technology) I; technology III

Techniker engineer II

Technikerin engineer II

Technologie technology III

Teddybär teddy I

Tee tea I

Teenager teen II; teenager V U2, 42

Teenagerin teen II

Teil part II

    oberer Teil top II

teilen to share III

teilnehmen (an) to take part (in) II

Telefon phone I

Telefonanruf phone call I

telefonieren to phone II

Telefonzelle telephone box II

Teller plate IV

Temperatur temperature V U1, 20

Tennis tennis I

Teppich carpet II

Termin appointment V U1, 16

Test test V U4, 90

testen to test II

teuer expensive I

Theater theatre; theater (AE) III

Theater- drama III

Theaterstück play III

Thema topic IV

Ticket ticket II

tief deep V U4, 98

Tier animal I

Tierarzt vet IV

Tierärztin vet IV

Tierheim animal rescue shelter I

Tierpark zoo IV

Tisch table I; desk II

Tochter daughter I

Toilette toilet V U2, 42

toll great I; amazing II; awesome III

Tomate tomato I

Tombola raffle II

Topf pot III

Tor goal III; gate V U3, 80

Torpfosten goalpost III

Torstange goalpost III

tot dead IV

töten to kill V U1, 11

Tour tour III

Tourismus tourist industry; tourism IV

Tourist tourist II

Touristin tourist II

Touristeninformation tourist information centre V U4, 90

Township (ehemalige Wohnsiedlungen für die schwarze Bevölkerung in Südafrika) township V U3, 62

Tradition tradition III

tragen to wear I

trainieren to train IV

Training practice I; training IV

Transport transport II

Transporter van IV

transportieren to transport IV

Traum dream I

traurig sad I; unhappy II

Treff club I

treffen to meet I; to hit III

    (sich) treffen to meet II

Treffer goal III

treiben to drive IV

trennen to separate V U3, 62

treten to kick III

Trick trick I

Trink- drinking V U2, 42

trinken to have I; to drink II

trocken dry II

Trompete trumpet II

Truthahn turkey IV

Tschüss. Bye. I; See you. II

T-Shirt T-shirt II

Tsunami (durch Seebeben ausgelöste Flutwelle) tsunami IV

Tuch scarf II

tun to do; to make I

    Tut mir leid. Sorry. I

Tür door II

Türkisch Turkish IV

türkisch Turkish IV

Türklingel doorbell I

Turm tower II

Turnschuh trainer II

Tüte bag I

Tutorial tutorial IV

U

U-Bahn underground I

über about I; above; across II; over III

überall all over; everywhere II

überallhin everywhere II

sich **übergeben** to be sick I

überhaupt ever III

überlegen to guess I

    sich überlegen to think about III

übernachten to stay I

überprüfen to check II

überrascht surprised II

Überraschung surprise III

übrig left III

Übung exercise; practice I

Übungsheft exercise book I

Uhr clock II

Uhr (Zeitangabe bei vollen Stunden) o'clock I

Uhrzeit time I

um at I; around III

    um zu to II

    um … herum around II

(sich) **umdrehen** to turn over III

Umgebung environment II

umkippen to turn over III

umsteigen to change III

Umwelt environment II

Umwelt- environmental V U2, 37

umziehen to move II

Umzug procession II; parade IV

unabhängig independent V U2, 37

Unabhängigkeit independence IV
und and I
    Und …? What about …? II
Unfall accident I
ungefähr about II
ungefährlich safe IV
unglaublich amazing II
unglücklich unhappy II
unglücklicherweise unfortunately
    V U2, 47
unheimlich scary I
Uniform uniform I
unmöglich impossible IV
Unordnung mess I
uns us II; ourselves IV
    uns selbst ourselves IV
unser our I
unsere ours III
unten at the bottom V U1, 28
unter under I
Unternehmen company II
Unterricht lesson I; class IV
unterrichten to teach IV
Unterrichtsstunde class IV
unterschiedlich different I
Unterstützung support V U4, 90
unterwegs out and about III
    unterwegs (in) around V U1, 10
unversehrt safe IV
Update update IV
Ur- great- V U4, 98
Ureinwohner Amerikas Native
    American III
Ureinwohnerin Amerikas Native
    American III
Urheberrecht copyright IV
Urkunde certificate V U4, 90
Urlaub holiday II; vacation *(AE)* III
Ururopa great-great-grandad I
US-amerikanisch US III

V

Vater father I
Vati dad I
Vegetarier vegetarian I
Vegetarierin vegetarian I
verändern to change II
Veranstaltung event II
die **Verantwortung** tragen (für) to be
    in charge (of) V U3, 72

verärgert angry II; annoyed IV
verbessern to correct II
    sich verbessern to get better
    V U1, 16
in **Verbindung** bleiben staying con-
    nected III
verbringen *(Zeit)* to spend II
Verein club V U4, 89
verfügbar available IV
Vergangenheit past III
vergessen to forget II; to leave III
sich **verirren** to get lost IV
verkaufen to sell I
Verkäufer assistant I; shop assistant
    V U4, 94
Verkäuferin assistant I; shop assis-
    tant V U4, 94
Verkehr transport II; traffic III
öffentliche **Verkehrsmittel** public
    transport III
Verkleidung fancy dress I
verlassen to leave II
    sich auf jmdn. verlassen to count
    on sb V U4, 90
    sich verlassen (auf) to rely (on) IV
verlässlich reliable IV
verletzen to hurt II; to injure V U3, 64
verletzt hurt III
verlieren to lose II
verloren gehen to get lost IV
vermeiden to avoid IV
vermindern to reduce V U4, 94
vermissen to miss II
verpassen to miss II
verringern to reduce V U4, 94
verrückt crazy V U2, 54
verschieden different I
verschiedene several V U2, 37
verschmutzen to pollute V U2, 42
Verschmutzung pollution V U2, 37
verschneit snowy II
verspätet delayed IV
sich **verständigen** to communicate
    V ZI, 9
verstehen to understand II
Versuch experiment II
versuchen to try III
vertrauen (auf) to rely (on) IV
vertrauenswürdig reliable IV
verunreinigen to pollute V U2, 42
verursachen to cause IV

vervollständigen to finish I
verwenden to use III
Video video III
viel a lot of; lots of; much I
    Viel Glück! Good luck! IV
viele a lot of; lots of; many I
    Viele Grüße Best wishes, I
vielleicht maybe II
vier four I
Viertel vor/nach quarter to/past II
vierzehn fourteen I
vierzig forty I
virtuell virtual V U2, 38
Vogel bird IV
Volk nation III; people V U4, 89
Volksstamm tribe V U1, 12
vollbringen to achieve V U3, 68
völlig quite II; completely V U1, 20
von from; of I; by III
vor in front of I; before II; of III
    vor ago II
vorbei (an) past I
Vorbild role model V U3, 68
Vordergrund foreground III
vorher before III
vorkommen to happen IV
vorlesen to read II
Vormittag morning I
vormittags *(Uhrzeit)* a.m. III
vorn in front II
Vorräte supplies *(pl)* IV
Vorschul- preschool V U3, 73
Vorschule preschool V U3, 73
vorsichtig careful III
jmdn. jmdm. **vorstellen** to introduce
    sb to sb III
Vortrag presentation III
Vulkan volcano V U4, 89

W

Wachs wax II
wachsen to grow V U2, 42
Waffe gun IV
wählen to choose III
während while; during IV
Wahrheit truth IV
wahrscheinlich probably IV
Wahrzeichen landmark IV
Wal whale IV

Walbeobachtungs- whale-watching IV

Wald wood IV

Walisisch Welsh III

walisisch Welsh III

Wand wall II

Wanderung walk I

Wandmalerei wall painting II

wann when I

Waren goods (pl only) V U2, 38

warm warm II

warten (auf) to wait (for) II

Warteschlange queue II

warum why I

was what I; which II

    Was hast du? What's the matter? V U1, 16

    Was ist los? What's the matter? V U1, 16

    Was ist mit …? What about …? II

    Was kann ich für euch/dich tun? How can I help you? I

Waschbär raccoon I

Wäsche wash II

(sich) waschen to wash II

Wasser water I

Website website III

Wechselgeld change I

wechseln to change II

Weg way I

    aus dem Weg gehen to avoid IV

weg away II

    weit weg sein to be a long way away II

wegen about IV; because of V U4, 98

wegfahren to drive off IV

weggehen to leave II

weglaufen to run away II

wehtun to hurt II

Weihnachten Christmas I

    Frohe Weihnachten! Merry Christmas! I

weil because I

Art und **Weise** way III

weiß white I

weit far II; long V U1, 11

    weit weg sein to be a long way away II

weitere more II

Weitsprung long jump II

welche what I; which II

Welle wave III

Wellenreiten surfing IV

Welt world I; earth III

    in aller Welt all around the world II

Weltraum space III

ein (klein) **wenig** a little (bit) II

wenige a few IV

weniger less III

wenn when II; if IV

wer who I

Werbung ad(vert) (= advertisement) III

werden to get I; will II

    etw. tun werden to be going to do sth III

    nicht werden won't (= will not) II

    (zu etw.) werden to become II

werfen to throw II

Werk factory III

Werkzeug tool V U4, 90

im **Wert** von worth of V U4, 94

wert worth V U4, 94

West- west III

Westen west III

Wettbewerb competition V ZI, 8

Wetter weather II

Wettlauf race II

Wettrennen race II

wichtig important III

wie how; like I; as II

    so … wie as … as III

    Wie alt bist du? How old are you? I

    Wie geht es dir? How are you? I

    Wie heißt du? What's your name? I

    Wie ist das Wetter? What's the weather like? II

    wie man … how to … IV

    Wie spät ist es? What time is it? I

    Wie viel (kostet/kosten) …? How much (is/are) …? I

    Wie viel Uhr ist es? What time is it? I

wieder again I

wiederaufbauen to rebuild IV

wiederholen to repeat V U3, 81

Auf **Wiedersehen.** Goodbye. I

wild wild IV

Wildnis wilderness IV

willkommen (bei/in) welcome (to) I

Wind wind I

windig windy II

Winter winter I

wir we I; us II

Wirbelsturm hurricane IV

wirklich really I

Wirtschaft economy V U2, 42

wissen to know I

    Ich weiß (es) nicht! I don't know. I

Wissenschaft science III

Witterung weather II

witzig sein to be fun II

wo where I

Woche week I

    in der Woche a week V U3, 73

    pro Woche a week V U3, 73

Wochenende weekend I

woher where I

    Woher kommst du? Where are you from? I

wohin where I

wohltätige Zwecke charity II

Wohltätigkeits- charity II

Wohltätigkeitsorganisation charity II

Wohnen living V U2, 42

wohnen to live I

Wohnung flat I; apartment (AE) IV

Wohnzimmer living room II

Wolf wolf II

Wolke cloud II

wolkig cloudy II

Wolldecke blanket IV

Wolle wool I

wollen to want (to) I

Workshop workshop III

Wort word II

Wunder wonder V U4, 99

wunderschön beautiful III

wünschen to wish V U4, 98

ich würde I'd (= I would) I

    ich würde gerne … I'd like (to) … (= I would like to) I

    ich würde nicht gerne … I wouldn't like (to) … I

    ich würde sehr gern … I'd love (to) … (= I would love to) IV

    Würdest du gern …? Would you like (to) …? I

wütend angry II

Z

Zahl number I

Zahn

Zahn tooth II
Zauberer wizard II
Zauberkünstler magician II
Zauberkünstlerin magician II
zaubern to do magic II
zehn ten I
Zeichen sign IV
zeigen to show II; to point V U4, 99
Zeit time I
Zeiten hours *(pl)* IV
Zeitpunkt date IV
Zeitschrift magazine IV
Zeitung newspaper III
Zeitungsstand newspaper kiosk II
Zelt tent II
zelten gehen to go camping III
Zeltplatz campsite III
Zentrum centre; center *(AE)* III
zerbrechen to break V U1, 11
zerstören to destroy IV
zerstört wrecked IV
Zerstörung destruction V U1, 21
Zertifikat certificate V U4, 90
zertrümmert wrecked IV

Zeuge witness IV
Zeugin witness IV
Zeugnis certificate V U4, 90
Ziege goat III
ziehen to pull I; to move IV; to grow
  V U2, 42
Ziel goal III
ziemlich quite II
Zimmer room I
zittern to shake IV
Zoo zoo IV
zornig angry II
zu to; at; too I
  auf … zu towards V U4, 99
  zu Fuß on foot I
züchten to grow V U2, 42
zuerst first II; at first V U3, 68
Zug train I
Zuhause home I
zuhören to listen (to) I
Zukunft future IV
zukünftig future V U4, 90
Zukunfts- future V U4, 90
Zulieferer supplier V U4, 94

zum 200. Mal for the 200th time III
zum Beispiel for example III
zum Glück fortunately V U3, 72
zumachen to close I
zunächst at first V U3, 68
zurück back II
zurückgehen to get back V U4, 98
zurückkommen to get back V U4, 98
zusammen together I; everyone II
zuschauen to watch II
zusehen to watch II
zuständig sein (für) to be in charge
  (of) V U3, 72
zustimmen to agree (with) II
zuverlässig reliable IV
zuvor before III
zwanzig twenty I
wohltätige **Zwecke** charity II
zwei two I
zweit- second IV
zweite second II
  aus zweiter Hand second-hand I
zwischen between III
zwölf twelve I

Instructions
Arbeitsanweisungen mit Operatoren

Act the dialogue with your partner.	**Spiele** den Dialog mit deinem Partner / deiner Partnerin.
Add more words.	**Füge** weitere Wörter **hinzu.**
Agree on the most important questions.	**Einigt euch** auf die wichtigsten Fragen.
Answer the questions.	**Beantworte** die Fragen.
Ask questions.	**Stelle** Fragen.
Ask your partner.	**Frage** deinen Partner / deine Partnerin.
Ask for feedback.	**Bitte um** Rückmeldung.
Change roles.	**Tauscht** die Rollen.
Change the dialogue.	**Ändere** den Dialog.
Check the sentences • your draft.	**Überprüfe** die Sätze • deinen Entwurf.
Choose one of the tasks • the right answers • the right words.	**Wähle** eine der Aufgaben • die richtigen Antworten • die richtigen Wörter **aus.**
Collect ideas • pictures.	**Sammle** Ideen • Bilder.
Compare the activities • the people • the things.	**Vergleiche** die Aktivitäten • die Leute • die Dinge.
Complete the dialogue • the sentences.	**Vervollständige** den Dialog • die Sätze.
Copy the table.	**Schreibe** die Tabelle **ab.**
Correct the wrong sentences • words.	**Verbessere** die falschen Sätze • Wörter.
Decide who can start.	**Entscheidet euch**, wer anfängt.
Describe the picture.	**Beschreibe** das Bild.
Discuss in groups.	**Besprecht euch** in Gruppen.
Draw a picture.	**Zeichne** ein Bild.
Explain.	**Erkläre.**
Find the answers • the names • the true statements • the words.	**Finde** die Antworten • die Namen • die richtigen Aussagen • die Wörter.
Find out about the country.	**Finde** etwas über das Land **heraus.**
Finish the sentences.	**Vervollständige** die Sätze.
Give a presentation.	**Halte** eine Präsentation.
Give feedback.	**Gib Rückmeldung.**
Guess.	**Überlege.**
Interview your partner.	**Interviewe** deinen Partner / deine Partnerin.
Listen, read and say.	**Höre zu, lies mit** und **sprich nach.**
Listen to the announcements • the dialogue • the interview.	**Höre** dir die Durchsagen • den Dialog • das Gespräch **an.**
Look at the photos • the pictures (again).	**Schaue** dir die Fotos • die Bilder (noch einmal) **an.**
Make questions • sentences.	**Bilde** Fragen • Sätze.
Make a chart • a dialogue • a list • a mind map • a poster • a table.	**Erstelle** ein Diagramm • einen Dialog • eine Liste • ein Wörternetz • ein Poster • eine Tabelle.
Make notes.	**Mache** dir Notizen.
Match the sentences • the words.	**Ordne** die Sätze • die Wörter **zu.**
Match the sentences with the pictures.	**Ordne** die Sätze den Bildern **zu.**

Organize your information.	**Ordnet** eure Informationen.
Pass on information.	**Gib** die Informationen **weiter**.
Plan your e-mail • your event.	**Plant** eure E-Mail • eure Veranstaltung.
Practise with a partner.	**Übe** mit einem Partner / einer Partnerin.
Prepare a presentation.	**Bereite** eine Präsentation **vor**.
Present your poster to your class.	**Stellt** euer Poster der Klasse **vor**.
Put in the right form • the right word • the right verbs.	**Setze** die richtige Form • das richtige Wort • die richtigen Verben **ein**.
Put the pictures • the sentences • the words **in the right order**.	**Bringe** die Bilder • die Sätze • die Wörter **in die richtige Reihenfolge**.
Put the words into groups.	**Sortiere** die Wörter in Gruppen.
Read, **say** and **listen**.	**Lies**, **sprich nach** und **höre zu**.
Read the dialogue • the story • the text.	**Lies** den Dialog • die Geschichte • den Text.
Read your sentences • your text to your class.	**Lies** deine Sätze • deinen Text der Klasse **vor**.
Report in class.	**Berichte** der Klasse.
Are the sentences **right or wrong**?	Sind die Sätze **richtig oder falsch**?
Say the names • the numbers.	**Nenne** die Namen • die Zahlen.
Show your brochure • your report to your group.	**Zeige** deiner Gruppe deine Broschüre • deinen Bericht.
Take notes.	**Mache** dir Notizen.
Talk about the film • the photos • your free time.	**Sprich über** den Film • die Fotos • deine Freizeit.
Talk to your partner.	**Sprich mit** deinem Partner / deiner Partnerin.
Tell the class.	**Erzähle** der Klasse davon.
Tell your partner **about** what you do at home.	**Erzähle** deinem Partner / deiner Partnerin, was du zu Hause machst.
Think about these questions.	**Denke über** diese Fragen **nach**.
Think of questions.	**Denke** dir Fragen **aus**.
Use your own ideas.	**Benutze** deine eigenen Ideen.
Watch the film.	**Schaue** den Film **an**.
What are the words?	**Wie** heißen die Wörter?
What (else) can you see in the photo?	**Was** kannst du **(noch)** auf dem Foto sehen?
Where are the things?	**Wo** sind die Dinge?
Which sentences are right?	**Welche** Sätze sind richtig?
Who is • says it?	**Wer** ist • sagt das?
Why (not)?	**Warum** (nicht)?
Work with the text.	**Arbeite** mit dem Text.
Write a diary entry • a draft • an e-mail • a text.	**Schreibe** einen Tagebucheintrag • einen Entwurf • eine E-Mail • einen Text.
Write sentences.	**Schreibe** Sätze.

Classroom phrases

Before or after the lesson

Good morning, Mr/Mrs/Miss	Guten Morgen, Herr/Frau ....
I'm sorry I'm late.	Tut mir leid, dass ich mich verspätet habe.
I'm sorry I don't have my exercise book / my homework with me.	Tut mir leid, ich habe mein Heft / meine Hausaufgaben nicht dabei.
What's for homework?	Was haben wir als Hausaufgabe auf?

Asking for help

What page are we on?	Auf welcher Seite sind wir?
Can you help me, please?	Können Sie / Kannst du mir bitte helfen?
What does … mean?	Was heißt …?
Can you say that again, please?	Können Sie / Kannst du das bitte wiederholen?
Can you write that on the board?	Können Sie das an die Tafel schreiben?
Can I go to the toilet, please?	Kann ich bitte auf die Toilette gehen?
Mr/Mrs/Miss …, I don't feel well.	Herr/Frau …, mir geht es nicht gut.

Asking for information

What page is it on, please?	Auf welcher Seite ist das?
What's the German/English word for …?	Was ist das deutsche/englische Wort für …?
How do you spell …?	Wie schreibt man …?
What's this in English, please?	Was heißt das bitte auf Englisch?
What does that mean?	Was heißt/bedeutet das?
Sorry, I don't understand.	Tut mir leid, ich verstehe das nicht.
Sorry, I don't know.	Tut mir leid, ich weiß es nicht.

Working together

Can we work in pairs/groups?	Können wir zu zweit / in Gruppen arbeiten?
Do you want to work with me/us?	Willst du / Wollt ihr mit mir/uns arbeiten?
Let's make/draw a	Lass(t) uns ein … machen/zeichnen.
Whose turn is it?	Wer ist dran?
It's my/your turn.	Ich bin dran./Du bist dran.
Who is going to do our presentation?	Wer macht unsere Präsentation?

Your teacher can say …

Listen, please.	Hört bitte zu.
Listen to the dialogue.	Höre dir / Hört euch den Dialog an.
Open your books at page	Öffnet eure Bücher auf Seite ....
Turn to page	Schlagt Seite … auf.
Read the text on page	Lest den Text auf Seite ....
Look at line	Schaue/Schaut in Zeile ....
Take out your pens.	Holt eure Stifte raus.

Show me your homework, please.	Zeigt mir bitte eure Hausaufgaben. / Zeige mir bitte deine Hausaufgaben.
Where's your homework?	Wo sind deine/eure Hausaufgaben?
Get into pairs/groups.	Bildet Paare/Gruppen.
Learn these words for homework.	Lernt diese Wörter als Hausaufgabe.
Look at the board.	Schaut an die Tafel.
Who can do number …?	Wer kann Nummer … machen?
Put your hands up, please.	Meldet euch, bitte.
Try again.	Versuche es noch einmal. / Versucht es noch einmal.
Sit down, please, and be quiet.	Setz dich bitte und sei ruhig. / Setzt euch bitte und seid ruhig.
Talk to your partner.	Sprecht mit eurem Partner / eurer Partnerin.
Talk about the pictures.	Redet über die Bilder.
Please speak up.	Bitte sprich lauter.
Well done.	Gut gemacht.

Abbildungsverzeichnis

I Dekelver, Christian, Weinstadt; **Cover.1** Avenue Images GmbH (Dave and Les Jacobs), Hamburg; **Cover.2** plainpicture GmbH & Co. KG (Angela Elbing), Hamburg; **8.1** .; graphitecture book & edition, Bernau am Chiemsee; **8.2** stock.adobe.com (mavoimages), Dublin; **8.3** Getty Images Plus (monkeybusinessimages), München; **9.1** ShutterStock.com RF (almonfoto), New York, NY; **9.2** Getty Images Plus (DGLimages), München; **10.1** Getty Images Plus (sarra22), München; **10.2** Alamy stock photo (Greg Balfour Evans), Abingdon; **11.1** Dekelver, Christian, Weinstadt; **11.2** Getty Images Plus (4FR), München; **11.3** Getty Images (Universal Images Group), München; **11.4** Getty Images (National Geographic), München; **12.1** Alamy stock photo (david a eastley), Abingdon; **12.2** F1online digitale Bildagentur (imagebroker.com), Frankfurt; **12.3** Thinkstock (esancai), München; **14.1** Alamy stock photo (Hideo Kurihara), Abingdon; **16.1** Getty Images Plus (Tim Kitchen), München; **18.1** ShutterStock.com RF (i viewfinder), New York, NY; **18.2** Alamy stock photo (martin berry), Abingdon; **18.3** Bláha, Marek, Offenbach am Main; **20.1** ShutterStock.com RF (Kristina Vackova), New York, NY; **20.2** Dekelver, Christian, Weinstadt; **22.1** Getty Images Plus (alvarez), München; **23.1** Thinkstock (esancai), München; **23.2** © BBC Motion Gallery — British Broadcasting Corporation — Media Centre, London; **23.3** © BBC Motion Gallery — British Broadcasting Corporation — Media Centre, London; **23.4** © BBC Motion Gallery — British Broadcasting Corporation — Media Centre, London; **23.5** © BBC Motion Gallery — British Broadcasting Corporation — Media Centre, London; **24.1** stock. adobe.com (Joe Gough), Dublin; **24.2** Bláha, Marek, Offenbach am Main; **25.1** Kramer, Peer (Peer Kramer), Düsseldorf; **25.2** Wolters, Dorothee, Köln; **25.3** Wolff, Steffen, Herzogenrath; **25.4** Schwarzstein, Jaroslaw, Hannover; **25.5** Ablang, Friederike, Berlin; **26.1** Alamy stock photo (David Wall), Abingdon; **26.2** ShutterStock.com RF (Alisia Luther), New York, NY; **26.3** Getty Images Plus (travellinglight), München; **26.4** ShutterStock.com RF (robert paul van beets), New York, NY; **26.5** Thinkstock (esancai), München; **27.1** Getty Images Plus (mollypix/iStock), München [Stanley Geebung (1956-): Kangaroo, Aboriginal Dot Painting, Ochre on Card, ca. 1995]; **27.2** ShutterStock.com RF (Peter Waters), New York, NY; **27.3** Getty Images Plus (tomograf), München; **27.4** imago images (UIG), Berlin; **28.1** ShutterStock.com RF (amophoto_au), New York, NY; **28.2** Alamy stock photo (JUPITERIMAGES/ STOCK IMAGE), Abingdon; **29.1** Bláha, Marek, Offenbach am Main; **30.1** Thinkstock (Wavebreakmedia Ltd), München; **30.2** Thinkstock (amazingmikael), München; **30.3** Thinkstock (ajr_images), München; **30.4** Thinkstock (123ducu), München; **32.1** Alamy stock photo (Rob Walls), Abingdon; **35.1** Bláha, Marek, Offenbach am Main; **36.1** Getty Images (Aleksandra Ladygin / EyeEm), München; **36.2** Getty Images (moodboard), München; **37.1** Dekelver, Christian, Weinstadt; **37.2** Getty Images (Jupiterimages), München; **37.3** Getty Images Plus (ra-photos), München; **37.4** Alamy stock photo (Aravind Teki), Abingdon; **38.1** Alamy stock photo (Stuart Forster India), Abingdon; **38.2** ShutterStock.com RF (CRS PHOTO), New York, NY; **38.3** Getty Images Plus (GCShutter), München; **38.4** Alamy stock photo (PhotosIndia.com LLC), Abingdon; **38.5** stock.adobe.com (Ray), Dublin; **39.1** Wolff, Steffen, Herzogenrath; **40.1** Alamy stock photo (Joerg Boethling), Abingdon; **42.1** stock.adobe.com (PRASANNAPIX), Dublin; **42.2** ShutterStock.com RF (David Davis), New York, NY; **44.1** ShutterStock.com RF (Indian Food Images), New York, NY; **44.2** stock.adobe.com (Phuong), Dublin; **44.3** stock.adobe.com (V.R.Murralinath), Dublin; **44.4** ShutterStock.com RF (Henk Bogaard), New York, NY; **44.5** Alamy stock photo (zah108 / Alamy Stock Foto), Abingdon; **44.6** Getty Images (Mint / Kontributor), München; **45.1** Getty Images Plus (SilviaJansen), München; **46.1** Alamy stock photo (Pictorial Press Ltd), Abingdon; **47.1** stock.adobe.com (Ray), Dublin; **47.2** Alamy stock photo (Science History Images), Abingdon; **48.1** Alamy stock photo (Jeffrey Isaac Greenberg 4), Abingdon; **48.2** stock.adobe.com (Ray), Dublin; **48.3** Thinkstock (Wavebreak Media), München; **48.4** stock.adobe.com (Ray), Dublin; **48.5** ShutterStock.com RF (Production Perig), New York, NY; **48.6** stock.adobe.com (Ray), Dublin; **49.1** © BBC Motion Gallery — British Broadcasting Corporation — Media Centre, London; **49.2** © BBC Motion Gallery — British Broadcasting Corporation — Media Centre, London; **49.3** © BBC Motion Gallery — British Broadcasting Corporation — Media Centre, London; **49.4** © BBC Motion Gallery — British Broadcasting Corporation — Media Centre, London; **49.5** stock.adobe.com (Ray), Dublin; **50.1** ShutterStock.com RF (nomads.team), New York, NY; **52.1** iStockphoto (DrRave), Calgary, Alberta; **53.1** Getty Images Plus (powerofforever), München; **53.2** ShutterStock.com RF (Matt Hahnewald), New York, NY; **53.3** ShutterStock.com RF (Paksongpob Kasempisaisin), New York, NY; **53.4** Getty Images Plus (hadynyah), München; **53.5** ShutterStock.com RF (Cavan-Images), New York, NY; **53.6** Alamy stock photo (Subhash Sharma/ ZUMAPRESS.com), Abingdon; **53.7** stock.adobe.com (Ray), Dublin; **54.1** Wolff, Steffen, Herzogenrath; **54.2** Wolff, Steffen, Herzogenrath; **54.3** Wolff, Steffen, Herzogenrath; **54.4** Wolff, Steffen, Herzogenrath; **57.1** ShutterStock.com RF (MD ZAKIR HOSSAIN SOHEL), New York, NY; **58.1** Alamy stock photo (Aditya "Dicky" Singh), Abingdon; **61.1** ShutterStock.com RF (Saurav022), New York, NY; **61.2** Bláha, Marek, Offenbach am Main; **62.1** ShutterStock.com RF (Robyn Gwilt), New York, NY; **62.2** Alamy stock photo (Adam Welz), Abingdon; **63.1** Dekelver, Christian, Weinstadt; **63.2** ShutterStock.com RF (Theodore Mattas), New York, NY; **63.3** Alamy stock photo (Roger Sedres), Abingdon; **63.4** Getty Images Plus (THEGIFT777), München; **64.1** stock.adobe.com (Ray), Dublin; **65.1** ShutterStock.com RF, New York, NY; **66.1** Wolff, Steffen, Herzogenrath; **66.2** Wolff, Steffen, Herzogenrath; **66.3** Wolff, Steffen, Herzogenrath; **66.4** Wolff, Steffen, Herzogenrath; **66.5** Wolff, Steffen, Herzogenrath; **66.6** Wolff, Steffen, Herzogenrath; **68.1** Alamy stock photo (RTNFreeberg / MediaPunch), Abingdon; **68.2** Picture-Alliance (REUTERS/Mike Hutchings), Frankfurt; **68.3** stock.adobe.com (Ray), Dublin; **69.1** Bláha, Marek, Offenbach am Main; **69.2** Bláha, Marek, Offenbach am Main; **69.3** Alamy stock photo (Africa Media Online), Abingdon; **70.1** stock.adobe.com (Ranta Images), Dublin; **70.2** stock.adobe.com (Daniel Ernst), Dublin; **71.1** ShutterStock.com RF (Africanstar), New York, NY; **72.1** ShutterStock.com RF (WAYHOME studio), New York, NY; **72.2** ShutterStock. com RF (Maridav), New York, NY; **73.1** stock.adobe.com (RichTphoto), Dublin; **73.2** stock.adobe.com (ajr_images), Dublin; **74.1** ShutterStock. com RF (JaneHYork), New York, NY; **75.1** © BBC Motion Gallery — British Broadcasting Corporation — Media Centre, London; **75.2** stock. adobe.com (Ray), Dublin; **76.1** Bláha, Marek, Offenbach am Main; **78.1** stock.adobe.com (WitR), Dublin; **78.2** Alamy stock photo (Bartek Wrzesniowski), Abingdon; **78.3** Alamy stock photo (Realy Easy Star/Giuseppe Masci), Abingdon; **79.1** Alamy stock photo (Africa Media Online), Abingdon; **79.2** Picture-Alliance (dpa), Frankfurt; **79.3** ShutterStock.com RF (Roger Sedres), New York, NY; **79.4** graphitecture book & edition, Bernau am Chiemsee; **79.5** stock.adobe.com (Ray), Dublin; **80.1** ShutterStock.com RF (Dirk M. de Boer), New York, NY; **84.1** Alamy stock photo (Gary Eastwood Photography), Abingdon; **85.1** Wolff, Steffen, Herzogenrath; **85.2** Wolff, Steffen, Herzogenrath; **85.3** Wolff, Steffen, Herzogenrath; **85.4** Wolff, Steffen, Herzogenrath; **86.1** ShutterStock.com RF (WitR), New York, NY; **86.2** ShutterStock.com RF (Moobatto), New York, NY; **86.3** ShutterStock.com RF (Elnur), New York, NY; **87.1** Bláha, Marek, Offenbach am Main; **88.1** Getty Images Plus (Robert CHG), München; **88.2** ShutterStock.com RF (sianc), New York, NY; **89.1** Dekelver, Christian, Weinstadt; **89.2** Getty Images Plus

(SolStock), München; **89.3** ShutterStock.com RF (atthle), New York, NY; **89.4** Alamy stock photo (Blaine Harrington III), Abingdon; **90.1** Wolff, Steffen, Herzogenrath; **92.1** ShutterStock.com RF (Gorodenkoff), New York, NY; **92.2** Bláha, Marek, Offenbach am Main; **94.1** Wolff, Steffen, Herzogenrath; **96.1** Wolff, Steffen, Herzogenrath; **96.2** Wolff, Steffen, Herzogenrath; **96.3** Wolff, Steffen, Herzogenrath; **96.4** Wolff, Steffen, Herzogenrath; **96.5** Wolff, Steffen, Herzogenrath; **96.6** Wolff, Steffen, Herzogenrath; **97.1** Getty Images Plus (fstop123), München; **99.1** Alamy stock photo (Moviestore collection Ltd/ Whale Rider, 2003), Abingdon; **99.2** Alamy stock photo (Entertainment Pictures/Whale Rider, 2003), Abingdon; **100.1** Getty Images Plus (FlairImages), München; **100.2** ShutterStock.com RF (StGrafix), New York, NY; **100.3** stock.adobe.com (ADESIGN), Dublin; **101.1** Alamy stock photo (eye35.pix), Abingdon; **101.2** ShutterStock.com RF (Peter Hermes Furian), New York, NY; **101.3** stock.adobe.com (ADESIGN), Dublin; **102.1** ShutterStock.com RF (Urban Napflin), New York, NY; **103.1** Getty Images Plus (Manchan), München; **104.1** ShutterStock.com RF (TDway), New York, NY; **104.2** stock.adobe.com (ADESIGN), Dublin; **105.1** stock.adobe.com (Dmitrii), Dublin; **105.2** Alamy stock photo (Wendy Johnson), Abingdon; **105.3** ShutterStock.com RF (Tim90), New York, NY; **105.4** ShutterStock.com RF (Paolo Bona), New York, NY; **108.1** Alamy stock photo (Gary Webber), Abingdon; **110.1** ShutterStock.com RF (vectorfusionart), New York, NY; **111.1** Bláha, Marek, Offenbach am Main; **113.1** Bláha, Marek, Offenbach am Main; **114.1** Alamy stock photo (Hideo Kurihara), Abingdon; **115.1** Alamy stock photo (martin berry), Abingdon; **116.1** Alamy stock photo (Joerg Boethling), Abingdon; **117.1** stock.adobe.com (PRASANNAPIX), Dublin; **117.2** ShutterStock.com RF (David Davis), New York, NY; **118.1** ShutterStock.com RF (Indian Food Images), New York, NY; **118.2** stock.adobe.com (Phuong), Dublin; **118.3** stock.adobe.com (V.R.Murralinath), Dublin; **118.4** ShutterStock.com RF (Henk Bogaard), New York, NY; **118.5** Alamy stock photo (zah108 / Alamy Stock Foto), Abingdon; **118.6** Getty Images (Mint / Kontributor), München; **121.1** Alamy stock photo (RTNFreeberg / MediaPunch), Abingdon; **121.2** Picture-Alliance (REUTERS/Mike Hutchings), Frankfurt; **122.1** Bláha, Marek, Offenbach am Main; **122.2** Bláha, Marek, Offenbach am Main; **122.3** stock.adobe.com (Ranta Images), Dublin; **122.4** stock.adobe.com (Daniel Ernst), Dublin; **123.1** Bláha, Marek, Offenbach am Main; **124.1** Wolff, Steffen, Herzogenrath; **125.1** Getty Images Plus (fstop123), München; **126.1** Klett-Archiv (Mo Büdinger), Stuttgart; **128.1** Klett-Archiv (Mo Büdinger), Stuttgart; **129.1** Bláha, Marek, Offenbach am Main; **130.1** Klett-Archiv (Mo Büdinger), Stuttgart; **131.1** Klett-Archiv (Mo Büdinger), Stuttgart; **133.1** Bláha, Marek, Offenbach am Main; **133.2** Klett-Archiv (Mo Büdinger), Stuttgart; **135.1** Klett-Archiv (Mo Büdinger), Stuttgart; **139.1** Bláha, Marek, Offenbach am Main; **146.1** Getty Images Plus (DigitalVision / Jacobs Stock Photography Ltd), München; **146.2** ShutterStock.com RF (Andriy Solovyov), New York, NY; **146.3** Getty Images RF (Photodisc), München; **146.4** Alamy stock photo (PhotoAbility), Abingdon; **146.5** BigStockPhoto.com (Jeni Foto), Davis, CA; **146.6** stock.adobe.com (Pavel Losevsky), Dublin; **146.7** ShutterStock.com RF (Alex Melnick), New York, NY; **146.8** iStockphoto (winhorse), Calgary, Alberta; **146.9** ShutterStock.com RF (Celso Diniz), New York, NY; **146.10** stock.adobe.com (Achim Thomae), Dublin; **148.1** Hesselbarth, Susann, Leipzig; **148.2** Jähde, Steffen, Sundhagen; **148.3** Reich, Bettina, Zwenkau/Leipzig; **148.4** Grafik wurde speziell für Redaktion F angefertigt und darf nur dort verwendet werden; **148.5** Fröhlich, Anke, Leipzig; **148.6** Wolff, Steffen (Steffen Wolff), Herzogenrath; **148.7** Wolff, Steffen, Herzogenrath; **148.8** Wolff, Steffen, Herzogenrath; **148.9** Wolf, Sylvia (Sylvia Wolf), Wiesbaden; **148.10** Wolf, Sylvia (Sylvia Wolf), Wiesbaden; **149.1** Rau, Katja, Berglen; **149.2** Wolff, Steffen (Steffen Wolff), Herzogenrath; **149.3** Ablang, Friederike, Berlin; **149.4** Wolff, Steffen, Herzogenrath; **149.5** Wolters, Dorothee, Köln; **149.6** Hochmann, Carmen, Gütersloh; **149.7** Wolff, Steffen, Herzogenrath; **149.8** Hoffmann, Martin, Stuttgart; **149.9** ShutterStock.com RF (Beny1), New York, NY; **149.10** Rockstroh, Myrtia, Berlin; **149.11** Wolff, Steffen, Herzogenrath; **149.12** Wolff, Steffen, Herzogenrath; **153.1** Kramer, Peer, Düsseldorf; **153.2** Wolters, Dorothee (Dorothee Wolters), Köln; **153.3** Wolf, Sylvia, Wiesbaden; **153.4** Wolf, Sylvia, Wiesbaden; **155.1** Hesselbarth, Susann, Leipzig; **155.2** Jähde, Steffen, Sundhagen; **156.1** Wolters, Dorothee, Köln; **156.2** Wolf, Sylvia (Sylvia Wolf), Wiesbaden; **161.1** Wolters, Dorothee, Köln; **162.1** Rau, Katja, Berglen; **163.1** Fröhlich, Anke, Leipzig; **163.2** Wilder, Marcus, Hamburg; **165.1** Schwarzstein, Jaroslaw, Hannover; **166.1** Burghart-Vollhardt, Martina, Kamenz; **167.1** Burghart-Vollhardt, Martina, Kamenz; **168.1** Nicolai, Axel, Sönnebüll; **169.1** Merkle, Helga, Albershausen; **170.1** Burghart-Vollhardt, Martina, Kamenz; **170.2** Kranenberg, Hendrik, Drolshagen; **170.3** Ablang, Friederike, Berlin; **232.1** Dekelver, Christian, Weinstadt; **233** Dekelver, Christian, Weinstadt; **234** Dekelver, Christian, Weinstadt

Textquellennachweis
98–99 From The Whale Rider, Witi Ihimaera, 2008

REPUBLIC OF SOUTH AFRICA

South Atlantic Ocean

Table Mountain
National Park

Cape of
Good Hope

Cape Town

WESTERN CAPE

Cederberg
Mountains

NORTHERN CAPE

SOUTH AFRICA

Upington

Orange

Orange

Bloemfontein

Kimberley

Port Elizabeth

Makhanda

Bhisho

EASTERN CAPE

FREE STATE

Drakensberg

LESOTHO

Maloti-
Drakensberg
Park

KWAZULU-
NATAL

Pietermaritzburg

Durban

Hluhluwe-Imfolozi Park

Indian Ocean

0

500 km

NAMIBIA

Kgalagadi
Transfrontier
Park

BOTSWANA

Klerksdorp

NORTH WEST

Mahikeng

Soweto

GAUTENG

Johannesburg

Pretoria

MPUMALANGA

ESWA-
TINI

Nelspruit

LIMPOPO

Polokwane

Kruger
National
Park

ZIMBABWE

MOZAMBIQUE

AUSTRALIA

0
500 km
1000 km

Indian Ocean

Ningaloo Reef

Monkey Mia

WESTERN AUSTRALIA

Perth

Darwin

Kakadu National Park

NORTHERN TERRITORY

AUSTRALIA

▲ Uluru

Alice Springs

SOUTH AUSTRALIA

QUEENSLAND

Cape York

Great Barrier Reef

Cairns

Townsville

Hervey Bay

Sunshine Coast

Brisbane

NEW SOUTH WALES

Adelaide

VICTORIA

Melbourne

TASMANIA

Hobart

Canberra

Sydney

Tasman Sea

Pacific Ocean

NEW ZEALAND